The Rise of Little Big Norway

The Rise of Little Big Norway

JOHN F. L. ROSS

ANTHEM PRESS

Anthem Press
An imprint of Wimbledon Publishing Company
www.anthempress.com

This edition first published in UK and USA 2020
by ANTHEM PRESS
75–76 Blackfriars Road, London SE1 8HA, UK
or PO Box 9779, London SW19 7ZG, UK
and
244 Madison Ave #116, New York, NY 10016, USA

Copyright © John F. L. Ross 2020

The author asserts the moral right to be identified as the author of this work.

Support for this project was provided by Det Faglitterære Fond and Fritt Ord.

All rights reserved. Without limiting the rights under copyright reserved above, no part of this publication may be reproduced, stored or introduced into a retrieval system, or transmitted, in any form or by any means (electronic, mechanical, photocopying, recording or otherwise), without the prior written permission of both the copyright owner and the above publisher of this book.

British Library Cataloguing-in-Publication Data
A catalogue record for this book is available from the British Library.

ISBN-13: 978-1-78527-193-9 (Pbk)
ISBN-10: 1-78527-193-8 (Pbk)

This title is also available as an e-book.

For Rebecca

Contents

Preface ix

■ ■ ■

Part I Settings 1

1 Little Big Country 3

2 A Directional Puzzle 31

3 Meanings of North 63

Part II Histories 95

4 A Fractured Timeline 97

5 Long Night's Journey into Day 129

6 Norway and the Dazzling Dutch 159

7 The Union of Weights and Wings 189

8 A Sporting Start 225

Part III Perennials and Currents 247

9 The Reluctant Unionists 249

10 Well and Truly Oiled 273

11 The Meaning of Nobel 303

12 Epilogue 327

Bibliography *333*
Index *351*

Preface

This is a broadly conceived work of exploration, which springs from two basic aims. One is to examine Norway's national development via some less familiar angles; the other is to elaborate on the unorthodox characteristics of a country celebrated for its simple virtues yet marked by relentless complexity. At its heart lies the interplay of geography and history—the "basic grid of time and space" as Norman Davies astutely frames it in his prodigious history of Europe—applied to one, quite special national context and in terms that might engage nonspecialist readers with an interest in the north.

In keeping with this spirit of duality, the exploratory theme is pursued by two different but, I hope, complementary means.

The first involves a search—a long-running, open-ended and at times quite personal one—to *find* Norway: to unlock its mysteries, locate its cultural heart, grasp its world role and intuit its distinctiveness especially, but not only, as regards its Nordic neighbors. These linked essays are suggestive sallies in this direction. As such, they might lend perspective to ongoing debates, especially over a post-oil future that carries such immense consequences for the world and for Norway.

I'm setting out, secondly, to probe aspects of Norwegian life that highlight an insistent national motif, namely *the search*. Norway has always struck me as a society relentlessly but purposefully on the go, and data from a recent survey have indeed confirmed Norwegians as the most mobile people on the planet in terms of working life. Norway has been, and still is, a conveyor belt of inquisitive globe-trotters with a deep capacity for surprise and a surprising capacity for going deep. While many societies are mobile, few are so thoroughly characterized by mobility. This to me is intriguing. Perhaps rashly, I take it as a symptom of deeper processes. For there is something truly striking about a country that is so organized, so successful and so ancient, yet so evidently and earnestly seeking its rightful place in the world.

As a non-Norwegian writing (in English) about Norway, I enjoy a certain freedom of expression that might elude a native. But liberty isn't license, and it is balanced by the caution required of anyone treading on sensitive ground. Fairly or not, outsider observations can easily get taken as a sort of litmus test of approval. Even the most cursory effort to convey a culture, especially one as intricate as Norway's, requires tiptoeing, not trampling, through the fields of cliché that sprout from the national soil. Norway's copious harvest ranges from knitted sweaters and sod-roofed mountain huts to blocks of brown cheese that, lo and behold, isn't cheese at all.

Such icons of old-timey innocence have held their ground through a commodity boom that transformed a congenitally hard-luck country into a preternaturally blessed *lykkeland* (land of happiness) within the space of a generation. Their tenacity speaks volumes about Norwegian continuity in the face of change. It also reveals a native talent for meshing opposites: complication and simplicity, speed and due deliberation, risk-assumption and risk-aversion, softness and steel. This flair for symbiosis, pulled off with the casual aplomb of conjurers in a circus act, is far easier to admire than to explain.

Arguably understudied as a subject, Norway has been inarguably underestimated as a country. It rarely draws attention to itself, unlike its neighbors Sweden, renowned purveyor of the just society; Denmark, the dominant market force in *hygge* (cozy living); and Finland, innovators in mobile telephony, educational reform and untranslatably dry humor. Oddly for such a forthright, open society, there is a puzzling ambiguity surrounding Norway. Having long eschewed a self-conscious world role, it has almost self-consciously eschewed such a role. No wonder it gets misconstrued or mistaken for its neighbors by otherwise intelligent people.

Norway stands out for *not* standing out, and its people seem remarkably unfazed by the fact.

That alone is quite the feat for a country which, in 2017, achieved two notable milestones in quick succession. Norway was tipped by the Sustainable Development Solutions Network as the "world's happiest country" in a study more serious than it sounds (it measures social capital, not laughter). Around that time Norway's sovereign oil fund—already the world's biggest—surpassed the incomprehensible figure of a trillion (US) dollars. True to form, Norwegians reacted to the news with insouciant shrugs and cryptic smiles. Then they headed out to ski.

The seeming interpretation of this extraordinary double act—that money really buys happiness, as if verifying the hoariest of clichés—barely scratches the Norwegian surface. Its most basic national features, from the language and history to the lay of its land, defy every notion of straightforward. It brings to mind the famous knot of ancient Gordium, which stumped visitors until Alexander the Great came along, unsheathed his sword and chopped it into two.

Norway is a Gordian knot of our time, a tenacious holdout to facile explanation. The paucity of outside writings on Norway, and the poverty marking some that do appear, amply attest to this characteristic. Careful disentangling is in order. Fool's errand it may be—and Norwegians don't impress easily or suffer fools gladly—I'm seeking to explain how a country so physically scattered and historically truncated that it shouldn't even *be*, has corralled its tinkering, inquiring and exploring impulses into the unprecedented twenty-first century national project that a half-comprehending world is only now waking up to in its midst.

It's not surprising that Norway, with fewer than six million mostly well-mannered people, flies below the radar in a world of galloping globalization and tribalized braggadocio. Yet Norway's catalog of accomplishment, and its burgeoning influence, can no longer be casually dismissed. Its oil savings, bound up in a pension fund, control upward of 1.5 percent of the world's financial markets. That fund, meaning Norway's people, has a guiding hand in the world economy and a direct stake in our future.

Norway has arrived as a world player, slipping in through the side door; just as typically, it has surpassed itself by summiting. It impels a fresh look at *norskhet*, "Norwegian-ness": at how the country slaved or stumbled into a golden age that dares not speak its name. Even now—especially now—there's a case for elaborating the Norwegian story from both sides of the national interface: as a unit with a certain mien and personality in the world, and as a set of inner works so finely tuned it could stump a master watchmaker in Neuchâtel.

Some readers might already sense that the book's title can be read several ways. Norway does rank high on plenty of world performance charts, as do all the Nordics. The Economist Intelligence Unit rates Norway as the world's most democratic country, while its work–life balance is the stuff of envy. Norway crowns its continent and reaches above the 80th parallel, while this famously hilly land's highest point, *Galdhøpiggen*, is the tallest peak in northern Europe. We call Tibet the roof of the world, but Norway has a stronger, three-dimensional claim to the title of *verdens tak*, the top of the world literally and not just figuratively.

There's also a touch of irony in my choice of phrase. If pushed, few observers would place Norway atop their list of world-beaters. Oslo, its monied but unpretentious capital, trails nearby Stockholm, Copenhagen and even Helsinki in the grandeur stakes. Few Norwegians would take such a haughty claim—that they're absolute best at anything (apart, of course, from cross-country skiing)—at face value. A people accustomed to downplaying themselves, especially in their own neighborhood, are prone to turn the very idea into slapstick comedy or brush the evidence aside as so much inconvenient truth. Telling sighs of relief greeted the news in 2018 that Norway had slipped a notch from the dual milestones reached the year before.

Yet the broader trend is the more persistent one: Norway has emerged with little fanfare as one of the most economically, ecologically, politically, diplomatically, juridically, architecturally, technologically and ethically influential countries on the planet. It has ascended into the rarefied air of global stewardship. Such influence is not simply a reflection of affluence. Some of it isn't even new. More than a century ago, pioneering Norwegians redefined theater, isolated the leprosy bacterium, beat the British Empire to the South Pole and, with a few deft brushstrokes on canvas, gave the modern world its indelible image of existential angst, courtesy of Edvard Munch's almost absurdly famous *Skrik* (Scream).

Norway's across-the-board contemporary impact craves the sort of critical scrutiny that reaches beyond the random blessings of geology and taps into the cultural wells that supply Norway with its mutedly contrarian spirit and marks out its people as quiet exceptionalists. As a fossil fuel provider Norway has managed to blend the volatile duo of big oil and big finance and even channel them into some greater good. Alone among Europe's 50-odd nations, Norway voted twice to stay out of "political Europe," then turned its seeming bloody-mindedness into uncanny foresight that somehow drew praise from *both* sides of the bitter Brexit divide. Seemingly alone among Western countries, Norway manages to deal rationally yet firmly with Russia, the troublesome giant it happens to border.

There is a suggestive abundance of *sui generis* about Norway. It wears an array of public hats ranging from trendy ecologist to winter sports juggernaut to crime fiction factory. One of Europe's younger states, Norway operates with a veteran's finesse as a global arbiter of peace, respected norm entrepreneur and floating fixer that's also respectfully in the Western camp, serenely riding out the Trump earthquake. Norwegians pop up everywhere, addressing the US Congress here and coining global buzzwords like "sustainability" there. It's quite a turnaround for a country that languished for most of its long history as poor, peripheral and only occasionally unforgotten.

While Norway's accomplishments impress, the country is also a potentially valuable object lesson, a microcosm of something far bigger than itself. Today's world is said to be split by a perceptual chasm, dividing those with localized mind-sets and superpatriotic hearts from some self-appointed and unchained global elite. David Goodhart employs the terms "somewheres" and "anywheres," the tribalists and the world citizens. Intriguingly, Norway exemplifies *both* tendencies, and in spades. Here we find the small-towner merging with the cosmopolitan, a special Norwegian concoction that epitomizes the global villager. The label is also reversible in a country of grounded globalists.

In a world fixated on identity struggles, Norway is an experienced hand that offers clues for how to approach, manage and potentially reconcile them. In a world of fractious division, it's an edifying example of soft-hued strength and rough-and-ready synthesis—and one that happens to have a front-row seat on the Arctic.

Norway mainly draws attention for its inanimate sides, from its achingly scenic glaciers, fjords and waterfalls to the fossil fuel storehouse that keeps on giving. Such emphasis isn't misguided, but it is incomplete. It underplays the society that occupies the timeless terrain and is now reaping the fleeting fortune. In turn, the Norwegian character is an elusive commodity. One recent study proposed three abiding national traits: egalitarian values, moderation and nearness to nature. Another examines "goodness" as a time-honored theme. Earnestness, its close cousin, crops up frequently. Themes of cooperation, fairness and benevolent compromise likewise permeate discussions of Norway.

These redeeming qualities tend to paint a misleading picture of agreeable idlers. For a doggedly disputatious country that exudes vitality, esteems the human struggle and rumbles with uncertainty, whose abiding images include the Viking longship, the ski pole and the *ryggsekk*, other qualities beg for attention too. Elements like dynamism, mobility and active engagement need factoring in. So do a flair for improvisation, a streak of defiance and that eccentric twist without which no account of Norway is complete. These elements add to the sense of a country that's easy to misconstrue and hard, figuratively or literally, to pin down.

Such features mark, for example, Norway's emergence as a global peace-broker, sidling into Sweden's traditional role with few people even noticing. They find physical expression in exploration and sport, pursuits Norwegians broadly identify with. Norway emerged as a land of thinker-doers, of autodidacts and polymaths, for whom a restless, probing spirit has been an abiding characteristic—and conceivably *the* defining trait—over the centuries. That is the Norway that occupies this work.

The idea of "seeking the seekers" is a promising vehicle for unraveling the Norwegian knot: a self-effacing collective molded by larger-than-life individuals in a certain heroic age and a global constructivist whose forebears epitomized an age of medieval terror. Remove the active, physical side of the Norwegian story, or neuter it intellectually, and something essential goes missing.

It took a perceptive writer and traveler from outside, Fredrika Bremer, to pose Norway as the ideal antidote to the "confined air of rooms" and the "dust of books."

Norway's subject appeal derives partly from its divergence from the cloying paragon of virtue it is sometimes taken for, the sculpted land remarkably unsullied by oil rigs, almost irritatingly full of really nice people. Norway is not without its blind spots, and chart-topping success has brought attention and occasional notoriety, not least for an environmental record that's decidedly patchier beyond the borders.

There is something intriguing, and instructive, about how a national champion of do-gooding produced a surfeit of history's dreamers and malcontents; about the electric-car-buying global citizens who still sell *hvalersalat* (whale salad) in my local and pump oil for a thirsty world; and about an officially bilingual country whose two written languages are both called Norwegian, clueing the newcomer to something unusual on his or her first, unsettling encounter with *Noreg*, the Nynorsk equivalent of *Norge*. It's all suggestive of the perceptual cul-de-sac Norway has long occupied and of the tenacious "cleavages" that gave me grad-student fits and still constitute blind alleys in the Norwegian maze.

Questions abound, and my thrust for answers is divided into three parts. Each addresses basic features of the Norwegian experience while exploring inner folds that often escape mainstream (especially non-Norwegian) treatment. The first part clusters around themes of geography: Norway's size dichotomy, coastal exposure and directional puzzles, along with its northern and Arctic dimensions that shape an infrequently recognized locus of national identity.

The second part looks at formative elements of the past: Norway's complex engagement with history, the ghostly thread linking the medieval country to the modern, the flickerings of progress along the way and the unions with Sweden that bookended an alleged national eclipse under Denmark. The final part tackles a trio of subjects having both long-term and contemporary national import: Nordic identity, oil and the Nobel Prize. It wraps with the suitably daunting task of summarizing a national cornucopia that poses, preposterously, as simple.

With so much attention gravitating to the Vikings and the modern "big three" of Munch, Grieg and Ibsen, formative centuries get pushed aside and a host of influential Norwegians swept under the rug. My own bias favors elements that are underexplored as subjects and overlooked as influences. Some, like the *Hollandertid*, are little known even to Norwegians. Others, like the country's sporting roots, often get trapped in puerile discussions about nature. Ditto for an Arctic element exasperatingly soft-pedaled in textbooks that paint the country into a dubious corner of the Baltic. A democratic breakout that led the Nordic way and a Nobel legacy it shares, rather uncomfortably, with Sweden further set it apart.

This work draws from a deep well of extant research on Norway, much of which languishes unfairly in minor-language purgatory. But it's not a work of narrative scholarship and makes no claim to definitiveness. My angle is too wide for that, my sourcing too deliberately eclectic, my nonuse of notes too obvious and my avoidance of obfuscatory jargon hopefully all too apparent. A piecemeal approach can at least help avoid the temptation to see Norwegian society as conveniently complete, "modeled" in the social-sciency sense. Modeling can limit our perspective on a country where adaptability and change are not just features of life but imperatives of it. Norway's array of national paradoxes, which gets significant play in these pages, just as often assign it anti-model status.

Model talk also feeds three persistent assumptions about Norway. One is that it is region-typical, a land of Swedish knockoffs, when it often begs to differ. Modeling also emphasizes the collective over the individual, which jars with the formative Norwegian experience. A third assumption, occasionally justified, rates Norway as a satisfied, complaisant place on cruise control, its edge dulled by conspicuous gains in prestige, comfort and worldly wealth.

Put another way, I'm exploring a Norway still in the throes of formation despite (or better yet, *in spite of*) its long and convoluted history, which fuel today's curious mix of vaulting ambition and conscious hand-wringing. "*Norway shows an extremely uneven profile,*" wrote Johan Galtung in a provocative 1960s essay (his italics), "probably one of the most uneven in the entire world community." Such a statement from such a prominent postwar scholar should give us pause whenever we assume bland conventionality to be a Norwegian staple. Norway has been labeled a "Hamlet among nations" (Linda Sangolt's pithy phrase), and it's a surprisingly common and not always flattering refrain.

The *essai* (meaning effort), which dates back to the sixteenth century and Michel de Montaigne, draws an occasional rap for assuming interpretive license. Yet the suitably grounded essay is a deft alternative to straight-up narrative. It can capture an unwieldy subject (like Norway) by stages. It has the virtue of open struggle in the spirit of inquiry and lends contextual color to empirical black and white. "Why is it generally assumed," historian Barbara Tuchman rightly asked, "that in writing, the creative process is the exclusive property of poets and novelists?" An interpretive essay is a kind of mental joystick, a tool that not only liberates but also disciplines. Besides, there's a lot to be said for nursing a subject along gradually, as opposed to bludgeoning it with an analytical sledgehammer.

My working model is the mosaic: an art form built from shards of colored glass out of which, given some distance and imagination, a unity starts to emerge. It's an apt image for a country whose defining dynamic has been bottom-up rather than top-down. In my own case, colliding inner impulses of the researcher, analyst and scribbler have shaped an arrayed perspective which I hope informs this work more than it detracts from it. Writers conjure images, social scientists build frameworks: I'm venturing to do some of both. It's underwritten by an Odyssean route to Norway that once seemed hopelessly diversionary but now seems decidedly Norwegian.

Via this textual mosaic, my hope is that a Norwegian portrait comes together for the diligent reader. My aim is to highlight exploratory aspects of Norway that lend some thematic unity. My wish is that it fosters interest in this enigmatic, unconventional and increasingly influential land we had best, and at last, pay serious attention to.

JFLR
Oslo, June 2019

Part I

Settings

Strange lands open their treasures more readily than the familiar world to the eye whose vision is bound by habit.
   Ralf Dahrendorf, *Society and Democracy in Germany*

The reader should bear in mind the principle which guided the traveler at every step and on every page: a pursuit of [...] history and culture. Guided by this principle, there's no chance of losing the way.
   José Saramago, *Journey to Portugal*

But, dear uncle, what have you to do with such quarrels? Is it not better to stay peacefully at home instead of roaming the world in search of trouble, not to mention that many who go for wool come home shorn?
   Niece to Don Quixote de la Mancha

It's easy to be dogmatic at a distance, and I dare say I could have made my half-baked conclusions [...] sound convincing. But it is one thing to bore your readers, another to mislead them. I did not like to run the risk of doing both.
   Peter Fleming, *One's Company*

What, then, is Norway exactly?
   Uffe Østergård, "The Geopolitics of Nordic Identity"

1

Little Big Country

Geography is clearly a fundamental part of the "why" as well as the "what." It might not be the determining factor, but it is certainly the most overlooked.
             Tim Marshall, *Prisoners of Geography*

What I wish to emphasize is the duality *of the human requirement when it comes to the question of size; there is no* single *answer.*
             E. F. Schumacher, *Small Is Beautiful*

Maps tell stories. At one, mundane level they're simply depictions, cold blueprints. The printed versions I prefer tend to fold badly, fall apart at the seams and draw snickers from teenagers on the sidewalk. But maps are also windows onto worlds and reflectors of reality. A finger on a page can quicken the pulse before a trip or unleash torrents of memory afterward. Cartographers know this instinctively. "Past and future," writes Denis Wood, demolishing notions that they represent some objective truth, "come together in my present through the grace of the map."

Maps of Norway have a particular resonance. "Political" versions, those that delineate boundaries, instantly reveal an ungainly, tadpole-like outline, broad sea exposure and peripherality. Physical maps unveil a deeper, three-dimensional untidiness befitting a glacier-gouged, island-pocked, peak-strewn and sea-carved land. Norwegians enjoy a reputation, even among their Nordic brethren, for being straight shooters, but the terrain they call home seems sculpted by geological jesters.

Anyone who begins to examine Norway from a perspective *other* than its Tolkienesque landscape is either very bold or exceedingly counterintuitive.

Strikingly, Norway's physical barriers have not been human ones. In north-central Norway, Finnish names tell of early-modern migrations from the east—the *Skogfinner* or "Forest Finns," later the *Kvener*—that lasted; in the farthest reaches of Finnmark, the names trend into Russian and Sami; in the deep south and distant north, Dutch names surprisingly proliferate. Place-names in the Norwegian Arctic were once so chaotic that an official commission had to impose etymological order, an effort that produced riveting titles like *Names on Svalbard*. The emergence of a cohesive society out of this miasma of nature and nomenclature could well be regarded as the, or at least a, Norwegian miracle.

If the story of Norway is bound up in a single idea—a big and tempting if—it is the timeless struggle to find, and define, their country's center of gravity. And if the patriotic proclivities of Norwegians boil down to one factor, it is their ability to overcome obstacles that are not just formidable but also seemingly insurmountable. A knack for surprising on the upside, for getting the better of expectation, is a justly celebrated Norwegian characteristic that plays out in human terms but originates in rock and ice.

Norway's political map is still evolving. In early 2017 the government announced a plan to consolidate the 19 *fylker* that long demarked the country's internal boundaries. While confirming Norwegian cartography as a growth industry, it was a revealing sign of a country willing to rejig, rename and redraw its own lines. Imagine the uproar if Nevada merged with California.

Another western state, Montana, sourced the name that best attaches to Norway. There, in June 1876, Lt. Col. George Armstrong Custer and his seventh army division were massacred by native tribes in a counter-raid forever known as Custer's Last Stand. Those events, and their blundering architect, went down at the Little Bighorn. The name echoes loudly in a Norway that exhibits exaggerated tendencies in both directions.

Norway has a built-in size paradox, one of many that mark Norway's history, culture and worldview. In the mid-1980s a perceptive German writer, Hans Magnus Enzensberger, described a Norway characterized by *utakt*, that is, anachronistic or slightly out of touch with the times. His teasing depiction of a nostalgic nation looking eagerly ahead—half folk museum, half hi-tech lab—rang bells even as it rubbed some Norwegians the wrong way.

Similar logic attaches to the metaphorical geography of Norway, where a soul of small is robustly counterbalanced by worldwide reach and outsized influence. Turn the image around and we have a country of globe-trotters ineffably characterized by small-townish modesty. These two Norways, the local-provincial and the global-worldly, are like two halves in search of a greater whole. Each is basic to the country's self-perception and its place in the world.

In 1972, then-prime minister Lars Korvald uttered a phrase that captured a prevailing spirit: *Norge er et lite land i verden* (Norway is a little country in the world). Two decades later, a second mantra was born when Gro Harlem Brundtland, a national mother figure and Norway's first female prime minister, told the nation that it is *typisk norsk å være god* (typically Norwegian to be good). It was intended to admonish Norwegians to be big-spirited Olympic hosts and cheer for all the athletes at Lillehammer. The two sentiments feed off each other.

The big/small paradox informed a 2002 book by Stian Bromark and Dag Herbjørnsrud titled *Norge—et lite stykke verdenshistorie* (*Norway—A Little Piece of World History*), which plays on this theme while turning it on its head. *Contra* Korvald, they argue the opposite, that Norway is *et stort land i en liten verden*, an expanding presence in a shrinking world. "Thinking big" became a Norwegian project ahead of the national centennial in 2005, when the Foreign Ministry hired a British advisor to spruce up Norway's image. Danish historian Leon Jespersen notes this tendency as early as 1618, when Dutch advisors were being hired "to explain the glorious past of the Scandinavian countries to the European public."

"Small" is a deceptively simple designation, vulnerable to public-relations spin. Relative by definition (big or small *against what?*), it can be measured variously. Modern analysts nearly always cite population numbers, but this flies in the face of history. Iver Neumann and Sieglinde Gstöhl, two small-state analysts, figure the upper population limit runs along Dutch lines. Seventeen million Netherlanders make their country, by this thinking, the biggest of the (European) small.

With a population around 5.3 million (but growing rapidly, mainly because of immigration and its consequences), Norway readily qualifies. Without ceremony it passed the five million mark in 2013. Norway remains the smallest of the "Nordic four" (Finland has roughly 5.5 million people, Denmark about 5.7 million and Sweden around 10 million). Norway ranks in the modest mid-20s in Europe.

Small-state analysis is a reliable cottage industry within the social sciences. The "study of small" is usually restricted to minor-nation Europe, stretching from the Alps to the Arctic. The two Alpine republics, the three Benelux countries and the five Nordic states constitute the heart of this group, with Canada thrown in for quasi-European variety. They lack formal identity but share ecological sensibilities, foreign policy postures designed not to rock the boat and propensities toward societal sobriety and order. Each exudes muted yet keen patriotism, a pride built on thriving among the sharks. Their export-oriented economies encourage niche enterprises. Their polyglot populations have cosmopolitan mind-sets, it being easier to think outside the box if you live in a small box. Yet if push comes to shove, they are eminently capable of raising the psychological drawbridge. They demark the parameters of Europe and embody much of its collective essence, not some forgettable fringe. The Nordics fit this profile to a T, but Norway bucks the trend in some surprising ways.

Bernd Henningsen, a cultural historian, traces the Nordic "appeal of small" back to Olof Rudbeck, an imaginative Swede who in 1679 wrote *Atlantica*, an idyllic portrayal that posited Sweden as the home of the lost Atlantis. The link from Rudbeck to our time, Henningsen holds, "lies precisely in smallness." Beyond a small-state mentality, it amounts to an overarching perspective on the world.

The association arises from the grandeur of Nordic nature and the instilled sense that humans are bit players—"little souls" to Swedish writer August Strindberg—in the presence of far bigger forces, from the stately boreal forests to the celestial curtains of the Northern Lights. "The human being becomes great by feeling himself small" is an enigmatic sentiment he traces to educator and women's activist Ellen Key. It captures a very Nordic notion, impelled by living in wide geographical expanses and capricious climates. It also clues us to the sensitivity of Scandinavians, who live near the margins of human habitation, to the challenge of global warming. A related aspect is broached by Barton, a cultural historian: that Scandinavians, who like Canadians live in quite large territories, tend to congregate in the far south. In mountainous Norway, they long clustered in villages separated less by distance than by terrain. Geography has been doubly important as a constricting factor.

History, too, weighs heavily. Among the Nordic fraternity, Norway is often said to be afflicted by a *lillebrorkompleks*, a "little brother" mentality owing to centuries of subjugation under the Danes and Swedes that are unraveled in Part II. A region riven and even defined by Danish-Swedish power struggles long made Norway the gimpy third leg of a fluctuating Scandinavian triad.

In 1889, Bjørnstjerne Bjørnson, the poet-nationalist who wrote the lyrics for Norway's national anthem, popularized the term *storsvensker*. Usefully from the national standpoint, the "big Swede" attribution conflated two different notions. One referenced the stifling social hierarchy of a country still dominated by its aristocracy. The other was a certain grandiosity of mind-set attributed to a country clinging, in his sharp view, to the tattered remnants of empire. Here's a big, size-based clue to Norway: Sweden, which to the rest of the world encapsulates the essence of a small state, has loomed exceptionally large in modern Norwegian experience. Within these sentiments lay a tendency to associate large size with nefarious intentions and its opposite: to link smallness with virtue.

Countless elements reinforce a Norwegian cult of small. The typical farm, or *jordbruk*, tends to be a smallholding, broken into plots and confined to dips and valleys of the landscape. Lines of vision are cut off, and horizons restricted, by that same folded landform that was "sufficient," wrote a visiting Mary Wollstonecraft in 1795, "to prevent the idea of a plain from entering the head."

A land traveler from the east can scarcely miss the contrast with south-central Sweden, especially Värmland and Bohuslän (once part of Denmark–Norway), with its wide vistas and generously scaled farmland. "There is scarcely an acre of level land" in Norway, wrote geographer Roy Millward in the early 1960s, a factor he boldly linked to the conservatism and poverty even then holding rural sway. Norway may conjure up a name like Little Bighorn, but it's not a big-sky country like Montana.

You cannot live long in Norway without being aware of a powerful rural aesthetic that evokes the smallholder and esteems the small producer. In contrast, Norway's landed nobility was always an embattled minority: deprived by nature of plantations, it was decimated by the Black Death, watered down by foreign blood and, after 1814, eliminated politically by parliament. Just one titled property survived into the twentieth century, the Rosendal Barony.

Urban life reflects the same pattern, with just six Norwegian cities having over 100,000 inhabitants, counting liberally. Greater Oslo barely cracks Europe's list of 100 biggest cities, ranking 97th on one scale. It's now in construction overdrive, but there's a lot of catching up to do and resistance to overcome. Oslo was long an object of provincial resentment for its concentration of power and wealth and Trojan horse associations with the Danish and Swedish crowns of old. For 300 years it carried the name of the Danish king, Christian IV, who rebuilt it after a fire in 1624. In a country of rural sensibilities, Norway's own capital long represented a disembodied and vaguely threatening presence. It's a prominent theme in Norwegian art, from Munch's expressionless faces on Karl Johans Gate to the pitiless anonymity of Knut Hamsun's novel *Hunger* to the urban bread-beggars in Christian Krohg's harrowing painting *Kampen for tilværelsen*. Ironically, Scandinavia's least overbearing capital has stirred the most animosity by nationals not living there.

In global affairs, Norway's smallness is accentuated by its chief external reference points. Its status has been defined less by Europe, a continent of mid-sized countries, than by the United States and Russia, quintessential big states. During the Cold War this became an urgent reality for Norway, a close ally of the former and an opposing neighbor of the latter. In fact, Russia and America have framed Norway's place in the world for over 200 years—in widely diverse ways, of course—which has exacerbated the perceived size differential. In 1809, czarist Russia snatched Finland from Sweden, intensifying a westward push begun under Peter the Great a century earlier, impinging on a Norway just finding its constitutional feet in 1814. In the early twentieth century, the Russian revolution stirred Norwegian domestic politics in unsettling ways.

The United States, meanwhile, became Norway's main physical outlet of the nineteenth century, its Great Plains and bustling cities drawing almost a million Norwegian émigrés fleeing poverty at home. It established a storied Norwegian diaspora. Since World War II, US political and cultural influence in Norway has been overweening, even if the old epithet "Americanized" seems dated in today's global, digitalized stew. Still, there is no denying a bedrock role of Americana in Norway and no reason to doubt the Norwegian official position that the United States is its main strategic ally, for all the intra-Scandinavian hobnobbing that goes on.

A David versus Goliath dimension of Norwegian thinking is a major side effect of these processes. Sweden, its eastern neighbor and cultural cousin, has been notably more insulated from both Americanization and Russian pressure. "Losing" Finland in 1809 gained the Swedes an eastern buffer, which in turn strengthened the neutrality that kept them out of NATO. For Norway, a proverbial minnow among whales, geopolitics has reinforced this defining motif.

"Little Norway" resonates as a cultural touchstone at home. The freeholder image, the bit player that counts, is a tenacious Norwegian trope. The farmers' political hand shaped both the 1814 constitution and the 1884 parliamentary breakthrough. Its societal attributions are endless. Norway, Bjørnson wrote, is a land of cottages not castles. The phrase applies the element of compactness even to patterns of home and hearth. A larger-than-life personality himself, Bjørnson spoke with authority on such matters. Yet this characterization is misleading; castles and cottages aren't mutually exclusive (Denmark has plenty of both, Sweden too). To his mind, Norwegians' dwellings were not just small in size but a direct reflection of an anti-opulent mind-set.

There are contemporary regional signs typifying this trend. Modern Swedish housing, reflecting a mania for postwar central planning, typically comes in apartment blocks of medium (four- or five-story) height. Norwegian housing still tends toward the *rekkehus* (row house), semidetached or multifamily dwellings, the *to-* or *fire-mannsbolig* (two- or four-family house). These are often rambling structures that have been divided up and sold or rented separately into a red-hot property market.

Oslo's Storo district, a transport and commercial hub, exemplifies this theme on a localized scale. It is home to a long-running communal holdout by a neighborhood of houses with wood frames and latticed fronts. *Ikke til salgs* ("not for sale!") protest signs dot countless awnings. It is a fascinating test of wills pitting gutsy homeowners against faceless, tower-block developers, even if the omens are unpromising.

Norwegian development pressures are surprisingly acute and arise from the fact that only around 3 percent of the land area is cultivable. It's a number to command our attention. Yet a casual visitor to the country's populous southeast might well regard this figure with disbelief, since that's where the richest farmland is. Mary Wollstonecraft called the Vestfold stretch from Larvik to Tønsberg "the most fertile and best cultivated track of country in Norway." Østfold, on the fjord's eastern shore, is equally productive.

Norway also marks its compactness in public life. Its officials walk the streets in ways inconceivable for bigger countries. In a Norwegian press frequently hailed as the world's freest, politicians are routinely referred to by their first names. It reinforces the sense that public Norway is like one big, unruly family, where the top brass is reassuringly answerable to a hoi polloi that, in turn, refuses to regard itself as such. Interconnectivity and relentless egalitarianism feed a national mind-set defined by compactness.

When corroborating details fit the broad framework, a picture starts to emerge. The Norwegian fixation with small is willful and insistent, not just subconsciously present but consciously belabored. It even marks out holiday tradition. Norway does not celebrate an all-knowing, well-girthed and big-spirited Santa Claus; its Christmas traditions are built around the *nisse*, an elfin figure that lurks in barns.

Size when combined with self-assessment helps shape a worldview. In this case it gives *janteloven*, the proscription on inflated self-opinion, a *collective* importance. Long ago it became a point of reference for Norway itself—a subtle form of national self-diminishment, born of submission to bigger forces ranging from the natural world to overbearing neighbors. Casting it aside is a work in progress.

This perspective pervades the publishing industry, where countless book titles belabor the theme of *den lille Norge* or "little Norway." A hefty volume on Norwegian intellectual history, *Norges idehistorie*, is subtitled *Et lite land i verden* (a little country in the world). Knut Frydenlund's *Lille land: hva nå?* reflected such thinking—ironically articulated by the foreign minister who presided over a massive increase in Norway's territorial shelf claims. A documentary TV series was entitled *Vårt lille land* (our little country), profiling plucky but unfamous individuals. The prefix *lille* proliferates among local place-names. A coffee-table book on the section of Nordmarka called Lillomarka describes it as *liten og variert* (small and full of contrasts), assigning a double diminutive to what is, in fact, a formidable expanse of forest. A reference source useful for this very work is wildly oxymoronic: *Lille norske leksikon* is a 1,200-page doorstopper.

The term shapes a national default setting that emerges in times of crisis. It irrupted anew after the Utøya tragedy in July 2011. In the emotional aftermath of 77 senseless deaths came searching questions as to how such a thing could befall a small and unthreatening place (or, for that matter, inflicted on it by one of its own). A touching commemorative book, a rare joint volume by two rival publishers, was entitled *Mitt lille land* (my little country). Ole Paus, a folk singer-songwriter, once penned a song by that name, which was then adopted for the title theme of a joint album released post-2011. The centerpiece was a small but beautiful land, indeed one seen as beautiful in part-reflection of its size.

Little Norway also reflects national purposes. It was the name given to an air force battalion formed in Britain and based in Canada during World War II. This unit, prompted by Norway's government-in-exile, formed the germ of the Royal Norwegian Air Force. Names like Bernt Balchen, a legendary pilot, became associated with this plucky unit with big ambitions and impressive record. Nowadays there is a beer on the Norwegian market called Little Norway, which is quite good and evidently brewed in honor of their bravery; fittingly, it's produced at a micro-brewery in the modest town of Arendal. The commercial spin on small pervades the chocolate market too, a significant bellwether in a country of active sports and deep winters. Freia, a firm that helped define independent Norway in its early years, has traditionally marketed its signature product as *et lite stykke Norge*, a less-than-subtle play on the same sentiment.

A sense of backseat identity was planted early in the Viking period. In bucolic countryside near Vejle in Jutland, west-central Denmark, rest two large rocks, covered in runic messages and nowadays encased in protective glass. These, the Jelling Stones, are the Danish equivalent of Mecca. Old King Gorm engraved one and his son and successor, Harald Bluetooth, the larger one in honor of his father and mother, Thyra. The tenth-century engravings were carved by "the same Harald who won all Denmark and Norway and made the Danes Christians." It leadingly suggests Norway's add-on status as a land civilized from the south starting around 965 AD—despite evidence that vestiges of Norwegian unity, under Harald Hårfagre (Harald Fairhair), predate either Denmark's or Sweden's. It was an interesting precedent nonetheless, literally chiseled in stone, which simultaneously made Norway's name official and, in neighboring eyes, vaguely secondary.

In the nineteenth century, the sentiment was reinforced by Norway's struggle to assert itself nationally. Prominent non-area scholars bought into the idea. David Thomson alluded cliché-like to "this little nation of less than a million fisherfolk and farmers" boldly standing up to the Swedish crown and aristocracy. Yet weakness was an ever-present corollary, reinforced by some powerful voices. Imputed Norwegian timidity in the face of German threats to Denmark riled Henrik Ibsen, a playwright who frequently chastised the parochial mind-sets of his countrymen. His published letters pulsate with withering put-downs that tar his countrymen with die-hard provincialism.

In Munich in 1877, Ibsen found "the conditions of the big world—freedom of thought and a broader view of things" that were sorely lacking in his native land. Two years later, writing to Bjørnson (an on-and-off friend and part-rival who was agitating, unlike the apolitical Ibsen, for Norwegian self-rule) Ibsen found Norway "independent enough," but added that "a great deal needs to be done."

Time hardly softened his attitude. In 1886, he wrote Georg Brandes, a Danish friend and cultural critic, that he was "repelled" by the "crude immaturity of Norwegian life," which he hoped might someday "be transformed into a culture with both form and substance." Even when he returned for good in 1891, he kept to himself and his circle, avoiding the political rabble-rousing all around him. It is probably a good thing that Ibsen predated Bertrand Russell, a twentieth-century philosopher with an equally caustic pen, who characterized "the peasant everywhere [as] cruel, avaricious, conservative and inefficient," as against the more usual tendency to venerate the little guy.

Ibsen's stigmatic portrayal was infused with a personal rancor that distance may have deepened. Given his youthful poverty and the harsh reception that greeted his early work, it was understandable after a fashion. But as Robert Ferguson's fine Ibsen biography points out, the playwright effectively shaped Norway's image for many. His damning portrait of a nation marked by attitudinal as well as budgetary parsimony was reinforced by Fridtjof Nansen's undisguised distaste for Norway's small-minded and compromise-ridden political meanderings post-1905. As late as 1928, in a Tønsberg speech, Nansen was lambasting the *all parti blindheten* (all-party blindness) he saw stifling Norwegian progress.

Little Norway became belittled Norway, pummeled by two of its own leading lights, who were not just notables but forbiddingly learned figures who had the world's ear. Others echoed this bitter sentiment. In his oddly combative memoir, polar pioneer Roald Amundsen looked askance on "the little Norwegian nation," less plucky than vindictive, a homeland that was quick to turn on him when his personal economy, like his advertised Arctic voyage, suddenly went south in 1910.

Even behaviorally these traits find expression. Norwegians tend to be a people of few words and small but meaningful gestures, the virtual opposite of the expansive Mediterranean gesticulator. Norwegians are rarely comfortable in the limelight. Look in vain for a Norwegian, especially the brainiest of the breed, to boast publicly of any achievement. This shy-away tendency may be changing in the digital age but a *jantelov* mind-set still holds substantially true.

Implications of this tendency, some touched on later, include a "tightly knit network of contacts and relations," an inbreeding tendency, a lack of meritocracy and a stilted public debate, all noted disdainfully by Ulf Torgersen some decades ago, and all shaping (as he doffs the other glove) an "elite [that] became nationalistic because they felt they owned Norway." This touches another bedrock Norwegian reality-cum-paradox, a small-nation image that was substantially crafted by larger-than-life characters and reinforced by an informational elite concentrated in a single university in Oslo. Modesty is a widely attributed Norwegian quality whose alkaline exterior can hide an acidic interior. In the public telling, clued long ago by Rousseau, small is readily associated with terms that are scarcely value-neutral, like well-meaning or peace-loving. Yet compactness in itself does not convey virtue.

Contrary arguments are made just as often. J. William Fulbright, founder of the educational exchange that bears his name, noted the same tendency among big countries. "A great nation is peculiarly susceptible to the idea that its power is a sign of God's favor [...] power confuses itself with virtue," he wrote in his cautionary work *The Arrogance of Power*. His undisguised reference was to Vietnam-era America, but the thread goes back to the Divine Righters and European colonialists of past ages.

Both sentiments can't be right. And perhaps neither is, if we agree with Marshall Singer's observation that "power itself is simply an existing capacity [...] a fact of life." All countries lace their prevailing narratives with sagacity and wisdom, so criticizing this tendency is a little like blaming human nature.

For all its culturally defining heft, Norway's fixation on small tells only half a story. From foreign policy to landscape to expansiveness of spirit, Norway has just as often attracted aggrandizing descriptions. Some, even those clearly post-Viking, are of long standing. Norway burst forth as a cultural force in the mid-nineteenth century and made its greatest exploratory impact before World War I. In public affairs its emergence was either stifled or delayed. But over the past half-century, Norway has undergone a dramatic expansion in attitude and outlook. Oil, discovered in quantity in the 1960s, is the convenient explanation, but it's not the only one and arguably not the best.

There is a messianic component to the Norwegian approach that long lay dormant. The Nobel bequest to Norway, his peace prize discussed in Chapter 11, contributed to tendencies already noticed by the industrialist and others. It burst forth in the economic sphere almost immediately on the heels of independence. In late 1905 Norsk Hydro became modern Norway's first industrial concern, initially as a fertilizer producer. It was predicated, in part, on the grandiose notion of "feeding the world" on the heels of a widespread agricultural shortfall. The later "green revolution" drew on the same idea, pioneered by Norman Borlaug, an American of Norwegian descent. But mid-century brought an official turnaround that the discovery of oil reinforced.

It took perhaps three generations for Norway to set aside the stunting legacies of delayed statehood, late industrialization and a paternalistic Sweden. An absolutely pivotal factor was the German wartime occupation of 1940–45, which forged both a greater unity and a stronger self-image in extremis, like sedimentary rock heat-pressured into the tougher igneous variety. It also gave Norway a putative moral leg up vis-à-vis the neighbors: on Swedes who avoided invasion and the attendant destruction and on the Danes who quickly abandoned their initial resistance. Norwegian willingness to fight Hitler against the odds stoked a lasting mind-set of stout-hearted resistance that is tirelessly reiterated in textual reexaminations of the war years.

This in turn was the basis for a new postwar identity built on foundations of institutional support from outside and the building of institutions from within. NATO membership, Nordic cooperation, managed trade and the welfare state were parts of the formula. So was globalism, with a generous percentage of Norwegian GDP, well over 1 percent, finding its way into world development projects, giving Norway an internationalist profile long before the oil fund turned it into a kind of twinned, public–private global player. Paul Johnson's intriguing distinction, in his mammoth work *The Birth of the Modern*, between a "world power" and the traditional notion of "great power" has relevance for contemporary Norway too, which grew along some strikingly unconventional lines.

Norway's emergence on the global political scene commenced fitfully after 1918. Its role in the interwar League of Nations was supportive but limited, driven by the singular figure of Fridtjof Nansen. He engaged in issues ranging from prisoner repatriation to refugee resettlement to relieving famine in Russia to finding a homeland for ravaged Armenia. But it remained conspicuously a one-man show that overshadowed rather than empowered Norway itself. And his legacy devolved to a private foundation, the Nansen Office for Refugees (which, like Nansen, won a Nobel Peace Prize) more than to the Norwegian nation or state.

The far more inclusive United Nations was the first real vehicle for Norwegian internationalism. It marked two distinctive Norwegian firsts as well. Thanks to the occupation, Norway was included in the "allied powers" allowed original UN membership in 1945 (51 in all). Denmark had similar status but neutral Sweden was made to wait a year before joining. The second factor was personal. A Norwegian was plucked from the diplomatic firmament to be the UN's first chief administrative officer: It was Trygve Lie, a former minister and Labor Party grandee.

An outsized figure with a taste for the limelight, Lie had a knack for attracting criticism that proved his undoing and inadvertently reinforced the small-Norway image. He had chaired the committee that wrote the UN Charter in early 1945, giving him visibility in world diplomatic circles, although he became secretary-general (starting a pattern) as a compromise figure. Lie became entangled in the nets of the early Cold War. The Korean War from 1950 quickened his demise; distrusted by the American government and disavowed by the Soviets, he resigned or was forced out in April 1953. This made him the first, and so far only, secretary-general to leave office before his term was up, which naturally makes him an ambiguous historical figure, not least among Norwegians. Much of his difficulty arose from his nationality (as the first and until 2017, the only) secretary-general to come from a NATO country). But he also personified an evolving yet undifferentiated Norwegian presence, a sort of partially emerged, half-cocooned national butterfly taking sluggish flight in mid-century.

Curiously given Lie's role but tellingly for Norway's emerging presence, he sustained ample criticism for his (Norwegian) provincialism, for failing to handle Korea adeptly because he could not grasp the "Asian point of view." The wounding implication was that Lie, the most visible Norwegian of his day, was insufficiently worldly. His relations with India's prime minister, Jawaharlal Nehru, were awkward; "there was no meeting of minds," Lie lamented in his memoirs. That Nehru later nursed friendships with influential Swedes, notably Alva Myrdal (a future Nobelist), contributed to this perception, among some, that Norway languished a regional step behind. Yet that factor too can be overstated since India and Sweden cultivated similar global postures—the one publicly nonaligned, the other officially but not legally neutral—denied to Norway because of circumstances. Norway's postwar adjustment pressures were consequently greater.

Perhaps, too, something of a chipped Norwegian shoulder lay behind Lie's attitude toward his replacement, an urbane Swede. As told in Brian Urquhart's superb biography of Dag Hammarskjöld, Lie opposed the Swede's appointment while disparaging his character. He memorably regarded Hammarskjöld—who proved a masterful interpreter of the Charter that Lie helped write—as "no more than a clerk."

For all Lie's visibility and seven years as a global lightning rod, his brilliant and far cannier Swedish successor may have done more to draw Norway out of its collective shell. Urquhart notes, for example, Hammarskjöld's reliance on a Nordic network of friends and advisors to vet ideas (a process the writer, a UN insider, was privy to). This was a lifelong Hammarskjöld trait, according to Sten Stolpe, his biographer and associate, a loose family substitute for a workaholic bachelor. An admirable desire not to show favoritism to his native land gave Hammarskjöld double reason to involve Norwegians. Norway was thus integral to the first big push toward UN activism and its earliest peacekeeping efforts, respectively UNEF (Suez) in late 1956 and, two years later, UNOGIL, the observation force in Lebanon.

In November 1956 the Norwegian delegation was invited (along with Canada, Colombia and India) to the very first, preliminary meeting on the Suez crisis; only in subsequent talks did Hammarskjöld bring in Swedes, Finns and Danes. Six days after the initial (4 November) meeting, the first advance troops, from Denmark and Norway, reached the staging ground outside Naples, from which they were flown to the Canal Zone. Eighteen months later, Norway—alone among the Nordics—was among the seven national contingents chosen by Hammarskjöld for an expanded advisory committee on Lebanon.

These were important precedents. Their effect on Norway and its world role was gradual and cumulative, as peacekeeping operations expanded in future years. They pointedly suggest that Norway's assumption of a postwar global role did not simply come in lockstep with Sweden's higher-profile globalism, and in some ways even prefigured it. Interestingly, there is a generational parallel as Hammarskjöld's father, Hjalmar, was instrumental in the birth of modern Norway. A longtime (and controversial) political figure and Sweden's first World War I prime minister, he had helped negotiate the end of the Swedish–Norwegian union at Karlstad in July 1905, just as his son Dag, the youngest of four, was born.

It remained quite a leap from these 1950s steps to the Norwegian activism of the 1990s, the Oslo Accords and the emergence of bold efforts as a "norm entrepreneur" and "moral superpower," terms that Christine Ingebritsen, a longtime observer, has generously attributed to Norway and the Nordics. They were but seeds, nurtured in ways and by figures that are rarely recognized as midwives in the process.

Norway's emerging internationalism by the 1960s found a counterpoint in its problematic regional links to Western Europe, which were repeatedly snagged by the question of joining the European Economic Community (EEC). Norwegian engagement became primarily transatlantic and internationalist, and only secondarily European. The free-trading EFTA was the most Norway was prepared to swallow organizationally, despite repeated applications by its governments to join the EEC (later EU). It suggests a flip side of the national psyche, one projected not in regional terms but in global ones for which the world, including its two poles, was the country's truer and wider frame of reference. "Norway is bigger than anyone realizes," wrote Nordahl Grieg, a prolific writer who died in World War II. He was clearly onto something.

Norway's recent growth in stature, self-image and ambition has been spurred by networks of cooperation and oil-fueled economic influence. But it also reflects physical enlargement of a rather unusual kind.

In one, important sense, Norway's boundaries have remained mostly intact since the mid-seventeenth century. Its landward borders were settled in the 1760s, apart from that with Russia in the distant northeast. Through successive political earthquakes, the boundaries did not budge. The late stages of Denmark–Norway, Sweden–Norway and independent Norway all operated within the same geographical space.

What has occurred is a shift in perception as Norwegians' *mental* geography has dramatically expanded. "Norwegians appear to have selected a basis for comparison which makes Norway the smallest among the great, instead of the greatest among the small," wrote Johan Galtung in the 1960s. This is not to be confused with growing "soft power," a term popularized by Harvard's Joseph Nye in the 1990s, although Norway does rank fairly (but not especially) high on such scales.

This disjunction between contiguous Norway's unwavering size and its expanding role is a rare thing in the international system. History is strewn with examples of territorial gains and losses accompanying power adjustments. Alsace-Lorraine, the best-known case, has passed between Germany and France as the bilateral balance shifted. The Baltic countries have seen their very independence hinge on regional power shifts. Even in its neighborhood, Norway's case is exceptional.

Denmark bled territory during a long decline starting in the early seventeenth century: it lost its Swedish foothold in 1658–60, Norway in 1814, Schleswig-Holstein to Germany in 1864 (clawing some back after World War I) and, in 1917, its Caribbean foothold to the United States. Sweden in turn retrenched from an overextended empire: first its Polish and Lithuanian possessions to the south, then to the east (Finland) and west (Norway). Finland, too, sacrificed territory after the war, both in the far north (its Arctic corridor) and, to the southeast, its Karelian heartland while absorbing half a million refugees. Compared to them, Norway's modern territorial stability, its physical continuity, is a striking constant.

It was a long time coming. Norway reached its maximum bulk around 1260 AD, in the late-Norse twilight. That realm included Jämtland, Härjedalen and Bohuslän (parts of today's Sweden), the Færoe Islands (now part of Denmark), Shetland, Orkney and the Hebrides (now Scottish island groups), the Isle of Man (now English), Greenland (now Danish, but since 2009 having home rule) and Iceland (independent since 1944). These territories gradually sloughed off, while during a fit of Swedish aggrandizement, Norway was actually cut into two. From that point (1660) Norway lost its direct border with Denmark, which continued to dominate it politically for another 150 years. And from that point the contiguous Kingdom of Norway became physically what it remains today.

Notwithstanding the plucky small-nation personality, Norway emits a powerful visual image of vastness. Its physical oddity is undeniable. Ungainly and stretched out, the national outline splays promiscuously across the west, north and northeast of Scandinavia, draping over the top of Europe like melted cheese. Swing Norway around as if on a hinge, it is said, and Hammerfest would reach central Italy.

What may look like a charming quirk of Mother Nature has had major consequences. It is a geopolitical twist of double proportions, taken up in the next two chapters: one gives Norway an overlooked but historically significant eastern exposure; the other gives Norway clear Nordic primacy in northern waters and Arctic affairs. Norway occupies not only Europe's northwestern corner but also its northeastern corner while also forming a double top for the region. Such location bestows not only political heft and visibility but also vulnerability, for Norway—oil-rich Norway at that—occupies the front-row seat on the melting Arctic that increasingly animates the global warming debate.

In another pertinent territorial quirk, Norway's few land borders are primarily in the High North. Sweden, a fraternal nation, is its sole neighbor along a south–north line stretching from Halden in Østfold into the Arctic—the central spine or "Keel" that serves as a watershed for the Scandinavian landmass. Only in remote Finnmark does Norway meet its other two neighbors, Finland and Russia. This may well create added psychological space for Norwegians living predominantly in the south. Border matters tend to be narrowly strategic rather than broadly national, and mostly escape everyday public attention, even if they're hardly out of mind for those paid to fret over such matters.

Norway is, in fact, Europe's sixth-largest country in land bulk when all its territory is included, and eighth largest on narrower metrics. The central statistics agency puts Norway on 385,203 square kilometers (slightly higher than *Wikipedia* figures). Minus Svalbard and Jan Mayen, a North Atlantic island populated chiefly by weathermen, the figure drops to 323,804. Full-size Norway is actually bulkier than Germany, Italy and Britain, each a modern great power with 10 or more times its population.

Land size, not population, is the bedrock of international law and traditionally the chief source of political prestige. Its acquisition was the primary motivator for state action down the ages. "Territory," as geographer Peter Taylor emphasizes, "is the platform for engaging in international relations," while sovereignty (merely) legitimizes it. The physical effect of the Norwegian landmass is further distorted by severe elongation. This generates a split-screen effect evident in visual representations of Norway. TV weather forecasts typically represent the country by cutting it into two, while printed maps place northern and southern halves of the country on flip sides. Norway is uncontainable on page or screen.

Within the country, access is an awkward matter that increases travel times and perceptual distances. Remoteness and isolation have been going concerns for everyone living outside the bigger cities. Most people associate Norway's national self-image with its great writers and painters. But the first postindependence national projects were mechanical in nature, involving engineers, land planners, road and rail builders and hydroelectric developers in remote areas. Many of the mountains that young Norway had to scale (or skirt, bore through or tunnel under) loomed right in their midst. Their challenges were both mammoth and mundane. ("The speed at which the engineer established himself in Norwegian society," Torgersen notes wryly, "is indeed remarkable.")

For centuries, the only feasible connection between Bergen and Oslo was by boat, looping around Norway's broad bottom. In turn Bergen and Stavanger, the second and fourth largest cities and not that far apart, have no rail or road connection between them. Trondheim, the third largest city up the coast, is reached from Bergen by sea or air but not by land. Further on, coastal communities, linked by Hurtigruten boats, are strung like pearls along the Atlantic littoral.

Norway is effortlessly beheld as a land of immensity—lengthy fjords, majestic waterfalls, mountains that seem higher than they are, sweeping vistas, post–ice-age outcroppings—the very stuff of sublime. An expansive, warrior-nation past lends historical subtext to the outsized-nation theme. These characteristics were reinforced in a nineteenth-century, Romantic-era European perception that was driven, first and foremost, by the paintbrush.

The grand landscape paintings of Johan Christian Dahl, first of the golden-age artists, contributed mightily to an image of Norway with vast, unrealized potential, a kind of European America in its undifferentiated rawness and frontier-like possibility. Norway's peripherality, both European and Scandinavian, has an aggrandizing dimension as well as a restricting one. Norway's essence was *on the physical edge*, with a hilly essence that gave it—as distinct from all its neighbors—a third, vertical interface with and exposure to nature.

More than a century ago Anders Beer Wilse's innovative photography dramatized the man-against-nature quality of Norwegian life while opening Norwegians' eyes to great swathes of their own national territory most didn't know existed. He had performed this same service for Americans in his years photographing and building railroad lines across the US midsection, forming impressions of purple mountain majesty. Through his bulky lenses, Wilse not only expanded native views of both countries but also underscored their dramatic physical personalities.

Norway's varied and frequently jaw-dropping scenery is an irrepressible national theme. The message is unsubtle: Norway isn't just grand, it encapsulates grandeur. This assignation provides a spoiled-for-choice backdrop for all manner of television, docudrama, film and commercial footage. It pervades nature documentaries that take prime-time viewing slots. There is no mistaking the contextual appeal of cross-country skiing, a national activity set against winter's natural wonders.

Landscape is a leading character in popular serials like *Farmen*, where groups of city-slickers return to the land, and *Alt for Norge*, featuring Americans reclaiming their Norwegian ancestry while performing open-air feats. It supplies the awe-inspiring, natural-cum-national backdrop for wholesome cheese-making and apple-picking adverts that, in turn, justify and sustain massive public subsidies for the indigenous farming sector. It frames real-estate shows like *Solgt!* (Sold!), conceivably inflating prices in a bubble economy as if to drive home the housing market's oldest axiom "location, location, location."

Norway's misty valleys provide the perfect sinister-like atmosphere for crime dramas. Scenery is the *dramatis personae* of gut-wrenching tales of heroism like *Den 12. mann* (recounting Jan Baalsrud's miraculous World War II escape) and the capricious villain of blockbuster films like *Avalanche* and *Skjelven* (earthquake).

The Norwegian landscape is a surefire staple of state-run NRK, which was the last in Western Europe to broadcast in color only to become, several better-funded decades later, the world's first to do so in all-digital format. Scenic magnificence is just as pervasive to the Norwegian image as the Engadine was for Thomas Mann's *The Magic Mountain* or stagnant canals for his poignant novella *Death in Venice* or Dublin for James Joyce's *Ulysses*. It reveals primeval forces bigger and older than Norway itself, a constant reminder of the might of nature and the evanescence of life struggling in its midst.

Norse mythology long ago fostered the image of an outsized Norway. It abounds with Frost Giants and Trolls, menacing but stupid, that lurk in the country's mountainous heartland. Norway's highest massif, Jotunheimen, means "home of the giants," where outsized creatures represented primordial barbarity. And in sharp contrast with prevailing Western notions of "first life," which depict evolution from the invisible world of single-celled minuteness, the pagan Norse vision built down from the opposite. Life originally sprang from the world's greatest creature, Ymer, the primal he–she giant whose corpse provided the raw material for the universe of giants, gods and mortals. The androgynous Ymer was the outsized source of all that followed. The great clash of gods versus giants symbolized the struggle of civilization against the untamed power of nature. Norway *was* nature and Norway's nature was a force to contend with.

While their populations are similar, Norway is by no means small in the Danish or Finnish sense. Finland's essentially horizontal landscape is accentuated by thousands of lakes. Denmark proper—setting well aside its immense dependency of Greenland—is compact, mostly flat and easy to negotiate. Hans Christian Andersen's homeland featured diminutive villages, thatched roofs and whitewashed churches, accentuated by the emblematic Little Mermaid gracing Copenhagen's outer harbor. Legoland, a big tourist draw in western Jutland, is a thoroughly Danish concept, built on interlocking toy bricks. The whole concept, like the toy village of Madurodam in the Netherlands, an even flatter land, would look out of place in Norway.

Everyday activities like bicycling are radically different propositions in a hilly Nordic country. Flattish Copenhagen and Stockholm pioneered urban cycling routes while Oslo's cyclists face punishing commutes, often without dedicated lanes. Many still do it anyway, with spiked tires in winter, which is revealing in a masochistic way.

This dichotomy also defies the small-state norm, characterized by the World Bank as "a small population, limited human capital and a confined land area." Norway has the first two covered but defies the third. More revealing still is the combination of people and land. Norway is continental Europe's least-populated country in terms of people per square kilometer (15.6), sparser even than Finland, at 16.2. (Russia's figure is lower, but it is a Euro-Asian landmass; Iceland's is lower still, but it is a North Atlantic island.) The European average is around 116 people per square kilometer, seven times as crowded as Norway.

Worldwide, Norway ranks a lowly 209th of 244 listed territories in population density. The world's bulkiest countries, from Russia, Canada and the United States to Australia and Brazil, typically have low population densities. Norway's main reference points density-wise are the global giants. This element has important knock-on effects in society that have shaped a certain Norwegian characteristic. A scattered population has produced a needs-driven tendency for people to combine jobs, multitask and be mobile to get by, emphasizing versatility as a national imperative.

Norway's continental coastline runs over 25,000 kilometers, already the world's seventh longest, longer than China's or America's. Depending on how it's measured—and the geographers' term "coastline paradox" indicates its slipperiness—it meanders far more if every rock, inlet and islet is included. The Norwegian Mapping Authority, discreetly flexing its statistical muscles, states a six-figure total of 100,915 kilometers, second in the world only to Canada. The upshot is that in two of the rawest forms of size measurement, outer borders and population density, Norway is a leading indicator of large. A Norwegian historian, Sølvi Sogner, noted that "Coastal Norway" was actually a separate political designation early in Norwegian history, and even carried military implications.

For 15 summers starting in 1751, a boundary commission pounded cairns into the soil, formally separating Denmark–Norway from Sweden–Finland. As Thomas Lundén emphasizes, it was a vital stabilizing step for both countries. Since 1826, apart from a 1944 adjustment in the far north, Norway's borders have been fixed and its geographical ambitions terminated.

Or have they? Outside Norway proper, territorial issues percolated in the twentieth century as the consolidation process discreetly began reversing itself. As indicated in Chapter 3, some of this was Arctic related. Norway successively moved to set its stamp on a northern swath from Greenland to Franz Josef Land. Less obviously and more impressively it included Antarctic territories that gave "polar imperialism" a distinct ring, and an unsettlingly Norwegian one at that.

This indirect physical expansion was a part-reaction to the exaggeratedly constricted posture that marked out Norway's first postindependence decade. As of 1915 the Norwegian Foreign Minister Nils Claus Ihlen was arguing against Norwegian annexation of Svalbard because of national weakness; by one account he actually contracted with Russian interests to buy out Norway's coal mining works there as a prelude to Russian sovereignty. An eleventh-hour strategic reversal salvaged Norway's interest in the northern archipelago—thanks to an adventurous Norwegian-turned-Russian, Jonas Lied—which affirms Susan Barr's broader assessment that Norway's polar thrust often reflected a "private, rather than a governmental success."

In the late 1920s certain factions in Norway, with discreet official backing, sought to reassert Norwegian interests in Greenland, based on historical settlement, sealing and other activity. A royal resolution was passed in 1931 setting down claims for a territory it called Eirik Raud's Land after Erik the Red, a ninth-century founder of Greenland. In a little-known follow-up the next year, a second chunk of eastern land was claimed (between 60 and 63 degrees north), designated "Fridtjof Nansens Land" after their famous compatriot who first crossed Greenland by ski. These official moves accompanied settler activity, led by explorer Helge Ingstad, building huts as a way of staking a (stronger) physical presence.

Norwegians had long bristled over a Napoleonic-era treaty (discussed in Chapter 7) that indirectly handed Denmark control over that hulking, ice-encrusted territory via the famous "parenthesis of Kiel." Post-1905 sovereignty allowed Norway to seek restitution by legal means. In April 1933, however, the Permanent Court of International Justice quashed that effort and "awarded" the entirety of Greenland to Denmark.

The Jan Mayen claim was more successful. This remote outcropping lies equidistant between Iceland and Greenland and far from the Norwegian mainland. Its chief landmark, Beerenburg Mountain, was known to Viking sailors. The place was claimed by the Norwegian Meteorological Institute in 1921, which erected a weather station the British later demolished during the war. To this day Norwegians are alert to weather systems spawned in the North Atlantic depression troughs near Jan Mayen—"the place," an old saying goes, "where weather is made." In May 1929 a royal decree announced Jan Mayen to be Norwegian, and "occupation" has been continual ever since. It is not a hot tourism prospect as it combines exposure, isolation, wind and incessant fog, surrounded by seas so furious they often deny experienced sailors the chance of landing.

During that same, ideologically fraught era, Norway laid claim to a vast chunk of Antarctica, some 1.2 million square miles (2.7 million square kilometers) between 20 degrees west and 45 degrees east longitude. It was christened Dronning Maud Land after Norway's queen at the time. This came a decade after Norway—pushed, again, by private interests, in this case whalers—also claimed a pair of isolated and uninhabited islands (Peter I Øy and Bouvetøya), both off the Antarctic coast. These are on opposite sides of the Antarctic Peninsula, so Norway's three dependent territories in the farthest south, claimed or actual, are themselves widely scattered.

The continental claim was made in haste. Clued by chance to Nazi designs on Antarctica, Norway's government claimed it preemptively in January 1939. The instigator was Adolf Hoel, a controversial but tireless advocate of a muscular Norwegian polar presence. It was not, understandably, advertised in the combustible language of neocolonialism. In many ways these various claims were quick-thinking responses to the designs of others. But expansive they were, multiplying nominal Norwegian territory several times over.

Norwegian names are sprinkled liberally across maps of Antarctica. One-time princes and princesses (Astrid, Ragnhild, Märtha, Olav) rule in spirit over uninhabited wastes with penguins as their subjects. Other names bear witness to Norway's exploratory phase there. Even Tryggve Gran—the sole Norwegian in Britain's tragic Antarctic party, whose reputation crumbled after he turned Nazi apologist—has his name forever affixed to multiple spots of the white continent.

The Antarctic claim has remained—metaphorically as well as literally—on ice since the Antarctic Treaty (drafted in 1959, ratified in 1961). That landmark document set aside all preexisting land claims, neither endorsing nor denying them. In the mid-1950s, when the treaty was still a distant prospect, Norway's Antarctic ambitions were dwindling; keeper of the flame was a Swede, Hans Wilhelmsson Ahlmann.

Postwar but pre-oil Norway could ill-afford a robust Antarctic presence. According to Peder Roberts and two coauthors, Norway had become so reluctant to claim Dronning Maud Land that it "actually required bribery from the United States (in the form of $150,000 toward base upkeep) to maintain a position" on the southern continent. In early 1959 Norway even ceded its Norway Station to the South Africans, already deep in the reviled Apartheid system. The rationale, or excuse, was tight money: Norwegian authorities felt compelled to choose between the poles and to prioritize the Arctic. Only through the fortunately timed treaty did Norway keep a foothold in Antarctica and a torch alight from the days of Amundsen.

For years it seemed a formality, but two decades later, things looked very different. Interest in Antarctic adventuring revived in the 1980s and took on a pronounced gender element thanks to Liv Arnesen, Monika Kristensen and other remarkable female explorers. Official Norway now holds that its Antarctic presence is a "national and moral duty," but this is possible largely because of an expanded scientific budget and the reenergized political will such things can bring. The fact that a prime minister (Stoltenberg) and his cabinet could fly to the South Pole to celebrate the centennial of Amundsen's triumph of 1911 reinforced this robust global presence while confirming the dramatic upswing in national fortunes needed to maintain it.

The result is a unique circumstance that goes unnoticed outside the inner sanctum of polar specialists. Norway is the world's only country with exogenous property, or claims to property, that lies *both* above the Arctic Circle *and* below the Antarctic Circle. And it all happened in a single, interwar decade, starting with Svalbard in 1920 and culminating, in 1929, with the claim on Peter I Øy (Bouvetøya, first claimed two years before, is technically sub-Antarctic). This officially made Norway, puns aside, the world's only bipolar nation; geographically, it became the most spread-out country on the planet. For a noncolonial power in the traditional sense, and a late-coming state besides, this is a remarkable reality. It's also an impressive feat of national consolidation, considering that Jan Mayen was named for a Dutchman, Bouvetøya for a Frenchman, Peter I Øy for a Russian czar (Peter the Great) and the capital of Svalbard, Longyearbyen, for an American entrepreneur.

Moreover, Norway has a privileged status at both ends. It is one of just five countries with Arctic Sea frontage, which gives it political heft of the sort emphasized in the 2008 Ilulissat Declaration—through which the fivesome politely announced to the world that they could handle Arctic disputes among themselves, without outside interference. Norway is likewise one of five countries maintaining formal claims to Antarctica (seven have them, although Argentina and Chile claim part of Britain's chunk), and it was the only original treaty signatory among the Nordics.

Physical Norway has expanded in other, equally surprising ways. In the 1970s, in conjunction with a series of UN sea-law conferences, Norway began to claim a 200-mile economic exclusion zone extending out from its extensive shoreline. This had the remarkable effect of quadrupling its effective physical reach. All this came at a critical time, the dawn of the national oil age, since most of the oil lies offshore—in waters now claimed as Norwegian and backed by international jurisprudence via the 1982 UNCLOS (law of the sea) treaty.

Norway is even expanding vertically, if ever so slightly. Isostatic or postglacial rebound has been lifting the landmass almost imperceptibly since the last ice age 13,000 years ago. Norway is rising on balance faster than the sea level. The process is still playing out; Norwegian coastlines are now some three to four meters (10–12 feet) higher than they were in the Viking period. It was a subject that intrigued the indefatigable Fridtjof Nansen, who immediately after collecting his Nobel Prize in November 1922 shifted his mental gears and completed a long-shelved study of this phenomenon, in the middle of Christmas. It's one of Norway's many anomalies that the global warming alarm is being sounded insistently by one of the few countries best insulated from its rising-sea impact.

Norway is awash in physical adjustment in other ways. The news each spring is reliably filled with footage of landslips and raging rivers that pull roads and houses into the sea. The "Forgotten Valley" inland from Ålesund is all that remains of an entire nineteenth-century village, buried under a giant landslide and still eerily visible from the nearby road. As recently as fall 2014, the Flåm valley, serviced by a world-famous mountain railway, was inundated by storms that forced an emergency evacuation. Local Norwegian news, especially around the equinoxes, can bring dramatic content.

It is the least visible part of Norway that has seen the most profound expansionary impact in the twenty-first century. Norway gained a recognized chunk of continental shelf when it settled a long-standing conflict with Russia in April 2010. That month the two countries inked a landmark agreement, which resolved ownership of a disputed area of the Barents Sea. The Barents triangle was so referenced because Norwegians measured the shelf territory via the coastline-extension principle—a line drawn straight out from the border where it meets the coast—while the Russian/Soviet position was based on the outdated sector principle, by which some states once claimed territorial extensions straight north from the borderline. In a rare political display of simple logic, the two agreed to split the difference and bury a hatchet.

Norway received a genuine inflationary boost from this settlement. It expanded the size of the potential shelf Norway can legally exploit under the UNCLOS treaty. That agreement enhanced the position of maritime states, and the ones with the longest coastlines came off best. Optimizing its specific situation within this favorable general context, Norway then reached its deal with Russia, boosting its prestige as a constructive Arctic trendsetter. In the process it secured a swath of undersea territory that someday will swell the national GDP via natural gas extraction and sale. Not least, it was a prime example of going head to head with Russia and coming out as a legal (and, in that context, geographical) equal.

Indeed as Geir Hønneland, director of the Oslo-based Nansen Institute, has described, the prevailing Russian narrative held that Norway shrewdly took advantage of "weak Russia" under Dimitri Medvedev's interregnum (both post-Putin and pre-Putin) to force through a deal that was inimical to Russian national interests. Another, equally perplexing angle was a Russian fear that Norway aimed to force Russian fishermen out of the rich fishing ground of the western Barents Sea, the unilateral Fisheries Zone that Norway has long patrolled around Svalbard while allowing the Russians access.

In this curious but revealing narrative, Norway not only emerges as an Arctic power to be reckoned with but was also being painted (by Russia!) as the neighborhood bully. Its weapons were not gunboats and diplomatic protests but the twenty-first century implements of coast guard patrols, environmental regulation and infuriatingly sweet reason.

Only the strong can afford to be magnanimous, and some in Norway have parlayed its Arctic position for neighborly purposes. It emerged in 2016 that Norwegian lobbyists were pressing the government to give Finland a mountain. Mt. Halti has its base mostly in Finland but its summit was artificially drawn into Norway. A small, 200-meter (600-foot) border adjustment would hand famously flat Finland the rest of a mountain, already billed as Finland's highest peak, in time for the country's centennial celebrations in December 1917. It was a very Scandinavian idea, while its ultimate rejection by Norway's prime minister was a testament to the limits of Scandinavian amity. Norway demurred— on reassuringly constitutional grounds.

2

A Directional Puzzle

Emerging from the coast we know that to north and south there open a thousand variations of the same labyrinth; we remind ourselves that we would not be able to see them all even in many years, and this leads us to a waking narcosis, to ecstasy or desperation.
　　　　　　　　　　　　Guido Piovene, *In Search of Europe*

The heritage of Byzantium can be found in unexpected places.
　　　　　　　　　　　　Judith Herrin, *Byzantium*

Life on the periphery demands a keen sense of direction. And in the riot of Norwegian irregularity, knowing how to connect physical points and grasp spatial relationships is essential. It follows that Scandinavians have mastered an activity designed to test all-around navigational skills from a tender age. Known as orienteering, it pits players competing to find a route from a starting point, usually deep in the woods, with map and compass through "control points" to a finish line, on foot and alone.

Orienteering is a consuming exercise in multitasking. It requires quick thinking, a rugged constitution, speed, endurance, a nose for nature and the ability to stave off panic. Mix an advanced Easter egg hunt with a crash course in map-reading, add breakneck sprints through soggy woods in the morning gloom and you have a fair approximation of an activity that is reckoned, in irrepressibly Scandinavian fashion, to be fun.

And Nordic it remains. The sport was invented in Sweden, the first major competition (in 1897) was held in Norway and the rules-making body is based in Finland. Swedes and Norwegians have dominated the international medals table. Østfold, southeast of Oslo, was the site of the 2019 world championships. Here we have Nordic exceptionalism, and a fair slice of Norway's essence, on ample display.

It translates surprisingly well to the small screen. An enterprising Norwegian called Lars Monsen, who spends big chunks of time alone (with his dog) in the Arctic wilderness, stars in a TV show built on the same principle. Dropped in some godforsaken spot, he must make his way to an assigned end point, aided only by a compass and his nose. Unfailingly, he manages. Another perennial, *71 Nord*, turns the idea into a group competition featuring bulging backpacks, bubbly personalities and the unbilled star of the show, Norway's scenery.

Geographical fundamentals beyond size have shaped the Norwegian perspective so profoundly that they bear dwelling on. Most country studies offer some boilerplate basics, dutifully setting the stage, but that clearly won't do in a country where nature *is* the stage. To outsiders like Piovene, it encapsulates a peculiar twist on Norwegian reality. Yet this is a delicate subject because Scandinavia was long subject to all-embracing theories about climate and location—that who they are reflects where they are—and misjudged because such deterministic thinking dominated learned circles.

In the mid-twentieth century, the thinkers' pendulum swung to the other extreme: societal advances convinced analysts that geography had been harnessed and the brute forces of nature broken. The seeming denial of geography (and of history) was an insidious side effect of the so-called behavioral revolution in the social sciences, with its impressive but disembodied emphasis on statistics that, in turn, reinforced notions of "Norway" as a singular, compact entity, suitable for comparative charts. The postwar decades also conflated geography, politics and socioeconomic patterns: West and East became bywords for Cold War tensions, while North and South became shorthand for questions of postcolonial development. The compass points were saddled with ideological baggage they have struggled to cast off.

Basic geography could never truly vanish from (the study of) Norway any more than the Norwegian landscape could fail to draw tourists. Yet Norway is a quadruple challenge to geographical normality because of its latitudinal, elevational, areal and longitudinal peculiarities, of which its neighbors fully share only the first. At such latitudes even small differences in elevation can bring staggering variations in weather conditions, vegetation and snow depth. Norway is a riot of microclimates and temperature inversions that set it apart.

Norway's severely elongated, spoon-like shape is another factor, which denies the country a geographical heart. Norway's center-point was once seriously thought to lie in Sweden; satellite precision now puts it at Steinkjer, inland from Trondheim, but the place carries little symbolic weight. In *The Story of England*, historian Michael Wood built a narrative around the chronicles of a central English town, Kibworth in Leicestershire. Such a project would never resonate in the Norwegian *midten*. An alternative candidate for centrality, Dovrefjell, is a barren, windswept upland. ("Until Dovre falls" was a unity pledge sworn at Eidsvoll in 1814.) Telemark, home of skiing, is another.

None represents navel-of-the-earth symbolism on the order of Delphi in Greece or folkloric Dalarna in Sweden; none conveys American heartland notions evoked by Kansas, or the kind of gut-level essence that Seamus Heaney, the Irish poet, felt for County Cork, his personal *omphalos*. Herein lies an indicator for modern Norwegian public policy, a knee-jerk resistance to centralization, as well as a clue to a culture that long sought a central thread for itself.

Ostentatiously, maritime Norway borders more seas than countries, including one bearing its name. And while it's not an island, Norway has sea on every side. The Skagerrak (east and south), the North Sea (southwest), the Norwegian Sea (west and northwest) and the Barents Sea, to the north and northeast, each lap its shores. One that doesn't—the Baltic—is the body of water most commonly linked to Scandinavia. This makes it a chronic source of Norwegian misconception, mirroring one further south, since Norway is no more Baltic than Portugal is Mediterranean. All but three of the country's 19 modern counties have sea frontage and are even numbered clockwise under International Maritime Organization (IMO) standards.

In practiced hands, the seeming liability of exposure has often been turned shrewdly to advantage. The Vikings may have been the first maritime culture, Phoenicians possibly aside, to escape the limiting convention of sailing within sight of coasts and to cross open seas in open boats. The dexterity they demonstrated established itself as a Norwegian characteristic. So, just possibly, was an advanced ability to read the seas. Whether this amounted to a maritime transport revolution is still a point of dispute. It depended on special conditions.

Research has confirmed the existence of mirage-like northern conditions caused by atmospheric refraction and temperature inversion. These conditions can produce optical distortion of the atmosphere, a "mirage horizon" which, some argue, enabled Norse sailors to "see" (for example) the Greenland coast from Iceland, 300 kilometers distant, or Helluland (today's Baffin Island in Canada) across the Davis Strait from northwestern Greenland. This *hillingar* effect produces a "saucer-shaped world" able to "visually bridge" large distances. The *hafgerdingar*, a related phenomenon, produces the appearance of walls or barriers in the distance. It was first theorized in 1917, and in July 1939, Canadian Captain Robert Bartlett confirmed this conjecture with recorded sightings on a clear day that were spectacularly off the actual mark.

So the notion that medieval Vikings had a kind of sixth sense about the sea, an extrasensory feel for direction, may not be fantasy. Less certain is their use of a mysterious mineral called cordierite, aka Viking sunstone, which has polarizing qualities that allegedly made it useful even on cloudy days. As Philip Parker reminds us, Viking sagas are full of stories of sailors being blown off course and winding up in strange places if not the bottom of the sea.

Norwegians toil "between the stones and the sea," the explorer Fridtjof Nansen mused in his diary in the summer of 1893 as the polar ship *Fram*, stuffed to the gunwales with provisions, wallowed northward on its maiden voyage toward its rendezvous with the Arctic ice. Horizontal and vertical, rock and water, land and sea: it's an ageless and thoroughly Norwegian contrast.

Norse mythology gave definition to this mingling of elements. A central figure, the god Njord (or Njorthr)—one of the good guys of that rough-and-tumble world of fable, the best of the band called Vanir—was worshipped as the protector of fishermen and sailors, and (thus) of wealth. Njord dwelt at Noatun, on the seashore, and was married to Skadi, a goddess who lived in the mountains. Theirs was an awkward union; she couldn't stand the cries of seagulls that kept her awake at night, while he resented the baying of mountain wolves for similar reasons. Unsurprisingly, they lived apart much of the time, although they managed to sire two famous god-children of their own, Freyr and Freyja. Both represented fertility and abundance, siblings who managed to be lovers in that murky mythical cosmos.

To the west, in fjord country, Norway's physical contrasts hit you with demonic intensity. In the east, they greet you with harmony. Cued by Edmund Burke, who dissected notions of natural beauty in a pre-Napoleonic essay, nineteenth-century Romantics distinguished between the beautiful (rounded, harmonic) and the sublime (untamed, awe-inspiring). Each label could have been coined with half of Norway—respectively east and west—in mind. Burke used the analogy of the bull and the ox, the one dangerous, the other benign. A landscape could be sublime "only when it suggested power, power greater than that of humans and threatening to them," adds Alain de Botton, who dissected these notions in a discursive volume. Sublimity not only implies high mountains; the icy Arctic equally qualifies.

Notions of east and west carry vast meaning in an upright country with copious exposure on either flank. Both directions have had outward, destinational importance; more surprisingly, they have been "inward" determinants of the nation as well. They took Norwegians far in both directions: Western waters led to the British Isles and the North Atlantic, while eastern rivers were gateways to southeastern Europe. Within Norway, the terms *Østland* and *Vestland* carry far deeper cultural implications than the map would suggest. They form identifiable bookends for the country, linked by the world's most storied east-to-west rail link, *Bergensbanen*, finished in 1909 and fittingly celebrated as independent Norway's first collective triumph.

Norway's east–west landform distinction is a surprising feature for tourists. Foreign visitors to Lillehammer, popular site of the 1994 Winter Olympics (and a decidedly eastern town), often experience a sense of letdown; arriving in breathless anticipation of snow-capped Alpine vistas, they instead find rolling hills more reminiscent of Appalachia. Despite the short distances involved, the east–west differences in outlook, spoken accent and climate are unmistakable.

They also represent a cleavage that resonates deeply in Norwegian popular culture and political life too. A postwar social scientist, Stein Rokkan, posited the southwest versus the southeast gulf—not the more intuitive north versus south—as the chief locus of Norway's "regionally differentiated party oppositions," the southwest being the home of countercultures in language, rural identity and even, via the peculiar politics of alcohol, of morality. Even today the area around Stavanger remains a stronghold of Norway's Christian Democratic Party. As John Madeley underscored, it's a distinctly different entity from anything by that name on the continent.

A promotional campaign for *Verdens Gang*, a Norwegian print daily, played cleverly on this age-old divide in fall 2018 in an effort to boost its flagging circulation. It was built around the "breaking news" of Bergen's decision to secede from Norway. For Norwegians the notion, while preposterous, touched a delicate pressure point. In 2013 the divide played out in politics when Jens Stoltenberg, scion of a multigenerational political family in Oslo and sitting prime minister, faced his functional opposite in Erna Solberg, a conservative from Bergen. Defying history, the West won.

Bergen and Oslo each served as the capital of medieval Norway. They have been historical competitors for primacy, much more than the bicoastal Swedish rivalry that makes Gothenburg, on Sweden's west coast, a sort of dressed-down, more relaxed semi-foil for Stockholm. Oslo to Bergen is a shorter distance than Stockholm to Gothenburg, yet for travelers it feels much further, almost like a continental journey because it crosses the Hardangervidda, high, treeless and snow-covered until June. At 1,222 meters, Finse is not just the highest point on the line but the highest station in Norway. Stockholm to Gothenburg is today a straight shoot by high-speed rail; Sweden's midsection was sliced by the Göta Canal by the early 1800s.

Outsiders too have noticed attitudinal distinctions. A visiting Mary Wollstonecraft delivered some scathing critique of "western" Norwegians even after she had left Norway for Sweden. "Particularly to the westward," she wrote in her 17th letter to Gilbert Ismay, "they boldly charge you for what you never had, and seem to consider you, as they do a wreck, if not as lawful prey." Left and right Norway, in her strong view, could be scaled by their attitudes toward commercial honesty. Norwegians of the east and north, she holds, "will not allow the people on the western coast to be their countrymen," such was their distaste for the moral iniquity they linked to west coast trading traditions.

The two Norwegian flanks are even divided by Christmas: the west's main seasonal delicacy is *pinnekjøtt* (smoked and dried ribs of lamb) while easterners tend to prefer *ribbe* (pork ribs) with *surkål*, something close to sauerkraut; in the north and south, fish is the feature. The sub-Arctic expanses in between may be short on people, but they carry reverse importance as the desolate national hinge.

Norway's directional puzzles are epitomized by its fjords. The fjord is Norway's geological signature, chief touristic selling point and locus of national pride. But as a signature it is illegible. Fjords are typified by the atypical, so marked by meander and contortion that they left a visiting Piovene, quoted above, more flustered than thrilled. River-like extensions of the sea with the preternatural calm of an inland lake, fjords have a mixed character and a singular beauty. Each is a world unto itself. Confusingly but unsurprisingly, their smaller branches assume new names as they cut inland.

In some, like sections of the Hjørundfjord, you can almost reach out from a boat and touch the vertical rock sides. Visitors to Geiranger can goggle over the Seven Sisters waterfall and feast visually on the mightiest of fjords. In serene Sognefjord, the world's longest and deepest, vineyards flourish on its sun-drenched southern shores. Hardanger—rolling, quietly panoramic, classic Gude-and-Grieg land—is quintessential Norway. Already by the twelfth century, monks were brewing apple cider from the orchards along its shoreline.

In Norway's midsection, Trondheim's eponymous fjord shelters rolling, productive farmland that seems out of place at such high latitude. It reaches inland toward the famed site of Stiklestad, not far from Sweden. Further north, Narvik's fjord services Sweden's iron ore industry. Its role was so critical in spring 1940 that the fight to control it led directly to the fall of the Chamberlain government and his replacement by Winston

Churchill, with all that implied for the direction of the war and the fate of the West. In the far north, the massive Vardøfjord upturns the norm, flowing in from the east.

The gentler Oslofjord is a wholly different proposition. It may be a mere "strip of water," in Per Egil Hegge's arched phrase, but others have remarked on the same benign quality. Thomas Malthus, who came collecting population data in 1799, called it a "river" in his travelogue. The very term *Oslofjord* needs immediate qualification. It is the northernmost extension of the rough Skagerrak, which is part of the North Sea which, in turn, conjoins the Baltic with the Atlantic. Humans are hardwired to classify, but with open bodies of water the labels are as fluid as the element they signify.

This is the fjord at its protective best, with a shape and effect that are almost palpably uterine. It is flanked and guarded, sentry-like, by a pair of regions, Østfold and Vestfold, which differ subtly in character but are equally jammed with historical association. These are the home waters of the nation's capital, signified by Færder *fyr*, the biggest and best-known lighthouse in Norway. From its wide opening at *Verdens Ende* (world's end) it narrows inexorably toward the capital, wrapped so splendidly around its headlands. It has served as the country's birth canal, launching countless voyages of exploration and royal send offs. Considering Oslo's status as the oldest of the Nordic capitals, it lays an extra claim as the birthplace of Scandinavia. It is Norway's only fjord that opens due southward, amplifying the life metaphor.

Flanking Vestfold, especially Larvik has produced the cream of Norway's shipping industry. Colin Archer built the *Fram* here. World explorer Thor Heyerdahl was born in Larvik in 1914, and Captain C. A. Larsen, who pioneered the messy industry of onboard whale processing, was another native son. Today the area is famous for another kind of water, its mineral springs that produce the Farris brand bottled variety sold in Norwegian convenience stores at an outlandish four dollars a pop.

In 1889 Nansen's return up the Oslofjord as the conqueror of Greenland, suitably a day of glorious weather, was "received by hundreds of sailing-boats and a whole fleet of steamers," making for "a day that I do not think that any of us will forget." September 9, 1896 capped even that with the boisterous return of the *Fram*.

They "met with a reception such as a prince might have envied," with "salutes, hurrahs, waving of handkerchiefs and hats, radiant faces everywhere, the whole fjord one multitudinous welcome," Nansen marveled. The home waters had become, for a day, like a colonnaded entranceway to the Roman Forum.

Fourteen years later, in June 1910, it became a trail of tears for an older Nansen, who watched helplessly as the *Fram*, with Amundsen at the helm, sailed south without him. "It was the bitterest day of my life," Nansen later told his son of Amundsen's departure. The Oslofjord was not just a watery conduit for such men; it marked a rite of passage for some very high-stakes journeys.

It is this subregion that Edvard Munch felt most attuned with, and in turn transformed into art. Born and raised in the Oslofjord area, the expressionist painter spent his happiest times in Åsgårdstrand, a tidy fjordside village in Vestfold. There he spent many summers in an unkempt cabin with a rolling lawn to the water, scandalized the neighbors by painting outside in the nude and once shot part of his finger off in a rage involving a woman and a gun. He immortalized the place. "Isn't it sad," Munch later remarked about Åsgårdstrand, "that I have painted everything there is to paint down there? To walk about the village is like walking among my own pictures." Even after leaving the town in 1908, it was still keenly in mind in the 1920s, featuring in his "Freia frieze" for the Oslo chocolate factory.

Munch famously shunned the western fjords and detested the Norwegian winter. His eastern associations make him pictorially unusual in the Norwegian context; style-wise he was a modernist opposite of Hans Gude and other National Romantics who affixed the "real" fjord country in the eyes of the world. "The soft contours of the Oslofjord region," wrote Rolf Stenersen in his richly anecdotal Munch biography, form "the leitmotif of his landscape art." Munch more than anyone else personified the link between Oslo and its "unrepresentative" fjord.

In the labyrinthine western fjords, directional anarchy is amplified by the absence of direct sunlight, blocked by perpendicular cliffs even on (distressingly rare) unclouded days. A single fjord services a chain of localized communities, while the panoramic larger ones sustain micro-climates determined by elevation. Fjords slash other coastlines too, in Alaska, New Zealand, Denmark and

Greenland, but Norway remains its symbolic home. They were known to the great mariners like Magellan. In 1520, as he inched his way through the strait that now bears his name separating Tierra del Fuego from mainland South America, crew members likened it to Norway's western waters, which they knew from prior voyages.

The fjords are glaciated remnants of the Pleistocene Epoch. Legacies of upheaval, the fjords not only splinter and distort but also manage to unite. The term derives from *fjordr*, to cross over, a root of our "ferry," "fare" or, indeed, "ford." Stumbling blocks to progress, sheltering sites and hiding places, they have also been pathways for culture and outlets to the world. For centuries their direct accessibility gave small communities closer links to Scotland and Holland than with Bergen or Oslo.

Even nondemonstrative Norwegians tend to overdo the fjordist terminology. On the Oslofjord's western flank, Tønsberg sits at the head of *Tønsbergfjorden*, which later silted up; further down the coast Sandefjord presides over, yes, *Sandefjordsfjorden*. West of Oslo, near Hønefoss, stretches *Tyrifjorden*, Norway's third-biggest body of inland water, but it's not connected to the sea. Its northern arm is called *Nordfjorden*, which means that a putative "northern fjord" is actually part of a southern lake. Just north of that lies *Randsfjorden*, a thin body of water snaking north from the Hadeland glassworks into the country's heartland. That, too, is enclosed, making it a lake in fact, a river in shape and a fjord in name alone. All told, it seems a telling aspect of Norway that the fjords that give it national uniqueness are characterized by a lack of definition, an excess of contortion and a multitude of misattribution.

Far from being a hindrance, the orientational challenge symbolized by the fjord has been in important respects the very making of modern Norway. Its peculiarities informed a kernel of modern Norwegian accomplishment. A trifecta of native sons, arguably Norway's three biggest world-exploratory names, each scored career-defining triumphs based on flouting conventional wisdom via feats that hinged, effectively, on turning directional logic on its head.

In summer 1888, Fridtjof Nansen scored an exploratory first by skiing (or rather climbing and trudging) across the Greenland ice cap with a handpicked group of companions and sledgefuls of exasperatingly faulty equipment. More to the point, he did so by a boldly counterintuitive plan, taking an east-to-west route over the great ice cap. He reasoned, against widespread ridicule, that success was more likely without a viable line of retreat, back to existing settlements. (Those in Greenland congregate in the sheltered western fjords.) He staked his life, and that of his companions, on a plan built on the principle of burning his bridges.

Sixty years on and half a world away, Thor Heyerdahl performed a similar reversal of directional expectation based on overwhelming received wisdom. His Kon-Tiki expedition of 1947 was designed to test his theory—against acid-laced rejection by the learned set and again with handpicked companions' lives in the balance—that east-to-west sea travel across the Pacific was possible, even in antiquity and by balsa raft. He (they) too made it, and the voyage's famously contrarian directional thrust left a deeper mark than did his theory about settlement patterns in Polynesia.

Coincidence or not, both men were Norwegian, and the success of both expeditions, with no loss of life or major injury, doubled the impact because they crossed the accepted grain. Both stories also became universal ones, Nansen through his best-selling account and Heyerdahl through an Oscar-winning documentary and an eponymous title that became one of the world's best-selling books of the twentieth century. The unmistakable message was that Norwegians were thinkers outside the box, conjurers of the unlikely as well as doers with tenacity.

Between the two came the most controversial of all directional somersaults, again pulled off by an audacious Norwegian. Roald Amundsen's consuming early-life ambition was to conquer the North Pole. His first "first," sailing through the once-fabled North-West Passage (1903–06), involved snaking through a dense labyrinth in the Canadian Arctic. That was meant as a tune-up for the big thrust further north. Amidst his preparations, word came from the United States that the Pole had been conquered, not just once but apparently twice. In the same week, Frederick Cook (who had been with Amundsen on the troubled *Belgica* expedition to Antarctica) and Admiral Robert Peary, a determined rival, each claimed to have achieved the pole in 1908 and 1909, respectively.

A crestfallen Amundsen performed a mental somersault, deciding to aim instead for the still unreached South Pole. He told only trusted aides and Leon, his lawyer brother. It was the trickiest of performances, preparing an expedition in the opposite direction, given his reliance on public funds and private benefactors, the goodwill of the esteemed Nansen (from whom he "borrowed" the *Fram* on the pretense of an Arctic journey) and a personal send-off by King Haakon VII.

Amundsen waited to tell his crew in tropical Madeira that his real aim was the South Pole. The old plan, convoluted in its own right, was to sail around Cape Horn and up the Pacific to Alaska. That was shelved. They would instead—he rationalized to the world—first make a "detour" to 90 degrees south, across the Antarctic ice cap. At best it was tortured logic, more deceitful than openly fraudulent. He escaped accusations of lying by later leading a multi-year expedition into the Arctic aboard another ship, the *Maud*, after Nansen, stripped of polar glory by his countryman, challenged Amundsen publicly in 1913 to make good on his promise.

Amundsen's decisions in Antarctica reflected further boldness bordering on recklessness. Staking his entire, redirected mission on another gamble, he set up camp not on the solid ice cap but on the "barrier." Now known as the Ross Ice Shelf, this expanse of level ice, the size of France, juts outward from the continent, high above the sea it floats on. Had it broken off and calved into icebergs, all would have been lost. The risk paid off; choosing that site, 100 kilometers closer to the South Pole than his rival Scott's camp at Cape Evans, helped him reach the Pole more than a month before Scott, despite departing from Europe two months later than did the British aboard the *Terra Nova*.

All three expeditions were more than just physical feats or benchmarks in perseverance. They involved decisive *conceptual* breakthroughs as well. The mental triumphs were just as impressive as the physical ones. Defiance of conventional wisdom was not just a feature of all three expeditions; it was the one element on which success or failure hinged, along with the lives of all involved. And their ultimate successes, logically dubious on paper, went far in affixing the Norwegian reputation and self-identity. They were not just capable of remarkable feats, but gifted at envisioning them from unusual vantage points—and at questioning bedrock assumptions, not least of geography.

Each compass point has a powerful, emotive and very different meaning for Norwegian culture and history. We tend to limit these to four, but the ancients told a more nuanced story. One of the great directional symbols of antiquity, the House of Cyrrhestus in the Roman Agora of Athens, was built by a Macedonian in the first or second century BC. Known as the Horologion, it was a monument to weather and time: a water-clock, a wind indicator and perhaps also a planetarium. It's not a four-sided square but an eight-sided octagon, today called the Tower of the Winds. Fittingly it later became, in Ottoman times, the headquarters for a sect of Whirling Dervishes.

For the Greeks, directions were assigned godlike characteristics and moods. North had not one but three names. Boreas was the bitter north wind; Sciron was its northwest counterpart while Caesias blew from the northeast. For southern Europeans, north was the most differentiated direction as well as the most feared (Boreas was depicted with snakes for feet). The medieval appearance of Viking raiders from the north reinforced some powerful images.

As below, so above: from a Nordic perspective, south would seem the overwhelmingly important orientation. It's no surprise that Norwegian has two designations for South, *sør* and *syd*, but just one for the others, *øst, vest* and *nord*. *Syden* is a more general or abstract term, as in birds flying south for the winter. *Sør* tends toward the locational.

Norwegians have an obvious orientation to the south; (almost) alone in the world they can genuinely refer to Poles, Germans and even Danes as "southerners." Raw reality conveys a wealth of cultural attributes. For peoples of the north, "south" evokes a state of mind. It stirs the blood; it represents poetry for a prose-addled people for whom Norway is part prison as well as part paradise, the revered homeland that needs escaping from at regular intervals. The far south of Norway, renowned for its bright skies, clapboard cottages and shimmering seas, is *Sørlandskyst* (the south coast) and coastal towns like Kragerø make passable substitutes for Mykonos. But to *gå sydpå*, to "head south" is Norwegian shorthand for going someplace with a tropical tinge, notably the Canary Islands off

North Africa, or to Spain, where entire Norwegian expatriate villages have cropped up.

All this is the stuff of generous disposable incomes and the triumph of tourism over travel. But historically, the south served as an artistic and intellectual touchstone for Norwegians, culture of a more exalted kind. Continental Europe nourished the Norwegian renaissance in the nineteenth century, a theme explored in Chapter 7. Munich, Rome, Paris, Leipzig, Düsseldorf and other cities attracted Norwegian writers, painters, ne'er-do-wells and assorted or self-styled intellectuals, where they formed expat communities and floated between cities whose appeal waxed and waned.

Partly because of these bohemian associations, Norwegians (and Scandinavians generally) long nursed a deep ambivalence about the South. It carries a trace of the forbidden fruit in the buttoned-down Lutheran world. Scandinavians' reputation as reluctant Europeans emerged, in part, from doubts, deepened by the Reformation, about the wisdom of mixing too freely with (other) Europeans and their licentious ways.

Lars Trägårdh, a Swedish social scientist, notes a four-fold, age-old bundle of Nordic anxiety about the South, the "four ks" of *konservativ europa, kapitalets europa, kartellernas europa* and *det klerikala katolska europa*—that is, a Europe shaded politically by deep conservatism, sullied economically by raw capitalism, corrupted by scheming cartels and pervaded by papist sentiment. It is a dark picture that few Americans could relate to, the same "Europe" often evoked stateside as a bastion of centrally planned and possibly aggressive social democracy. Yet such ideas and prejudices have persisted, in some attenuated form, into the age of cheap flights and second homes in the Mediterranean. It may contribute to the strong Nordic engagement with the developing world and the guilt-complex often said to saddle the contemporary Scandinavian.

The pull of the south can easily obscure the importance of the eastern and western dimensions of the outward national orientation. These have strong cultural heft but remain frustratingly unreliable demarkers nationally. Name-confusion, apropos the fjord, can easily follow.

When the Vikings, led by Erik the Red, first migrated to Greenland around 982 AD, they settled in two fjord regions on the southwest coast, one north of the other, and called them the Eastern and Western Settlements. This quirky nomenclature later caused problems for archaeologists, leading to some futile Viking digs on the wrong side of Greenland. In *Fresh-Air Fiend*, Paul Theroux notes a similar confusion in Britain, thanks to the same Norsemen. Sutherland, in Scotland's northernmost reaches, took that name from Vikings for whom it represented their south. In greater Oslo, the county of Vestfold is firmly, and to outsiders confusingly, part of Østland.

Famously upright Norway actually trends southwest to northeast, a stepladder not a needle pointing north. This brings longitudinal questions sharply into play. Lindesnes to Nordkapp, the south-to-north stretch of Norway, is well known. Utvær to Vardø, the east-to-west spread, is not. It forces us to rethink our ducks-in-a-row image of the Nordic subregion that mechanically places Norway in the west, Sweden in the middle and Finland to the east. Reality begs to differ.

Nordkapp, at roughly 25 degrees east longitude, is not just well east of Oslo (at 10 degrees east); it is further east than Stockholm, Helsinki and even Tallinn, the capital of Estonia (and once a Soviet, hence "eastern," city). It's actually 200 kilometers or 130 miles closer to Helsinki than it is to Oslo. Vardø, Norway's easternmost town, lies further east than St. Petersburg or Istanbul. The country assumed to taper off and peter out into northern nothingness actually expands anew and spills further east as well as north. This alters the perspective of travelers who manage to get that far. East of Nordkapp, the coastline direction veers south. The sea, including the massive Vardøfjord, indents the land from the east. Travelers since the days of Ottar, who sailed increasingly southward for nine days after passing the North Cape, have been nonplussed.

Norway's Varanger *halvøya* (peninsula), in Finnmark, is a touch beyond 31 degrees east longitude. This puts easternmost Norway (technically at Vardø *fyr*) further east than the entirety of Sweden, nearly all of Finland and parts of Russia too. It also perpetuates a modern time distortion. Norway, which has a single time zone, is officially at GMT +1, an hour behind Finnish time, which is GMT +2. As a single time zone stretches from 5 degrees east longitude to 31 degrees east, the midnight sun actually comes well before the appointed hour. Hopeful travelers, beware.

Factoring in Svalbard too, Norway's eastern border reaches just shy of 34 degrees east, on a par with Sinai or Cyprus, two places the world consigns to the Orient. Kirkenes is further east than Bucharest or Minsk, cities once deep in the Soviet bloc. Finland is commonly marked out for its eastern as well as western identity, especially if we accept Huntington's association between civilization and religion; onion-domed cathedrals in Tampere, Helsinki and other cities all show this element in architecture. Norway's eastern stretch, while more physically pronounced, has generated fewer standard cultural attributes.

Jan Mayen apart, Norway's western extremity is placed at *Utvær* lighthouse, in a skerry in Sogn og Fjordane *fylke*, north of Bergen. At less than 5 degrees east longitude, it lies further west than Amsterdam, and the entirety of Denmark. Going purely by the grid pattern of latitude and longitude, Norway seems to stretch further east-and-west (26 degrees) than north-to-south (12 degrees latitude, or about 20 degrees including Svalbard). This is striking, yet it's also a cartographical distortion (with other implications explored in the next chapter).

"For the teller of folk tales," relates W. R. Mead, "all of Norway lay east of the sun and west of the moon." In mythology the western wind, the Zephyr, has traditionally been an agent of change: a harbinger of spring, filler of sails and bearer of rain showers. The western wind has had a good press ever since *The Odyssey*, when Odysseus, seeking his way home to Ithaka, was helped by Aeolus's gift of "a firm and fair West Wind to blow my ships and ourselves along." And outside liberation twice came to modern Norway, both times from the west: in want and in war.

The sea gave the west a pivotal importance for Norse society, as an outlet for an often crowded and quarreling land. Norsemen hopscotched across the Atlantic in a slow-motion exercise in expansion. Centuries later America, and specifically the Upper Midwest, exerted a powerful pull. Waves of Norwegians joined the quixotic crusade launched by Cleng Peerson, who loaded the *Restauration* for its inaugural New World voyage in summer 1825. The "Sloopers" became bound up with Norway's history of transatlantic emigration. Most who left wound up in scattered farming communities of the Dakotas, Minnesota and Iowa; less famously they swelled the migrant populations of New York and Chicago. Even for today's third- and fourth-generation expatriates, nursing ancestral ties and caught up in pleasantly diffuse time warps, Norway serves as a sort of symbolic home. Scholars like Odd Lovoll have documented the deep importance of these ties for both countries.

The nineteenth-century westward exodus was a fundamentally different proposition from the southern flow to Europe. Both represented freedom and new beginnings, but the transatlantic flow was economically driven and far more psychologically fraught. Above all it implied permanence; most émigrés to North America bought one-way steerage tickets and stayed. Yet perhaps a quarter ended up back in Norway, a daunting step redoubled. Some traveled back and forth, like Knut Hamsun, Ole Bull and Anders Beer Wilse. Still, the Atlantic was more than a wide Skagerrak.

The war years of 1940–45 brought liberation from the west on a different scale, with America (and Britain) acting not as passive magnets but as active agents. Norway's "Americanization" in the twentieth century was stimulated by the long-term consequences of both. Norway's government-in-exile was based in London along with the king and the crown prince, while the crown princess and her children stayed in the United States and enjoyed privileged access to President Roosevelt. In due course this led variously to the decision to abandon neutrality, adhere to NATO, join the Marshall Plan, participate in Fulbright and other educational exchanges, and generally align itself strategically to the west— though not so much with the European west. A third agent of transformation then blew in from the west: oil strikes in the late 1960s, courtesy of US-based Phillips Petroleum.

Norway and North America, especially the United States, share affinities that made policy overlaps possible. In no particular order, these include a hankering—in theory and often in practice—for freedom; a cultural narrative built on homespun wisdom, nurtured in log cabins; expansionist tendencies; a west/ east coastal dichotomy; a pronounced individualism; a fixation on sport; an unfettered and still surprisingly innocent kind of patriotism; influential pockets of conservatively inclined religion;

and, for many citizens in both countries, an inherent and often healthy distrust of goings-on in the nation's capital.

The saga accounts of Leif Eriksson's North American voyage, the richly storied emigrant experience, modern economies and politico-strategic ties all link Norway overwhelmingly with the West in the broadest civilizational terms. Yet historically Norway's eastern reach and relationships have been crucial too. East is where its land borders are, not just primarily but exclusively. Beyond them lie Norway's only immediate neighbors.

At 1,619 kilometers or roughly 1,000 miles, the Norwegian–Swedish land border is one of Europe's longest. It splits Scandinavia into two distinct halves, geologically as well as geographically and politically. The challenge of defending that sparsely populated border country has brought strategic grief over the centuries. The Keel figured in the last stages of the Great Northern War, where in 1721 an army of 3,000 froze to death; it was the scene of a brief war with Sweden in 1814; and in the tense period before late 1905, Norway fortified its eastern fortresses, their decommissioning becoming a sticking point in the final "divorce" negotiations in Karlstad. The fortress of Fredriksten, which looms above Halden in Norway's extreme southeast, was never intended for anything other than to defend against Swedish invaders. During the German occupation of 1940–45 much of the worrying was on the other side as Sweden kept perilously out of the war.

East also means Finland, Norway's frequently forgotten other neighbor in the north. From 1917, when the Finns gained their independence from revolutionary Russia, until 1944, Finland was Norway's protection against Russian incursion. That year the geopolitical relationship changed. As a result of having attacked and fought Russia in 1941–44 as a "co-belligerent" of Nazi Germany (the so-called Continuation War), Norway lost Finland as a buffer to Russia, and the Pasvik River came to mark the adjusted border with Russia.

Norway has a long eastern lineage, but today's Norwegians do not relate comfortably to this directional marker. Painter Harald Sohlberg, who made the mining town of Røros famous, called it a "Russian village of the steppes" and was heartily disliked for the implication. Accomplished historians likewise tend to downplay the eastern theme; the authors of *Viking Empires*, for instance, note that "Swedish Vikings mainly sought their fortune" in the East, in Russia and Byzantium, while "the Norwegians and Danes turned toward [...] the west," to Britain, Ireland and the Atlantic. Yet three great figures of Viking Norway spent formative time in the east. Olav Tryggvason who founded Trondheim spent early years in Novgorod as an escaped slave, while another, Olav Haraldsson ("the Stout"), the future saint, sought refuge there in 1028. A third, warrior-king (and Olav's half brother) Harald Hardråde, married there after amassing an immense fortune, along with experience, during an adventurous stint in Byzantium.

The eastern component of the Norwegian past remains trapped in memory mists, because those areas that today make up western Russia had their development arrested and their origins obscured in the centuries that followed. East has also been an unsettling source of directional controversy in Norway; Thor Heyerdahl, who late in his adventurous life theorized about the Near East origins of Norse gods, took some serious lumps because of it. Scandinavians have been noticeably more reluctant to embrace the "Germanic" side of their culture than vice versa, so it's not surprising that overt associations with the more distant and "barbarous" east can rattle the westernized Norwegian mind.

It also battles a two-fold Western historical association, a Protestant one dating back 500 years and a 500-year stretch before that, when Norway was a physically remote part of the church in Rome. This, long obscured Catholic connection was rescued through the novels of Sigrid Undset. While broadening Norway's historical associations they further burrowed it into the Western civilizational framework as shaped by the "Latin" world.

Yet long before the Saga age about which she wrote, Viking- and early-Christian-era Norwegians were playing a foundation role in lands to the east, in Novgorod, Smolensk and Kiev, where pockets of settling Norsemen formed the Kievan Rus, a kernel of early Ukrainian and Russian society. Those eastern imperial courts also served as asylum havens for Norwegian tribal chiefs escaping civil war at home. There is long-running debate about the Nordic versus Slavic roots of Russia, although much of the past evidence has been airbrushed from Russian historiography since Ivan IV, aka the Terrible, razed Novgorod in the sixteenth century and established Muscovy as the center of political Russia.

As mentioned, it's common to link this movement purely to Viking-age Swedes pushing southeast. But as historians Bente Magnus, Håkon Stang and others have shown, the Norse push southeast started well before the Viking era—perhaps as early as 500 AD, in the so-called *romertid og folkevandringstid* ("people-wandering time" or, better, "migration period") that qualifies as Nordic prehistory. It also drew a smattering of farmer-boys from Norway. A single but tantalizing runestone in Sweden refers to one such figure "*som fant döden i Vitaholm*" (who met his end in Vitaholm).

Further afield, Norsemen from Norway were instrumental players—both directly and indirectly, through their Norman descendants—in the Byzantine eastern half of the Christian world. Dating (plausibly) from 324 to 325 AD, when Emperor Constantine founded Constantinople, it took shape after the first formal splintering of the (Roman Catholic) Church in 395. Eventually it stretched from Italy to the Tigris, surviving incessant tumult until the final, Ottoman conquest on May 29, 1453. (The issue of direction-identity does not plague Norway alone: The Byzantines called themselves Romans, while in Europe they were referred to loosely as Greeks, tarred as apostates and resented by the Vatican for their power and proximity to Jerusalem.)

Norsemen, including Icelanders and Norwegians, played a formative and even stabilizing role in the eastern Mediterranean, the Near East and southwestern Asia. Norse influence there peaked during a crucial century or two that marked major inflection points in both Norwegian and Byzantine society. It overlapped with the Norse transition from paganism to Christianity: its shift from a raiding to a trading society and its people from plunderers to pilgrims and settlers. Transitions are often dismissed as staging posts for something greater, and here that problem is laid bare. Early Norse roots were eased from a Russian historical picture increasingly shaded in Slavic hues; Byzantium itself evaporated in the mid-fifteenth century with the sack of Constantinople, its treasures looted and its manuscripts carted off, mainly to the West.

Tracing the Nordic/Norse/Norwegian impact in those eastern regions and vanished civilizations is no easy task; positing influences the other way is harder still, despite growing evidence (mainly archaeological) attesting to a two-way influence and reach. Other clues, such as two separate runic carvings, essentially old graffiti, inside the great sixth-century AD church of Hagia Sofia, indicate a long-running Norse presence in those parts. More titillating still is growing evidence of Norse exploration yet further east and even earlier than previously thought. Centuries before the Viking heyday, astonishingly intrepid adventurers sailed down the Volga River through the Caspian Sea to the caliphate of Baghdad, called Serkland.

Viking-era Norway, especially pre-Christian, is generally seen as a producer not a consumer culture, which left an impact far deeper than anything it received. Evidence of Byzantine influence is piecemeal, like much else in the Viking era, which is a concern in a land of rationalists who also happen to be Viking descendants. Yet if Steven Runciman, long the doyen of Byzantine scholars, is right that "throughout its whole existence the Empire continually exercised an active influence on the civilization of the world [...] Western Europe was perpetually in debt to her," and that its centerpiece, Constantinople, was "the unquestioned capital of European civilization [...] a fairy-tale city of which men dreamed in France, in Scandinavia, in England," then we brush off its possible influences at some peril while reinforcing asymmetries in perspective.

"Oh, East is East, and West is West, and never the twain shall meet." These lines of Rudyard Kipling, written in 1889, referenced Britain's colonial–military rule in India and even then indicated what seemed like an unbridgeable chasm of understanding. Yet by the eleventh century Norway gave lie to these sentiments. At that time it produced a singular figure that shaped the future trajectory of *both* East and West—a bridge-builder with a warrior stripe who is also credited with founding Oslo.

Harald Sigurdsson, aka Hardråde ("hard ruler") and half-brother of *Olaf den Helige* (St. Olav), was the most famous and infamously notorious Scandinavian active in the Byzantine capital, its far-flung provinces and the Holy Land a thousand years ago. Two decades after his return, in 1066, the same man headed a Norwegian army that invaded the northern English coast, and at Stamford Bridge, near York, came within an ace of defeating a Saxon army that stood between him and the vacant throne of England. Harald, more than any other individual, personified this astounding, and never since matched, Norwegian reach from west to east. His life story was Hollywood epic-worthy, while through him Norway straddled two genuine tipping points in world history.

As related in Snorri's tale an injured Harald, having fled the battlefield of Stiklestad in 1030 where Olav was killed, escaped east, first to Sweden, down through Russia (called Gardarik) and on to Constantinople—called Miklagård—via Kiev and the court of Jarislav. There he paused to make acquaintance with the grand duke's young daughter, Ellisiv, whom he eventually wed. Harald made his way to Constantinople by 1034. He did not go alone, leading a 500-strong contingent of axe-bearing warriors while endeavoring to keep his royal aspirations back in Norway under wraps. There he spent roughly a decade serving the Byzantine court and its military while amassing an unprecedented fortune.

An imposing physical specimen, Harald stood out for his martial qualities. His bravery and strength were matched by artful cunning in battle, while his natural leadership skills quickly landed him the role of chief of the *Værings*, or Varangian Guard. This crack unit was central to the success of the empire's mercenary-based army and crucial to the life of its embattled emperors. It served several purposes, as mobile military or paramilitary units and, at home, as an elite palace unit. The Varangians' makeup changed over time. Once dominated by Russians, including the fierce Druzina, it became primarily Norse and, after the Norman invasion of 1066, English. Under Harald the guard was reorganized to take advantage not only of his outsized talents but also to utilize the itinerant Nordic adventurers who had found their way to Constantinople and into the imperial services.

Harald served an empire marred by erratic leadership with brutal distinction. He probably arrived well before December 1034, when Emperor Romanos III Argyros died after a six-year rule, possibly in suspicious circumstances. Most of Harald's time overlapped with the seven-year reign of Emperor Michael IV (the Paphlagonian), an epileptic who had been Empress Zoe's lover and who took the crown by marrying Zoe in December 1034 on the very day of Romanos's death. He, Harald, remained in the imperial service until some unspecified point following the blinding and forced demise of Michael IV's short-lived and unpopular successor, Michael V, in April 1042. His departure was allegedly precipitated by that orchestrated attack, giving rise to the possibility, unprovable to us, that he had a direct hand in regicide.

Harald himself was a beneficiary of an established Viking reputation for loyalty and ferocity. By roughly 930 AD, a full century before Harald arrived, Norsemen were flocking to the eastern Mediterranean. J. J. Norwich, author of a three-volume history of Byzantium, cites the pivotal role by Norse Varangians in a raid in 960, as part of a force under renowned general Nicephorus Phokas that successfully stormed Candia (today's Hania) in Crete, clearing the island of a Saracen threat. Nine years later the same Varangians were forced to watch—then immediately switch allegiance—as John Tzimisces, another pretender, had Phokas killed.

While famed as warriors, killing took a professional back seat to fortune hunting for the Norsemen. Constantinople, which along with Baghdad then represented the epitome of world civilization, was by 1000 AD idealized in the Nordic lands for wealth so fabulous that they associated it with the godly Aesirs. The city was, in fact and in name, "The City," Miklagård meaning essentially the same in Norse. (By the same token, Greeks long referred to it as "Stin Poli," "the city," which gave rise to today's bastardized name of Istanbul.)

The timing of the Norse arrival may have been fortuitous, but it was practically ideal for both their purposes and the empire's. They played a key role in the late stages of the misnamed Macedonian dynasty (whose founder, Basil I, was in fact Armenian), during a phase commonly regarded as a high point of the thousand-year empire. Byzantium's apex in military–security terms came under Basil II, *Bulgaroctonus* or "Bulgar slayer" and ruler, either alone or in regency, for over 60 years. Basil's annihilation of the upstart Bulgar Empire in 1014 (blinding 15,000 captured soldiers who were then led, in groups of 100, back to Tsar Samuil by half-blinded guides) cleared the empire's western reaches of a major peril. By 1019 most remaining pockets of resistance had been flushed out of Italy and the Balkans. Here was a rare quiet moment for a chronically besieged empire.

The Varangians under Harald were credited with helping to pacify the outer provinces—the sprawling empire itself being divided into Asian/eastern and European/western "themes," or theaters—and in securing a modicum of peace by the mid-eleventh century. Harald at first operated in tandem with the

Greek commander, George Maniaces. But the Scandinavian warrior soon clashed with his erstwhile superior. Harald quashed rebellions in distant imperial corners including North Africa, Sicily, northern Greece and the southern Balkans, in the process drawing his own fearsome nickname "burner of the Bulgars."

He helped to clear the Aegean of the troubling menace of pirates. He took a page from Homer's *Iliad* and pulled off, via the use of hidden tunnels, a Trojan Horse–type raid on an unsuspecting Sicilian town. He torched another by setting alight birds that flew back to their tinderbox nests under the town's eaves. Such ingenious tactics served a broader, strategic imperative of stabilizing the empire or, rather, consolidating the stability achieved by the time of Basil II's death in 1025.

What is less acutely understood is the exceptional moment of time into which the Vikings under Harald stepped, and on which they placed their stamp. They did not just serve a great empire or powerful dynasty; they bolstered it at the imperial peak while deepening its cosmopolitanism. The three decades from 1025 to 1055 represent the Byzantine version of a hinge of fate. In this, the empire's Middle Period came a fleeting phase that combined lavish wealth with a newfound if tenuous groundwork of stability. The empire, while overstretched, had entered a phase of relaxed maturity that fostered art and lavish court life as well as learning, later personified by the studious Emperor Michael VII.

It was a delicate balance that was fleetingly enjoyed in the post-Basil interim, a philosophical and cultural golden age that, like others of its kind, proved evanescent. It bears a heady resemblance to Periclean Athens, which completed the Parthenon in less than a decade before the Athenian empire splintered in the wars with Sparta. The Byzantine equivalent came in 1054 with the Great Schism with Rome and a pair of military defeats to the Seljuk Turks at Manzikert in 1071 and, further west in the same year, to the Normans. By an immense stroke of repercussive luck, the Norsemen appeared in greatest force at perhaps the empire's greatest hour. They then drew off much of its wealth at a time when those riches were most conspicuous. They had a direct hand in shoring the empire up from within while, indirectly through the Normans, they later undermined its foundations from without.

Consolidation, more than conquest, was the military byword in Harald's time. The Arab threat had been seen off (if temporarily), the upstart Bulgar Empire crushed in 1014. Action was mainly limited to mop-up operations that were easier to execute. The imperial court had relaxed from the austere regime of Basil; it attracted men of learning, such as theologian John Mauropus, John Xiphilinos and above all Michael Psellus, a Platonist, perhaps the greatest of the Byzantine philosophers and the first great humanist. Psellus later wrote of Harald's influence in the region, giving us verification, from the other end of Europe, of the Norwegian's key role and impact. The empire's subsequent disintegration—via the ruinous tax relief granted to the landed aristocracy, which weakened the state; stagnation in the army; currency debasements; and, in 1054, the momentous break with Rome—was a smudge on the horizon that grew ever larger in the decade following Harald's dramatic departure.

Runciman emphasizes the unusually fertile environment in which Viking or post-Viking figures—not just as imperial henchmen and shock-troops but as pilgrims, as traders and, eventually, as crusaders—came to play a formative role in the wider Near East. Miklagård was the big draw, with riches beyond measure. But getting there was long the chief obstacle because of distance, cost and danger. Thus another, hidden role of the imperial Norsemen was their work in securing the conditions of people movement, which in turn increased the allure of the Holy Land as a destination from the Latin West.

Securing the Mediterranean basin for travelers was only part of it. Another Norse role was in "taming" the vast regions that mark the diffuse boundary between eastern parts of Europe and the steppes of western Asia, amorphously called the East Realm. And there a finely timed combination of Nordic expansion and Byzantine evangelism fostered an incipient civilization where roaming tribes, notably the Pechenegs, had long sowed terror as successors to the Huns, Ostrogoths and others.

The empire and specifically Thessaloniki, its secondary center, delivered civilization into the Balkans and Russia in the form of scripture, liturgy and the Cyrillic alphabet, courtesy of two peripatetic monks, the brothers Cyril and Methodius, and their disciples. Largely unseen, far to the east of Rome, Byzantium from the south and Norsemen from the north had a joint hand in the development of a wide swathe of territory, a sort of corridor of the like-minded, or in Norwich's phrase "a Slav people organized by an alien aristocracy" of Nordic provenance.

Hungary became Christianized in 975 AD; so too, and more dramatically, did the incipient state of Kiev in 989—sealed in that case by a rare purple marriage, when Basil II gave his sister Anna's hand to Vladimir, prince of Kiev, in a religious ceremony that would have immense political and cultural impact. One of its more practical consequences was safer land travel from the north to Constantinople, turning perilous zones of passage into friendlier or at least more negotiable territory. By easing the tribulations of whose who came overland, it encouraged more movement of the purposeful kind.

Norsemen from Norway not only came east, and in force; their role in the eastern empire helped pave the way for others to follow. Pilgrimage was also being encouraged from the other direction, by the popes of Rome, as a redemptive form of penitence. (And harsh—some paid their celestial dues by walking barefoot over mountains; not all survived.) The exploitation of new routes to the east and the dusting off of old ones like the Via Egnatia, an old Roman east–west route, in turn paved the way for a later and infinitely more destructive form of collective travel, the Crusades, launched with fanfare in Clermont in 1095 AD. And while there is less evidence to this effect, the Norsemen, expert mariners, may have helped to shore up the Byzantine navy, the chronically weak component of an overstretched military. Harald's common way of getting around was the Greek corsair, a sailing vessel, and his success in clearing out the pirate menace is amply documented.

Miklagård, and the Holy Sites of the Near East, may also have played a more peaceable destination in a sort of medieval Grand Tour for Norsemen esteemed for their adventurism as well as fearlessness. "Most Scandinavian pilgrims liked to make a round tour," Runciman avers, "coming by sea through the Straits of Gibraltar and returning through Russia." It is an astonishing testament to a peripatetic spirit, and to a traveling culture that was just as capable of overland-and-river treks (in both directions, to and from Scandinavia, with or without longboats) as of lengthy sea voyages. Judith Herrin points out, for example, that the lower

Dnieper River, which empties into the Black Sea, was notorious for its seven treacherous cataracts, one named Essoupi, meaning "Do not sleep!"

Runciman also notes that the Varangians themselves, as converted Christians, were known for taking leaves to travel on to the Holy Land for pilgrimages of their own. Harald Hardråde made one such trip, probably in 1034, as head of a delegation to restore the Church of the Holy Sepulchre in Jerusalem, which had been sacked by Arabs earlier that century. This was some decades after repeated "sightings" in the Holy City of Olaf Tryggvason, the Norwegian king and founder of Trondheim, who had mysteriously died (and presumed drowned) during a battle around 1000 AD. As important as Constantinople was for the Norsemen living in the material world, it was, in spiritual terms, but a stepping stone to a higher realm.

The Norse role in Byzantium had changed complexion by 1081, when Norman raiders (their descendants) defeated the Varangians, now dominated by English soldiers. The loss prompted further upheaval as the brief Ducas dynasty was subsumed within the Komnenian, ushering in an era of deceptive stability in a fragmenting empire. Yet the post-Viking Norsemen still came. It was that glittering but brittle phase, personified by Alexios I Komnenos, which extravagantly greeted a visiting Sigurd Jorsalfar (the Crusader) around 1100, at the tail end of the First Crusade.

Sigurd cut a magnificent figure on a youthful, three-year trek there and back via Portugal, Gibraltar and Greece. He and his entourage entered Miklagård mounted on horses wearing shoes of gold, and he disdained the lavish presents offered to him—giving the appearance of immense wealth and power to an imperium of immense wealth and power. The impression he imparted eventually returned to Norway as legend along with the man himself. "It was the talk of men," Snorri relates, "that no one had gone from Norway on a journey of greater honor than this." Another century and three destructive waves later, the sack of Constantinople in 1204, with terrible irony at the hands of Christians of the Fourth Crusade, marked the definitive end of this era. The prohibitive costs of funding foreign mercenaries may have speeded these events.

Harald's final phase in imperial service is unclear. He likely remained there well into the 1040s. The saga version has him making a daring escape after blinding the roundly detested emperor of six months' standing, Michael V (Caliphates), a fit of apparently justified rage marking a notorious event datable to April 1042. Harald's precise role in the plot is opaque. It is not helped by Snorri's account of his subsequent flight (in defiance of Empress Zoe's wishes). A stirring tale, it makes a faulty reference to Emperor Constantine IX Monomachus who only later entered the imperial picture, which makes us question the broader narrative.

Jailed after the attack, Harald was hauled out by rope, helped by a rescuer who had seen a vision of Harald's half brother, St. Olav. He gathered his Varangians and put out to sea. Their way was blocked by an iron chain across the Bosporus Strait, but their leader's ingenuity helped them escape. With some men manning the oars, the rest ran aft as the galley was stopped by the chain. In the crucial pause, Snorre relates, "He bade all his men run forward. Then the galley Harald was on plunged forward, and after swinging on the chain, slipped off." The other galley was less fortunate, and men were lost. But Harald escaped, entered the Black Sea from the west and headed up the Dnieper River back to Novgorod (Holmgård). There he wed Ellisiv and gathered the vast fortune he had forwarded for safekeeping by his future in-laws.

If the Norsemen, Harald in particular, were beneficiaries of the empire at its biggest, richest and fleetingly most stable, their rewards were greater still because of upheaval at the imperial heart. After Basil's death (1025) came the *Epigoni* or "little ones," weak leaders that followed in rapid succession (13 in a stretch, 56 years to 1081, which was briefer than Basil's reign alone). Basil's nieces Theodora and Zoe ruled, mostly behind the scenes, as *porphyrogenitoi* or "purple-born" princesses, for the quarter-century after Basil. This period included Romanos III Argyros, who had married Zoe and died in December 1034; Michael IV, Zoe's second husband, who died in December 1041; Michael V, who was blinded and deposed the following April; a brief and disastrous dual rule by fractious sisters Zoe and Theodora; then a longer but still volatile stretch under Constantine Monomachus, Zoe's third husband, who survived until 1055.

This turmoil in the imperial inner sanctum mattered enormously because the primary beneficiaries of any inherited spoils were in fact the loyal Varangians. They, principally their leader, had first legal and physical claim and obvious heft to ensure it. After a decade in Constantinople, coupled with conspicuous successes as a sanctioned raider, Harald had collected vast riches, multiplied by three because of the royal turnover.

His time coincided with the regimes and deaths of Romanos and the two Michaels, which provided sufficient spoils to secure his position back in Norway—first as joint king with Magnus Olavson and subsequently as supreme Norwegian ruler—for the next two decades. Its nature is obscure (per Snorri's reference to "all the goods and many kinds of costly things") but its essence was gold and its effect was clear. "There was so much wealth," the Icelander continues, "that no man in the Northlands had ever seen so much in the possession of one man." It remained a fabulous fortune even after being shared with King Magnus. Little wonder that one of Harald's tangible legacies was the minting of a Byzantine-like coin as legal tender in his northern realm.

Harald may also have left a smaller but equally tantalizing footprint in the form of carved initials on one of medieval Athens's symbols, namely the lion of Piraeus, which was hauled off to Venice in the seventeenth century and still graces St. Mark's Square. As these tales of Sigurd and Harald and the wider sweep underscore, it is a convenient myth that Swedish Vikings went east, the Danes south and the Norwegians west. And their outsized personalities should not obscure the fact that they also symptomized a crucial Norse role in the eastern Mediterranean at a turning point for both.

The pivotal Byzantine centuries underscore the prodigious nature of the Viking achievement. Their impact on an imperium that lasted a thousand years was time-specific, so it inevitably gets soft-pedaled in massive compendiums like Ostrogorsky's. Yet it's precisely this timing that gives this phase special prominence in both Norse and Byzantine narratives. The pilgrimage and crusading cultures that followed—those who opened up the Near East for the West, both for good and ill—could point to the late- and post-Viking role in the southeast Mediterranean as path-making. It was far more substantial than a focus on Harald or the Varangians would indicate. In this, Byzantium's so-called first encounter with the west, the Norwegian/Norse role was central and its influence long term.

In the other direction, what the Norsemen took home could be measured in visible wealth: hoardable and mobile treasure and all the influence it could buy. Venturing there for riches, they (or those who survived the long journeys) surely found it. But they brought back intangibles too: glimpses of an immense civilization and prideful knowledge of their hard-won ability to profit from it.

They also returned having been steeped in the qualities marking out the empire. The term "Byzantine" was long saddled with negative associations and a bad Western press. It never quite recovered from the disdain of Edward Gibbon, the eighteenth-century rationalist and Roman chronicler who described the "Oriental Romans" as hidebound and fatally tied to religion. Western critics have focused on the extravagance and corruption that marked its court. Still, that is only part of the story. The Constantinople they knew was finally in control of a sprawling realm, run by an administration that in Runciman's estimation was "extremely efficient" and no more violence-prone than the medieval world it represented.

It was also a place where women could be empresses as well as emperor-makers; Zoe, revered into old age, outstaged the three men she married and who nominally ruled. Law-based governance and gender equality are not qualities generally associated with Byzantine (or Viking) life, but they too informed the environment the Norsemen soaked in and the experience they took back.

Another unheralded Byzantine practice that found a Norwegian echo was the general use of non-hereditary titles, which is intriguing given Norway's post-1814 elimination of formal aristocracy. Others include individuals' recourse to the justice system and, far from least, a military culture that was primarily defensive in nature and oriented increasingly toward managing a vast realm. Such elements cannot but have filtered back north, mixing with preexisting Norse qualities of rough honor while shaping the man one describes as a "Byzantine emperor on the Norwegian throne."

Any effort to draw a direct thread between Byzantium and post-Viking Norway, or to assert direct causation, is strewn with mines. Still, it would be rash to deny such links because of their alien provenance or their removal from our time. Just because Norsemen returned from the Bosporus far richer does not mean they failed to bring back, resourceful types that they were, treasures that carried no price tag.

While immensely valuable, Snorri's histories describe what kings like Harald Hardråde did, rather than what they thought. He deliberately excludes the extraneous or the unverifiable. In Harald's case the precise or even approximate lines of influence aren't clear. His increasingly ruthless exercise of power upon returning to Norway is well known, but so is his resourcefulness. He is described as a man of understanding. "There never has been a ruler in Norway," Snorri asserts, "who was so deep-thinking or of such good counsel as Harald." We don't know how this translated into governance practices of early-Christian Norway—and Norway itself radically changed course after his death—but we don't know enough to brush aside the possibility of longer-term or indirect impact. And then there is the suggestive parallel between two civilizations at opposite corners of Europe—each one, Norse and Byzantine, overstretched and riven from within, where wary leaders with organizational talents clung to hard-won gains.

Such mixing did not stop a wall of cultural suspicion from going up between west and east as the Norse and Norwegian impact faded and the Slavic component came to dominate Russian historiography and collective memory. Just as Norway is an often overlooked modern frontline with Russia, its tenth- and eleventh-century eastern thrust is a forgotten factor in its early development and a recipient of lessons from the East Realm—unless we regard those who went there as opportunists and bullies, incapable of repatriating knowledge gained elsewhere.

3

Meanings of North

Norway is the farthest country of the world [...] the most unproductive of all countries, suitable only for herds.
     Adam of Bremen, History of the Archbishops of
                Hamburg-Bremen

Well, the land of Fogs used to be thought by the ancients to lie in the north, where all confused ideas come from.
     Bjørnstjerne Bjørnson, The Editor

Take Arctic travel out of our history, and will it not be poorer? Perhaps we have here the greatest service [Norway] has done humanity.
     Fridtjof Nansen, In Northern Mists

Most visitors to Norway know, or think they know, that *Nordkapp*, the North Cape, marks the northern extremity of Europe. Roughly 200,000 tourists flock there each summer in the service of this alleged certainty. It's the motorized, secular equivalent of the old Pilgrim's Way that once drew the pious to Nidaros Cathedral, and still pulls the faithful to southern shrines like Santiago de Compostela, in northern Spain, and Fatima in Portugal. In this case the destination is not a holy site but a stupendous sight: cliff-faces that drop 300 meters (ca. 1,000 feet) into a frigid sea. Weather permitting, visitors can watch the sun dip low before it begins another early-hour rise. For 77 consecutive days, the sun lingers above the horizon.

The leadingly named Fatima project links the mainland and Magerøy, the sprawling island with North Cape at its tip. Its hefty costs are recouped by an entrance fee that gallingly applies even to hikers. Beyond the tourist-trappiness there's a surreal touch (a statue of French King Louis Philippe, who visited in 1795) along with a whiff of untruth about the place. Another 1.5 kilometers northwest is Knivskjellodden, which gets but a trickle of visitors.

Then again, both markers are off. *Det Bestes Store Veiatlas*, the book of maps in a country that needs them, marks Kinnarodden at the northern tip of Nordkinnhalvøya, to the east as *Europas nordligste fastland*. Magerøya's island status technically disqualifies it (Nordkapp is not marked the "most northerly" anything). At any rate, once you've gazed down on these places from the comfort of a window seat on the northbound flight to Svalbard, the notion of "northernmost Norway" becomes a tangle of ambiguity.

If for many Norway stands for a northern essence, what does north itself signify? And how has its northern half shaped Norway's national trajectory? Whether as a place, a destination or a state of mind, "the North," *Norden*, packs a powerful punch. ("Nordicity," the idea of a common Nordic identity, is taken up in Part III.) No other directional indicator can command a prefix like "true" or exalt a famously fixed star. But north is less a trope than a whole range of them. It has become an all-purpose metaphor in the Western canon, a cosmological kitchen sink of myth and allegory, which complicates understanding of the one country said to exemplify it.

North emerged in modern thought, Henningsen suggests, as an attributed mix of mysticism, beauty, piety and innocence, coda for a cold-weather paradise, but these qualities were transposed onto older ones shaded in darker hues. Clarity tinged with goodness and confusion stoked by malign forces are the two poles around which humans have engaged mentally with the far north. Both derive from the physical world, the seasonal swings of night and day that become extreme in the high latitudes. These are perceptual realities, mental states shaped by physical ones.

Confusion arises because morally opposite notions of evil and good both became assigned to the one direction humans have relied on physically to find their way. Its physical basis is found in Polaris, the North Star. Polaris has been a nighttime navigational guide for travelers and sailors since antiquity. Its fixed presence in the Little Bear constellation, 430 light-years away, derives from the earth's axial tilt of roughly 22.5 degrees from the vertical. The polar axis points at it, and the earth's rotation makes the other stars appear to move around it. Scouts everywhere know its value and, at least in theory, how to spot it with a naked eye. Its qualities turned it into humanity's ethical lodestar. "I am constant as the Northern Star," says Julius Caesar in Shakespeare's famous Roman tragedy, "Of whose true fix'd and resting quality there is no fellow in the firmament." Its uniqueness, however, has not gone unchallenged. Sir William Herschel, discoverer of Uranus, hypothesized in 1774 that Polaris might be two stars in conjunction.

Fixity has a stern side as well. Another northern attribution is the pitiless truth-teller, the stripper-away of societal obfuscation. This north imposes a monastic-like moral order on those who dare venture into its midst. It becomes a less-is-more kind of symbol. Frozen yet full of life, it has a desolate beauty that derives from its very desolation.

Nansen wrote frequently about the purifying element of the (far) north, where few people go and where civilization had not yet laid its dirtying hand. His (Arctic) version of north rewards bold initiative and reveres the solitary figure pushing forward against mighty odds—the impetus for christening his ship the *Fram* ("forward").

This theme was pursued by a pair of late-century adventurers. Erling Kagge, an extraordinary Norwegian who became the first person to achieve the "three summits" (North Pole, South Pole and Mt. Everest), posits the polar region(s) as an aural phenomenon, the ultimate repository of absolute silence, in a well-received book of that name. Børge Ousland, an adventuring compatriot with whom he reached the North Pole in 1997, poses the north's visuals as the great unveiler.

On this theme Ousland's chronicle of numbing slog through the icy monochrome waxes lyrical. "The starry sky stretched over me like a huge dome of light in the endless darkness," he wrote. That night he "almost jumped" at the sight of the aurora, which he found "unworldly, a symphony of light in exaggerated colors" that made polar aloneness a scintillating as well as solitary experience. Then, at dawn, a third vision: "the vault of the sky is like no other," resplendent in "rich, clear colors of blue, red and gold." Here we have three life-enhancing celestial sights, all unfolding in a single, frigid and very solitary evening at 81 degrees, 24 minutes north latitude.

In the early twentieth century, north took on a veil of innocence that conjured Disneyesque, Snow-Whitish interpretation and forged its now-inseparable Christmas link with Santa. A variant of this theme underlies the 1939 film *The Wizard of Oz*, based on a novel by L. Frank Baum. A road movie of the imagination, it assigns the compass points very definite moral attributes with Glinda, the good witch (itself a head-turning notion), representing the north. Soft in spirit, she is a discreet helper on Dorothy's perilous journey to Oz. The bumbling wizard has the black bag of tricks, but white-gowned Glinda is Dorothy's directional guide and ticket home.

The '60s cartoon TV character Dudley Do-Right represented another ethically colored northern angle. The Royal Canadian Mounted Police, his employer, exercises upright, soft-glove authority of a sort highlighted (in a very different context) in a memorable cross-border crime scene in the 1987 film *The Untouchables*. The Dudley character was depicted in terms (naïve, well-meaning, cheerful) that any Norwegian would recognize. And if we are tempted to pass such images off as adolescent concoctions, we misread their beguiling side and underestimate their power to shape perceptions.

The north sealed its connection with Christmas in a post–World War I commercial push. Fighting off its hard-luck reputation, Finland emerged as the winner of a good-natured rivalry with Norway for the rights to Santa's true home. A combination of Arctic Circle location and shrewd advertising has transformed Rovaniemi, a Lapland town burned to the ground by retreating Germans in 1945, into a sprawling holiday complex. It draws nearly 600,000 yearly visitors, mostly Asians willing to pay through the nose to experience the dubious charms of a Finnish winter.

This modern association with jollity and virtue was a conscious counter to traditionally darker attributions. The medieval perils of the dense northern woods were brought to life through Hansel and Gretel and other tales by the Brothers Grimm. In the worst imaginings, the north was portrayed as a bubbling cauldron of satanic forces, embodied in images of Lady Macbeth and the witch hunt, of devil worship and shamanism—the sum of all fears flowing from an ignorance that has brought so much human calamity to the far north.

The mental haziness ascribed rather lightly by Bjørnson alludes to the whiteouts, freeze-fogs and other sources of sensory dislocation that are special to the north. Viking explorers were often flummoxed by the *hafvilla* phenomenon, a disorienting mix of fog and wind that would follow exceptionally clear conditions. Fog was also the characteristic northern condition for Hans Christian Andersen, an avid if self-consciously neurotic traveler. "Wrapped in a cold raw fog," he wrote in 1841 on his return from the Orient, "Hamburg's towers lie before us. We are in the north!"

The physical north can be a trickster. Weather conditions can change in a flash. Proximity to the Magnetic North Pole—a physical oddity that itself migrates—makes compasses act strangely. Fierce cold brings desert-like conditions of low humidity. Sharp solar angles create visual distortions, like the famous double-sun effect that mesmerizes skilled photographers. Constant summer daylight gives way to months of winter night. Such conditions could hardly leave the human psyche unaffected.

Earth's northern reaches have been tainted in both literature and politics. Macbeth, the darkest figure of Shakespeare's tragedies, was a Scottish king of the eleventh century. In the 1590s a real-life monarch, Scotland's James VI, personally prosecuted alleged witches of North Berwick for sabotaging his wedding plans. Across the pond, Salem, in today's New England, was famously if more briefly convulsed.

Diabolism, conniving with the devil, was the worst charge, and the upheavals of the Reformation brought furious efforts to seek out and destroy those responsible. To the Lutheran Church, northern Norway was long regarded as *Satans Rike*, devil's country. Witch hunt victims tended to be women, partly linked to the scourge of syphilis brought back to the Old World by Columbus's crews. In Denmark more than 1,000 women were put to death, in (mostly north) Norway around 350, with over 1,400 prosecutions that continued into the nineteenth century. Curiously, though, in Iceland it was men who mainly stood accused. The genders may have switched, but the northern association remained.

The Sami, the indigenous people of northern Scandinavia, traditionally feared the polar winter because they saw the Northern Lights as a sign of God's wrath. The Vikings took the celestial aurora to be Valkyries or messengers of death. These associations later animated Swedish writer August Strindberg, whose family had distant roots in Norrland. In his fervid inventiveness, Lapp blood coursed through his veins. As told by his biographer Olof Lagerkrantz, Strindberg became convinced of his indigenous magical powers based on this loose association.

Magical thinking has long shadowed the rationalist mindset more typically associated with the modern north. Trolls, elves and sprites populate the northern folk tales. In Jonas Lie's popular collection *Troll*, they manifest in human "temperament, will of nature and explosive power." Nordic lore is full of heroic imagery and forbidding vision, fittingly for a region that resisted Christianity until very late.

Even today Nordic popular culture nurses a subtext of fascination with the supernatural. It lingers in the cultural firmament, like background radiation in the outer cosmos. A perennial hit TV show with various Scandinavian permutations, *Åndenes Makt*, purports to document the workings of ghosts in old buildings. Similar notions inform the unceasing deluge of crime literature, the "Nordic noir" that dominates the world of fiction. Still another, very public tangent was broached by the daughter and eldest child of King Harald, Princess Märtha Louise, who for a decade jointly ran an *engleskole* ("angels' school") designed to help participants access their divine sides until it ran into (economic) problems of a more mundane sort.

Northern mythmaking has a long pedigree. To the ancient Greeks, the north was a nether land populated by *hyperborei*, people who lived "back of the north wind," the bitter *boreadis*. They were said to live in harmony and perpetual sunshine. A similar myth hypothesized a balmy land, a *terra australis*, at the other earth's end. Herodotus, the first great Classical-age historian, situated the *hyperborei* in southern Russia, from where they made regular offerings (wrapped in straw) to Apollo's sanctuary at Delos, appearing only by proxy.

He also imagined lands beyond that, so climatically cursed as to be uninhabitable. "I think myself that it must always be snowing in these northern regions," he adds dryly, "though less, of course, in summer rather than winter." (In that he was not wrong.) Herodotus is to ancient Greece what Snorri Sturluson became for Viking Norway, a worldly chronicler whose anecdotes can be unreliable in factual terms.

The far north's first "discoverer" was a rank outsider from the other end of Europe. Pytheas was a Hellenistic-age trader and explorer from Massalias, today's Marseilles, in the northern Greek province of Gaul. Around 325 BC he sailed from the Mediterranean into the Arctic: past Carthage, through the Pillars of Hercules, across the Bay of Biscay to Cornwall and up Britain's west coast. From the tip of Scotland he continued north. After six days' sail he reached land he called *Thule*.

His descriptions leave room for doubt about where he ended up. He found slushy sea ice and almost round-the-clock sunshine, so he made it near the Arctic Circle. Along with Pytheas the explorer (and the commercial scout, seeking tin and amber) was Pytheas the social analyst. He was first to distinguish between the *Keltoi* of the west and the Germanic tribes (*Germanoi*) that became cultural demarkers within northern Europe.

His account, *On the Ocean*, is lost to history, possibly consumed in the fire that destroyed the ancient library of Alexandria. (In a nice modern twist, Norwegian architectural firm Snøhetta won the global competition to design the modern Bibliotheca Alexandrina, which opened in 2002.) Pytheas's feats come to us indirectly, through later geographers like Polybius, Pliny and Ptolemy, who scorned his accounts as fantasy. The Thule he encountered was likely either Iceland, to the northwest, or Norway. It seems he entered the Baltic and found amber and encountered tilled farmland not possible in (then) empty Iceland. Nansen, in his underrated tour de force *In Northern Mists*, argued the Norwegian option while Barry Cunliffe, a classicist, opts for Iceland.

Wherever it was, Thule long stood for the "farthest known point north." It's still an Arctic place-name (in Greenland, denoting an air base), but gradually it assumed symbolic value as an indicator of human achievement. The term *Ultima Thule* referenced the literal end of the earth and came to mean the ultimate accomplishment for an explorer—even an unmanned one. It's the fitting name assigned to a lump of rock at the edge of the solar system, the destination for NASA's New Horizons spacecraft that was launched in early 2019.

In such ways did north come to transcend location or direction. It was *aspirational*, representing achievement in the highest degree, a notion that Nordkapp-bound roadsters can relate to. Such imagery conceivably made it easier, in the twentieth century, to posit a "Nordic model" as a higher form of public virtue. But Scandinavia's complex ethical associations—a mix of social virtue and hidden vice, a cross of well-meaning aid worker and bleak-minded *Wallander*—have even deeper roots.

Northern confusion was also sewn by the ancient amber trade. The world's first widely exchanged gemstone, amber lined the walls of Mycenaean palaces and was fashioned into jewelry. Most of it originated in the Baltic, the Mediterranean's northern counterpart, and the amber zone formed an ill-defined border between civilization and "the other."

Amber is organic, the fossilized excretions of conifers or "tears of trees" as Victoria Finlay, biographer of gems, appealingly puts it. "Amber was the color of sunlight," she writes. "It was exotic and mysterious, and it came from far away," which fed imaginings of the north as a warm and sunny place. Phoenician traders controlled the amber routes, adding to its mystery and upping its worth. Amber pushed early trading cultures northward; Finlay even suggests that it brought the Bronze Age to the Baltic. But there it stopped. The lands beyond it remained *terra incognita*.

Southern Europeans broadly associate the north with territory "beyond the Alps." This Germanic link was solidified by Tacitus, a Roman official and historian active around 100 AD. The son-in-law of Agricola, a governor of Britain, he wrote admiringly of disciplined, racially pure northerners in his *Germania*, a kind of ethnographic study, comparing them favorably with louche Roman ways. Charlemagne, eighth-century founder of the Holy Roman Empire, demarked north by the River Eider, which cuts through today's Schleswig-Holstein. He reputedly flung a spear into the river, exclaiming "This is the Empire's frontier!" In modern times, central Europeans and Brits have tended to trace a line in the Baltic lowlands. "Stettin in the Baltic," now well disguised as the Polish city of Szczecin, was Churchill's famous northern terminus in his 1946 Iron Curtain speech.

Oddly enough, north suffers distortion at the hands of the cartography industry we rely on for geographical clarity. Its instruments diminish it in some respects while accentuating it in others. It is surprisingly common, for example, to see maps of Europe shorn of Scandinavian territory north of Oslo, Stockholm and Helsinki, all of which bestride the sixtieth parallel that slices through the bottom quarter of Norway and Sweden and brushes southernmost Finland.

No less a place-name authority than the *Oxford Dictionary of the World* lops off all of Scandinavia above Lillehammer, Gävle and Turku; its two-page spread of "Europe" displays more of Algeria than of Norway. Imagine a Europe deprived of the Balkans or Sicily, and the indignity of this severance becomes apparent. To unsuspecting map-gazers Scandinavia is a chronic amputee, and out of sight means out of mind.

This is a special shame because to a true Scandinavian, "north" is restricted to the upper latitudes, the High North. The term *Arctic* is derived neither from "arc" (as in map lines) nor from the Biblical Ark (a store of ancient wisdom) but rather from the constellation Arcturus, the Little Bear. On earth it is the land of tundra and permafrost. Natural scientists, given to definitional severity, restrict the High North to the very top of Europe that is now the preserve of Norwegians alone.

It also comes bundled with cultural attributes. To southern Europeans, the prevailing northern image is still that of people who are tall, blond and cool in character, but to Scandinavians, northerners get vaguely portrayed as short, kitted in blue-and-red dress and furry boots with curled toes and herd reindeer for a living, a ready-made package of regional cliché all its own.

What the image-makers take away, they can give back. Mapmakers since Claudius Ptolemy in the second century AD have exalted north by placing it atop their rudimentary representations. Doing so was a matter of practicality, since the world's land masses are bunched in the northern hemisphere (something known even in his time). A friendly nod to readers became a bedrock principle of cartography thanks to repetition and shared Eurocentrism. This tendency was reinforced with the refinement of longitude in the eighteenth century, courtesy of John Harrison's H4 chronograph.

Longitude is determined by meridians, the gauging standards for points east and west. Unlike latitudinal parallels, the flat lines on a map, meridians converge inexorably at the poles, pulling the eye upward. Marked on a globe, they perform an immense psychological service for the north. North became the marquee name in a providential spot, thanks to accidents of nomenclature and geography. A kind of positive prejudice is built into the picture. Meridians conjure up the vertical lines of a Gothic Cathedral, a defining image for northern Europe since its first appearance in eleventh-century France. Pointed arches and ribbed vaulting were distinctive Gothic tweaks on the semicircular Roman basilica (and the horseshoe-shaped Moorish archway). They created sight lines that "soared from the earth like great forest groves [...] to recreate the sacred landscape of their culture," in Osborne's phrase, lifting the medieval gaze to the heavens. Gothic remains a compelling northern image and a suitably contradictory one, linked both to spiritual grandeur and punk barbarism.

Northern regions also benefit from the phenomenon of map distortion, which arises from efforts to squeeze a three-dimensional reality, the earth sphere, onto the page via projection. The one fashioned in 1569 by Gerardus Mercator, a Dutchman, is still widely used because it preserves the integrity of straight or rhumb lines between points, helping ships navigate. It is conformal, meaning it preserves shapes, but this accuracy comes at the expense of areal correctness. The distortion rate increases exponentially the further north you go.

Mercator's main drawback is indeed that it "cannot be extended to the poles," according to geographer Norman Thrower. This produces the famous Greenland effect that gives northern landmasses, including Alaska, bloated dimensions on world maps. Northern Scandinavia benefits in a minor way from these distortions. The world's most popular mapping schema can't relate the high latitudes accurately, making them difficult to grasp either as concepts or as physical realities.

The evocative aspect of meridians stirred Colin Thubron, a deft chronicler of direction and remoteness. *In Siberia*, his tableau of the forsaken landmass he calls Russia's Elsewhere, describes a trip down the Yenisei River (i.e., heading northward in the perverse way of most Russian rivers) into the High Arctic.

"You wait in childlike anticipation," he writes, "the globe of the earth steepening as all the lines of longitude converge in front of you." The notion takes wing in another sense: "Soon, you conceive, the earth must level out under the crushing weight of sky, and through that slit in the horizon [...] you will glide over the top of the world and begin to slide down into the south." We willingly follow.

These jumbled messages long lent a kind of cultivated imprecision to the north. Distant, sparsely populated, rarely visited, distorted by maps and itself poorly mapped, the whole region, including its migratory peoples, long remained mysterious, even to Scandinavians. In the eleventh century Adam of Bremen stoked imaginings by speculating about "heathens [...] superior in the magic arts," where women grew beards and men lived in the woods wearing only animal skins. Images of the north as wild and untamed were powerfully reinforced by the Berserker and other excesses of the Viking Age.

To many others the north was long seen as soulless as well as lifeless. Mary Shelley situated the final, bleak scenes of *Frankenstein* there, the scientist-creator chasing his creature to the North Pole, two lost spirits in the desolate ice fields. (The daughter of Mary Wollstonecraft, a Nordic traveler, she may have had a seed planted for her.)

The first modern thinker to link geography with temperament, Montesquieu in 1748 believed it froze the northern character. "You must flail a Muscovite," he averred, "to make him feel." To him Scandinavia was important mainly as a physical barrier against Arctic winds, making Europe's climate more hospitable. The north as windbreaker: yet another fanciful image bequeathed us by the wise men of the Enlightenment.

In the late fifteenth century, practical interest in the north was sparked by dreams of a shortcut from Europe to the Far East. Imaginations were fired by the dictated travelogues of Marco Polo, a Venetian who traveled to China in the thirteenth century along the fabled Silk Road, consorted with Kublai Khan and returned with tales both fantastical and unverifiable. Soon the Arctic became connected to the spice trade as pepper, cinnamon and nutmeg made their lucrative way to European commercial centers from their Pacific island gardens.

Portugal and Spain had a crucial head start, and their bid to divide the world into hemispheres of control, via the Treaty of Tordesillas in 1494, received the papal nod. Their northern (Dutch, English, Danish) competitors were forced to seek a different route east. A mix of greed and ignorance led them northward on voyages that brought accidental discoveries like those of Barentsz, the Dutch explorer who happened upon Svalbard on his way to China.

Mankind's two "hardiest geographical illusions," writes John Noble Wilford in *The Mapmakers*, were both polar. One was the *Terra australis incognita*, the "great unknown southern continent" that was long thought to connect with Africa, South America or both. The other was the North-West Passage from the Atlantic over Canada to the Pacific Ocean. A third and equally potent illusion, unmentioned by Wilford, was the North-East Passage over Norway and Russia. All three polar "myths" ultimately were shown to have an attenuated factual basis, which gives them a strange, proved-false-before-being-proved-true historical twist.

The Arctic thrust wasn't without foundational logic. With the southern routes around the Capes of Horn and Good Hope accounted for, north was the one option left. The rounded earth also made it attractively shorter. But it proved an icy siren that cut short countless lives of feckless crews by scurvy, exposure and starvation.

The hunt for the North-West Passage, says Wilford, was driven by "wishful thinking [rather] than observed fact," making, in Jon Balchin's more arched view, for "a story of almost tragically comical proportions." It warrants a brief digression for what it says about the tenacity of northern fantasies and about the bareback enterprise by which a handful of Norwegians, led by Roald Amundsen, quietly succeeded where a string of well-funded colonial enterprises fell conspicuously short.

The push began soon after Columbus's first New World voyage of 1492. Giovanni Caboto, aka John Cabot, sailing for Henry VII of Britain in 1497, probably landed in southern Canada and returned safely; the following year, his flotilla of four ships (a fifth having mutinied early on), along with all hands, was lost at sea.

Sir Martin Frobisher sought it out on repeated failed voyages in the 1570s, and John Davis a decade later. Sir Francis Drake at the same time, who circumnavigated the earth on pirate raids, may have tried to reach it too. Before those Englishmen, Giovanni da Verrazzano thought he espied China on the far side of North Carolina's Outer Banks, such was the reigning confusion.

Frobisher's three voyages set an oft-repeated pattern of triple expeditionary failures. His first, in 1576, lost one ship to a storm and a second to desertion. The remaining ship found a tantalizing passage he called Frobisher Strait, which later proved a dead-end bay. He then diverted his attention to local mining, returning to England with heaps of black ore he was convinced, falsely, contained gold ore; it was instead pyrite, fool's gold. His second voyage was dedicated to mining these false riches, and on his third and most ambitious expedition, in 1578, he found an actual sail-through (now Hudson Strait), which he believed a dead-end, calling it "Mistaken Strait."

The pious hopes merely fueled interest. In 1610 Henry Hudson, sailing for Holland, having failed to find the North-East Passage, turned west, floundered and was ultimately set loose in a dinghy by his mutinying crew and left to die. In 1615 William Baffin went further into Hudson Bay but concluded, erroneously, that it was a dead-end. The next year he discovered an actual passage, Lancaster Sound, but was stopped by ice.

Denmark, victorious over Sweden in war, then joined the calamitous fray. This also, in effect, meant Norway. In 1619 Jens Munk, an Arendal-born Norwegian sailing for the Danish king, set off in search of a western passage with a pair of ships and a crew of 65; just three, including their leader, survived the scurvy-ravaged ordeal while iced up in Hudson Bay. The bedraggled trio returned, minus their teeth, only to be grilled about the loss of a ship by King Christian IV. The passage's false allure even survived the doubts of the incomparable James Cook in his third and final voyage of 1778–79, when he reached above 70 degrees north off western Canada and penetrated the Bering Strait before being stopped by ice.

The defeat of Napoleon brought renewed interest in finding the fabled route. By now the practical value of the passage was in severe doubt; it was a matter of national prestige for the British Admiralty. It brought further catalogs of (heroic, British) disaster, typically in triplicate, and in search of something even more nebulous than a lust for faraway riches.

Sir John Ross set out in 1818, got as far as Lancaster Bay, then turned around for home when he was misled by a mirage and assumed, wrongly, that he had reached an impasse. It took two decades to clear his name from the public pillorying that greeted his unforced retreat. A second voyage, ending in 1833, led to four years in the ice, crushed ships and a narrow escape that, failure notwithstanding, restored his name. A third and final voyage to rescue the lost John Franklin came up empty-handed. Franklin, in turn, made three voyages into the Canadian far north, two via inland rivers, the third, in 1845, by sea from the north. Each came to grief, with his last ending in the loss of all 129 crew. It was the worst calamity in the annals of Arctic exploration and earned him, like Scott in 1911, a kind of fallen polar hero immortality.

Franklin's loss spurred other voyages in the area, ostensibly in search of the lost men. A contemporary of Ross and Franklin, William Parry, likewise, took three voyages in search of the passage, one from the north, one from the south, both stopped by ice; his third, in 1824–25, was aborted, unsurprisingly, because of ice. James Clark Ross, John Ross's nephew and perhaps the greatest of nineteenth-century polar explorers, himself sailed on Parry's three searches for the North-West Passage. His retirement was interrupted by yet another, and another futile, venture, this time in search of Franklin. Knowledge accumulated with these voyages, but the reputational and financial losses were enormous.

Only in 1905 was the passage successfully negotiated, by Amundsen in the tiny *Gjøa*, a converted fishing smack with a shallow draft and rudimentary diesel engine. His crew of six had a budget so stretched that they had to launch in a midnight downpour in order to escape impoundment by creditors in hot pursuit. After two winters stuck in Canadian ice, they made it through in mid-1905, the summer of Norwegian independence. His low-key professionalism earned for Norway Arctic bragging rights, denying the British before he again did the same, six years later, at the bottom of the world. His passage to Alaska is now but a footnote to a fabled career and makes for an ironically low-key final chapter to three centuries of misplaced hopes. This made it the ultimate anticlimax in exploratory annals—and a thoroughly Norwegian sort of denouement.

But it was the North-East Passage over Scandinavia and Russia that first excited maritime interest in the European Arctic as a destination in its own right, not just as a zone of transit. It stimulated a pathbreaking commercial enterprise, the Muscovy Company, founded in 1555 to capitalize on transit business. Barentsz's (re) discovery of Svalbard, coupled with Henry Hudson's reports of whale-rich northern seas, lured Danes, Dutchmen, Englishmen, Basques, Pomors and others, sparking a killing orgy at the eightieth parallel. Greed now doubly drove interest in the Arctic waters.

It also set a precedent for successive resource races to fuzzy Eldorados of the high latitudes. The amber trade, whale- and later seal-hunting, the spice trail and later the Klondike, Alaskan and Siberian gold rushes all blazed a cautionary trail to today's equivalent, the gas fields beneath the Barents Sea. Each brought feverish excitement followed by ruin. Fears of a twenty-first century Arctic resource war, soberly postulated by Roger Howard, draw on a noxious past littered with grab-and-scram tales that today's fossil fuel industry would be well advised to ponder.

Where does modern Norway slot into this syncretic scene? The country's very name conveys meanings half-hidden in plain sight. Unlike those of most countries, it is explicitly geographical; it's also directional and conveys a sense of movement. The Norwegian name, like its location, packs a lot of punch.

The far north has played a more central role in Norwegian life than is generally realized. An unexpected eruption in 2018 of anger in Troms, over the planned merger of their county with Finnmark and Nordland, is just one recent manifestation of its impact, while the ghostly militarization of Arctic waters, including by the likes of China, adds a dose of deeper contemporary worry.

In sheer bulk, the Norwegian north asserts itself. Of modern Norway's 19 counties, three of the biggest four lie north of the Arctic Circle. Finnmark, in the extreme northeast, is by far the largest in size (and the smallest in population). Nordland is second biggest, Troms a strong fourth. One of the most underrated of Norwegian accomplishments, building on Hansa and Danish precedents, has been to incorporate this far-flung territory into a single administrative unit and cultural expression while preserving something of its special character. It is a *bureaucratic* achievement of the first order. The north's importance nonetheless tugs at Norwegian national priorities even as it lends it a distinctive profile.

As nonplussed visitors learn the hard way, there are multiple "physical norths" even in mainland Norway. *Saltfjellet* (salt mountain) is the traditional starting point for vastness stretching to the Barents Sea. This, Norway's *nordområde*, contains a tenth of the population and a third of the country's mainland landmass. Beyond that is submerged, continental-shelf Norway, the vast seas to which Norway lays solid claim—having been the first Arctic-rim country to have its shelf claims submitted, and approved, by the UN body administering the 1982 UNCLOS (sea-law) treaty. Here Norway operates a complex fishing-zone and exploratory-block legal regime.

Further on is Bjørnøya (population: nine), the southern tip of the Svalbard island group. This archipelagic Norway bears separate legal imprimatur and is run directly from Oslo by a resident governor. A couple of thousand hardy souls, though outnumbered by polar bears and surrounded by postglacial eeriness, live surprisingly regular lives there. Jan Mayen (population: 18) lies halfway to Iceland but is administered via Nordland.

Few Norwegians would link Trondheim to the Arctic, but discussion of Norway's north really begins with this, the country's third city at its narrow midsection. It is attractively set on the broad arm of a fjord reaching well inland from the west coast. "Beyond Trondheim," writes geographer Roy Millward, "lies another Norway [...] an outpost of Europe on the edge of the empty Arctic." It forms an intangible border on the order of the Mason–Dixon Line in pre–Civil War America.

Because of its setting, Norway attracts the labels of northern, Nordic, Scandinavian, Arctic and polar. Yet none is self-evident. Nor-way, *Norvegr*, essentially means "road to the north." (A companion term with a static connotation, *Norregr*, refers to "realm of the north.") Unusually, this northern country ushers our attention *to* the north as well. The *Kystriksveien* is a coastal road that winds northward spectacularly from Steinkjer to Bodø starting in Nord Trøndelag. The main sea route, Hurtigruten, plies the west-coast waters from Bergen to Kirkenes in the manner, if not the style, of old tramp steamers, a mobile lifeline.

Norway makes for an unexpected point of transit. Its sea-passage associations date back 3,000 years, while in the late Middle Ages the "sacred way" to Nidaros, the world's most northerly cathedral, gave landward routes other importance. The earliest known Norwegian explorer, Ottar (Ohthere), lived at the time of Harald Harfågre (Fairhair) in the late ninth century AD. He hailed from "the furthest north of all the Norwegians," a place he called Hålogaland, near today's Tromsø. From there he set out "to examine how far the land stretched to the north," partly to see whether anyone lived there. An early multitasker, he managed a trade network that reached down to Hedeby in today's Schleswig, over a month's sail away. He later made his way to Ireland and England. In Wessex he dictated his extraordinary story to King Alfred, who in turn recorded it. His trips thus provide the earliest account we have of the first native Norwegian sailor to venture out for the sake of it, not just for food or plunder.

The sparsely populated north suffered post-Viking human drainage, exacerbated by the Little Ice Age that followed the relatively clement Medieval Warm Period (or Climatic Optimum). Southern drift worsened after the sixteenth-century Reformation that desecrated the shrine of St. Olav. But countervailing efforts to "rescue" the north were also underway.

Olaus Magnus, a Swedish Catholic priest in Rome, wrote a tract (his *Description of the Northern Peoples*) extolling the wonders of territories lost to the Church because of Luther. If Olaus was the region's chief publicist and mapmaker (via his *carta marina*) of his time, he was also a truth-spinner. His work pulsated with fantastic tales of sea beasts and strange customs befitting a land of perpetual winter storms. It's no surprise that the north later began to attract proselytizing Pietists, who sniffed ripe territory. It was the battle for hearts and minds, as much as spices, fish and whales, which stoked early-modern interest in the far north.

For a time Sweden became more tightly identified with the north than Denmark, which nominally controlled its farthest reaches. Swedish King Karl IX launched a church-building venture in far-northern Norway that was halted by the Peace of Knäred in 1613. But Sweden continued to assert its interests in other ways. In Henningsen's reading, the north later emerged in the public mind as a function of Sweden's great power era, as "a symbol of the power and splendor" of Sweden's Karl XI—and this, in turn, was a conscious political counterpoint to France. These two countries share surprising links, forged early in Sweden's power era when continental capital, art and know-how flowed north. A human connection was Nicodemus Tessin the Younger, son of the architect of Drottningholm Palace outside Stockholm, which was modeled on Versailles.

This Arctic connection with Sweden deepened via the writings of Olof Rudbeck. The "Nordic Leonardo" (who was also, as Anne Simonsen notes, the great-great-grandfather of Alfred Nobel) proposed a Swedish connection with the fabled Atlantis, 40 years before Carl Linnæus redirected it to the firmer truths of science. In the late eighteenth century, Swedish King Gustav III promoted Sweden as a guardian of civilization in the far north, consciously mirroring France's self-styled civilizational role on the continent. Thus the Swedish decision, in 1810, to import a Frenchman to establish a new royal bloodline was less arbitrary than it seemed. Four years after that, this Franco-Swedish connection roped in Norway via the Kiel Treaty.

Gustavian Sweden posited itself as a (northern, Protestant, lunar) reflection of France's Louis XIV—the Sun King and, not coincidentally, Sweden's frequent political ally against Denmark. It found all manner of expression. One is the Royal Order of the Polar Star (N*ordstjärneorden*), created by King Fredrik I in 1748 and still bestowed on those whose good work "knows no decline" and, naturally, advances the good name of Sweden.

Carl von Linné (aka Linnæus) first brought scientific acumen to the far north. In May 1732, on the eve of his 25th birthday, he set out "for the purpose of investigating the three kingdoms of Nature in that country." It was no leisurely jaunt. In *A Tour in Lapland* he recounts losing horses from underneath him, nearly freezing to death and going a month without bread. His focus was not the coniferous northern *taiga* but the fragile ecosystem of the High Arctic. His classification system for plants and animals is still used today, gained after grueling trips to catalog the north's unsuspected botanical richness. Linnæus shared his northern fascination with Anders Celsius, one of his sponsors and eponymous father of the centigrade scale. Less famously, Celsius helped determine that the earth is not circular but flattens slightly at the poles—thus adding still another physical twist on normality in the north.

As the region's dominant player in the seventeenth and eighteenth centuries and, for most of the nineteenth, effective suzerain of Norway, Sweden had territorial, cultural and political claims, now backed by scientific authority, to supremacy at the top of Europe. Hemmed in by Danish control over Baltic access, Swedes looked north as an antidote to encirclement and a source of easy income (by taxing the Sami peoples). The association went deep. *Jag vill leva, jag vill dö i Norden* ("I wish to live and die in the North") is a line from the de facto Swedish, not Norwegian national anthem. Written in 1844 by Richard Dybeck, it underscores the peremptory, if by then increasingly shaky, Swedish claim to northern as well as Nordic preeminence.

The Swedish thrust that came to involve Norway ultimately led to its displacement *by* Norway. Norwegian territory was a launching pad for Swedish exploration in the union period. Baron Adolf Nordenskjöld (born in Finland but associated with Sweden), whose *Vega* expedition in 1878–79 was the first to achieve the North-East Passage, set off from Tromsø. Six years earlier he had built the "Swedish House" on Svalbard in a quixotic bid to mine for phosphorus—another baleful object lesson for the high north. As the century wore on, northern Norway became the preferred launching pad for adventurers trying, and failing, to reach the North Pole by ship, sledge, airplane, airship, balloon, ski and, in one particularly imaginative (German) scheme, by train.

In 1897 Salomon Andrée, a Swedish engineer, set out with two companions from northern Svalbard in a silk hydrogen balloon. Attempting to reach the North Pole they crashed, then survived a harrowing, two-month trek across the ice before perishing, as revealed in diaries found decades later. The group had lifted off with champagne, but without Arctic ballooning experience, in what became the most celebrated and tragic instance of absurdist (and in this case Swedish) Arctic dreams. Five years before, a pair of Swedes (Björling and Kallstenius) were lost off northwest Greenland seeking a route to the North Pole. If one national failure is unfortunate, two in a decade suggest a pattern. Norway, the union's chafing lesser half, was doubly primed for a turn-of-century Arctic thrust that became the wellspring of breakout triumphs.

The north's remoteness, however, remained an awkward constant. At the Eidsvoll constitutional gathering in spring 1814, Finnmark and Nordland weren't represented because their delegates could not reach that southern nook in time. But the wider trend, from the eighteenth century, posited the north as a place of economic promise. Reverse migration brought new regularization of life, the towns of Tromsø and Vardø indicatively being established in 1794, Hammerfest in 1789.

Interest from outside followed, but slowly. Of the foreign travelers who reached Norway before the late nineteenth century, few ventured inland and fewer still north; their literary versions of Europe's north mostly conveyed the Scandinavian south. One exception was a curmudgeonly American, Bayard Taylor, who reached distant Vardø and left an unflattering Norwegian portrait as of summer 1857. Two decades before, William Hooker blazed a similar trail as a med student in Samiland near the Alten River, writing of mosquito plagues (the "persevering phlebotomizers" that still torment campers) and yoiking, now a celebrated Sami singing tradition. Yet even the dyspeptic Taylor noticed qualities that set "real" [Norwegian] northerners apart. "They are in every respect more agreeable and promising specimens of humanity than their brothers of Southern Norway," he wrote, despite "the dark and savage scenery amidst which their lot is cast."

Nor did the nineteenth-century stirrings of Norwegian culture inevitably embrace the country's own north. The great landscape paintings of Dahl and his successors featured the greener, softgrand landscapes of the south and west. A major exception was Peder Balke, who despite poverty traveled north in 1832 and returned with a portfolio of works depicting bleakness and stormy winter. His austere, almost primordial images, like those of Lars Hertervig, who went insane, offered a jarring counterpoint to the prevailing, summer-in-mountain scenes being promoted in Germany by the likes of Adolph Tidemand and Hans Gude, who packaged Norway's physical appeal in benign ways.

Gradually, Norwegians engaged with the far north via science, mining and exploration. Bear Island and Svalbard drew expeditions, and this preliminary work added depth to the late-century exploratory feats of Nansen and Amundsen. Otto

Sverdrup, the forgotten third man of this triumvirate, mapped huge sections of Greenland and Canada while skippering the *Fram* on its marathon second voyage.

Russian trappers had mostly ceased to operate on Svalbard, last overwintering, by one account, in 1851–52. By contrast, Norwegians increasingly figured in Svalbard "firsts." Baltazar Mathias Keilhau, a geologist, spearheaded Scandinavian scientific interest there, running through names like Lovén, Torell and Nordenskjöld, a mentor of Nansen's. In 1863 the *Jan Mayen*, skippered by a Norwegian, became the first ship to circumnavigate Svalbard. And in 1899 an unknown Norwegian shipper brought the first known load of Svalbard coal to the mainland. The following year a Trondheim syndicate became the first to sink a coal shaft at Advent Bay, finding a seam three meters (10 feet) thick. In 1903 a coal industry was founded in Longyearbyen, which invigorated Norwegian coastal zones. It was providential for a nearby country on the cusp of independence but whose northern claims were still shaky and its ability to fund expeditions chronically hamstrung.

Though late to a northern mind-set, the Norwegians were gradually establishing the Arctic as a vaguely national enterprise. On his Greenland crossing (1888) Nansen had included two Sami and relied on Danish funding. Five years later, his fame growing along with tensions with Sweden, Nansen permitted neither Swedish scientists nor its backing money on the inaugural *Fram* expedition. Yet Nansen himself reflected widening Arctic interest. Norway was among the 12 countries participating in the inaugural International Polar Year (1882–83), the first cooperative initiative focused on polar research.

With Norway's national awakening came a corollary awareness of the north's political value. Nord-Norge was politically "invented," according to Niemi, around 1894 by an elitist internal diaspora based in Kristiania (Oslo). The north was the last part of Norway to be formally embraced while it continued, in Niemi's view, to be treated as a colonial appendage. Soon after, a north–south rivalry prompted Sørlanders to create their own pseudo-political identity for Norway's far south.

In the 1930s a "North Norwegian Rising" movement emerged, faintly paralleling other nationalist movements of the era (like

Finland's Lapua), only to be interrupted by the war. Yet its aim was economic modernization and political inclusion, not separatism, so in this respect there is no parallel with Italy's Northern League, which today is a genuine political force. The surprising upshot is that any politico-cultural differentiation between Norway's south and north is less pronounced than the visuals suggest, and demonstrably weaker than the perceptual gulf separating the country's southwest from its southeast—or for that matter, Scotland from England.

Ironically, Norwegian independence in 1905 marked a setback for the region. Reflecting a wider academic vilification of neo-imperialist thinking in the 1960s, Per Otnes wrote of the north, especially Finnmark, as "a little known chapter of the general history of colonialism" of the internal rather than exogenous variety. The desolate north had long been treated, by Sweden and Russia as well as Norway, as a kind of Lapp patchwork quilt (*lappeteppe*), an area ripe for economic exploitation. Mixed motives long attached to the north in a political sense.

Norway, at first via Denmark, came to dominate, he argued, in four phases: a mercantile phase from around 1600, strengthened by trade monopoly till 1788; formal colonialization, helped by establishment of firm borders from 1751 and (with Russia) 1826; and a third phase of "practical" colonialism via measures restricting reindeer herding (1883, 1897), the building of *Ofotbanen* to service Kiruna's iron mines and, in 1902, a law forbidding the sale of northern land to non-Norwegian speakers. All these were aimed at cultural dominance of the north by "real" (i.e., ethnic) Norwegians while institutionalizing a legal inequality. School policy took on the same strategic urgency, building on the religious schools of Thomas Weston in the 1700s. The picture Otnes paints is the shadowy side of the Norwegian awakening. Growing numbers of Norwegian settlers flowed north—a domestic corollary to the mass people flow across the Atlantic (freer life, cheaper land).

Norwegian independence materially worsened native conditions. This, according to Aubert, a social analyst, deepened discrimination in the name of consolidating the state and "Norwegianizing" the area. In this fourth and harshest phase of Otnes's, the stated aim was to turn the Sami into "good Norwegians" while making them a permanent minority in their own homeland.

Most damaging was Norwegian abrogation, in 1905, of the old Lapp Codicil dating back to 1751 that had allowed them free migration across borders.

It is important not to overlook the context of these draconian measures. In 1905 a still-weak Norway emerged into a world of expansionist nationalism; within the decade came a world war, and a generation later another, along with Nazi occupation. From the late 1940s a Cold War raged on Norway's northern border, with the far north nursing fresh memories of "liberation" by Soviet troops and still haunted by terrible uncertainties in 1944–45 about whether the Russians would respect the established border. This relentless twentieth-century catalog of political pressures from outside helps to explain, if not excuse, inequities that persisted until the 1970s.

Norway's north attracted fin de siècle attention of a positive sort as well, not least literary. Prolific novelist Jonas Lie grew up in Tromsø and wrote of the sea and of family life; after two decades in Paris he returned to Norway in his last years. Knut Hamsun grew up in Hamerøy, on a farm called Hamsund, and talked up the north as a hope for the future. He returned to the sub-Arctic of his boyhood late in life and memorably situated one of his most celebrated works, *Pan* (published in 1894), in the northern woods.

The north developed a range of associations, especially ethical and political, that tied it to attributed Norwegian values. The Lutheran ethic resonated deepest in the chilly north and the severe values said to prevail there, the northern "three S's" of silence, sorrow and suffering. Such notions became linked to the Nordic welfare state, a slate of policies to relieve material want. The Labor Party, which dominated Norwegian politics for a century, got its breakthrough not in the urban southeast but in the far north, winning its first parliamentary seats there in 1903. One of the party's, the country's, and the history profession's most prominent twentieth-century figures was Halvdan Koht, another Tromsø native. He too advocated a vigorous upgrade of northern Norway's political standing.

The qualities that Norwegians associated with north Norway were broadly those attributed to Norway by Europe, namely (in Niemi's words) as a region that "would [...] infuse new vitality into the miserable life of the aging southern relative." But its embrace was still restricted to the Norwegian ethnic north. Open discrimination persisted until the 1970s, when regional identities were recognized as a separate category of third-generation human rights by the United Nations—a development that made the Sami the only recognized indigenous culture in Europe.

The north's true political emergence coincided with the fledgling environmental movement. A hydroelectric scheme on the Alta River was the unlikely spark. Local protests escalated into mass marches in downtown Oslo, which drew vocal support from Helge Ingstad and other esteemed Norwegians. They even prompted hunger strikes by political sympathizers. Such flirtation with extra-parliamentary methods finally forced an official turn. Within a decade, in 1989, a Sami parliament (*Sámediggi*) was inaugurated and new respect flowed to the region's scattered peoples and their intricate culture. It was a highly unusual case of direct action that threatened, fleetingly, to breach the unspoken rule against violence in Norwegian politics. But there was no mistaking its sociopolitical impact, a fusion of north and south by way of ecology and minority rights.

It wasn't the first time Norway's north had altered national priorities. In the early 1960s a fatal mining disaster at King's Bay in north Svalbard, coupled with a botched commission of inquiry, compelled the resignation of a (Gerhardsen-led) cabinet—effectively ending a remarkable run of Labor-led governments dating back to 1935. Derek Urwin, who later put the two events into context, calls these 1963 developments "a watershed for the [Norwegian] party system."

The Norwegian north has also shaken things up on the outside. Nordland twice put up fierce resistance to joining Europe, voting by three to one against in the 1972 EC referendum and decisively rejecting EU membership in 1994. In the 2018 regional referenda, both Troms and Finnmark massively (by over 80 percent) rejected government plans to merge them administratively. The tussle with the "people down south" (i.e., Oslo) goes on. Yet the broader picture shows a newfound and hard-won synthesis in which confrontations resemble skirmishes rather than wars and development funds salve many a bruised ego.

Norwegian independence was the obvious game changer for the far north. The northern awakening was sealed, politically, by three events separated by four decades and two world wars. The top of Europe switched in 1905 from Swedish to Norwegian responsibility. Despite losing their Arctic Ocean frontage, Swedes kept up a robust presence, notably in Svalbard, but that in turn was undercut by the second change: the decision by the victorious allies, at the Versailles Conference of 1918–19, to hand Svalbard—now with proven mineral wealth (coal) to go with its strategic location—to Norway. The Treaty of Spitsbergen that was signed in early 1920, together with Norway's own Svalbard Act of April 1925, confirmed Norway as the managing power in the (officially demilitarized) archipelago, which is also an economic free zone and, in Ny Ålesund, a scientific center. Sweden sold its interests in Pyramiden, a mining town, to the Soviets—who much later, as Russia in the cash-strapped 1990s, abandoned the place overnight in 1998. The spooky result is the ghost town with the hammer-and-sickle statuary that greets intrepid tourists today.

The third change came in 1944, when the Finns relinquished their Petsamo corridor to the Arctic Ocean. With the loss came a bitter irony; Finland also lost its only year-round, ice-free harbor. For Finland, like Sweden 40 years earlier, this shifted attention to the south and east. For Norway the effect was just the opposite: it brought undisputed primacy at the top of Europe, responsibility for a Barents archipelago and an adjusted border with an expansionist and militant Soviet Union—a huge change and immense new responsibility for any late-coming state.

Finland, Sweden and Norway each has vast tracts of land above the Arctic Circle, their shared *Nordkalotten* (skullcap). Sweden still bravely touts its northern primacy. Stockholm is the self-styled "capital of Scandinavia," ABBA recorded albums in the Polar Studios and a Romantic-inspired *Nordiska Museet* nurtures a pretense of Nordic amity. Yet the north image resonates in contemporary Norway in ways it can't quite attain in Sweden or even in Finland, both of which have fundamentally inland-sea exposures (Helsinki, a showpiece for Czar Alexander I, is tipped traditionally as the "daughter of the Baltic").

Norway's positioning became pivotal to both the Allied and Nazi war efforts. Hitler identified it as his *Festung Norwegen* or "Norwegian fortress," stationing 400,000 German troops there. Commanded by a fanatical Nazi called Terboven, who enjoyed unusual decision-making leeway, they were constantly reinforced because of Hitler's obsession with an Allied invasion of Norway which, in the end, never came.

Meanwhile a system of Arctic convoys, the "Kola run" over the North Cape to northern Russia, kept the anti-German alliance literally afloat even as it sustained punishing losses under appalling conditions. Perversely, the convoys were safest in the winter cold and dark, away from the airborne eyes of the *Luftwaffe*. The Barents Sea was also the scene of a little-known turning point in the war, the sinking of the *Scharnhorst* in the Battle of the North Cape at Christmas 1943, half a year before the Allied invasion of Normandy. Dogged research by Richard Woodman has given the Kola merchantmen, pressed into wartime service in the Arctic Ocean, their belated due.

Norway's northern, Arctic and polar sides are chronically underplayed in the broader narrative, with social science texts, emphasizing the Fenno-Scandinavian collective, especially culpable. Officially this all changed in 2005, when a newly elected Stoltenberg government (prompted by a preparatory White Paper by the Bondevik government that preceded it) declared the Arctic to be Norway's chief strategic focal point. Less obviously, this initiative represented a culmination of trends and revealed the value and risk bound up in its northern reaches.

Fully a third of mainland Norway lies within the Arctic Circle compared to 15 percent of Sweden and a quarter of Finland. And its *nordområde* is important in different ways than is Sweden's, which has navigable rivers, farmable land, swathes of forest and rich iron ore deposits that, a little gallingly from a Norwegian angle, are sold to world markets via a Norwegian port (Narvik). With none of these assets, the Norwegian north may still be more vital to Norway than Lapland is to Sweden or to Finland.

Northern Norway's saving grace is its year-round accessibility, thanks to its dominant maritime feature, the Gulf Stream. This miraculous ocean-river flows northeastward from the Caribbean, cuts across the Atlantic at an obliquely right angle and washes the Norwegian seaboard before splitting off, as the North Atlantic Drift, in the frigid Arctic. Its warming waters guarantee year-round shipping far above the Arctic Circle, enrich the fishing grounds and keep the country's coastal zone far milder than any comparable latitude on earth. Its natural and human consequences are beyond measure.

Access is not limited to the sea. The Arctic Highway, which runs for 1,500 kilometers (nearly 1,000 miles) from Mo i Rana to Kirkenes, opened land access to vast tracks of territory beyond the railhead at Bodø. An intrepid Brit, John Douglas, has chronicled its turbulent history in an overlooked research effort. Infrastructure brought new life to inland territory, courtesy of Nazi occupation. In a bid to fortify their stronghold the Germans built road and rail connections in Norway with Soviet, East European and Yugoslav slave labor. The resulting roadwork is known as *Blodvei*, the Blood Road, for this history.

Norway emerged from the heroic age (which ended with the deaths of Amundsen in 1928 and Sverdrup and Nansen in 1930) as a self-described "polar nation." Language was corralled for the purpose; Spitsbergen became Svalbard, the northeastern Atlantic the Norwegian Sea. Ships were christened to underscore the link (*Nordstjernan* was the Norwegian liner that brought Alva and Gunnar Myrdal home to Sweden from their first US sojourn). As a place-name root, *Nord* proliferates in everyday Norwegian usage on a par with *lille*.

Is some of this for show? Close observers, notably Susan Barr of the Norwegian Polar Institute, have questioned whether modern Norway actually qualifies as Arctic, a term vaguely defined. Classic texts on Svalbard, like Martin Conway's *No Man's Land*, downplay any special Norwegian involvement in the centuries before independence. As we've seen, the frisson of post-1814 interest long prefigured sustained Norwegian activity.

Barr describes Norwegian official engagement as "mediocre," with Arctic attention running hot and cold for over a century. "Norway," she lets slip, "obviously chooses to bask in the real or imagined glory of being called a Polar Nation," a designation so subject to spin that it has no objective importance. A former foreign minister, Knut Frydenlund, corroborated this sentiment, noting in his memoirs that Norway went without a full-on parliamentary debate over Arctic Svalbard for half a century to 1974, by which time it was being reprioritized along with the north generally.

For all that, important segments of Norwegian national life are explicitly oriented northward. Some, notably fishing, have been all along; others are postwar products. Access by water is perennial, road connections a Nazi legacy and working airports a function of modern life. In strong contrast, civilization in Sweden and Finland tends to peter out in the southern Arctic—notwithstanding the commercial triumph of Rovaniemi—with a wholly inland orientation mostly inaccessible except by chartered small plane. Their only coastal access, on the Gulf of Bothnia, is iced up during the long winter.

All three countries' northern reaches suffered postwar depopulation. Norway too experienced drainage into the 1980s, while a crop failure in 2010 was another spur to farm closures and departure. Norway's *Finnmarksvidda*, doubly challenged in altitude and latitude, is as desolate as can be, scarcely relieved by inland Sami outposts like Karaskjokk and Kautokeino. For much of Norway's north, there is no coastal hinterland in the national name, since most of it lies across the border in Sweden.

But Norway has also done more to anticipate the depopulation trend and counteract its effects, starting with its *Nord-Norge Planen* of 1952. This effort had the twin aims of developing the north economically and integrating it politically with the rest of the country. Bodø was to be the locus and mining, fishing and power generation its chief activities. The program was bitterly criticized in some circles (notably by Ottar Brox in a 1960s riposte) for its mechanistic and centralized conception. Still, it prevented wholesale human flight, and the bulk of the people movement was to area towns. It reinforced a key national priority of keeping all corners of the country populated, active and vibrant.

Today a host of Norwegian towns dot the Atlantic littoral north of Trondheim. Each is a living metropolis with ports, bustling commerce, quirky cultural milieus and thriving tourist trades—winter as well as summer—built around whale spotting, spring skiing, ice hotels and the Northern Lights. The term "regional policy" has a dreary ring to it, but in north Norway it has been almost a Kantian categorical imperative, and the results are increasingly self-sustaining.

Bureaucratic relocation—feasible in the computer age and sensible in a hyperinflated real-estate market—has been key, buttressed by the state's prominent role in Norwegian life. Civil servants, along with industry, fish, oil and art, provide the unlikely link. Brønnøysund, a town of 5,000, is widely known, and less widely loved, as the home of the bureaucracy monitoring Norwegian companies. Hard by is Vega, famous for its duck-down industry and now a UNESCO world heritage natural site. Mo i Rana's tax offices give it plenty of national heft, even if the Hurtigruten boats don't stop there. Mo, too, was a postwar priority. In July 1946 Norway established a national ironworks there, drawing on local ores and fired by coal shipped from Svalbard. The decision transformed the place. This presaged the North Norway Economic Development plan mentioned above, which prioritized the wider area.

Further on, Bodø is Norway's northern railhead and the jumping-off point to the picturesque Vesterålen and Lofoten islands. Two centuries ago its name was linked to a rum-and-tobacco smuggling ring, the famous "Bodø affair" that involved and embarrassed the Swedish and British foreign ministries. Reputations have since improved. Now Bodø is home to the Arctic Philharmonic Orchestra, a base for the Arctic University and a promoter of high-level polar dialogue. It's also a focal point for North Sea energy: the mammoth Aasta Hansteen gas project, in the Norwegian Sea 300 kilometers to the west, has aroused opposition from the World Wide Fund for Nature (WWF) for environmental and even economic reasons. Built between 2013 and 2018, its estimated 51 billion cubic meters of natural gas will make it a presence for decades to come.

Art, too, has found its way into the northern heart. Since the 1990s the Nordland Sculptural Landscape project brought dozens of modern works to unlikely spots. It was conceived in the spirit of ancient rock art and instilled a desolate coastline with a quiet vitality and contemporary feel. Art veers in another direction in inland Alta: the place famous for its *helleristninger*, ancient rock-paintings, now draws music DJs for an international week of tub-thumping electronica.

Tromsø, an attractive university town, twice achieved renown in World War II. It was the departure point for King Haakon VII, who escaped from there to England in 1940 (with baleful coincidence, on Norway's independence day of June 7). Later in the war the elusive German battleship *Tirpitz* was sunk there. The town got a big reputational boost when the Norwegian Polar Institute (NPI) was transferred there from Oslo in the early 1990s. That move, in turn, helped to secure the home offices of the Arctic Council, an intergovernmental body that oversees Arctic cooperation and research. But the move was controversial and politically driven, less for territorial than for party-political reasons.

Narvik is the outlet for Swedish iron ore, hauled there hourly from Kiruna on specially built trains. Hammerfest, touted as the world's northernmost incorporated town, is a center for gas production, the onshore outlet for the huge *Snøhvit* (Snow White) gas field and Norway's first liquefied natural gas works. Energy innovation is nothing new for the first city in Europe to install electric street lighting, in 1891. Hammerfest is yet another northern phoenix: in 1945 exactly one building, a chapel, was left standing after retreating Germans torched the rest.

Even unloved Kirkenes, in the remote northeast, is a hub of commerce and information. Fish, shipping, journalism and climate change politics are all active local concerns. Its waters too are ice-free the year-round. *The Independent Barents Observer*, an online publication that even has a Russian-language portal, is produced there. Kirkenes is a much-touted focal point for the fledgling Northern Sea Route over the top of Russia.

Northern Norway is vital for Norway's present, but it hasn't escaped the past. Medieval depopulation, Sami struggles, wartime devastation, marginal agriculture, eight-month winters and an indefinably heavy spirit still pervade its far-flung areas. In many ways the region embodies Norway's unspoken national sorrow. The psychological scars have yet to heal, although a new generation is doing its best to overcome them with hipster appeal, and oil revenues keep the infrastructure current.

In many ways Norway's postwar rebuilding never stopped. In contrast to Denmark, Sweden and Finland it is the Barents Sea, not the Baltic, which is the truer point of Norwegian reference, a reality deepened with the 2010 agreement with Russia. North is increasingly seen as Norway's destiny and a newly appreciated determinant of its past. But it was not always so, and as Barr and others insist, the idea has been oversold. In 2018 a searching critique of Norway's Arctic policy in *Internasjonal Politikk*, a scholarly journal, held that governments have been persistently wrong-footed in the Arctic ever since reprioritizing the region in 2005.

The Arctic seems to have a mind of its own, displaying an elusiveness that complicates Norway's engagement with it. This inscrutable north is Norway's true backyard—with a frame of reference stretching from the heavenly to the hellish.

Part II

Histories

The phases of history that offer least evidence are open to the widest interpretations, offering ample opportunities for the present to impose its own views on the past.
                             Roger Osborne, *Civilization*

Norwegians were and still are to some extent divided as regards the past.
  Glenthøj and Ottosen, *Experiences of War and Nationality*

4

A Fractured Timeline

Whatever progress we can observe in history is certainly not continuous either in time or in place.
   Edward Hallett Carr, *What Is History?*

"Here is the old but ever young Norway," enthused Fredrika Bremer, a peripatetic Swedish writer of German extraction and Finnish birth, who was active in the early to mid-nineteenth century. Keenly observant and endlessly prolific, she spent some formative years in Norway, performing a literary double act: seeing her native land through fresh eyes while unveiling Norway, a recent Swedish acquisition, to a curious public back home. Later she headed to the United States, where she marveled over the languid pace of life in the antebellum Deep South when not recoiling from its slave society. She then roamed in Greece and Asia Minor, often on horseback. Her novels are largely forgotten but her impression-filled letters and diaries shape a rich literary legacy.

Bremer penned this particular paradox during a stay in Dovrefjell, a bleak expanse of high plateau in south-central Norway that she, reflecting a wider sentiment, considered the country's spiritual heart. It touches an essential truth about Norway. The national timeline is no unbroken thread, as Danes and (to some extent) Swedes claim theirs to be, but one of fits and starts.

Twice, in the Viking Age and again in the nineteenth century, Norway held Europe in thrall: the first by sowing violence, the second by purveying virtue. The long stretch in between has seared its way into the national consciousness in the manner of a hyperextended Dark Age. It also holds countless clues to today's Norway. Simplified to the core, Norway in 1000 seemed invincible; by 1500 it had vanished into the Danish maw; by 2000 Norwegians again seemed atop the world. Yet such swings go underexplored because Norway was largely hidden from view and effectively banished from the polite society of mainstream European narrative, at the very time that narrative was being fashioned. Throughout the great movements of modernity—Renaissance, Reformation, Enlightenment, scientific revolutions—Norway languished at the back end of a political hyphen.

Such discontinuities imbue the Norwegian narrative with mystique and *faux*-heroism, but they also instilled qualities like mutability, forbearance and humor in diversity that shaped the Norwegian character and mark the country out as the ultimate national survivor. They also give Norway, *pace* Bremer, a double age paradox.

Norway is frequently characterized as an old nation but a young state. On traditional reading, late statehood is plain fact, as is Finland's and Iceland's. Norwegians wrested their sovereignty from Sweden in 1905 peacefully, some say, because the nation was fully formed, a people getting their just desserts. Yet things are not so clear-cut.

In the fevered months before the break, esteemed explorer Fridtjof Nansen penned a pamphlet aimed at foreign audiences, explaining why the union with Sweden was unjust as well as unhappy. Norway, he insisted, was actually a very old state, with established institutions that were interrupted, but not eviscerated, after the thirteenth century. This wasn't just nationalist cant. Post-Viking Norway was, in fact, one of the best-organized states in all of late-medieval Europe.

It got an early start; a kernel of Norwegian unity formed in the late ninth century, datable to the battle of Hafrsfjord, outside Stavanger in the country's southwest, in roughly 871 AD. It began to coalesce during the "Viking centuries" (roughly 800–1100), corresponding with the great period of Norse expansion. It survived forced Christianization from the late tenth century and was itself reinforced by rulers' determination to bend their subjects' will to Biblical tenets they scarcely understood themselves.

Norway, or some semblance of it, survived many decades of civil war starting around 1120, only to reemerge with unity and broader reach once those upheavals had played out. That alone is telling when we consider how deeply a four-year Civil War marked US society, or how Denmark was upturned by a three-year "Counts' War" (1534–36) or a brief *Sonderbundskrieg* reshaped the Swiss Confederation. It shows surprising resilience by a predemocratic society that lacked a public administration as we know it.

The events of 1905, in which Nansen played a key role, highlighted the element of lapsed time, of *non-contiguous continuity*, in a pointed and personal way. The new king was Prince Carl of Denmark, already married (to a British princess, Maud) and a father, who assumed the name (and old-style spelling) of Haakon VII. His young son, Alexander, was unsettlingly renamed and whisked off the land he would serve as King Olav V.

The two choices made a vigorous double statement, even a quadruple one. Håkon is a characteristically Norwegian name, while the number rebooted an old kingly line that halted in 1380, some 525 years before, with the death of Haakon (VI) Magnusson. The name Olav hot-wired another connection left dangling since 1387 with the death, aged 16, of Olav IV. The tentacles reach into our time; King Harald, born in 1936, is the first Norwegian monarch born in Norway since the fourteenth century. All this was a conscious attempt to repair fractured conduits with a late-medieval past so riven with disaster that the need to refashion new links was just as urgent.

As for nationhood, matters could equally be switched. Cultural continuity withered on the Danish vine for centuries. Vestiges were cobbled together in the nineteenth century, as the reemergence of Norway sparked the emergent *study* of Norway and new sources of bonding glue were identified. Norway has never lacked national symbols with deep roots, because they have been so earnestly sought out. It is part of an incessant Norwegian "search within" that informs an old trope and fuels insider jokes among Scandinavians. A traveler to Norway in the 1850s, Bayard Taylor, wrote of an "excessive national vanity" in Norway, a "love of *Gamle Norge* [...] manifested in such ridiculous extremes." It seemed to him like puffed-up cultural nationalism to make up for some chronic deficiency.

The upshot is one complication within another: an old nation and a new state is also its opposite. Winston Churchill memorably described the Soviet Union as "a riddle wrapped in a mystery inside an enigma": few observers would assign Norway to such company, yet as Barton and other cultural historians insist, Norway has a contradictory image that itself is remarkably persistent. All this poses an intellectual puzzle and little else. It does, however, offer an intriguing historical corollary to Norway's geographical paradoxes, a fractured timeline to match a broken coastline. It behooves us to examine the subcurrents driving it along.

The Swedish "case" is a counterexample of progressive development. It evolved via a 500-year gradualist process, built on a strong sixteenth-century founding monarchy whose bloodline was interrupted just once, in 1809–10. Its largely peaceful democratic breakthrough appears to us inevitable. Its wide swings in foreign policy orientation, from its great power era to its later tradition of flexible neutrality, flowed from this established system.

Danish continuity is more striking still. It is sometimes argued that an unbroken royal line extends back almost a thousand years, reaching up to Queen Margrete II. The *Dannebrog*, the Danish white-cross-on-red flag, first flew in 1219 (fluttering down, legend has it, straight from heaven in the midst of a battle in today's Estonia). This makes it the oldest continuous-use national flag in the world, whose 800th anniversary was celebrated in June 2019 with a flourish in Tallinn.

Almost perversely, seekers of modern north European history are far more exposed to Denmark, which was in more or less chronic decline from the early seventeenth century, than to Norway, which was quietly on the ascendant during the same period. The best, and often only, way to examine historical Norway has been comparatively via its neighbors, and that of course touches relationships among kinsmen who are not immune to petty bias. Otherwise we are more or less stuck with the purely national—that is, Norwegian historians writing about Norwegian history, mostly and naturally in their own language.

This may not matter much to Norwegians, but for interested outsiders the result is a deep and chronic lack of context. Peripheral and politically eclipsed Norway was *intellectually* sidelined as well, with effects that were less obvious but more insidious. For anyone who learns by comparing, this presents an awkward and pernicious problem.

Misapprehension about Norway and its region has been perpetuated in some truly influential works. Shakespeare, who in *Hamlet* wrote of rot in the state of Denmark and who as a young actor may have trod Danish floorboards in the 1580s, was conspicuously ignorant of the region. In this, his one play set in Scandinavia, he casts "ambassadors from Norway," a state supposedly in conflict with Poland, when it had long been a part of the Danish realm.

Continentals were equally clueless. Jean-Jacques Rousseau, who echoed Montesquieu's belief in climate as a behavioral factor, cited Poland and England as his "northern" examples; "and," he adds unhelpfully, "let us ignore everything further north." Hegel, the German philosopher of dialectics, showed little interest in Scandinavia while to Engels and Marx, historical determinists who fashioned their theories of working-class empowerment on Hegelian thinking, the region was a distant and (for their purposes) hopeless peasant economy.

Like much else in Friedrich Nietzsche's combustible prose, the "splendid blond beast" is a misattribution. It appears in *On the Genealogy of Morals*, but almost in passing, via an obtuse reference to (Viking) Scandinavia. As his translator Walter Kaufmann argues, it was not a racial reference at all, or anything specifically Teutonic or Nordic; it was simply a shaded cultural quality, "a hidden core [that] needs to erupt from time to time." Yet it too managed to reinforce prejudice at the expense of knowledge, adding to a hazy image of a harsh region populated by dried-fish-eating, paganistic recalcitrants. The picture, says Printz-Pålson, was "amazingly constant and depressingly jejune." And importantly, Norway suffered even worse from the inattention because its external identity had been all but snuffed out.

Without diplomats, without native governments, without autonomous kings and princes and for centuries without armed forces either native or mercenary—without, that is, the stuff of sovereignty in the Westphalian age—Norway effectively *did not exist* in the standard historical sense, whatever its farmers and merchants and fishermen were doing in real life. Jean Bodin, the seventeenth-century sovereignty theorist, would have had little to say about a country whose independence had slipped away just as it was starting to matter in the era of the fixed border, the sovereign nation-state and the nonfiction book.

Small states are readily buttonholed when not being overlooked. But Norway has managed to buttonhole itself through what can seem, to the uninitiated, like a blinkered approach to the national history that mixes the painstaking with the parochial. The belated establishment of Norway's first university (1811) had something to do with it, as did the fact that for the rest of the century there was no other. This concentration of elite-guided interpretation jarred with a decentralized and democratizing society. Few other Western countries have been marked by such a double perceptual gulf, one external and one internal.

This oddity has contemporary consequences. Today's Norwegians can justifiably claim that few outsiders truly understand their country. Such claims often betray a touch of collective self-satisfaction, since the typical Norwegian—educated, traveled and clued-in—knows far more about the rest of the world than vice versa. The result is a persistent intellectual crevasse. Two-way understanding gets stifled in the smugness of small, reinforced by all manner of regional peculiarities and cultural trip wires. Perhaps it is the way of Norwegians, more than Danes or Swedes, to prefer (or even societally to need) this state of abnormally unequal comprehension. And as we'll see, others' ignorance can be and often has been their gain.

The time gaps also pose problems for the formulation of collective memory. Today's famously peace-loving Scandinavians can all hark back to militaristic ages. They shared the same amorphous Norse society and common language prevailing a thousand years ago, Viking cultures as we understand them. But Denmark and Sweden had post-Viking, early-modern great-power eras as well. These were histories recorded in written documents, palatial architecture, grand-master portraits and battlefield memory. There are two major differences between Norwegian history writ large and the Dano-Swedish variety. One is that Norway's is *less tangible*; the other is that its telling traditionally was *foreign in origin*.

The gilded palaces we see today, the Fredenborgs, Amalienborgs and Frederiksborgs dotting the bucolic Danish countryside, is mostly vintage sixteenth and seventeenth century. We can trace the career trajectory of Christian IV, for 300 years the namesake of Oslo, from young swashbuckler to the one-eyed washout of his final years. Sweden's great power age came still later, erupting in the Thirty Years' War (1618–48), peaking by 1660 and flaming out in 1718. Both left distinctly national histories with an objective substantiation that is especially marked in Scandinavia (Sweden being the first European state to record population figures).

In sharp contrast, Norway's twin great-power apex, its Viking and Saga eras however rendered, was essentially prehistorical and pre-Gutenberg. It transpired in an age of scholasticism, when knowledge was squirreled away rather than shared, literacy was a privilege and leaders were unbothered with recording things they did, other than through *skalds* whose task was to glorify their exploits and bravery. History was passed on orally, a remarkable skill largely lost to time. We know it primarily through the imprecise science of archaeology. Most written Viking history was a literal postscript, set down centuries later in Snorri Sturluson's *Heimskringla* and other works of Icelandic, Orkney and similar provenance—when not from the jaundiced hand of victims like the monks of Lindisfarne.

Snorri still looms, Fuji-like, over the Norwegian historical landscape; his remarkable *Saga* histories and *Prose Edda* remain central pillars around which an era is understood. Yet he was often opaque and, as we've seen, prone to factual goofs. Historians today cut him and other medievals, like Saxo Grammaticus (author of *Deeds of the Danes*), ever less slack, Forte, Oram and Pedersen calling their works "literature masquerading as history." And the late-medieval Saga era only came into focus with the works of another Icelandic historian, Tormud Torfæus, whose *Historia Rerum Norvegicarum*, published in 1711, recounted the major events up to 1387.

Post-1814 this pattern reversed itself: Norwegian history became a consuming concern more or less to the exclusion of others. The search for continuity suddenly had urgent practical implications for a country plunged into a nation-building process *after* it had promulgated an independent constitution. History writing became a cultural imperative, not just a way to understand the past, while subsequent reinterpretations assumed their own corrective urgency. It is a reason why Norwegian history can seem trapped in a maze of interpretative detail and wrapped in a cloak of claustrophobia.

Paucity of written records, as Osborne points out, puts a premium on physical evidence. Yet the organic essence of Norway's medieval past has also largely vanished, stonework not finding its way to Norway until the thirteenth century. Apart from some wonderfully reconstructed Viking burial ships and Bergen's medieval old town, most of it lies at or below ground level. Evidence must be disinterred, not just deciphered. Archaeology is doubly important for understanding a Viking culture that prioritized burial customs designed to give a fitting send-off to the afterlife in Valhalla. "We may speculate, but we can never be certain," caution the authors of *Viking Empires*, alive to the danger of conflating "remains with records."

Knowledge of old Norway is fated to be rough-edged and approximate; it has been vulnerable to academic cherry-picking and aggressive theorizing as well as political exploitation by neo-Nazis intent on parading their inner Viking. Quisling and Breivik, two notorious modern Norwegians, might be considered cracked edges of the imagined Viking legacy. All nations emphasize golden ages and buff their heroes, but the task is more inviting if the esteemed period is distant. It is not surprising that the mid-nineteenth century yearnings for Scandinavian unity (exemplified by Swedish poet Esaias Tegnér, Danish reformer Grundtvig and others) harked back to the prenational Vikings, not the national Vasas and Oldenburgs.

For outsiders, nineteenth-century Norway was a canvas against which to project aspirations. It became, to anticipate Chapter 7, a nation of and for the world at large, leapfrogging the constraints of its regional setting for an amorphous wider one. Somewhere in this heady brew was a country whose essence many foreigners thought they intuitively grasped, yet few actually knew about beyond the bare outlines.

Lacking dynastic or other vestiges of continuity, Norway has conjured a bewildering array of elements that have been seriously proposed as nation-builders: the battle-scarred language issue, shipping, fish (especially cod or *klippfisk*), the great outdoors, simplicity of lifestyle, societal trust, the exploratory impulse, skiing, wintertime, brown cheese, Asbjørnson and Moe's folk tales, anti-centralizing attitudes, May 17 celebrations, Grieg's piano concerto in A minor, fjords, stave churches, mountain huts, Peer Gynt (character and play) and, not least, the fragmented timeline and the unique national trajectory it has wrought.

The historians who expounded on these themes long played an unusually prominent role in Norwegian society. They produced master narratives often built on the notion of the heroic struggle into which they insinuated themselves. Historicists—those who believe that events flow with a kind of inevitability—tended not only to crowd their profession but were often co-opted into politics, as if to make the history while also writing it. It was a deliberate symbiosis between scholarly and public life, with distinct echoes of the old skaldic tradition.

Some, like Ernst Sars (brother of Eva Sars, Fridtjof Nansen's first wife) and before him Peter Andreas Munch (an uncle of the famous artist Edvard; people-wise, this is a small country) wrote penetrating, politically tinged historical narratives—Sars's paragraphs can run several pages, almost stream-of-consciousness style—which set a tone for later generations and emboldened other formidables like Andreas Holmsen.

Sars was active in the Liberal Party; other historians, like Edward Bull Sr. and Halvdan Koht, later served in high office, Koht being Norway's foreign minister in the dark days of 1940. Jacob Aall, a force at Eidsvoll and later in Parliament, was a translator of Snorri's *Heimskringla,* Eilert Sundt a sociologist whose field studies later pushed Norway, not just Norwegian scholarship, in a modern direction. The latter two have had Oslo streets named after them, a public honor not often accorded to social scientists. Scholarly suasion may even have launched the "miracle at Eidsvoll" in 1814. Professor Georg Sverdrup is credited (by Norway's soon-to-be king-regent, Christian Frederik, in his diary) for convincing him, in an apparently compelling private audience on February 16, of the folly of trying to rule as an absolutist king, thus reorienting the country in a constitutional direction.

Among various notions, one explored by Jacob Rudolf Keyser and Munch in the nineteenth century (and later exploited by the Nazis) posited pre-Christian Norway as representative of the "pure" Scandinavia, with roots to the north and east, as opposed to the Svear who conquered Sweden from the east, and the Teutonic

Goths who came from the south. This was a doubly useful idea as it also exaggerated differences between the Nordic peoples, which were starting to separate perhaps as early as the ninth century AD. It was a wordy indication of the exaggerated need for Norway to emphasize its atypicality—and perhaps for historians to present themselves as societal guiding lights. With good reason, German historian Stefan Berger calls Norway "one of the most historical countries in Europe."

Historians' concerns in Norway followed a thematic arc ranging from hyper-nationalism to watered-down Marxism, and on to the severely positivist, skeptical prism that still obtains. In the process, questions replaced certainties as social scientists went back to the classroom and the drawing board. The trumped-up image of the gallant Norwegian, rising against evil foreign designs, now seems passé to the point of embarrassment. Yet Norway still nurtures an exceptionally complicated relationship with its own history, one that mixes hyper-patriotic May 17 celebrations with a relentless modernism and odd but telling flashes of indifference to the national patrimony.

The modernism dominant from the late nineteenth century frequently had the effect of denying the very history that Berger claims to hold sway. Having been chronically overlooked the Scandinavians were forced, believes Printz-Pålson, essentially to reinvent themselves, "in opposition to the massive neglect and even mistrust" elsewhere, which resulted in a "sudden, complete reversal of the Scandinavian image," especially in Germany and specifically in regard to Norway.

After World War II another modernist eruption, this time in urban planning, led entire neighborhoods, some assuredly slums, to be razed ("renovated" in the going euphemism) in Scandinavia's capital cities. This was part of a feverish push not just to develop but to put the past, still associated with mass exodus and poverty, behind them. This drove the then-celebrated (but since widely lamented) demolition, among much else, of Stockholm's old Klara district to make way for today's concrete, wind-swept Sergels Torg and the adjacent, wishfully democratic *Kulturhuset*. Oslo's *Gamle By* suffered cavalier treatment in the early rail era that it still struggles to reconcile.

All over Scandinavia, the old became the enemy after 1945 in a modernist leap prosecuted, like the welfare state itself, in the name of people's progress. It was a wider Western trend, burnished by Keynesian thinking and postwar faith in progress and the modern secular state. But the muffling of history that was the postwar welfare state's dark side was taken to its greatest lengths north of the Baltic and extended to include aesthetic judgments. Oslo's harborside town hall, completed in 1950, symptomized this brutalist approach, even if the decades have softened the initial and quite virulent opposition to its very presence.

We get a startling glimpse of this mid-century mind-set from *The Oslo Book*, a compiled publication—bursting with pride, a touch defensive—intended to showcase the capital's postwar rebirth. A thousand-year-old city is described as an "unfinished town," with a willful aversion to memory. "Oslo has shown a remarkable capacity for obliterating all traces of those buildings [that are] worthy memorials of a distant past," one contributor wrote. To another, growth-happy Oslo had become "a mechanized big production community," a chilling descriptive penned with evident approval. "It may be a pretty idea to preserve all memories of past ages," chief editor Vilhelm Bjørset writes high-handedly, "but it is surely much more important that our town should develop according to the plans and standards that are agreed on today [...] modern in the best sense of the word." History, Scandinavian style, has had to slug it out with modernism epitomized by Scandinavia, leaving history as the frequent loser. The years since 2000 have brought a fundamental rethink about the priorities of Oslo, which is even repositioning itself physically back toward Ekeberg hill, east of Bjørvika, and reevaluating itself to the core in ways not possible in a city and country with greater continuity.

Fitful progress through muted conflict has been a Norwegian hallmark. The country was forged at the interface between the theory of opposition and the practice of accommodation, where matters often went to the brink but rarely beyond it. The incessant references, in today's otherwise conspicuously comfortable Norway, to themes of titanic struggle and tales of gallant comeback—and here the widely read novels of Karl Ove Knausgaard come to mind—spring from fertile soil and practiced invective. Many fault lines have imprinted Norwegian history, and they in turn have often been exaggerated by those attempting to speak for the national soul. Literary Norway has been shoehorned conveniently into "writerly battles" (Welhaven vs. Wergeland; Bjørnson vs. Ibsen) that were in fact complicated, often ego-dominated competitive relationships. Later they appeared in politics (liberal/socialist vs. conservative) and in language via the "two-cultures" debate pitting *Bokmål* against *Landsmål.* As we've seen it is also a feature of Norwegian topography, as land vs. sea; of perspective, as west vs. east; of orientation, as north vs. south; and of development, as town vs. land.

But the fault lines also tend to be crosscutting, not reinforcing. This, along with a practiced pliability to circumstances and what Asle Toje rightly labels a "thick" culture, mitigates tendencies toward direct or open conflict. It can produce the sort of milquetoast compromise that outsiders associate with the Nordic world. In Norway the welfare state has papered over such distinctions, and oil wealth has smoothed them out further. A smiling culture can give the impression that they have vanished altogether. But they emerged with a vengeance in 1972 and again in 1994, during (and after) the two punishing debates over Europe.

Divisions still rumble beneath issues like Arctic oil drilling, immigration and assimilation policy in a still freshly multiethnic culture. To suggest that Norwegians stand as one on such issues is to overlook Norwegian realities. They speak to tensions of interpretation and clashes of will that contributed to the building of a rough Norwegian consensus and which haven't died away. Norway's posture is that of a small country, but its debate often reflects the tangled complications of far bigger ones—even if the tone is decorous and the emotions modulated.

That part of Norwegian history we call Viking or Norse is so expertly covered elsewhere that it seems redundant to attempt more than a brief synopsis here. A phenomenon of the Middle Ages, it qualifies as prehistory, yet to many minds it encapsulates Norwegian history. While this testifies to a powerful legacy, it siphons attention from subsequent eras that shaped modern Norway's contours, as opposed to animating its myths. Knowledge is reliant on digs, post hoc sagas, cryptic runestones (few of which are actually in Norway), intuition and educated guesswork burnished nowadays by satellites and geothermal imaging. Key Viking centers like Borgund near today's Ålesund, Borg in Lofoten, Kaupang outside Larvik (once called Skiringssal), Hedeby in north Germany, Ribe in Denmark and Birka in the Stockholm archipelago have either vanished or morphed (like Ribe and Aarhus) into modern towns.

Understanding of the Norse period is complicated by modern prejudices, not just untruths like horned helmets. Better that we not trap ourselves into specific time periods or firm borders. The, or a, Viking Age "eludes almost any attempt at packaging and labeling," cautions Robert Ferguson, a fastidious chronicler of that period. The Vikings may have fostered an outsized Nordic impact by besting the pirates in an age of piracy and by shrewdly adapting imported sailing technology during relatively mild centuries that minimized the ice menace in the North Atlantic.

A characteristic feature of Viking history is its plasticity, as it continues to generate reinterpretations and new lines of inquiry. Historians are drawing away from old certainties including dates that once reliably bookended the High Viking era, namely the Lindisfarne raid of June 793 and the battle of Stamford Bridge, outside today's York, in September 1066. Far earlier incursions into Britain and Ireland are now thought to have taken place, to match the wanderings far to the south and east. Likewise, the end of the Viking era is no longer hostage to Anglo-Saxon interpretation. Danes tend to use 1085 as the preferred date while for Scots, 1263/66 forms both a temporal and physical division that won them the western isles from Norse rule. In other senses the fourteenth-century Black Death (see below) marks the end, while the extinction of Norse Greenlanders in the early fifteenth century is another, equally poignant marker.

Notwithstanding the lack of parameters, there are obvious reasons why the Viking Age is so avidly evoked. It is ceaselessly picked over by historians, archaeologists, anthropologists, ethnologists, political scientists, migration specialists, shipbuilders, filmmakers and racy-novel writers. Even feminist theory has punctured that seriously macho world; women held the keys to the farm, and somebody had to till the fields when the men were out "a-Viking," which was a mostly warm-weather activity even for the toughest of races.

They were not just heathen raiders but also explorers, traders, mariners, craftsmen, farmers and masterful shipbuilders. Their hit-and-run tactics stoked universal fear, making violence and mobility two persistent themes. Early unification that built outward from local successes was reinforced by sword and hammer. The relentless expansion so characteristic of Norse society was a part-result of civil wars and banishments.

Yet the feared raiders are now acknowledged as the tip of a much bigger iceberg, a gradually identifiable people with distinct societal practices. Notions of self-government were based on *thing* tradition, clans and kingships for which Midsummer festivals made for an annual gathering ritual. Iceland, a Norse (and "Norwegian") colony settled in the ninth century, birthed the modern world's first parliament-like body, the Althing; on the Isle of Man, the open-air Tynwald still meets annually. Viking Norway must be among the least appreciated *political* innovators of history, and their mobile administrative capacities among the least recognized elements of Norse-era life. Clan patronage, internecine rivalries, penal banishment, colonial outpostings and the use of Norway itself as a home base or "mother ship" all complicated the pattern of roving kingships and traveling courts that mark medieval Norway as a source of bewilderingly complicated and fluid politics. Foreign, colonial and domestic elements were intertwined, and mobility the common trait that enabled it to function.

Their distant reach could conjure astonishing outcomes. Morris Bishop, a medieval chronicler, tells of how the Sultan of Damascus in the twelfth century wound up with the unusual gift of a live polar bear, courtesy of Emperor Frederick II; what's not mentioned is that Frederick received it from Norsemen bearing gifts, relayed from Greenland in what must have been a spirited set of exchanges.

While scarcely celebrated for scientific acumen, Viking society pioneered nutrition, surviving long sea voyages with dried fish (lighter to carry) and berries (staving off scurvy). Another overlooked aspect was their advanced level of fitness, explored in Chapter 8. Physical stamina enabled them to cover astonishing distances in open boats, their cramped space often shared with livestock. As we've seen, northern (including Norwegian) adventurers ventured into the Eurasian heartland, forming civilizational pockets like the Kievan Rus. Norsemen, called "Danes" but often Norwegian, conquered eastern England, while those from Norwegian coastal areas settled in western England, Ireland and more persistently in Scotland and the island groups including the Orkneys, Shetlands, Færoes and the western isles including the Hebrides and Man. They also went north; Jan Mayen and almost certainly Svalbard (the "land of cold coasts") were known to them.

They were exploring the British coast by the 780s AD, founded Dublin (around 841), settled in Normandy, marauded through France, rounded Gibraltar, sacked Seville, conquered Sicily, traveled up Russian rivers, attacked the same Byzantium they later served and ventured beyond the Caspian Sea. They played determinative roles in Baltic, British, Irish, Icelandic, Greenlandic, Iberian, Italian, Balkan, North African and Byzantine life. They later swelled the ranks of the Crusaders. They dominated an era between the Franks and the high Middle Ages.

And of course they hopscotched across the North Atlantic, which became for some centuries a Viking lake. The earldom of Orkney became an extraterritorial center of a growing chain of settlement. At first an offshore base for conducting Viking raids, Orkney animated Scottish concerns in the eleventh century even as it came to serve as a cultural bridge between Norway and the outside world; Thorfinn, Earl of Orkney, paid a papal visit in 1050.

By roughly 870 AD Norse sailors reached Iceland, until then mostly uninhabited save for some Irish monks, using the Færoes as a stepping stone. From Iceland, around 980, Erik the Red took settlers and ships, settled at Brattahlid farm and colonized southwestern Greenland. And from there, led by one of Erik's sons, Leif Eriksson, Norwegian settlers in Greenland reached what is today's Newfoundland.

Perhaps the most exciting archaeological find at L'Anse aux Meadows in Newfoundland—still the only site offering proof that Norse people spent more than a passing summer in North America—was a spindle wheel, used to spin wool into clothing. It was an item of unmistakable domesticity, suggesting that they went there intending to settle, and took women with them. This was a civilization on the move, not just hit-and-run bands of seasonal raiders and wood-gatherers.

It's one of those underplayed but arresting facts that the three pivotal figures of 1066—heralded, ominously, by an appearance of Halley's Comet—were all Norsemen in fact or by direct descent. Harald Hardråde, who swept across the North Sea from Norway (by way of Orkney) to claim the English throne made vacant by the death of Edward the Confessor, was surprised and annihilated by Harold Godwineson at Stamford Bridge. William the Conqueror, a Viking descendant of Rollo who sailed from Normandy in a rival bid for the same throne, defeated Harold's weakened forces at Hastings three weeks later. The fate of modern England was shaped by internecine Norse conflict writ widely. Its northern reaches were once the realm of the Danelaw. Knut, a Dane, was king of England until his death in 1035. York (Jorvik), long a Viking stronghold, was older still; Constantine the Great, founder of Constantinople, was crowned Roman Emperor there around 325 AD.

A mobile society is by definition a flexible one. Their absorptive capacity mentioned in Chapter 2 gave them a niche role in the medieval world's rudimentary trading system. Their ability to insinuate into other places and cultures has long been underplayed by interpretations that fixed the brutalist and unbending Viking reputation in modern consciousness. The gently insistent revisionism of Forte, Oram and Pedersen, who emphasize the "easy integration of the Scandinavians into mainstream European society" draws our attention. "A crucial aspect [...] was the adaptability of the Scandinavian settlers, and the relative ease of their integration" in the places they went, which in turn created "new bonds of mutual interest between colonists and conquered" that encouraged mixing between Norsemen and the Pict, Irish, Frank and other cultures whom they once were supposed to have only ravaged, looted and left to unhappy fates.

Another theme is the importance given to generational connectivity and blood ties. The "legacy society" was exemplified, in late 1263, in Kirkwall, where Håkon IV lay dying while the feats of his ancestors were read to him. The convoluted line of succession that preceded him may actually have contributed to this need, even in the Saga Era, to forge continuity in the wake of the Baglar–Birker "civil" wars of the twelfth century.

The question of where the (Norwegian) Vikings had their political center of gravity has long animated historians. Nineteenth-century nation-builders insisted that the Oslofjord region in the southeast, especially Vestfold, was the place. They pointed to evidence like the Gokstad and Oseberg ship discoveries, the even older burial grounds at Borre, the eastern origins of kings Olav Haraldsson and Harald Fairhair, local place-names like Vika, and the battle of Nesjar (around 1016) that won for Olav the Norwegian throne. More recent research concentrates on the southwest, the area of the *Gulating*, of Hafrsfjord near today's Stavanger, as the real birthplace of modern Norway. And true to Norwegian form, the discovery of a buried Viking ship near Halden, in Østfold, in late 2018 may herald yet another shift of attention to the Oslofjord.

What seems more pertinent and interesting is that tribal peoples and petty kingdoms were established in both areas, as well as in Trøndelag to the north, three centers of activity with good farmland but poor land connections between them. Norwegian kings and courts were ceaselessly mobile. It was a practice of *itineration*, of incessant movement, which came to mark early patterns of governance in a country where transport relied largely on the sea, although Norse culture was also a ski culture. Viking adventurism abroad is rightly acknowledged, but their local mobility and its role in governance is equally worthy of attention.

Christianity came to Scandinavia famously late. It is frequently dated to the conversion of a Danish king, Harald Bluetooth, around 960 AD, arriving (less gently) in Norway a generation later and soon thereafter in Sweden. As the Roman church gained a foothold, which became a political lock by 1153 in Norway, it became a power center to match those of royalty and nobility. And whereas it filtered into the countryside only gradually, the sign of the cross was delivered on Norwegian shores with fanfare after its first, tentative introduction by Håkon the Good earlier in the tenth century.

King Olav II (Haraldsson) provided a spark. Baptized in Rouen in 1014 after a raiding career notorious for excesses even in his time, he initiated the full-scale conversion of Norway. However, it was his short-lived predecessor, Olav Tryggvason, who died in battle in 999 or 1000, who is often credited with (forcibly) introducing the faith, as opposed to Harald Bluetooth's more accommodative approach a generation before.

From England, Olav II and his forces invaded and strong-armed their way to power by around 1015. In his policy of forced conversion he also instigated a social turn, gathering together the isolated yeoman farmers of inland areas as against coastal peoples. Chased out of Norway to Sweden in 1028 for his high-handed methods and opposition from his enemy Knut, king of Denmark and England, Olav returned with a vengeance and a scratch army reminiscent of Napoleon's return in early 1815 from Elba.

Olav was cut down at the battle of Stiklestad on July 29, 1030 and returned to Trondheim for burial. He was subsequently exhumed and pronounced a saint after miracles were attributed to him. Near St. Olav's gravesite arose the cathedral of Nidaros in today's Trondheim. For nearly 500 years the shrine was a cult and pilgrimage destination, only to be removed and hidden away in the tumult of the Reformation. The Olav site, revered and lost, is a source of lively speculation and messy digs in the backstreets of Trondheim.

An English writer of the old, sweeping historicist tradition, Arnold Toynbee, dismissed the post-Viking downshift as a long-term cultural demise at the hands of the christianized Franks whom they had previously terrorized. Christianization introduced new uncertainties into northern Europe, and many Norwegians hedged their bets. The stave churches that have dotted the Norwegian countryside since the Middle Ages (only 30 or so have survived intact) were frequently festooned with dragons and other pagan images to ward off evil spirits. The same symbols were resurrected in the national romanticism of the nineteenth century; even today they adorn the faddish end of the housing market. The original stave churches, most dating from before the twelfth century, were largely built during the reign of Olav Kyrre (the peaceful) after 1066. Olav Kyrre's nonviolent ways after those of his predecessor set an early Norwegian pattern of kings reversing the ruling style of their predecessors.

The "Saga period" that is considered post-Viking yet still fundamentally Norse ranged up to the fourteenth century. This, the early Christian era, was a rocky road for Norway. The pagan hinterlands resisted the new faith. Political consolidation was slow, while Danish king Valdemar the Great extended his rule through Norway, stamping Denmark's influence in Norway decisively and foreshadowing things to come.

The twelfth century initiated a period of civil violence and disputed claims on the throne. The 1163 law of succession raised the stakes for any faction that could win out, this being an era when illegitimate offspring complicated the royal bloodlines. Competing dynastic claims, amounting to protracted civil war, raged until roughly 1240. Yet by the twelfth century slavery had been abolished in Norway, whereas in Sweden it persisted until 1335.

This period is linked to the legends of the Birkebeiners ("birch-legs") as the native champions as against evil (rich, Catholic-ecclesiastical, Danish) Baglar overlords. A potent foundation myth is encapsulated in the stirring tale of an infant king, the future King Håkon (IV) Håkonsson. Holder of a slender claim to the throne as the grandson of Sverre Sigurdson, he was whisked to safety (by ski) across the countryside to be crowned at Nidaros—a royal deliverance that is implicitly, and all too easily, likened to modern Norway's.

Norway emerged in the thirteenth century with a renewed sense of purpose, while it consolidated a colonial presence that peaked around 1260. *Norgesvelden*, the Norwegian realm, was never bigger before or since. In terms of influence and physical reach, the 1260s marked a decisive turning point for late-medieval Norway.

In 1261, Greenland submitted to Norwegian rule; Iceland, closer and more coveted, followed in 1262, again under the wing of the archbishopric of Nidaros. This brought not only vast new territory and prestige but also burdens; roughly 5,000 Greenlanders relied precariously on annual supply ships. Yet the very next year (1263) Håkon IV died in the Orkney capital, following the desultory Battle of Largs that was meant to reinforce Norwegian presence in the western isles. Three years later his successor, Magnus Lagabøte (the Lawmender), mortgaged the Hebrides, together with the Isle of Man, to the Scottish king (Alexander III) in return for annual payments. Thus began a slow-motion unwinding from the overextended and haphazard Viking sprawl. At the time it was not seen that way, since Norway was strengthening its hold on the Shetlands, Orkneys and, further out, the Færoes.

Håkon's rule ended almost as dramatically, and just as peripatetically, as it began. But while he presided over Norway's imperial peak, his managerial effectiveness is still debated. His reign brought Germans into Norwegian commercial life via his agreement with Lübeck in 1250 (later, in 1294, bound in a Royal Charter), which initiated a centuries-long Hansa stranglehold over much of Norway's commercial life and its all-important fishing industry.

It did, however, usher in 80 years of relative peace. This era extended through his successors Magnus Lagabøte, who introduced the law of succession, through Erik Magnusson and from about 1299, Håkon V (Magnusson). In spirit it could be likened to Antonine Rome of the second century AD, an era esteemed by Gibbon as "the fairest part of the earth and the most civilized portion of mankind."

This late golden age stands in stark contrast with the convulsions racking its nearest neighbors. Sweden, following Magnus Ladulås's death in 1290, descended into internecine wars involving King Birger and his brothers Eirik and Valdemar, which Håkon V was increasingly dragged into. (It was Eirik's incursion up to Oslo in winter 1308–09, with the aid of German mercenaries, which framed the dramatic finale for Sigrid Undset's novel *In the Wilderness*.) And in Denmark, the murder of Erik Klipping in 1286 ushered in half a century of political instability, marked by royal battles with the assertive Danish nobility.

This period was a hinge of fate for Norway in other respects too. In the reign of Magnus, Norway reached its Gothic apogee with the building, in Bergen, of Håkon's Hall, a striking, elongated stone structure that still stands (albeit rebuilt after severe damage in World War II) as the defining symbol of west-coast political power in the old Norway. Yet within a few years the iterative tendencies would reassert themselves and the political seat shifted east, to Tønsberg and Oslo. And the king who prompted this move, Håkon V, was the same ruler who signed, in 1294, the Royal Charter with the Hanseatic League, based in Rostock and Lübeck. This established a Hansa foothold, most visibly in Bergen, that persisted to the eighteenth century—and now draws legions of tourists to its brightly colored waterside wooden district once known as The Office. Yet the country's southeast was also a Hansa stronghold.

A splintering of Norway, and foreign control over its choice parts, was at hand. Premonitions of loss of control over his realm tormented Håkon V in his last years, especially after his only legal issue, daughter Ingebjørg, was married to Duke Eirik of Sweden—a man with active ambitions in Norway, one of the many influential royal figures of history who never took the throne himself. The Oslo marriage of September 1312, in fact, was a double wedding, bringing together another Ingebjørg (the king's niece) and another Swedish prince, Valdemar. Liberal mixing among Swedish and Norwegian royals was now a (decade-old) reality.

Already by the late thirteenth century, certain characteristic Norwegian elements were in place. These included an established church hierarchy and resident national saint (Olav) in Nidaros; a west-coast trade system, buoyed by early-Hansa connections via Bergen to northern Norway; North Atlantic settlements reaching as far as Greenland; a highly dispersed population with bicoastal political centers; and, not least, a pattern of social relations that was hierarchical only in part, including a smallish nobility co-opted by royals within a tradition of *konungs skuggsjá*, a king's code of honor. Norway was by no means democratic, or developed, or egalitarian, but important seeds had been sown.

Norway was distinguished from both Denmark and Sweden by having suffered protracted civil war and dynastic confusion at an earlier stage. It now had an independent archbishopric, with a political heft enhanced by more extensive land ownership than the church enjoyed in neighboring countries, and a controlling influence in far-flung island dependencies that actually made northern Scotland, not mainland Norway, the country's geopolitical centerpoint for two centuries. The rudiments of a central administration had been laid down earlier by the archbishopric of Hamburg-Bremen, which sustained early Christian Norway from without.

In Denmark, a tradition of noble councils empowered to select kings flourished, as they did in Sweden. Norway was at the scale's other end; its nobility was smallest and weakest, its farming culture the most fragmented; its crowns were traditionally inherited but also frequently disputed. And in Norway a relatively free peasantry featured from early on. Sweden gets typecast between those extremes: fairly free peasantries, limited feudalism, and a strong but pliable noble class that was alternately indulged and kept in check through successive "reductions" by kings bent on military adventurism.

This did not make for a peaceful region or era. Just as the Vikings brought progress along with devastation, the early Christian centuries were marked by conflicts between church and crown and violent struggle among ruling families. Yet for a time Norway escaped the gratuitous violence that afflicted Sweden in the last decades of the Folkunga dynasty, founded by Birger Jarl in 1250.

Much of that centered on dynastic claims and counterclaims. The "game of Håtuna," associated with King Birger Magnusson and his rivalrous siblings, was the most notorious. Birger had followed King Magnus of Sweden (1275–90), whose reign was marked by prosperity and peace. Yet his accession in 1298 brought fierce intrafamily rivalries involving his two brothers, Duke Eirik and Duke Valdemar, which effectively split Sweden into three sovereign realms.

During a visit in 1306, Eirik had playfully locked up his brother Birger, the king (at Håtuna, near Sigtuna) and forced him to grant special privileges. Sweden seemed doomed to disintegration. Eleven years later, Birger returned the favor in a deadlier version at a pre-Christmas feast at his castle at Nyköping. He locked Eirik and Valdemar, both very drunk, in the dungeon, and threw the key into the river. Both starved to death, their fates twinned to the bitter end. Birger was soon driven into Danish exile (his wife, Märta, being the sister of Danish King Erik Menved), and the turmoil that convulsed the whole region from the fourteenth century's second decade was at hand. It was pan-Scandinavianism of the worst sort, and a fateful diversion for Norwegian autonomy.

In Norway the final years of Håkon V (Magnusson) also marked the last of a royal line that extended back three centuries. Upon taking the throne in 1299, Håkon shifted the political center decisively, and irrevocably, from west to east. The foundation stone for Oslo's Akershus fortress was laid at that time—not long before the great cathedral at Nidaros was completed and another fortress, Vardøhus, begun in the far northeast. He lived in Oslo with his bookish queen, Euphemia, who commissioned translations of romances and ballads. (Even in death they have migrated; buried in *Mariakirken* in old Oslo, their sarcophaguses now rest in the gloomy depths of Akershus.) Tønsberg, in Vestfold, was fortified as well, as was Bohus to the south.

Norway's precarious independence was undercut by a succession issue in 1319 that brought Sweden, as well as Denmark, squarely into the picture. Magnus Eriksson, newly king of Norway, was crowned king of Sweden at Mora in July. It was Norway–Sweden's first personal royal union and an early foretaste of 1814.

A tendency toward peasant unrest was another Norwegian feature, underscored by Njåstad. The Oslofjord revolts of the late Middle Ages were followed by riots in the 1490s and early 1520s, directed at the harsh rule of Denmark's Christian II. Later the Loftus riots of 1765 manifested a new spirit linked to the end of the Hansa monopoly and the prideful emergence of the Norwegian merchant fleet, much of which operated out of the west coast. The stone-throwing episode involving Carsten Anker, a local mogul, 30 years later (witnessed by Mary Wollstonecraft) was in this mold. As ever, the activist and self-aware, but nonrevolutionary, peasant lurks near the center of the Norwegian story—a narrative that shifted course in the mid-fourteenth century.

Pesten, dauden, svartedauen, den store mannedauden, byllepest, the Great Pestilence, the Year of the Mortality, the Distemper, the Plague, the Black Death: no other event marks the literal as well as symbolic end of the old Norway, the turn of turns. Like "the media" in our time, the plague was no singular thing. Bacterial as well as viral, it came in various bubonic, septicemic and pneumonic strains both primary and secondary, all highly infectious but the airborne pneumonic type virulently so. Plague came in European waves over a period of centuries, hastening new generations to a premature grave, but in Norway it destroyed a way of life peculiar to Norwegian conditions.

Beyond certain basics, expert agreement over the Black Death—its causes and consequences, what data to trust, why it disappeared, even what it was—is conspicuously lacking. Perhaps the most intensive study, by Cohn, pointedly summarizes what it was not: that it was "any disease other than the rat-based bubonic plague" that was discovered in 1894 but whose symptoms, ever since, have been erroneously extrapolated backward, the epidemiological evidence readily "imposed on the past" by overeager historians. Analytical sins of commission, in his view, have been added to those of omission. A kind of "source pluralism" is now the going if loose explanation for its uneven spread and diversity of symptoms.

Ersland and Sandvik, who cast a critical eye over this still powerfully emotive subject, note at least 16 known and major pest outbreaks in northwestern Europe from 1348 to 1494 alone—centuries before England's notorious plague epidemic of the mid-1660s about which Samuel Pepys diarized. These episodes turned a catastrophic event in 1348–50, in which perhaps a third of the Norwegian population perished within a few months, into a recurring humanitarian nightmare. It hastened independent Norway's demise and contributed to economic and demographic tailspins lasting into modern times.

Its arrival into a vulnerable continent—the first, that is, in 700 years since the famous Justinian Plague—was singularly devastating. Acemoglou and Robinson, authors of *Why Nations Fail*, call it one of history's true critical junctures: "A major event [...] disrupting the existing economic or political balance in society." They might have added its transformative social impact, but the point is taken. Norman Cantor, author of a general study of plague-era Europe, suggests it was unique—a "biomedical holocaust" of its time—because it combined a primarily bubonic (and secondarily pneumatic) outbreak with a lethal anthrax contagion. The initial complexity may also have distinguished the first wave from later ones.

Whatever its science, the plague became a folkloric catch-all. It was ruinously symptomatic of the rotting structures and attitudes of late feudal Europe, with its terrible sanitation and pervasive superstitions about personal hygiene and public health, perpetuated by a primitive knowledge base. In Barbara Tuchman's classic study of the fourteenth century, the plague emerges as the source of wider social and moral pathologies ranging from anti-Semitism to the granting of monetized indulgences by Pope Clement VI (based in Avignon, in connection with the Jubilee Year of 1350 that took pilgrims to Rome). In turn and in time, this led ineluctably to the Protestant Reformation—even if temporarily it was the Church alone that emerged institutionally stronger from the plague (becoming "richer if not more unpopular"), thanks to a sharp rise in bequests by the terrified. But more fundamentally, "the absolutes of a fixed order were loosed from its moorings; the end of an age of submission came in sight," she wrote powerfully of a pestilence that marked out the "unrecognized beginning of modern man."

Its deathly tentacles spread widely, carried by the unknowing and unwilling, as is typical with pandemics. Here was a truly democratic disease. It took time to spread, unlike today, on the order of one kilometer (two-thirds of an English mile) a day on land—although scholars of the era are prone to note its relative speed, which suggests person-to-person contagion. The plague likely came in waves from the Orient. Its arrival (October 1347) in Messina, in southern Italy, aboard a Genoese cargo ship, its stricken crew dying or dead, is widely documented. Common assumption, derived from saga accounts, holds that it was summer 1349 before the flea-borne, rat-carried pestilence arrived in Norway. Bergen is traditionally cited as the entryway, via an English ship, before its killing wave washed over the Norwegian countryside from south to north and west to east, and from there into Sweden.

This line of argument was pursued by P. A. Munch and has been passed down to modern historians, fueling the common view that Norway was far worse hit than other countries including Denmark and Sweden. Such a view has been perpetuated by a blatant misattribution, where the brown rat in Britain mistakenly (and much later) took on the name *Rattus norvegicus* on assumptions that it had arrived from Norway via a timber ship in 1728. A noted eighteenth-century taxidermist, Charles Waterton, waged "a lifelong vendetta of unsurpassed ferocity" against the mislabeling of this scourge according to John Keay, a Waterton chronicler, which had brought undeserved disrepute to the Norwegian name in British medical circles.

Ingmar Bergman's 1957 film *The Seventh Seal* gives a searing portrayal of the gloom and emptiness of the postplague Swedish countryside, while historian Dick Harrison has written of its importance there. Still, the plague is a focus of Norwegian historiography beyond that of its neighbors. It differentiates the national experience, although—in apt reflection of the wider neglect already discussed—Norway's possible singularity does not feature in general studies like Cantor's and Tuchman's.

Plague ravaged Norway's island dependencies like Orkney and Shetland, reaching as far as the Færoe Islands—but because of its rapid maturation it spared more distant Greenland, while Iceland saved itself by banning ships from Norway. Finland too was initially spared, although it was devastated in a later contagion, as was Iceland (twice) in the fifteenth century.

Plague was the most feared late-medieval public health nightmare but it was not the only one. Typhus came to Europe via returning Spanish troops; smallpox was a perennial that left Queen Christina of Sweden and Russia's Catherine the Great facially disfigured; syphilis appeared in Naples in 1495, centuries before penicillin, and predictably spread. Leprosy distressingly hung on in Scandinavia through the nineteenth century, primarily in Norway; it was a Norwegian researcher in Bergen, Armaur Hansen, who isolated the bacterium in 1873, a case of need generating a solution.

But the plague wreaked immediate devastation. The bubonic strain, which (some argue) predominated in Scandinavia, brought agonizing death, usually within three days of the first, ominous egg-sized blotches and suppurating glandular swellings in the armpits and groin. The pneumatic strain brought fever, coughed blood and even quicker death. Whatever the form, it struck massively but randomly. For those temporarily spared it prompted a sense of cheapened life under the terror of God's indiscriminate wrath, bringing an all-consuming uncertainty and sense of impending doom. Its debilitating effects on the survivors, in turn, worsened the subsequent waves. Within the decade a terrifying strain of "children's plague" (*barnedauden*) hit the most vulnerable segment and presumably worsened the long-term population crisis. It arrived around 1357, killing among others Sweden's King Erik and his entire family. Another pest wave arrived in 1371.

Norway was possibly the first and, some historians suggest, the hardest hit of all the Nordic lands. Swedish sources tend to put the death toll at a third of the (Swedish) population; Norwegian ones range from half to two-thirds, *sex av ti* (six of 10) being the prevailing guesstimate, from a total preplague population of roughly 400,000. Neil Kent, who looked broadly at Nordic health matters over time, believes the two-thirds figure applied "in parts" (i.e., regionally) rather than countrywide. Overall it probably also applies to the longer-term loss over the oncoming century.

Is subtle dramatization at work? A chronicler of Swedish–Norwegian relations, Alf Henrikson, hints at Icelandic exaggeration in regards to the two-thirds figure. Acemoglou and Robinson, the failure chroniclers, insist that "everywhere a similar fraction of the population perished," roughly half, which in Europe would amount to 20–30 million victims. Yet there is compelling evidence that western parts of Europe were hit harder than points further east, and that the devastation in Norway cut especially deep. An otherwise sober analyst, Holmsen, did not mince his words: "The downturn took an especially catastrophic character, [it was] an economic catastrophe of fantastic dimensions," he wrote *apropos* of Norway.

Recorded land sale prices, for example, dropped in some farming areas by up to 75 percent, tithes to the church (which owned nearly half the land in late-Middle-Age Norway) by similar amounts. Farms were abandoned in their thousands, while at those hanging on, production plummeted. In this, economic sense Norway would have been especially vulnerable: it was even more rural than its neighbors and barely sustained more marginal farms due to its peculiar topography. "As between landowner and peasant," Tuchman avers, "the balance of impoverishment and enrichment caused by the plague on the whole favored the peasant," with the mass abandonment of hill farms cited as crucial.

The plague spared neither the powerful nor the devout: at Nidaros the archbishop and all his church officials save for one (Lodin) died; in one church in a single day, 80 corpses were found, among them 20 bishops. The devastation prompted a foot-pilgrimage to Trondheim by King Magnus Eriksson from Stockholm to St. Olav's shrine in 1350. Perhaps it helped; he survived, for a time. In 1355 he was deposed as Norwegian king, though he hung on in Sweden for almost another decade.

After the initial devastation, a reeling society was agonizingly slow to recover. A Middle Age historian, William Chester Jordan, thinks that Norway took far longer (until 1750) to reach its preplague population levels than did, for example, Normandy or England, which may have recovered by 1600. Holmsen cites other factors as to why Norway may have been hit harder than Denmark or Sweden: more farms further north, and a climatic cooling spell that made them productively marginal.

An alternative view is put forth by Ole Jørgen Benedictow, a student of Holmsen who reviewed medical literature largely overlooked by Munch and those who followed his painstaking lead. (Cohn, in true scholarly spirit, savages Benedictow's research as narrowly selective.) Contrary to saga accounts, he argues that the pandemic arrived first in the Oslofjord area, perhaps as early as autumn 1348 and probably from Denmark or England. There it lay dormant, he thinks, only to explode in the warm months of 1349—bubonic plague's essential agent, the rat-carried flea, being confined to a narrow temperature range.

More importantly, he offers a convincing explanation for the biggest mystery, namely why the pestilence spread into the remotest corners of Norway. Typically plague, like other pathogens, is said to affect the close quarters of cities the worst. Defoe suggested as much in his *Journal of the Plague Year* a cleverly fictionalized version of the great London Plague of 1665 he had experienced in childhood. There, contagion was partly contained by "the shutting up of houses [...] a public good that justified the private mischief." But in arguing counterintuitively that the pathogen hit rural areas even harder than towns—thanks to prevailing social habits, a traveling culture and tighter ratios of rat colonies to individual family units—Benedictow believes that a "radical rewriting" of the plague history, so central to the national narrative, is in order.

He cites practices that encouraged both local transmission and long-distance migration of the disease. These included an inbuilt communal tendency for remote villagers to draw together in times of distress, and specifically the ruinous ritual of gathering in the homes of the dead prior to burial. Tenacious social customs—notably "funeral feasts" that doubled as inheritance parties, where valuables like clothes and bedding were sold second-hand or inherited at the bedside of the newly deceased—encouraged its spread at the closest of quarters. Rather than isolating the dead or afflicted, which might have stanched any contagion, the opposite happened. The newly dead became the plague's chief purveyors *after* they succumbed, a process reinforced by poverty, ignorance and clannish tendencies.

Economically, too, medieval Norway was structured to encourage pestilential spread. Norway operated on surprisingly intricate, and highly mobile, trade-based conduits forged during the rapid population growth in the stable thirteenth century. It linked larger towns, coastal villages and far-flung "proletarian-rural" settlements that operated on the margin. Grain grown at lower altitudes was readily exchanged for animal products cultivated upland via a complex chain of goods, which encouraged specialized production and included salt exchange as well as grain. *Xenopsylla cheopis*, the black rat–born flea that carried the pathogen, could live (he argues) for stretches off the stashes of grain that were constantly moved around and which served as a barter currency, taking the deadly carriers effectively into any place in Norway where people lived and ate. The plague was both systemic and lethally systematic.

Still another factor—and again one with strong Norwegian echoes—was known as *Wandertrieb*, an "urge to wander," by which a frightful reality, such as rampant disease, compels migrant people to take to the road and head for home. The result was "the extraordinary powers of plague to reach the most peripheral districts and localities," spreading with devastating efficiency into areas that he calls "the external margin" flourishing in late-Middle-Age Norway.

What emerges is a picture of a highly specialized but unmonetized and fragile trade system, a "fine-meshed network of commercial exchange" linking coast and mountain, by which arable farming and animal husbandry exchanged their products according to caloric need. And it was this specialized, intricate arrangement, not just the people involved, which was destroyed by the plague, sending peasants from the remotest areas if they were lucky to survive.

The upshot is that it was not a depraved, isolated or failed society that fell apart in fourteenth-century Norway, but a carefully modulated trading system, built on specialized forms of production and lubricated by incessant movement. Perversely, this pattern invited the pathogen into the tiniest hamlets and remotest areas. Norway may have suffered no worse than other places, in terms of overall depopulation (which Benedictow pegs at 64 percent in the first postplague century) or in its regenerative powers.

At the same time, the Norwegian effects appear far more devastating, and the long-term impact more fundamental, because the pestilence destroyed a rural economic arrangement that not only reached into localities but depended on their role in sustaining the chain. The plague eviscerated a finely tuned, premodern socioeconomic system—one based on barter, product specialization, close neighborly connections and incessant movement, vertical as well as horizontal—which, in his studied view, set the stage for a transition to a very different way of life in a depopulated, ravaged land. It encouraged, or forced, "people mixing" and landholding to a wider extent than that occurring in neighboring countries or in more urbanized places like England. Michael North terms this an "upward leveling process," and in Norway it empowered most of the population in the long term, especially the freehold and leasehold peasantry. The quick initial devastation also seems, believes Benedictow, to have ameliorated the effects of later waves as "the epidemic dragon drew its own teeth."

A contributing factor now increasingly appreciated was environmental in the modern sense, namely a long-term cooling spell from the late thirteenth century. Failing crops in already marginal farms in the decades before 1349 unquestionably worsened the Norwegian effects once the infestation(s) did arrive. Conditions of want do not make for a stout defense against aggressive infection. The plague, while uniquely devastating, contributed to a downward spiral whose vehicle, with a full complement of irony, was a specialized commodity system that hinged, as is so common in Norway, on mobility.

The political effects were also quicker to appear in Norway, and there again the regional imprint appears deepest. Magnus Eriksson, who clung to power in Sweden (against attacks by the council and by his aggrieved son, Erik) until 1364, lost his Norwegian throne in 1355 to another son, Håkon VI (Magnusson). The Norwegian nobility, already constricted and consequently vulnerable, suffered a permanent reduction in its numbers and role. This was a structural change that allowed the *riksråd* (king's council) to be infiltrated by foreign blood from Denmark, Germany and Sweden. Surviving titled landowners were forced to till their own land. There seems a consensus view that the plague thinned the ranks of an already weak Norwegian aristocracy, reducing its power and paving the way for the Danish power thrust later that century. Both social and sociopolitical relationships underwent a sea change.

If in the long run this produced the grassroots "farmer democracy" of the nineteenth century, in the shorter term it made Norway—already locked into a personal union with Sweden—ripe for foreign takeover. This was especially the case since overwhelmingly rural Norway also lacked an urban-burgher class to provide support for indigenous power centers.

The surviving peasantry was pressed into official positions (as jurymen, local officials and de facto judges) in a process driven by urgency, which empowered that entire segment of society. Just as importantly, this peasant empowerment was local; they were not "kingsmen" (i.e., royal representatives). Another impact was on the church, whose numbers—but not, it seems, its organization or influence—were cut sharply; of 300 priests in Nidaros diocese before the plague hit, the number was just 40 in 1371. Ecclesiastical authorities had to petition Pope Clemens VI for a special dispensation allowing them to appoint orphans as church officials. Surviving priests, called on to administer rites and bless the dying, passed on the contagion unknowingly. The Bishop of Hamar, in the east, succumbed in September 1349, that of Stavanger in January 1350, the last known name to perish.

The consequences have passed into rural myth. A complex pathogen amplified human pathologies; in monasteries, flagellation and self-mutilation were commonplace, while outside the walls, Jews were persecuted in the search for scapegoats, and shamans sought out for miracle cures. Yet some sectors benefited; fisherfolk, for example, found ready new markets and were largely spared by working in the open air. Some people migrated north. The abandonment of marginal farms for better land actually minimized starvation going forward. The countryside reeled from an experience that was seared into the folk memory—but the people there saw their long-term position strengthened by its consequences.

The burning image of medieval Norway remains that of Pesta, the fearsome hag with the rake, broom and haunting eyes, an image molded for posterity by Theodore Kittelsen in his *Svartedauen* series, executed in the unlikely milieu of his idyllic lakeside retreat at Lauvlia. In its way the Pesta figure is as emblematic of old Norway's pathologies as Munch's *Scream* became for the upheavals of the new. Another of Kittelsen's images portrayed the Soaring Eagle, majestic yet black and menacing. The plague was long thought to be an airborne phenomenon, carried by birds, rather than rat-borne fleas that were the actual, ground-level bubonic purveyors. Insofar as pneumatic plague was involved, Kittelsen's image conveyed a real truth after all.

What seemed like the end of the world in fact wasn't. The Great Plague swept aside much that went before and, in the emptiness of time, set the stage for a new beginning built on empowerment of the localized, grassroots variety.

5

Long Night's Journey into Day

What is it I'm looking for? I know it's something I lost.
Eugene O'Neill, *Long Day's Journey into Night*

Because modern Norway secured its independence by breaking with Sweden, the 91-year Swedish–Norwegian union remains the backstop for modern Norwegian memory and Sweden the nation's chief point of reference. Norwegians, however, lived for a great deal longer than that under Denmark. Exactly how and how long are matters of dispute that concern this chapter as they occupy the mustier corners of Norwegian historiography. For example, the role of Danish civil servants or *embetstanden* in Norway (helpers, modernizers, oppressors?) animates a range of interpretations that are gamely unveiled by Rian in a dedicated volume but are likely to sail over most non-Norwegian heads.

"For four whole centuries," proclaims Huhu, a character in Ibsen's *Peer Gynt*, "the simian race / Brooded in darkness [...] such long nights leave their mark upon a people." Thus was born, almost in passing and from the mouth of an Egyptian lunatic, the 400-year night trope of Norwegian history. This period of rule is generally labeled the *dansketida* or "Danish period." More accurately, it represents a lengthy phase of usurped power and cultural strangulation that is primarily associated with Denmark but is bookended by two separate phases of personal union with Sweden. Stretched to its limit it approximates a *sekshundreårsnatt* or 600-year night, which is staggering in its implications. In Europe only Finland and parts of the Balkans suffered such long-term eclipse.

The long-night notion underscores the problem of historiography noted in the last chapter, the writing of history itself, which almost inevitably focuses on crises and turning points, whereas "phases of consolidation" generate yawns and footnote fodder. For Norway those centuries also titillate because they are surprisingly full of nonevents: Rubicons approached but not breached, crises narrowly averted, lines drawn in the sand. Post-Viking Norway presents multiple births but few open revolts or fundamental crises. Glimpses of violence are unaccompanied by revolution. Poverty was endemic, yet famine scant. The outward face of Norway is equally perplexing. Historically it is a game of shadows.

How did Norway, in whatever form, survive such a lengthy period of eclipse? How did it emerge as anything but emasculated? How has it shaped the country of today? The questions are worthy but the answers are elusive and the causal connections diffuse. There are, however, some promising developmental lines.

First, Norway's post-Viking consolidation was sufficiently strong to form a core of stability capable of surviving centuries of often humiliating foreign rule. Second, Norway's postmedieval fate—infiltrated by Swedes, Danes and Germans in the fourteenth century, then entrapped by Denmark until its "recapture" in 1814 by Sweden—was not a chronic condition of subservience but a time of fitful evolution. Third, these successive overlordships were themselves more erratic and less onerous than they might have been, often leaving Norway more or less to its own devices while keeping a modicum of rules-based (religious, civil) control.

Fourth, Norway became a periodic point of contention between the Danish and Swedish royal houses, which came to an inevitable head because of Napoleon early in the nineteenth century. And fifth, Norway became an unwitting political football in the complex, pre-democratic internal politics within Denmark and later Sweden, making it an instrument in turns neglected and seized upon by domestic factions competing for influence. Norwegians grew skilled at parlaying a chronically weak situation to their own increasing advantage, without resorting to rebellion or militant nationalism. In this way Norwegians proved adept early practitioners of the *art of strategic weakness*, maximizing opportunities that came their way and squeezing the best out of the poor hand they were dealt.

The latter two factors in particular gave Norwegians subtle leverage, backhand influence, room to maneuver and space to grow. These were enabling conditions that together allowed Norwegians to turn seeming deficiencies into covert strengths that would serve the country well when it emerged, belatedly, from its shell. They tell more of resilience and fortitude than of the raw opportunism of the weak. And they positioned Norway to pull off that rarest of feats, a (mostly) peaceful national revolution—and in fact to do it twice within a century, the long nineteenth, that was otherwise marked by the societally disruptive forces of nationalism, industrialization and democratization.

The long night is coincidental with the *dansketida* but not identical to it, while their longevity makes both hard to characterize. Was Norway a Danish dependency, an appendage, a protectorate, a province, a vassal state or perhaps a fiefdom? J. E. Sars employed the pungent term "annex." One descriptive rarely heard is the politically supercharged one of colony. Its emotional milieu is suggestive of passivity and its legacy vaguely colored by shame, while the changes it brought about warrant not one big chapter but several smaller ones.

Norway's "long night" was not a night at all but rather a twilight period marked by subterranean currents: social and economic in the main, cultural and political on a lesser scale. The notion intrigues partly because it puzzles. As indicated in the last chapter, Norway was coming off a period of renewed stability and expansiveness that has a Victorian ring about it and which posits Håkon IV (1217–63) as a Norwegian equivalent of the British imperial monarch. (Norman Cantor, a medieval chronicler, takes the analogy wider by twinning the thirteenth and nineteenth centuries as eras of European stability.) Yet half a century later, ostensibly on the trifling matter of a male heir, the royal edifice tottered; the Swedes moved in, society was hit by crop failures and then, prompted by plague, it collapsed.

Question-begging it is, the way all broken histories, from Easter Island to the Lost Colony of Roanoke to the lost Norse settlers of Greenland, can be. Jared Diamond's book *Collapse* dissects a series of civilizations that imploded and points a learned finger at environmental self-sabotage. But this surely is a different dynamic. Norway did not suddenly disappear but was caught in a gradually tightening noose. In different ways 1302, 1319, 1380, 1387, 1397, 1450, 1469, 1502, 1520, 1536 and 1660 all mark datable downshifts in Norwegian autonomy, principally vis-à-vis Denmark.

The country that sprang to life in spring 1814 was no thawed-out version of late Middle Age Norway but something else entirely. Thus it helps to regard 1814 not in its usual light—as the "miracle year" that spawned a text of that title by Karsten Alnæs—but rather as a *culminating* point for a quietly defining period. Norway emerged in 1814 behind enlightened figures capable of seizing the moment, penning a modern constitution, going toe to toe with covetous Swedes and ensuring the nation's autonomy going forward. None of it was luck or happenstance. De-dramatizing 1814 can give it perspective and expose its underpinnings. These include independent political awakenings, associated with a power shift to the country's southeast; the birth of a Norwegian military; settlement of most of its borders; consolidation of the Protestant Reformation; the stirrings of proto-industry; new patterns of foreign trade; the weakening and final severance of the Hansa monopoly; and the foundations of the shipping power that Norway was, once again, to become.

All these changes find a curious parallel in Eugene O'Neill's gripping family drama. Norway, like the Tyrone family, suffered a series of collective setbacks, first in the century-long stretch of civil war following the Vikings, then ineluctably in the submission to Denmark and, much later, in 1814, when independence flickered briefly only to be snuffed out. And his signature play, *Long Day's Journey into Night*, does seem to resonate in Norway (and in Scandinavia; its stage debut was in Sweden, where O'Neill became a Nobel laureate at just 48).

It was the chosen vehicle for the actress Liv Ullmann, after 50 years away from the national stage, to get reacquainted with the Norwegian public in 2007, taking O'Neill's drama on the road throughout the country. The big difference, of course, is that Norwegians managed to write another and bolder family act, using the setback of 1814 as a springboard.

Norway's unheralded path to modernity amounted to an invisible renaissance, organic and unseen. Societies are protean entities that develop at multiple speeds, just as clouds can cross in various directions and oceanic currents in the salty depths.

Early-modern Norway is Exhibit A for such tendencies. Even as official Norway saw its existence slipping away from the fourteenth century, everyday Norway was experiencing a slow-motion rebirth.

Of the above dates, 1380 is most commonly cited as it marks the passing of the last Norwegian-born independent king, Håkon VI. His death brought on the short-lived rule of Olav IV, who died in 1387 while still a teen (which poses that date as another candidate). That in turn led to direct Danish rule of Norway via the formidable Margrete, Håkon VI's widow, a queen herself but more importantly a determined kingmaker. After defeating an army of Mecklenburg at Falköping in 1389, she proceeded to pull Sweden into her realm as well, engineering the Kalmar Union of the three crowns. Running from 1380 to 1814 would give a 434-year night—and a stretch of some 14 Oldenburg kings, later alternating between Frederiks and Christians in the Danish way.

Yet 1319 seems a more defensible starting point for Norway's slippage into foreign control. Two pivotal events that year proved terminal symbolically as well as literally: the death of Norway's Håkon V in May and, in November, that of Erik Menved in Denmark. In the same year, the Norwegian and Danish kings both died heirless—the former without male issue, the latter childless—which sparked decades of regional turmoil. Succession crises racked both countries, with regencies, feuding councils and power struggles undermining stability, and both dragged Sweden into the mix. Amidst the upheaval came famines and then the plague.

In May 1319 Magnus Eriksson, aged 3, became the titular king of Norway; in July he came into the Swedish crown as well, where the new era was also marked by the Letter of Privilege, sometimes called Sweden's Magna Carta. This brought a very Scandinavian (and more generally, north European) type of rule: a personal union of crowns, often in the precarious form of a child monarch. Personal royal unions later marked the Danish hold on Schleswig and Holstein; another connected the Russian czars to Finland from 1809 and, starting five years later, Sweden's kings in Norway. With the crowning of Scotland's James VI as James I in 1603, Scotland and England were similarly linked by personal union; Great Britain only emerged under Queen Anne in 1707.

Well-meaning but ineffectual, the adult King Magnus Eriksson never managed to govern either land. His reign became cosmopolitan via his marriage to Blanche of Namur, of French and Flemish ancestry, who became queen of Sweden and thus, in 1335, of Norway. Her reputed beauty and breeding could not save a binational reign by Magnus that was marked by calamity. Nidaros Cathedral, Catholicism's great northern bridgehead, was finally completed in 1320 only to burn down eight years later. National debts mounted. Magnus pawned castles to the Germans and ruled ineffectually over two countries devastated by the Black Death. In 1353 his second capital, Oslo, burned to the ground. In 1355 his son, Erik, became a rival king of Sweden, again dividing the two realms. He faced relentless internal opposition. He lost territories of Skåne, Halland and Blekinge to the resurgent Danes under Valdemar Atterdag, in 1360; the following year the strategic island of Gotland was also lost to (and pillaged by) the Danes. Later he was jailed, ransomed and, in 1371, drowned when his ship sank. A new phase emerged from this parade of misfortune with the passing of Håkon V in 1380 and the emergence of Margrete as the region's chief power broker.

Margrete represented recovery on the Danish side of this turmoil. Her marriage to Norway's Håkon VI in 1363 made her a pivotal regional figure. She was the daughter of Valdemar Atterdag, who had managed to stabilize a Denmark still reeling from a decade during which the country went without a king (a weak ruler, Christoffer II, had been forced to sign a charter of accession). Later Valdemar took Gotland by force before suffering a blow by the resurgent Hansa. Valdemar's reign gave way, in 1375, to Olav IV, who became king of Norway through his father after inheriting the Danish throne via his mother: quite the double act starting from the age of 5. Twelve years later he was dead.

Into this chaotic breach stepped Margrete, his mother and Håkon VI's widow, who emerged as the dominant Scandinavian personality by the century's end. Though never the titular ruler of the Kalmar Union, she was the driving force in its formative years until her death in 1412. She had recruited a relative, a Pomeranian prince called Bugislav—then all of 12, yet another child ruler in a vexed time—and placed him, as Erik of Pomerania, on the

Kalmar throne. In a region that has spawned many strong queens, she stands alone.

So if we use 1319 as the marker—the start of the twilight years, Håkon V's justly feared beginning of the end—then the "Norwegian night" ran for five centuries. The 700th anniversary of those events in 2019 ensures that more will be written, presumably not all of it in Norwegian, on a subject of almost intimidating complexity.

During this period the country's southeast assumed an importance that derived from location and proximity. Østfold and Vestfold are natural partners and joint guardians of the Oslofjord, and both became strategic territory with the shift of the capital to Oslo *circa* 1300. Yet they are fraternal rather than identical twins. Larger and flatter Østfold abuts Sweden and was long an invasion corridor. Inland Vestfold is more rugged and rustic, more authentically Norwegian in its way, while its meandering shoreline, cut by countless inlets, gives it a protective character. It helped make Kaupang, now an archeological site outside today's Larvik, one of the larger settlements in Viking Norway, home to roughly a thousand people in its trading heyday.

By the fifteenth century, both areas had developed rebellious reputations. In 1436–37 Østfold erupted in peasant revolts, associated with a gentryman called Amund Sigurdsson Bolt; in 1438 Vestfold followed suit, prompted by one Halvard Gråtopp. These stirrings led to more Danish crackdowns. But a restless tradition of local self-assertion in the Oslofjord, whether the perceived enemy was the local merchant class, tax officials or Erik of Pomerania, made a strong early mark in both places.

Outsiders who paint the Scandinavians as a collective unit do so partly because of these convoluted dynastic ties and mixed marriages of past centuries. Yet even under the Kalmar Union (formally 1397–1523, in reality far less than that), its founding charter gave each country leeway to run its own affairs, via their Councils of the Realm. As Michael North notes, this was the result of an open-ended constitutional struggle: an Act of Coronation, monarchist in character, quickly took precedent over a Union Document that might have cultivated deeper political union. The loosely federative nature of Kalmar was seemingly reinforced at a 1436 gathering, but the delicate balance was in turn upset after

1450 by a rising Denmark under Christian I of Oldenburg, the founder of a new bloodline.

The chief fillip came via the establishment, in 1429, of the Sound Toll, by which the Danish crown levied fees on every ship passing in and out of the Baltic. At first levied per-ship, it later became a value-based fee that dramatically expanded the royal income. Its archive has emerged, belatedly, as a valuable resource, as a recent anthology shows. The increasingly uneven power balance contributed to centuries of intra-Scandinavian wars that were often inconclusive or unnecessary, marked by peace deals with obscure names and limited remit; the times of peace in between were filled with ceaseless jockeying for advantage.

Outsiders, from Hansa traders to the English to the Dutch Estates-General, were all too happy to exploit these differences as Sweden sought to adjust. One of the Sound Toll mysteries was how and why Sweden permitted Danish collection for another two centuries after 1658, when Denmark lost its foothold in (today's) southern Sweden via the Treaty of Roskilde and might well have been challenged.

The Kalmar Union itself was bookended by a pair of massacres that became notorious even in grisly early-modern Nordic annals.

In 1361 Valdemar Atterdag forcibly ended Gotland's great age as a medieval entrepot for Baltic trade. The town of Visby, now a UNESCO-protected medieval gem, had grown rich and could afford a building spree of churches, the legacy of which is still very present. A (later) painting by C. G. Hellqvist depicts Valdemar's ransom of Visby, when he marched an army to the city walls, defeated a ramshackle peasant army, entered the city center, set up three empty ale vats and demanded that residents fill them with gold and silver to win their freedom. Paying up paid them few dividends as Gotland passed into Danish hands. Presumed divine intervention then sank Valdemar's treasure-laden ship in a storm. Yet two years later it was his daughter Margrete who, by marrying Håkon VI, turned this dark episode into the germ of Kalmar, the ill-fated experiment in common governance.

The mid-fifteenth century delivered two further blows to Norway's sense of self. The accession, in 1450, of Christian (I) of Oldenburg as joint king of Norway and Denmark siphoned off much of Norway's lingering autonomy through a formal act of union. Then in 1469 the impoverished crown, no longer able to sustain a lifeline to Greenland, threw in another towel closer to home. King Christian pawned the Orkney and Shetland island groups (for 50,000 and 8,000 florins, respectively) in lieu of a dowry to James III, the Scottish king, who was marrying (another) Margaret of Denmark. The pledge of two island groups for dowry purposes was a political expedient that was later interpreted as a blunder of historic proportions, turning a manageable shortfall into a permanent loss. The joint crown could ill-afford to buy the island groups back as intended, although in any case Scottish cultural creep had watered down the once-dominant Norwegian influence in both places.

In 1520, at the last stages of Kalmar's terminal decline, came the second and more precipitous horror. King Christian II of Denmark was set on taking back regional control in the name of Denmark, more resolutely than Christian I had managed in 1471, when he was defeated by Sten Sture the Elder. In severely overreaching, Christian II instigated the birth of modern Sweden, brought on the Reformation he didn't want and engineered his own downfall.

He is less known, at least outside Norway, for terminating his own career with military adventurism *in* Norway. As crown prince to King Hans, he fought in the campaign to subdue an uprising led by Knut Alvsson, a Norwegian–Swedish noble, in 1502. Alvsson's death, the result of alleged treachery during safe passage by Henrik Krummedige, was a huge psychological blow to Norway. Thirty years later, in 1531–32, Christian's dramatic attempt to recapture his lost crown came to naught with his abortive attack on Oslo.

Christian II comes to us with an almost schizophrenic reputation. Most historians regard him as brilliant but half-cocked. To Swedes he was a butcher; to Danes, especially the lower classes, he was revered as a people's hero who stood up to the nobility as well as to Sweden. His subsequent (Danish) reputation as the commoners' king grew after he took up with a marketplace girl, called Dyveke Sigbritsdatter, whom he met in Bergen. It was an unlikely match that turned bizarre when Dyveke died suddenly and the girl's mother became an influential royal advisor. And in Norway, where he earned his political spurs as resident crown prince in 1501–02, Christian is vilified for stamping out resurgent Norwegian nationalism by decreeing the murder of Knut Alvsson, the insurgency's leader. None other than Henrik Ibsen posited that event as "plucking the heart out" of the Norwegian spirit. The year 1502 thus presents itself as yet another point of encroaching nightfall for Norway.

The events of 1520 were by any standard shocking in their brutality, scale and outright deceit. In a time of civil war he met and defeated the forces of Sten Sture the Younger, who died after the battle. The Danes then marched onto Stockholm but were stymied by forces defending the old Tre Kronor's castle, buoyed up by Christina Gyllenstierna, Sture's widow, in a siege lasting some four months. Entering the city, a victorious Christian promised an amnesty and was duly crowned king of Sweden to go with his Danish and Norwegian titles.

On November 4, after three days of feasting, Christian turned on his celebrants. Swedish nobles, bishops and burghers (including the father and two uncles of future King Gustav Vasa) were condemned for heresy, the worst possible crime, and executed in the marketplace of today's Gamla Stan. Some 82 were put to death, while Sture's corpse was disinterred and thrown atop the pile to amplify the local lesson. Numerous other executions were carried out elsewhere in Sweden, an estimated 600 all told. Along with the cream of Swedish society, the cause of Nordic unity was deader than dead, and the stage was set for the peasant-backed Swedish uprising instigated by Gustav Vasa. Later, Christian was unrepentant; "mild measures avail nothing," he told Erasmus, the great humanist, who questioned his genocidal tactics. "The medicine that gives the whole body a good shaking is the best and surest."

Yet Harald Gustafsson, a historian, gives a spirited defense of the notion of a common Nordic history that was alive even at that point of desperation. After Christian II's massacre, dissident Swedes found refuge in Norway, which was by then firmly under Denmark. The charter of his successor Christian III, who promulgated the Reformation in Denmark and Norway, applied also to those activist Swedes on the run—another argument, Gustafsson believes, for a common early-modern Nordic narrative. Still, dreams of a unified Norden were snuffed out forever in this era, not even allowed to pass away naturally.

Norway's "nightfall" can also be more recently and perhaps decisively dated to the Protestant Reformation, which was imposed in 1536. Its sudden arrival in Norway mirrored its unexpected insurgency further south. In contrast to the halting seepage of Christian ideas north of the Baltic, the movement launched, unwittingly, in 1517 by Martin Luther swept through northern Europe within a generation. It did not start with much: a hammer, a nail, paper and pen, a disgruntled churchman. But the day that Luther, a reform-minded German preacher, scholar and monk, posted his 95 Theses to the Archbishop of Mainz (and later, legend has it, nailed to a church door in Wittenberg), in hopes of prompting debate over official practices, he unleashed a tide of change that overturned life as north Europeans knew it.

Until the sixteenth century, Norway was simply part of the Church. Nidaros drew pilgrims while the archbishop became a source of authority—and increasingly, a bothersome presence—to the Danes intent on consolidating control. The archbishop's palace was a power holdout in a fast-weakening Norway, which gave it outsized visibility (and distant Trondheim tenacious residual power); the country otherwise lacked direction, and Luther's ideas held little attraction. A key figure in the drama was the last Archbishop of Nidaros, Olaf Engelbrektsson. The verdict on him is divided: condemned by some for his militant-retro Catholicism (and for allegedly looting Nidaros archives), he also promoted a strong, independent Norway at a time when national champions were in short supply. Stripped of his power base, he was evacuated from Trondheim to Holland on Easter Sunday in 1537, never to return. Any Norwegian fighting spirit seemed to drain away too.

Reformist by name, the Reformation was built on protest, hence the term Protestant. Luther's ideas lit a fuse because of the slide into corruption by the late-medieval church. His main objection was the selling of "indulgences" to a faithful flock compelled, after a fashion, to buy their way to Heaven. The aim of halting such practices mushroomed into a movement to sweep away the Church that sanctioned them. The 1521 Diet of Worms sealed his fate as a renegade and turned his protest into a revolution.

The tensions split the continent: Catholicism proved more resilient in southern Europe. But like many sweeping tides, the

Reformation itself fragmented. Ulrich Zwingli preached one interpretation in Zürich, John Calvin another in Geneva (the Reformation's spiritual home), firebrand John Knox a particularly shrill version in Scotland. Today's Methodists, Lutherans, Baptists, Presbyterians and other sects emerged later, united in basic faith yet divided by liturgical detail. All, too, were emboldened by the Counter-Reformation that tried to stop the dissent with more success further south. The tensions later boiled over into the terrible destruction of the Thirty Years' War (1618–1648) which started, but did not end, as a religious war.

Soon Christian II was discussing Luther's insurgency with converted Germans invited into his court, but he never took the bait himself. Gustav Vasa decreed a Swedish Reformation in 1527; nine years later, Denmark followed suit. Christian III, an elected monarch, emerged victorious in August 1536 from the "Count's War," a short but violent period following Christian II's abdication. Christian III, his successor of a very different stripe, became forever known as the Clergyman King. For all his virtues, his decision amounted to a ruthless power play which, at a stroke, changed the faith, eliminated Norway's Council of the Realm along with its former ecclesiastical autonomy and ended the polite fiction of a dual kingship.

From that date, Norway's institutions of state ceased to be; Norway, as Jespersen phrases it, was "incorporated but not integrated" into Denmark—that is, no longer formally independent yet *informally* still separate, a halfway house that offered considerable wiggle room. And in fact, Norway's saving grace soon became the cut and thrust of Danish domestic politics at the high-water mark of Danish world influence—an altered relationship that made a weakened Norway a useful bargaining chip between kings and the powerful nobility. But here matters get distressingly complicated. In order to understand early post-Reformation Norway, we must factor in not only Dano-Swedish power-posturings but also internal machinations in Copenhagen and, later on, those in Stockholm. Sixteenth-century Danish politics may seem a Norwegian subject too far, but the main lines are fairly straightforward.

Many historians believe that Christian III's decree marks the nadir of Norway's fortunes and a genuine national catastrophe—an insult to the injuries of 1531–32, when a resurgent Christian II entered Oslofjord with a fleet, besieged Akershus and torched part of the city. For the restored Danish crown four years later, it was part of a double coup that turned Norway into the provincial rump it would remain until 1814. Norwegians had special reason for linking the Reformation with power politics, as it represented the new order that jolted their Sunday expectations while extinguishing their independence for the next 280 years.

But the same Reformation that brought upheaval also, in the longer term, heralded political consolidation. Royal houses in early-modern Europe—bastions of traditionalism and purveyors of absolutism, clinging perilously to power—found its subversive ideas surprisingly useful for their own purposes. By decreeing Protestantism they could undercut the church bishops and the aristocracy, their chief rivals in governing Councils of State. Christian III mastered this strategy at home. In turn the Reformation empowered merchant classes and, in Scandinavia, farmers and peasants. In this way the Lutheran upheaval speeded the formation of national states and state churches—Henry VIII's Church of England being an awkward pioneer—that were independent of Rome and Papal authority. Confiscations brought church lands under state control, while tax rolls guaranteed royal houses a solid economic base and dynastic wars ample opportunity to spend it.

But even in receptive northern Europe the Reformation took time to settle. More than a century after Gustav Vasa forced through Lutheranism in Sweden, Queen Christina—the daughter of a king, Gustavus Adolphus, who fought and died on behalf of Protestantism—abdicated as a converted Catholic in 1654. In England, Catholic King James II was forced out in the Glorious Revolution of 1688—exactly a century after (Protestant) Queen Elizabeth's defeat of Catholic Spain with its Armada.

The Reformation that convulsed Denmark had other, practical effects in Norway. Oslo's medieval churches (*Mariakyrken*, St. Hallvards Cathedral) fell into ruin. Soon a new cathedral, the indifferently situated *domkirken* of today, went up in stages further west. Today's scattered ruins of *Gamle By*, the old town, barely whisper to the grandeur of the earlier church-and-state power structure.

It also marked a cultural eclipse for Norwegians unhappy with the new faith's austere tenets. The liturgy and other trappings of service were presented in formal Danish, the oppressors' tongue, which jarred with traditional practices. It all made Protestantism seem for a long time awkwardly, fundamentally and irretrievably foreign, and thus a double imposition. Old strongholds of Norwegian Catholicism were "more starved to death than crushed," in Neil Kent's pithy words. Norway's "language question" originated in those smoldering centuries when Danish became associated with suffocating officialdom and a foreign, though not alien, culture for which Oslo served as its Norwegian bridgehead. Functioning churches changed too, as the rich accoutrements of Catholicism, including statuary, vanished almost overnight. Church interiors were whitewashed and the past painted over. Even bell-ringing took on a different sound.

The transition was abrupt and unsettling but its handmaiden, a Lutheran austerity, became a byword for Norwegian lifestyles. In time it provided one of the foundations for the modern country built on notions of the good society. It fit naturally with a diligent, no-nonsense people. There was also something indefinably democratic about a faith built on a direct relationship between the individual and God.

The political–institutional arrangement, however, remained opaque. Olaf Riste notes, for example, that Christian III's Accession Charter of 1536 stated that Norway was to be thenceforth treated as a province (via the so-called Norway paragraph). Yet subsequent treaties in 1544 and 1546 still refer to the "kingdom of Norway," which retained the principle of hereditary monarchy (as opposed to Denmark and Sweden, where the elective-kingship tradition held sway).

King Frederik II of Denmark–Norway ushered in a new chapter of this uneven union. His role is insufficiently heralded, sandwiched between the reformist upheavals of Christians II and III that preceded him and the great-power associations of his son and heir, Christian IV. In a reign stretching three decades to his death in 1588, Frederik visited Norway exactly once, in 1585. Yet his rule underscored both Norway's emerging importance and his personal investment in it. He instituted changes that flowered under his more illustrious and impetuous son.

Frederik warily monitored the rise of Elizabethan England's naval power in the late sixteenth century—he died just months before the defeat of the Spanish Armada—along with the countervailing rise of the seagoing Dutch. To his mind the North Sea, to Denmark's west, constituted the "king's stream," but his chief maritime interest lay to the east and the Baltic. Astutely, he reconfigured the Sound Tolls to charge ships by the value of their cargo, not by vessel size, which effectively tripled the crown's income. The impressive rise of sixteenth-century Denmark was a precipitating factor in the arranged marriage between James VI of Scotland and Anna, princess of Denmark, in 1589, which was sealed in a shotgun wedding in Oslo.

The maritime fillip was sorely needed given the drainage of the Northern Seven Years' War (1563–70) fought against Sweden with little help from Norwegian peasant-soldiers, who proved reluctant to take up the fight. The protracted conflict ended in stalemate at the Treaty of Stettin. The compensating toll revenues not only paid the war bills but also funded the castle of Kronborg in Elsinore (Helsingør). Completed in the 1580s, it still looms impressively over the entrance to the Sound. At the same time the greatest of the Danish palaces, Frederiksborg in nearby Hillerød, was reconstructed and became yet another kingly namesake.

Frederik had been shocked with the ease at which marauding Swedes ravaged the Norwegian countryside. He strengthened the office of *stattholder* to keep a personal eye on affairs in Oslo. And in 1567 he fortified the city that still bears his name, Fredrikstad, strategically set at the junction of the Glomma River and the Oslofjord.

The seas west and north of Norway were a third (or fourth) watery frontier that took on sudden new importance in the late sixteenth century, for reasons mentioned in Chapter 3. One was the discovery of massive whaling stocks in the vast northern seas; the other was the developing interest in routes to Asia. These developments quickly turned Norway into a strategic asset for Denmark. The timing was again auspicious; Frederik's son and successor, Christian IV, came of age in 1596—the year that Dutch explorer Willem Barentsz accidentally discovered Bjørnøya and subsequently Spitsbergen in the High Arctic. The arrival of Henry Hudson then opened the floodgates for competitive exploitation of northern waters and landward incursions by Sweden.

Christian famously doted on his Norwegian possession, visiting for the first time in 1591 before he had taken the throne. Christian traveled there a second time in 1597, while his third trip, in 1599, became an Arctic expedition. He traveled under the deck-name of Kristian Fredriksen, with a fleet of eight ships commanded by Admiral Børge Trolle. This three-month adventure demonstrated that Norway in its totality was a special concern for the Danish crown and Christian personally.

The 1613 Peace of Knäred, far better known for Sweden's expensive ransom of Älvsborg fortress on the west coast, near today's Gothenburg, was important in this regard. Swedish designs on the far north had expanded under Karl IX, piqued by the whaling and passage interests of the Dutch, French and Basques. After two decades of Arctic jostling for commercial and political supremacy, the 1613 agreement dealt a double if still modest setback for Sweden. The Älvsborg ransom was soon enough resolved through payment, skillfully arranged by Chancellor Oxenstierna and funded by Dutch loans, but Sweden's relinquished claims in Finnmark gave Denmark–Norway a freer hand. Russia thereafter became the big outside concern in those parts. Gustavus Adolphus, for all his repute as the "lion of the north," thenceforth shifted his attention to Sweden's southern flank, its acquisitions below the Baltic, consolidating a foothold on the continent that lingered, at least on paper, until 1903.

Christian's consolidation of southern Norway and his personal role in rebuilding Oslo after the fire of 1624 tend to obscure his crucial role in securing the country's northern flank and pushing the Swedes (and Russians) east. Since Gustav Vasa the Swedes had assigned bailiffs to levy taxes across the far north to Lofoten, while Karl IX had styled himself "king of the Lapps" and built churches there, so the northern push was economically shrewd as well as strategically astute.

The war with Sweden in 1611–13 may well signify the high-water mark for Denmark's great-power era. At a stroke Christian scored a triple victory: outflanking the Danish nobility that opposed a fight with Sweden, besting the Swedes in a crucial interregnum of their own (Karl IX had died in 1611 from stroke complications; his successor, Gustavus Adolphus, was still a precocious teen) and consolidating Denmark–Norway into the bargain. Even at the beginning of Denmark's general decline it was stamping its authority both to its north and in Norway's far north. In all Christian visited Norway more than 30 times, but it was the peculiar nature of this attention, a tangle of personal, economic and above all strategic interest, which set Norway on a different footing.

Anxious to stamp his authority, Christian IV in 1596 also turned the office of Norwegian *stattholder*, or viceroy, into a more or less direct office of the Danish crown. The move had economic motives, for Norway represented a threefold source of wealth. Aside from its northern maritime allure, its west coast was prized by the German Hansas who might help him in his struggle with Sweden for mastery of the Baltic. Norway was also prized for its underground wealth, which could help pay for his military adventurism and craze for castle construction. In a bid to make Norway self-sufficient, he opened Bærums Verk ironworks in 1611. Hankering for currency, he opened the royal silver mines at Kongsberg in 1624 and, two decades later, the copper mines of Røros.

Norway proved useful for Christian IV's ongoing tug-of-war with the strong but recalcitrant nobility. In this aim, Norway's hereditary-king traditions became a practice to flaunt and a card to play. He and his successors were anxious to keep Norway partly free, notionally independent and sufficiently happy in a manner that left many Norwegian traditions intact and the Norwegian economy ripe for development. Modest levels of taxation, and pressure to keep them down, were one way of doing this. Subservience at one level meant relative freedom at another. And Norway, at any rate, differed in matters of law, administration and social class from that obtained in Denmark. Thus did Norway's long eclipse, deepened by a pair of external body blows—one, the Plague, biomedical in character and socioeconomic in effect, the other, the Reformation, politico-religious in nature and culturally transformative—become a time of slow and almost imperceptible consolidation prior to entry into the modern world.

A single example demonstrates the pitiless politics at work. Tycho Brahe, an early-modern astronomer on a reputational par with Copernicus and Kepler, was also a prominent member of the sixteenth-century Danish nobility and Regency Council. His renown extended widely and he was lavished with attention by Frederik II, whose life had once been saved by Brahe's father. The king provided him with an observatory on the tiny island of Hven, which lies mid-channel in the Sound between Sweden and Denmark, without it being formally chartered. Royal favors also delivered for him a public income and fiefs in Norway.

As told by J. R. Christianson, a Brahe biographer, these titles could change hands repeatedly according to royal whim, and in his case, Norwegian property in Nordfjord came and went repeatedly from Brahe's possession. This all changed when Christian IV came of age in 1596. The imperious nobleman-scientist and the brash young royal clashed; inevitably Brahe became the example and the victim. Stripped of favors and with royal prosecution pending, the self-consciously great man fled Denmark in the spring of 1597, never to return and dying in Prague.

Late in his checkered reign, Christian IV solidified Norway's position while seemingly diminishing it. In 1642 he appointed his son-in-law, Hannibal Sehested, to the *stattholder* job and appointed another in-law, Corfitz Ulfeldt, as *rikshovmester*, a lesser post. Christian visited Oslo yet again in 1643, at the outbreak of another war with Sweden. This was a crucial period after his disastrous intervention in the Thirty Years' War in 1625 (followed, five years later, by Sweden's far more successful intervention). A losing campaign against Sweden starting that year (1643) had produced the Peace of Brömsebro, in which Norway lost Jämtland and Härjedalen, while Christian lost an eye, among other injuries, leading a naval battle off Germany. For Denmark it was a costly catastrophe; in a desperate bid to raise revenues, Christian raised the Sound Tolls nine times in 10 years, along with export taxes on Norwegian timber, while being humiliatingly compelled to lower the charge on the Dutch fleet to the level of 1628.

Sehested seized on the war to solidify his independent position. In April 1643 he gained crucial royal assent to raise monies in order to fund a Norwegian farmers' battalion of 8,000 against the Swedes. By becoming a military overlord in Norway, with independent powers of taxation and backed by a rudimentary public administration, all with the blessing of the Danish king who was also his relative, Sehested carved out a virtual *eneveld* (autocracy) in Norway, which in turn became an indirect beneficiary of his personal ambitions. The war he fomented was almost a private sideshow, unaffectionately known as "Sehested's feud."

It was no surprise that Christian IV's eventual successor, his second son Frederik III, who played a longer and shrewder game, came to regard Norway as hereditary property. Norway and Sehested's version of it both became cards in the convoluted succession game in 1647–48 that started with the death of the crown prince, also called Christian, in late 1647, and was not decided until months after his father's death late that winter. King, peasants and clergy became united against the nobility, while the noble ranks were themselves torn—a classic early case of what's now commonly called a two-level political game.

Once enthroned in mid-1648, Frederik III worked to solidify Norway as a royal pet project, creating new positions in mine administration, forest protection and similar fields. In 1651 an outmaneuvered and widely detested Sehested left Norway and his stash of riksdollars and agricultural goods at Akershus to the king. (Still later he reemerged as a champion of *rapprochement* with Sweden.)

During the 1650s the powers of the Danish aristocracy continued to be undercut by the king, while a national emergency from 1657 to 1660 placed power by necessity in royal hands. All this created a new situation and a new opening for Norway. Over the course of a century and three kings, Norway went from being a depleted and overlooked part of the Danish realm to a fast-developing, geopolitically strategic, resource-rich and substantially autonomous unit. This, in turn, helped the Danish crown maneuver politically at home while turning its attention to Germany.

Thus a still more recent and still less often recognized "eclipse point" would be 1660, a red-letter date in Danish and Swedish history that ineluctably became one for Norway too. It marked the exhausted terminus of two furious wars waged by Sweden's Karl X against Denmark, when Denmark was on the cusp of annihilation and Norway easily could have been absorbed into Sweden some 150 years before it actually was.

Derring-do marked Karl's campaigns. With entire armies he famously crossed the frozen Little Belt and then the Great Belt during the frigid winter of 1658. A besieged Copenhagen had to be rescued by the Dutch navy, but Denmark was still forced out of its long-standing territories in southern Sweden in the subsequent settlements. These territorial shifts, presaged in 1645 at Brömsebro and in 1658 at Roskilde, were finalized—more or less permanently—through the Treaty of Copenhagen in May 1660. Despite Denmark's losses, Norway emerged as a more substantial presence that built on the initiatives of Sehested. Even in a losing campaign the forces gathered two decades before managed to keep Fredriksten fortress out of Swedish hands while gaining back Trøndelag—in effect keeping a loss from becoming a rout.

The immediate comeuppance within Denmark–Norway was a coup by Frederik III against the nobles in the *riksråd* and the dramatic reemergence of absolutism. History has painted the Danish action in a dim light, especially because of its staying power; absolutism finally and belatedly ended only in 1848–49. Yet Denmark's backslide into autocracy was far from exceptional. The foundations for the great palace of Versailles were laid in 1661 by Louis XIV, who ruled there for the next half-century, while the Spaniards were wreaking long-distance colonial havoc in Flanders a decade later. In Sweden too, the "great reductions" of that era materially weakened aristocratic holdings to the crown's direct benefit.

Norway was by now in the nominally degraded position of a northern colony, increasingly also shorn of the personal interest shown by Christian IV and Frederik III. In terms of history from above, it marked another Norwegian low. But in other, quieter ways, Norway's situation was entering a new phase. Its citizens were newly placed on an equal, if equally poor, legal footing with Danes. At the pulpit, from which power was exercised in the provinces, it was another question. Sermons were strictly regulated and clergymen regaled their listeners with unsubtle metaphors of a (Norwegian) flock lovingly tended to by a (royal, Danish) shepherd. Øystein Viken, who has analyzed this sermon content, likens the effect to *sharia* law.

Absolutism, power concentrated in a king, had an unexpected general effect, according to Perry Anderson, author of a densely argued and influential 1974 volume on the subject. It was a seemingly retrograde step that ultimately became a force for modernization. In particular it sped the transition to the kind of rationalist, centralized, civil–administrative qualities that Max Weber, a prominent German sociologist, a theorist of the modern state, later linked to northern, Protestant and industrial Europe.

Modern Norwegian bureaucracy may be a direct legacy of Danish rule, yet everyday people, not just bureaucrats, were winners in this process. A letter that took 12 days to be delivered from Oslo to Skien, 180 kilometers (110 miles) away, in 1645, took just two to three days by 1660 thanks to Sehested's post office reforms. And in other respects Norway retained its special qualities. It had lower tax status within the Danish realm; a sense of agricultural empowerment, flowing from Frederik's sale of state lands to reduce debts; and a growing commercial class with outward contacts of its own. By this stage Norway was more independent from Denmark than Finland was from Sweden. But it was also less of a unit. In Jespersen's view, Norway was split by divergent economic pressures; Norway's North Sea coast was "not oriented toward Copenhagen, but to the west," the British Isles in particular, while the southeast was the political–administrative focus of Copenhagen and the north still attracted sporadic interest from outside.

In 1700 over nine-tenths of Norway's people still lived rurally. But the traditional Western dominance of Norwegian life was changing. In 1530 Bergen still had 70 percent of Norway's urban population; by 1700 half of Norway lived in the towns and villages dotting the Oslofjord. The shift had a long-term social and economic impact. The country at large was recovering smartly from the traumas of the fourteenth century. One source of growth was foreign trade, in fish but now also in mining and timber, with Norway selling a third of its production abroad.

Two other trends took root after the 1660 shocks. One involved a Danish geopolitical pivot, impelled by rumblings south of the border. Frederick William, the Great Elector, was refashioning Prussia into a solvent modern entity on the ruins of the old Teutonic state and the Thirty Years' War. The Treaty of Oliva (1660) had set Prussian borders, within which the Hohenzollern dynasty later consolidated their rule. (Danish) King Frederik III had studied German theology, been *stattholder* in Holstein, and had a German queen. The Oldenburg kings were traditionally also dukes of Schleswig-Holstein, so any drift of attention southward had an institutional anchor as well.

Denmark's internal balance was affected; Frederik's precipitate coup against the nobility brought an influx of Holsteiners that swelled the ranks of the minor aristocracy. French Huguenots also came to Denmark, while Louis XIV of France stoked other worries during decades when Sweden, under Karl XI, was less of an immediate threat, focused as it was on domestic consolidation while digesting its land acquisitions from Denmark.

The other trend was mundanely but importantly administrative. U. F. Gyldenløve served as *stattholder* in Norway for 35 years, reinforcing a sense of continuity while strengthening state control over the church and administrative life. He lived mostly in Copenhagen, an absentee reformer. Yet Norway showed few signs of restiveness. Indeed on one reading the Norwegian response to the Danish royal coup was almost perversely passive, "a revolution," in Derry's words, "which was accepted seemingly with indifference." The notion that Norway sheepishly accepted rule by a king who was officially "above all human law" seems incomprehensible but for another legal fact post-1660, which was that for the first time Norwegians and Danes were "on the same humble level as equal subjects of an all-powerful sovereign."

Norway was seemingly backsliding while in fact it was progressing. But consolidation faced an uphill battle and plenty of countervailing pressures, given the geopolitical irreducibles. Sixteenth-century Norway (in Rian's words) had "no natural center; it was more like a conglomeration of regions with limited mutual contacts," coupled with an array of foreign connections ranging from the North Sea to the western Baltic. And it is easy to overstate the heavy hand of Denmark. There was a marked tendency, notably under Christian IV, to run Norway haphazardly. Revenue collection in particular was inefficient, even in the lucrative timber and mining industries. Ironically, by being treated more as a royal pet project than managed efficiently as a unit—by being, in other words, simultaneously more and less than a full-fledged colony—Norway was able to retain much of its fundamental character and chart its course even as power drained away at the top.

Power was also drifting eastward. The Danish-Swedish wars of 1643–45 and late 1650s shifted the Nordic balance of power irrevocably toward Sweden. In the former conflict, prosecuted by

Torstensson and ending with the peace of Brömsebro, Denmark lost its Norwegian provinces Jämtland and Härjedalen, about halfway up the Keel and today forming parts of Sweden just north of its Dalarna heartland. It also lost strategic Gotland, which it had controlled since 1361. The bleeding continued with the Treaty of Roskilde of 1658, when Denmark lost its last properties in Sweden proper (Blekinge, Halland and Skåne) while Norway lost Bohuslän to the Swedes.

Even central Trøndelag was sliced from the Norwegian center, effectively creating two separate Norwegian exclaves, before being restored two years later. The treaties of Roskilde and Copenhagen stand as punctuation marks for Scandinavia. Decades of war were still to follow, mostly fruitless attempts by Denmark and later Sweden to take or capture more land. But the borders of today were more or less set. Norway was a mostly unobtrusive beneficiary of the new order being laid down.

By the eighteenth century the Hansa merchants that long played a controlling role in Norway had their power stripped away. The long-standing monopoly was terminated in 1757, and Norway's shipbuilding capacity and merchant marine quickly shot up in size; from 80 ships it rose, by Napoleon's time, to over 1,000 vessels. A thriving fish industry along the coasts and, in the interior, the growing timber trade kept Norwegian commercial exports robust. After the upheavals of Struensee (see below), this period actually marked a brief golden age for Denmark that touched Norway too, principally via removal of the Danish corn (i.e. grain) monopoly in Norway.

Militarily, Norway was an insurgent presence. In 1612, a ragbag band of locals defeated a company of Scottish mercenaries passing through by means of a natural ambush, using rock and felled trees as rudimentary weapons. Intermittent decades showed how unreliable Norwegian troops could be in another country's service. Yet by 1715 the Danish–Norwegian navy, under the commanding presence of a Norwegian, Peter Wessel (aka Tordenskiold or "thunder shield"), had turned Norway indirectly into a naval force.

The eighteenth century dawned with Norway still far removed from European trends; by the century's end, some Norwegians were soaking up the latest in continental fashion. This startling shift is on display at the small open-air museum of Tønsberg, one of the many across the Norwegian countryside. On one side of a gravel path stands a reconstructed early-modern house, of a type prevailing in 1700: tiny windows, dark interiors, rough-hewn logs, a low doorway forcing the visitor to stoop, heavy furniture, massive fireplace-cum-stove, one room and no privacy: all in all a frightful living prospect for us moderns. Across the way stands a two-story pile of 1780s vintage, customized with faux-brick doorframes and roof tiles. Its spacious rooms have upholstered furniture and full-sized doors. Servants' entrances and quarters in the back, discreetly set off from the rest of the house, give abundant evidence of prosperity befitting an upwardly mobile and clever farmer who simultaneously operated a thriving convenience-store trade for passing travelers from a corner of his living room.

The juxtaposition speaks of unheralded transformation. Norway in 1700 was isolated, remote; by 1800 it was consciously European and aggressively in pursuit of more. On the cusp of a breakthrough often attributed to farmers and egalitarian spirit, Norway at the time of the French Revolution was in fact immersed in a sustained bout of social climbing and commercial grasping. Mary Wollstonecraft, a committed social reformer who was alert to such signs, found many Norwegians to be "extravagantly fond of courtly distinctions and of titles [...] and are easily purchased"; even their horses were garnished with hogs' bristles as odd-looking "trophies of nobility."

The end of Hansa and the consequent, rapid expansion of native trade brought a welling of socioeconomic pressures. Norwegian commerce was rapidly liberalized in the 1780s from Finnmark to Lofoten and Senja to the far south. Yet chronic inefficiencies ensured that even the silver mines of Kongsberg, opened with fanfare in 1624, were a drain on the treasury. And little of this energy translated to politics. There was a near-absence of Norwegian fanaticism in the face of Danish rule that, in turn, was absolute on paper only. A key reason was that the up-and-coming social classes, the merchants and local bureaucrats, benefited from ties to Copenhagen and had much to lose should Norway break away.

By now the internal wobbles and changing external priorities of Denmark were unmistakable. In 1767, via another Treaty of Copenhagen, Denmark took effective control of the regions of Holstein and Schleswig, signaling urgent new attention to matters German. Caroline Mathilde, sister of Britain's King George III, was a Hanoverian who had married Denmark's King Christian VII. Caroline and Christian were swept up in the charms of Johann Friedrich Struensee, a German physician with keen political instincts, a reformist bent and an ultimately fatal tendency to overreach. He effectively ran Denmark for a brief stretch in the early 1770s, pushing through a raft of liberal reforms.

In a fall just as swift as his rise, Struensee was exposed and finally destroyed by Julianne, the Queen Dowager. Along with his collaborator Enevold Brandt, Struensee was executed, publicly and gruesomely, in April 1772 in a Copenhagen square. Caroline was exiled to Germany and died, possibly by poison, in 1775. Ironically their (illegitimate and half-royal) son became the same Frederik VI who became regent from 1784 and later ruled as a reformist king. Many of Struensee's reforms ultimately survived him. Christian's descent into madness had been early and swift, yet he remained alive and on the titular throne until 1808.

The entire episode unfolded as a slow-motion exercise in moral and political collapse that echoed strongly in Norway. But it also reinforced a trend toward passive Danish neglect. After the settlement of 1721 Sweden had abandoned expansionism, turned inward and basked in its Age of Liberty, relieving Denmark of a chronic source of trouble. While Norway was stable and growing, the Danes weathered self-induced turmoil that then unexpectedly brought a sharpened sense of purpose. While much is made of Norwegian nationalism in the nineteenth century, it is easy to overlook the earlier resurgence of *Danish* nationalism that altered the mutual state of play. And just as Struensee's emergence was a symptom of German influence in Denmark, his short rule sparked a violent reversal in Danish sentiment; xenophobia took hold as relations with Germany tensed. Before 1770 Germans were free to settle in Jutland and took noble titles; after 1772 the door was shut as non-Danes were excluded from official posts.

Some 50 years passed between Danish royal excursions to Norway, until Crown Prince Frederik paid an extended visit in 1788—a telling sign of other priorities. Into the vacuum stepped the Swedes, where King Gustav III actively cultivated interests in Norway. Just as Germany had a growing impact in Denmark, Russia under Catherine the Great was another rising force to contend with and sealed a landmark "League of Armed Neutrality" with Denmark in 1780. Sweden, which increasingly feared encirclement, signed too, but by 1788 Denmark and Sweden nearly came to blows. By 1789 Norway factored in Danish foreign policy more than its domestic politics, its position about to be upturned by the French Revolution.

The Struensee aftermath also brought a phase of stability and modest but meaningful progress in Denmark, a fleeting age of Enlightenment before the Napoleonic storm. It was marked by growth and timely land reform that improved the lot of long-suffering peasants and Scandinavia's largest cottar (rural and landless) class. These changes reflected wider ones. For example, in Habsburg Austria Empress Maria Theresa adopted land reforms while her son and successor, Joseph II, imperial patron of Mozart, attacked Catholic privileges at home and in Belgium.

Yet Danes in the mid-1790s seemed, to a visiting Mary Wollstonecraft, to have a blinkered view of the world. Comfortable and self-deluded, they were oblivious to the upheavals in France from which she had just escaped (she had watched from her window as Louis XVI was carted to the guillotine). Signs of distress abounded. The royal palace in Copenhagen was destroyed by fire in 1794. A year later a quarter of the city burned, including the town hall and a thousand homes; she was practically "treading on live ashes" in its wake. The country, nominally absolutist, had a nonfunctioning king while the chief court figure, Count Bernstorff, was a mollifier given to side-stepping problems. Danes seemed unconcerned over Swedish works on the Trollhättan canal, designed to link Lake Vänern to Gothenburg and the North Sea and thereby skirt the Sound Tolls that Denmark still depended on. While Denmark was being undermined from near and far, the Norwegians, scarcely unaware of the possibilities, were disinclined to take advantage of them.

Still, in Norway Wollstonecraft breathed the unexpected air of liberty: "Though the king of Denmark be an absolute monarch," she wrote, "the Norwegians appear to enjoy all the blessings of freedom." Norway was neither desperate nor trampled asunder: "the people have no viceroy to lord it over them, and fatten his dependants with the fruit of their labor." Authority fell between two stools, and local mayors wielded relative but not absolute control. The essence of this freedom was self-owned farms; "for not being obliged to submit to any debasing tenure," she says, "they act with an independent spirit." Functionally liberated already, Norway also had a small—but still very influential—aristocracy that would be instrumental in the coming turn.

Wealth was increasingly in the hands of merchants, which made it more authentically open in her strong view. The national economy ran a healthy trade surplus (the export of rye and corn/wheat was still restricted). Consumption taxes were a constant, but "the officers are not strict [in enforcing them]," producing "a lenity that almost renders the laws nullities." She paints a Denmark afraid of its own shadow, "fearing to appear tyrannical" to their nominal subjects to the north. Already by 1770 Struensee had abolished the office of governor of Norway, loosening another shackle before it could be restored. All this was contrary to the strong-armed English practices in Ireland. In the law too, judicial appeal was available to the average man—except that, following three convictions, the chronic Norwegian lawbreaker still faced branding and chains of iron. The famous legal reforms would have to wait.

Another factor also loomed: an alternative Norwegian patron in the shape of Sweden. King Gustav III (killed in 1792) had assiduously cultivated such ideas—up to that time Sweden was the only country, apart from Denmark, to have officials stationed in Christiania—while important landed and industrial figures in Norway began to push the idea of a Swedish interregnum. Carl Emil Vogt's biography of Herman Wedel Jarlsberg, an enterprising count of this persuasion, is a helpful counter to the all-too-standard view that Norway was birthed in 1814 by restive farmers and Haugean revivalists alone. Swedish–Norwegian business interests had a growing stake in a new and deeper relationship, the prospects for which dramatically improved along with Napoleon's rise.

Wedel Jarlsberg, a wealthy cosmopolitan, was a major force behind the *Selskap for Norges Vel*, a society for promoting the idea of Norwegian self-awakening. Prompted by the palace coup in Sweden that felled King Gustav IV Adolf in March 1809 and brought a new more liberal constitution, Wedel Jarlsberg pushed his dual ambition of a self-standing Norway in union with Sweden, possibly guaranteed by Britain. It was a vision that came largely true but also to grief.

The prospect of a northern pivot seemed to animate the Norwegian spirit. Wollstonecraft found "little appearance of active industry" on the streets of Copenhagen compared with "the sprightly gait of Norwegians, who in every respect appear to have got the start of them." The difference she chalked up to Norwegians' greater level of freedom, "a liberty which they think their right by inheritance," compared to Denmark's "domestic tyrants [who] dogmatically assert that Denmark is the happiest country in the world." The harassment and early death of (disgraced royal consort) Mathilde, at just 24, seemed to her an appalling symptom of ethical collapse that brought on her *cri de coeur*. "What a farce is life!" And this was the country still nominally in charge of Norway.

During that simmering century, Norway's diversity became something that could work to its national benefit. Oslo was drawn increasingly toward Denmark (and later to Sweden), while Bergen retained a Germanic character and Trondheim was becoming Anglicized. Though decentralized and oddly rudderless, Norway was no longer centrifugal; it was shedding its more introverted leanings and finding its feet. Outlying territories like Greenland (starting with Hans Egede's theological mission in 1721) and Svalbard (thanks to A. E. Keilhau's scientific initiatives) both received new attention; in 1795 Norwegians overwintered in Svalbard for the first time.

What by appearances was a prostrate Norway was, in fact, a country finding strength in the widening cracks and offsetting priorities of foreign rule. Yet there was a diffuse sense of collective self, little self-identification as a polity and no knee-jerk rejection of political Denmark. "They love their country, but have not much public spirit," Wollstonecraft said of Norwegians' half-hearted embrace of the era's possibilities. Count Bernstorff, the Danish prime minister, was actually saluted by Norwegians for his abilities and virtues; French revolutionary ideas were openly, and (to her horror) favorably, discussed in a remarkably free press.

The national goal, such as it was, centered not on politics but on education in a country which, as of 1800, still lacked a university or scientific establishment worthy of the name. Another focus—and point of urgency once the British blockade of Napoleon's Nordic allies, enforced from 1801, began to bite hard in Denmark–Norway—was the lack of an issuing bank in Norway. It was economic emergency, prolonged and sharpened from outside and channeled by some masterful diplomacy by the likes of Wedel Jarlsberg, which together prized Norway away from Denmark and, by 1809–10, had passed it ineluctably into the Swedish orbit.

Noticed, too, by Wollstonecraft was another set of character traits. Norwegians, she wrote, were "a sensible, shrewd people" which despite a "second-hand government" had managed to keep their heads down, focusing on their livelihoods rather than fanning the flames of liberty. Economic opportunism was the implied impetus. If Norwegians have an aptitude for understatement and a tendency toward inward rebelliousness, then such traits were being perfected in the late Danish period, when loyalties were torn and caution necessarily trumped boldness. Norway never broke away from Denmark; the Danes, rather, squandered their inheritance in their ruinously loyal embrace of Napoleon.

Thus at the other, modern end of this malleable timeline, the terminal date for Danish control over Norway proves almost as elusive as its starting point. If the formal break came in 1814 and the de facto end in 1809–10, the beginning of the end, in Sars's estimation, came in 1772, a year of upheaval in Sweden as well as Denmark. Struensee's fall and execution that year came on the heels of the Stockholm palace coup that brought to the throne Gustav III—a king who instituted his own, modified form of absolutism and, more importantly, had a sharp eye on Norway.

Here again, dates mean little when shorn of their context; this was a time, believed Sars, of broadly shifting social sentiments in which "the well-developed Danish aristocracy was seen as a [Norwegian] weakness, and what was seen as Norway's shame, that it was a land of farmers, now became the country's force and strength." Here, in fact, was the kernel of the political alliance that later led Norway, in the 1880s, to a decisive political breakthrough.

The last and most dramatic act commenced in 1807. A furious, three-day British bombardment of Copenhagen—just six years after a lesser attack—followed by Britain's confiscation of the Danish fleet precipitated a fateful decision by King Frederik VI to ally with Napoleon. Norway was dragged into a war not of its choosing, against its better instincts and counter to its interests. A crucial private meeting at Bærums Verk in August 1809 arguably sealed the final break with Denmark while shifting tacit Norwegian support to the conspirators in Stockholm.

There seems a kind of tragic inevitability about the demise of Norway–Denmark, the predestined end of a long unfolding personified by two successive kings—the first (Christian VII) mad, the second (Frederik VI) misguided—who were but dimly aware of the shifting winds. Frederik's preening in 1809–10 to become king of Sweden and reawaken the spirit of Kalmar gave his early years a delusional aspect, yet he survived until 1839. Rising in the east was a man, Crown Prince Karl Johan, who was already angling for Norway, far more keenly attuned to the shifting geopolitical winds and more ruthless in his methods.

All told, the long-night notion is more axiomatic than accurate as a description of Norway's post-Viking and pre-independence era. It makes a formidable image in the hands of Ibsen, shaping a sort of national allegory. The same obscurity that marks it out, and sets early-modern Norway apart from the rest of the Western world, molded a propensity for non-confrontational change and a bent for nontraditional solutions that was to shape the country's modern personality.

6

Norway and the Dazzling Dutch

The transition, in a Völkerwanderung, *from [...] passivity to a sudden paroxysm of storm and stress produces a dynamic effect on the life of any community, but this effect is naturally more intense when the migrants take ship than when they trek over solid ground.*
Arnold Toynbee, A Study of History

All their Norway mariners are run in to the Hollanders' service, for want of employment at home, and if [the Danish king] should command them back, the [Dutch] states would not be able to put their fleet to sea.
Gilbert Talbot, English Envoy Extraordinary to Copenhagen, 1664

It's the first thing you see in Norway, before you even get there. From the air a carpet of evergreen stretches into the distance, giving on to the great swathe of boreal forest that rings the globe at the upper-middle latitudes and brings life to the monochrome of winter. As the plane descends, forest gives way to trees. Once inside you're stepping on its product, the warm and welcoming floorboards of Gardermoen's arrival hall.

Trees, and all that derives from them, are a perennial Nordic hallmark. Even today forestry dominates rural life north of the Baltic. Roughly a quarter of Norway is tree-covered; in Sweden the figure is over half, while Finland, three-quarters forested, sustains an industry of truly national-strategic import. Yet it is Norway where wood most powerfully drove the preindustrial national story, shaped its architectural legacy and formed its chief interface with the outside world. There are reasons why it was Norwegian not Finnish wood that sparked a Beatles tune and, more recently, birthed a surprise bestseller borrowing from the same title.

Wood with a Norwegian stamp was lifting musical spirits long before the age of rock. From the 1660s, violin maker Antonio Stradivari was fashioning his famous instruments from wood culled from a variety of Norwegian spruce that thrived high up in the Val de Fiemme, in northern Italy. A rare microclimate (ravaged by twenty-first century storms that some blame on climate change) encouraged the slow forest growth needed for extra-dense wood which (along with a special varnish) provided the exquisite resonance that, in turn, gave his string instruments their mystique at the dawn of the symphonic age. It is a fitting testament to Norway's stealth-like impact on the early-modern world.

Fish, metals and timber have formed a commodity trifecta for Norwegian development. But timber was in many respects the most crucial for the national story. Fishing is a coastal affair and mining an underground proposition, but a wood industry involves both landward and waterborne operations. Timber cultivation was also more indigenous, involving local ownership and operation. Norway's great forests also stimulated two-way people movement. It lured Finns to Finnskogen, in eastern Norway, to settle in the sixteenth century. It brought Dutchmen, Scots and others deep into Norwegian fjords. In the other direction it stimulated the first, post-Viking Norwegian emigration and launched its first modern diaspora.

It was also critical to national development at crucial phases. Timber was the chief source of wealth for patrician families like the Ankers, whose properties hosted the 1814 constitutional conventions at Eidsvoll and Moss. Within a few years the industry's collapse in 1817–19 sent shock waves throughout Scandinavia. Through centuries of managing and mismanaging their wooded endowment, Norwegians internalized some painful economic and ecological lessons about building a national economy around a fickle organic commodity. Anyone looking for historical lessons for today's oil economy need look no further.

Ancient civilizations often worshipped everyday objects for their life-giving properties. Pagan-era Vikings, too, revered what was alive and at hand. In their case it was the native forests that put a roof over their heads, warmed their homes and took them to distant lands. Special reverence was attached to the evergreens that gave reassuring, year-round evidence that life had continuity as well as upheaval. For Norse civilization it was the tree, so ubiquitous and vital, that served as a kind of universal symbol.

In Norse cosmology this keystone was *Yggdrasil*, the "world tree." It linked the three realms of Åsgard, Midgard and Utgard (or Niflheim), respectively, heaven, earth and the underworld. It was seen as the ultimate conduit, reaching from the sky deep into the earth. It was an *axis mundi*, the "pivot of the world," around which life itself revolved. The word derived from *Ygg* (another name for Odin, god of wisdom) and his horse. Odin himself, so the legend went, hung in its branches for nine days in a bid for greater understanding and departed clutching his valuable runes. The tree thus became associated with the timeless quest for knowledge. The connection hasn't been lost; it takes striking artistic form in the murals decorating the great staircase in Norway's National Library.

As a timeless symbol of Norwegian culture, the tree can scarcely be bettered. The stave church forms the preeminent image of old Norway, wooden inside and out; a few dozen have survived the peril of errant candles. The wooden *hytte* is an equally strong countryside symbol of today. And as a workaday enabler it long reigned supreme. Native timber (*tømmer*) produced long-distance Viking ships; the search for exploitable forests took Greenlanders led by Leif Eriksson to the New World in the late tenth century. Norway's first rail line (Eidsvoll to Oslo, which opened in 1854) was built to transport harvested timber to the Oslofjord. Wooden skis took Norway to the pinnacle of the winter sporting world. Even now wooden road bridges are a common sight over highways in central and southern parts of the country, notably on the road from Oslo to Lillehammer. These scattered but compelling symbols give today's Norway a visible link to its medieval past and demonstrate the continuing importance of this living commodity.

For a crucial time, no other Norwegian market topped that of the Netherlands during the Dutch Golden Age. It was a match made in economists' heaven, a classic case of comparative advantage: each country had in abundance what the other one lacked and needed. Economically stagnant Norway had timber in excess, easy to harvest and sell. The Dutch, riding an imperial tiger, were bereft of native forestland at a time when wood was the basis of nearly everything that mattered. On this pairing hinged one of the pivotal factors behind Europe's modern development—and one of Norway's largely untold chapters.

It is hard for us moderns, living in cities of steel, asphalt and industrial glass, to fathom just how critical wood was to the preindustrial world. Strong, malleable and remarkably durable, it formed the backbone of Dutch colonial life and served as the irreducible ingredient of a seaborne imperium. Timber felled along Norwegian fjords worked its way into every crack and crevice of the Dutch empire. Later Britain became Norway's main commercial market, but the Dutch link was singular. "Amsterdam is standing on Norway" became a much-noted (and misquoted) phrase of the time; more completely, the city was said to be "built on pillars of [Norwegian] pine and resembles a subterranean forest." (By another connection, noted by Øystein Rian with bleaker humor, "Norwegians warmed themselves at the fire of London" in 1666.) The Amsterdam town hall alone, it was noted with unsettling precision, rested on 13,659 wooden piles hammered into the River Amstel's mud, each one of Norwegian origin. The city eventually rested on five million such piles and pillars—roughly one for every man, woman and child in today's Norway.

The connection went deeper still, for the Dutch empire was also *floating* on Norway, thanks to timber imports that sustained its North Sea shipyards which, in turn, built its naval and commercial fleets. Another, equally subterranean dimension followed, namely an unsung and largely hidden labor force of expatriate Norwegians who flocked south and buttressed Dutch society in its headiest growth phase. It was all part of *hollandertida*, Norway's "Dutch period."

This era represents far more than a giddy phase of chopping trees for fast money. It was a powerfully formative period that opens a window onto Norway itself. It forms a bridge in three crucial respects. First, it linked *Norway*—not Denmark–Norway—to the Netherlands, the insurgent star of Europe's early imperial age. This opened vast new horizons and established postmedieval Norway's first true émigré community.

Second, it knocked a dormant domestic economy into higher gear, promoting cultivation of an exportable commodity run on a local basis and introducing the first, tender shoots of industry. The rudiments of capital markets and a money economy also found their way to Norway via the humble tree and less humble Dutch moneymen. And third, it links the country's late-medieval and modern eras, providing an overlooked element of continuity in Norway's broken timeline.

It would not be a stretch to say that the Dutch link, fueled by timber, was Norway's chief road to modernity. Timber pulled a land deep in provincial torpor into the heart of an incipient global trading system. It drew Norwegians not just *to* Holland and its booming cities but to the world's four corners, *via* the Dutch, in a sort of global piggyback effect. By venturing afield and exploiting their native forests, Norwegians effectively manned, fueled and floated the first trade-based world empire and, in the process, kick-started a new era at home. Norway may not have been the heart and soul of the Dutch colossus, but it formed its root and branch.

If we dare take things further, Norwegian products and people effectively facilitated Europe's world economic supremacy on the cusp of the Industrial Revolution. And anyone tempted to dismiss such claims as self-serving professional blather might instead spare a thought for someone trying to convince busy readers why they should care whether a remote Danish colony was selling trees to Holland in the sixteenth century.

Thematically, Norway's "Dutch period" resembles a subplot of a complex novel, a secondary narrative that slips in unseen and subtly alters the main story. In the midst of Norway's long subjugation to Denmark, an upstart Dutch empire appeared on the horizon, and like a fresh wind it shifted Norway's colonial fortunes and national focus. How it did so, and what it meant, has long been disputed. This period is often characterized as anomalous, like a sudden winning hand during a dismal run at the poker table. Recently it's been credited as a time of transition for Norway.

The Dutch empire and Norway's "long night" may be relics of a distant past, but that era's main lines remain highly pertinent even today. Three of modern Norway's fundamentals—its reliance on an extractive industry, its niche role in the global economy and its mobile and influential expatriate community—all find direct antecedents in the *hollandertid.* Commodity dependence and mass people movement, what Arnold Toynbee described as "transmarine migration" and considered pivotal for political and cultural development, directly marked Norway's Dutch phase. It turns out that we have seen this movie before, and can't quite recall the ending.

History tends to reflect two different processes. "Hard" history comes down from above, via events with some official stamp that can be assigned a date or a famous face. "Soft" history reflects broader trends and subtler changes over a longer period. While much is anonymous, it can be far more important for the long term. History "from below" tends to percolate to the surface—the stirrings of nationalism, say, or early social movements. Gradualism is an implicit element.

Norway's Dutch period falls unmistakably into the latter category and is easily overlooked as a result. Its timeframe is disputed; it gets swallowed up by the lengthier Danish period (*dansketid*); a fragmented archival record is the despair of historians; it rarely gets dignified as a "national era" or is mixed up with the *skottetid* that brought Scot traders to Norwegian waters at the same time and for the same purpose. The very term *hollandertid* is fairly new and not universally accepted. It is easy to dismiss because it lacked the overtly strategic elements driving history in its "hard" form. There is little war-and-peace component to lend it historical heft or narrative pizzazz.

The Dutch influence on Norway is in fact often dismissed as short-lived, locally focused and broadly negative. The timber trade responsible for it is often assessed as another of the ruinous boom-and-bust cycles that left Norway's resources, from whales to fish to copper, decimated, at the behest and for the interests of foreigners. The common historical reading is tainted by post hoc interpretation of unusual severity, one associated with false dawns, dependency and renewed heartache. It is not generally thought of as a nation-building process at all or a bridge to the world, yet it was both.

At the other end, some first-rate analysts of *het gouden eeuw,* the Dutch Golden Age of Hals, Vermeer and Rembrandt, have reinforced an impression of a minor Norwegian spoke in the giant Dutch wheel. Mary Lindemann, who compared life in the great merchant cities of Amsterdam, Hamburg and Antwerp, saw this urban trio as collecting points for the "flotsam and jetsam of early modern society," notably itinerant Norwegians who flocked there for work but often wound up as social nuisances. These were conveniently labeled, in Erika Kuijper's choice phrase, as "poor, illiterate and superstitious" and typified, according to Simon Schama, author of a suitably sprawling work on the Dutch imperium, by "seamen who kept showing up in tavern and street brawls." Then as now, nations are tempted to downplay the role of immigrant labor or to credit the foreigners who toil in their midst. The Dutch, for all their traditional reputation for cosmopolitanism, are no different, yet the Dutch miracle relied heavily on two cut-rate and seemingly inexhaustible Norwegian assets: timber and labor.

Early-modern Holland was a magnet for humanity. People flocked there as internal migrants, notably from the Spanish Netherlands (later Belgium) or from farms to cities, for work. Many others, individually or in groups, came from outside: asylum-seeking Huguenots and other religious refugees, writer-dissidents like John Locke and Baruch Spinoza, Germans and Scandinavians.

The whole period is complicated by the quasi-colonial role by which the Netherlands seemingly trapped Norway in a double bind of dependency. Norwegians were under the thumb of Denmark, but both countries were affected by the rising power, ambition and unpredictability of the Dutch. Thus on one melancholic reading the Norwegians were nothing more than cut-rate enablers of both empires. Another Netherlands chronicler, Jonathan Israel, holds that Norway merely supplied low-value forest products, not just wood but timber in its rawest, uncut form. He rates this role as clearly secondary to more valuable commodities flowing to Holland, like grain from Danzig and iron ore from Sweden.

Yet there is ample scope for projecting the *hollandertid* onto a bigger canvas and assigning it a national role in Norway, beyond the local curiosity, regional impact it had in places like Tysvær, Flekkefjord and Son. (To the Dutch, the Oslofjord was *Soen Waater*.) Recent research in Norway and elsewhere has highlighted the relationship as a cultural turning point for Norway. More surprisingly, it has been posited as crucial for the Netherlands too;

Conway, for one, argued that the Dutch role in Svalbard whaling helped to unify the squabbling Dutch states in the seventeenth century. The notion that this bilateral relationship forged a greater sense of unity in both countries is an intriguing one that, if true, only magnifies its importance.

Sølvi Sogner, an historian, and Margit Løyland, an archivist and author, two Norwegian chroniclers of that period, both lean toward recognizing the Dutch era as having national import in Norway. Some outsiders do too. J. W. Moore calls southern Norway, and south Scandinavia, a "vital resource zone" for the capital-rich city of Amsterdam. Dutch innovations, notably in new ship design, were catalyzed by access to Norwegian expertise. A clutch of Dutch analysts also posit the era as one of breakthrough. The picture is fragmented, and there's more to be said. It forms part of the Norwegian mosaic—and represents a crucial piece giving on to the whole.

The Netherlands played a formative part in Norway for 200 years, roughly marked, by Løyland's reckoning, from 1550 to 1750. Even that may be conservative, considering the pivotal Dutch role in the crisis of 1536–37 that had such major fallout in Norway. This concerned the flight of the last (Catholic) archbishop and staunch Norwegian nationalist, Olav Engelbrektsson, from Trondheim to Amsterdam on Easter Sunday in 1537—the point at which Norway submitted to Danish rule and the Lutheran Reformation—in a flotilla organized in Holland by a Norwegian expatriate, Christopher Trondsson.

Engelbrektsson followed in the even heavier footsteps of disgraced Danish (hence also Norwegian) King Christian II, who fled to Dutch sanctuary in 1523 following his disastrous intervention in Sweden. Christian was also notorious in Norway after precipitating the death of nobleman Knut Alvsson. Christian's earlier dalliance with Dyveke Sigbritsdatter, aka the Little Dove, was a Dutch matter given her ancestry and her mother Sigbrit's later role as unofficial royal advisor (which included claims of extrasensory powers over Christian, reminiscent of Grigori Rasputin's influence at the last czarist court of Russia). Even at that early juncture the two chief characteristics of imperial Dutch life, namely freewheeling trade and a tradition of asylum, were well established and known in Norden.

From roughly 1500 the North Sea territories that coalesced into the seven United Provinces, and eventually the Netherlands, were an emerging trade outlet for Norway. From mid-century the Dutch initiated the first of the great post-Iberian expansions. Accordingly, they were the first to reap the commercial bounty that Cabot, Dias, da Gama, Columbus, Magellan and Vespucci had prized open in the first great age of sea exploration.

For precisely a century, from the Dutch revolt from Spain (commonly dated to 1572) up to the Anglo-French invasion of Holland in 1672, the Dutch were the overachieving envy of the world. They operated a sprawling maritime colossus with Holland as the provincial leader and Amsterdam at its epicenter. Whether the Dutch imperium was a passing and unsustainable phase (like Sweden's great-power period) or amounted to the first modern world empire remains a matter of general dispute. What no longer is—in its broad lines if not in every detail—is the multipronged Norwegian role within it.

Netherlanders, it was said, were the best housed and fed people of early-modern Europe. Amsterdam was Europe's third-largest seventeenth-century city after London and Paris, a boom town on a scale never before seen and a prototype of urban innovation. Dutch towns were planned and functional; they were trade and finance centers, not just manufacturing hubs. They were living spaces built to a human scale, accessible by water, surprisingly clean and pioneering in their use of gas lighting and paved streets. To outsiders, especially Norwegians, they were magnets of opportunity.

In its heyday, the Netherlands was a country in double or even triple transformation. Periodically its growth was stifled and its fragile unity undermined by domestic convulsions. The Protestant Reformation in the north was followed by a slow-motion revolt from its long-distance rulers the Habsburgs of Spain, even as royalist interests tussled with republican forces for supremacy, so the national economic flowering took place amidst religious, external and domestic political upheaval. Prosperous Amsterdam merchants lived the good life, but Dutch society was anything but settled. A diverse collection of seven provinces that eventually unified, it resembles an early postcolonial America with its associated growth pains and shaky epicenter, claimed in this case by the House of Orange. Despite this uneasy arrangement—or conceivably, because of it—the United Provinces looked outward, parlaying these energies into a world economic powerhouse with phoenix-like character.

By their nature, empires feed on outside suppliers. And for all their outward sophistication, the main European empires were sustained by a handful of commodities, the "basic trades" like naval stores, timber, cloth and grain. These unheralded but intensely strategic materials represented, in Michael Pye's pithy words, "the perfect opposite of all the crafted, gaudy bits and pieces once shipped about for the benefit of kings and grand persons." Most attention, and most wars, revolved around goods of higher monetary value: silver and gold extracted from Latin America, sugar from the Caribbean, tobacco from America, spices from the Far East, slaves from Africa. But the basic trades constituted the sturdy, hidden framework of empire.

Europe's empires were like octopi, with long tentacles reaching back to a central *entrepôt* that served as both a commercial center and a point of transit or "turntable" serving distant markets. Holland's location offered convenient ports of call via the North Sea, Atlantic coast and Baltic. Amsterdam emerged as the clear first among urban equals as the crux of a north–south trade route to Lisbon and Leghorn. And its siting at the mouth of the Rhine gave inland access to central Europe and northern Italy, where modern banking and finance got their start. The Dutch made up for their unhelpfully low-lying geography with a location that was spectacularly well suited for outward trade.

Why the Dutch came to matter so much to Norway, as opposed to the other way around, is not as immediately obvious. Norway was not contiguous to Europe. It did not border any Dutch provinces or, after 1660, even Denmark. Ruled from Copenhagen, Norway's commercial life was controlled by the same Hanseatics who were competing with the Dutch. The answer probably lies in the complex, triple-tiered nature of the relationship, one with direct, indirect and tertiary elements.

First, the Dutch were expert mariners, many of whom knew their way around Norwegian waters as early as the mid-fifteenth century, when their traders first won the right to access Norwegian markets. Their presence was felt both on land (via the timber trade) and in its waters (as coastal fishermen). Their commercial activity spread from the Oslofjord around the southern coastline and up to Trondheim. From around 1600, as indicated earlier, Dutch whalers initiated a new rush of opportunity much further north. One Svalbard legacy is a host of unlikely place-names like Smeerenburg and Amsterdam Island, which served as seasonal whaling bases. They fought off competition from the English and Swedes, who had long claimed northern Scandinavia as their own. By the Peace of Knäred (1613) the Swedes conceded the Dutch commercial entitlement to the far north. Dutch influences later extended into the Norwegian heartland, to places ranging from Trøndelag (the chief exit point for Røros copper destined for Amsterdam) and the Oslofjord right up to the Danish (subsequently Swedish) border.

More indirectly for Norway, the Dutch were pivotal players in the Baltic region, home of their so-called mother trade. Once granted permanent access to that inland sea, by the 1544 Treaty of Speyer, Dutch traders became a Baltic commercial force, challenging the presumed Danish–Swedish duopoly (the *dominium maris Baltici*). As a Danish province with a maritime character, port towns and untapped trade potential, Norway had a special, if also tangential, interest in this Baltic activity as it remained chiefly an Atlantic presence.

Via its location and Sound Tolls, Denmark controlled outsider access to the inner Baltic resources of Poland and Livonia. Danish–Dutch tensions were inevitable and clashes frequent. Norwegians were often dragged willy-nilly into an edgy codependent relationship. The Sound Toll record shows that, for the indicative year of 1640, the Dutch paid nearly 70 percent of the total sum collected for that year (some 446,496 riksdaler), so they had every incentive to find commodity sources that would skirt Elsinore and the Øresund altogether—like Norway.

And third, the Dutch controlled vast overseas territory and seas stretching from the Caribbean to East Asia. For a time this included an American colony in the Hudson Valley, called New Amsterdam, which eventually (under the English) became New York. Running a far-flung empire required manpower, ships, organization and a willful blurring of commercial and security interests. It also brought a ruthlessness of purpose, especially in the Far East, that belied the benign reputation of the Dutch at home. Notorious massacres of English seamen in the Spice Islands in 1621 and Amboyna in 1623—the fraught subjects of Giles Milton's engrossing work *Nathaniel's Nutmeg*—underscored this messily two-faced reality.

Given their endemic lack of resources the Dutch, power traders with finesse, were especially acquisitive. Norway supplied sailors and the timber for the imperial ships they worked on. The Dutch provided a physical and highly mobile link between isolated Norway and a heady but risk-filled new world of strategic commerce. In the process, Norwegian horizons grew far beyond the North Atlantic world that was first opened in and by the Viking age.

In turn, Dutch visitors—traders, fishermen, cartographers—shaped Norwegian developmental history and, more importantly, its sense of national consciousness. As foreign traders, the German Hansas dominated by rigid social separation while controlling monopolized routes with an iron fist or, as one put it, with a "dead hand." The Dutch were different, necessarily less domineering in their approach. "They did not act like a master race," wrote one observer of their operations in Oslofjord. "They made room for Norwegian initiative." Through these Dutch channels Norway became abruptly internationalized, thrust—but not compelled—into a nascent world trading arrangement.

The Dutch also pioneered the development of precapitalist credit markets. Already by 1602—the founding year for the Dutch East India Company—it had a functioning *Beurs*, arguably the world's first stock market. The Dutch quickly became go-to creditors for both Sweden and Denmark, with the power to fund industry through present and future money (cash in the form of silver coinage, and credit, both as brokers and as suppliers). Some of it flowed back to Norway, not unlike the way modern remittances sustain struggling countries from outside.

The Norwegian–Dutch link ultimately went deeper than trade and migration, beyond trees and money. Dutch historian Johan Huizinga, in a thoughtful essay written in 1939, underscored the catalytic nature of this bilateral link for two countries whose points of departure were totally different. Sixteenth-century Norway was poor and isolated, seemingly a spent force; the Netherlands, with a tenth of Norway's physical size, was orchestrating an empire and strutting the world stage. In Huizinga's view, an attraction of opposites pulled them along a convergent path to modernity as independent, self-assertive democracies. There was also a shared cultural aesthetic, an earthiness that prevailed in Dutch Golden Age art just as it later marked the Norwegian National Romantics.

Yet for all the grand themes of modernization, historical convergence and pictorial art, Norway's Dutch role has to be seen as fundamentally practical. For all their differences, *because* of those differences, the relationship was mutually beneficial even if it was far from equal. It was the crux of a wheel of fortune that transformed them from odd-couple opposites to the partners in public virtue we see today.

History has been kinder to the Dutch than their contemporaries ever were. A vague but tenacious *hollandophobia* gripped their many enemies, who were quickly tired of being outmaneuvered and grew envious of Dutch wealth. The Dutch had pioneered the conversion of sea to land by an ingenious polder-and-dike system, while throwing off Spanish rule and forging an empire that controlled a lucrative spice trade. As conspicuous success rarely goes unpunished, an anti-Dutch reflex was understandable, but this often went to extremes. It agitated seventeenth-century figures like George Downing, along with Cromwellian political pamphleteers who forced through clampdowns on Dutch access to English ports. Two centuries on, English cultural critic John Ruskin was railing against "soulless" Dutch painting, with its real-life (genre) themes, absence of spiritual overtones and supposed lack of depth.

Such attitudes spilled into politics. France under King Louis XIV, traditionally a land-based power with an agricultural heart that produced the Physiocratic intellectual movement, was said to be "satanically" opposed to the Dutch and all their seaborne society stood for. It drove his English alliance and their joint invasion of Holland (by land) in 1672, which turned out to be his biggest foreign policy disaster.

Foreign policy in a loose political amalgamation like the Netherlands was necessarily built on pragmatism. It combined naval muscle with a studied avoidance of permanent political ties.

Not surprisingly, the Dutch championed the principle of freedom of the seas, best represented in the juridical writings of Hugo Grotius. Freedom to sail and trade was an irreducible essential for a seaborne trading power, and it provided the root of a lesson that later informed Norwegian attitudes up to World War II. This did not always win the Dutch friends or stave off enemies. Even in its heyday the Netherlands fought wars against each of the imperial big four of Spain, France, Sweden and (three times in 25 years) England. Its perch was ever shaky, and its dominance of trade routes, the essence of its power, was undercut by reactive and deliberate counterstrategies that came to be called mercantilism.

Mercantilist strategy aimed at building national wealth by importing little, exporting more and hoarding precious metals. It was a zero-sum calculation that drove Swedish and Danish thinking and dominated British and French policy. It ultimately proved Holland's undoing. It was embodied in England's Navigation Acts, a series of restrictions against foreign traders starting in 1651. France had its own mercantilist twist (the so-called *Exclusif*) which further dented the Dutch carry trade. It was out of those same great power counterstrategies that the Norwegian merchant marine would grow, flourish and eventually dominate entire segments of world shipping.

Dutch interests in Scandinavia were refreshingly free of heavy-handed political considerations. Outright Dutch takeover of mainland Norway was scarcely in question. For Sweden and Denmark, things were very different. For both, the Dutch link touched sensitive power relationships.

The Danes and Swedes competed for control of Baltic granaries, timberlands and iron foundries. The Netherlands adeptly played them off against each other in a restless power triangle. In the sixteenth century this meant siding with the weaker Swedes; a century later the Dutch helped the Danes resist the ascendant Swedish empire. A stance as much as a policy, it resembled Britain's role as the European "balancer" in the nineteenth century, only more subregionally delineated.

Such considerations led to striking political shifts. The Dutch navy helped to rescue Copenhagen when it was besieged in 1657–58 by Sweden's bellicose Karl X. This came just 13 years after the Dutch, with a 400-vessel fleet under Witte de With ("Double

Witt"), had humiliated Denmark, and the same King Christian IV, who had been ramping up the Sound Tolls, by sailing unmolested through the Sound as Christian looked on helplessly from Elsinore castle.

The Swedes were frequently wrong-footed by the Dutch too. Dutch credit repeatedly helped Sweden ransom the Älvsborg fortress (long its only foothold on the North Sea); it also bankrolled the copper and iron foundry growth that dominated Sweden's exports and enabled a succession of warrior-kings to prosecute foreign wars with substantially mercenary armies. A Low Country entrepreneur, Louis de Geer, built Sweden's metals industry (the *Bergslagen*) while Elias Trip, his brother-in-law, birthed an armaments industry. Yet just four years after joining, in 1668, the Triple Alliance with Holland and England, the Swedes jumped into the French camp; in 1676 they paid a hefty price as a Dutch–Danish force sank a Swedish fleet off Öland. The nimble Dutch ability to play things both ways was never as apparent as in the Baltic.

Because of its location, Norway was out of that overtly strategic game. Its Dutch links must be measured by a different, primarily socioeconomic metric. That said, T. K. Derry, a historian of both Norway and Scandinavia, argues that the Dutch role was even more important in Norway than in Sweden, where they founded industries and entered the aristocracy, or in Denmark where they designed and built many Copenhagen landmarks. Put another way, for the Swedes the Dutch link was formative; for Norway it was closer to transformative.

Dutch demand for Norwegian wood first came from Hoorn, then quickly from other towns after 1500. Orders exploded late that century, in the second "wave" of Dutch Baltic expansion that commenced around 1590. It peaked by 1650, when 130,000 *last* were exported from Norway, a figure representing some two-thirds of all Dutch timber requirements (one *last* equaled three cubic meters of bulk or two tons in weight). The corresponding figure in 1750 was just 38,000 *last*.

The Dutch had other timber sources too, including the upper Rhine and the inner Baltic. Yet both were limited. The Rhine was narrow, flowing and even then heavily regulated, while Baltic sources were distant and served many other markets.

Norway offered an ideal combination of proximity and availability. Just as importantly, Norway's landward production was (at least for a time) fairly uncontrolled. Norway was a few days' sail away; it had quality product in abundance; and timber was easily accessible, near sea or fjord level. Norway was closer than Sweden or Finland, so ships had less far to travel (the outward leg was typically made empty, under ballast), which lowered transit and crew costs. And this trade was effectively toll-free, since it avoided the Sound and Baltic. And as explained below, the timber industry in Norway was a special, more freewheeling market than other forms of trade.

In timber, Norway benefited from its own backwardness. The lack of industry kept domestic demand subdued, beyond basics like house construction. In Sweden things were different; most wood went for making charcoal to fire the domestic iron industry, keeping exports below a quarter of the total product. Only with introduction of the steam saw in the mid-nineteenth century did Sweden (and Finland) become big exporters of timber, pulp and paper. In this crucial period it was Norwegian wood that mainly figured in wider markets.

The range of uses for wood was almost inexhaustible and demand, in an expanding empire, insatiable. An entire vocabulary grew up around it. Public buildings required piles and beams as support structures on marshy ground. The well-known Dutch housing preference for the vertical required great quantities of boards (deals). Fishermen and bulk traders required barrels, staves and hoops to deliver their produce to market. Miners required beams as props to avoid fatal collapses underground. Wooden supports shored up the dikes that held back the sea. Furniture was impossible without it. Even the tools used to put pieces together were themselves made of wood.

Raw wood was also fuel, not least for warming houses and cooking. Vital cottage industries, notably ceramics and glassmaking, required quantities to fire their production, the Dutch being pioneers of telescope and spectacle making. (An Iberian émigré philosopher, Baruch Spinoza, was a lens grinder in Holland.) Printers needed paper which required trees, and seventeenth-century Amsterdam was eclipsing Venice as a world center of book printing, bookbinding and mapmaking. Some fuel needs could be met locally, via peat reclaimed from salt marshes, but imported wood was far superior in most every respect.

The needs of Dutch shippers were never ending, since no ship ever sailed on a keel of peat. The Dutch navy and merchant fleet had wooden hulls, masts and fittings. This was of course part of the times; Henry VIII's famous flagship, the *Mary Rose*, was similarly based, throughout, on wood, as was the *Vasa*, which sank in 1628 during its maiden voyage in Stockholm harbor. The founding of joint-stock companies by these two countries—the British East India Company in 1600, the Dutch VOC two years later—in turn required still stronger ships for longer hauls. In 1614 a Dutch Northern Company followed, and in 1621 a corresponding West India Company to develop Dutch interests in the Caribbean. Such companies were practically states within states.

Dutch shipyards became such renowned models of efficiency that Peter the Great, bidding to make Russia a world power, spent several months in 1697 there (supposedly incognito) learning the tricks of the trade. He came in 1716 on another "Grand Embassy," bringing back to Russia more experts as well as expertise, some of it Norwegian.

All this activity had other knock-on effects, including ever-escalating replacement needs. With an estimated 10,000 Dutch ships afloat in the heyday, hundreds each year were damaged, decommissioned or lost. Pirates and privateers were another persistent scourge; in 1631 the Spanish impounded over 25 Dutch ships in Norwegian waters alone. Hundreds were captured by the English during three wars and by "Dunkirkers" and other privateers based on French coasts.

Norwegian timber was also the main staple for the *fluyt*, the technically innovative yet workaday cargo ship on which Dutch life and wealth depended. It was an ideal response to need: the *fluyt* was midsized (300–500 tons) and had a shallow draft, with ample below-deck space for cargo (notably timber); a crew of 12 could operate one.

The timber trade with Norway operated at several levels. The regulated, "legal" end of the business was increasingly concentrated in prominent family firms with names like Marselis and Berns, who also dominated the copper business centered in Røros and exported out of Trondheim. The timber trade also had a big shadow side that both Dutch and Danish officials fretted over. Only in 1647 was a thorough audit carried out at the Dutch end; up to that point, no one knew how extensive the trade actually was. Suddenly it emerged that 397 Dutch-registered ships were plying Norwegian routes, often several times a season, making for over 1,000 shipments annually, most of them untracked.

Timber was not the only Norwegian product exported to Holland; fish, whale oil and hides were also lucrative commodities. And the Netherlands was eventually eclipsed by Scotland and England as Norwegian export markets. But to a remarkable degree this relationship, so vital at both ends at a crucial period for both countries, was built around this one, all-purpose commodity. Human activity followed.

Some of the expertise gained in Dutch service and in its shipyards rebounded back to Norway. *Skuder* trading vessels in north Jutland, built along *fluyt* lines, were built to order in Norway, giving an early shipbuilding impetus. There was a competitive dimension to this, since Norwegian builders were also contracted by the Spanish, the Netherlanders' traditional nemesis, to construct vessels. An indigenous Norwegian shipping industry stimulated by foreign competition—and ultimately, the outlines of a naval force—emerged in fairly quick time out of this North Sea trade.

Wood's significance lay not just in its economic role but in the nature of the industry. Early on it emerged as a partial exception to mercantilist practices, while its nature made it resistant to the very notion of managed trade. As early as 1443, Amsterdammers had secured the freedom to import what they wanted from Norway; in 1558, Danish and Norwegian peasants won the right to buy and sell the commodities they chose. This had established, at both ends, a legally attained freedom to trade with each other.

Timber enjoyed a longtime exemption from normal (Danish) rules that required exported goods to be channeled through customs posts that were located, naturally, in the bigger port towns. Norway had 15 such facilities. Felled trees being bulky, heavy and hard to maneuver, this exemption had big consequences. Ship owners and captains could potentially avoid freight registration (especially for cargo destined for transshipment), and thereby dodge export duties or, at the other end, those on imports. The whole timber trade had an unregulated, Wild West aspect to it, much of the business remaining off-the-books. Smuggling and indiscriminate cutting proliferated. Eventually and naturally, this hit both the Danish and Dutch treasuries.

In 1579 King Frederik II, fretting over the loss of revenue, granted Stavanger a stronger grant of privilege, yet timber was not covered by it. In 1602 his son and successor, Christian IV, banned the export of Norwegian oak, a hardwood much in demand but in fast-dwindling supply. Other clampdowns followed in the 1630s and again in the 1680s. Most were ineffectual, like trying to secure the barn door after the horses have bolted.

In 1717, still grappling with the problem, a Danish royal resolution decreed that all timber had to be funneled through town channels (which, on the west coast, meant Stavanger). The same year Scots were forbidden to enter Norwegian waters in search of wood. All this accelerated an ongoing decline in Dutch fortunes that was signaled by the *guerres de commerce* with Britain and France launched in the 1650s.

Tracking the trade was hardly easier in Dutch waters. Thanks to Rotterdam (still Europe's biggest seaport) we have an impression of the Netherlands today as an efficient port administrator. But in its heyday it was a diverse semi-entity at home, partly masked by its strong-armed presence abroad. Only around 1580 was there an attempt to coordinate freight registration. Up to then, each port and town had to fend for itself. A beggar-thy-neighbor kind of competition reigned supreme. The physical reality, with ports strung along the coast and the Zuiderzee offering protective cover, also made it hard to manage. Thus at both ends of this trade there was ample scope, not to say incentive, to skirt the regulatory state.

Officialdom was especially easy to avoid in Norwegian fjords branching deep into the countryside. Farmers, who owned most of the forestland, sold their product on site, while individual Dutch shippers bought and loaded their cargo with skeleton crews. They paid in cloth, herring, salt and a variety of other goods like wine, spirits, ceramics, cheese, tobacco, spices, dried fruit, soap and glass—products that made life a little more pleasant for everyday Norwegians. Intermediaries and middlemen were mostly cut out of this strange amalgam of bulk product, international trade and mom-and-pop ownership. After 1650 or so, the timber market grew more consolidated and merchant-controlled in a way that stimulated middle-class concentration of wealth.

Whereas the Scots tended to pay in kind, bartering malt or barley, the Dutch also increasingly paid in silver. This introduced, by way of Latin America, a money economy into northern Europe. The use of credit—buying goods against future payment—became common and eventually widespread thanks to the Dutch role in Norwegian and Nordic economic life. And unlike Scotland, where relations with Norway were tainted by ancient disputes over Orkney and Shetland, the Dutch seemed like moderns and harbingers of a rosier future. With fewer geopolitical axes to grind, they, in refreshing contrast, could focus on commerce.

The result was a timber trade that maximized entrepreneurship and flexibility while minimizing state interference at both ends. It stimulated a wealth of human contacts in a way unmatched by other forms of trade. The Dutch were already adept at skirting either gild or Hansa regulations. They thrived in this "living" dimension of the business that prioritized personal relationships and direct dealings.

Traders came and lingered on Norwegian shores and in their homes, paying frequent visits and generating a human multiplier effect. It was a transnational trade link with a distinctly human face. The story that emerged from it, as Sogner emphasizes, was a *collective* one, built on countless individual and mostly anonymous life chapters. Coastal traders, as Kirby and Hinkkanen, coauthors of an authoritative history of the Baltic, nicely put it, "made their own connections and created their own intimate world."

The everyday, consumerist implications of all this were intriguing. An upwardly mobile Amsterdam merchant, hankering for a canal-side address in a choice district, could hire a *fluyt* (or better still a *houtvaarder*, a converted timber ship with deeper draught and extra loading gates) with crew and dispatch them to Norway. There they could slip into a fjord unnoticed, renew an old contact and cut a deal locally, while the crew took a breather amidst some sublime Norwegian scenery. Then it could load up, head back south and sail into the Zuiderzee (which was an inland sea before it was enclosed as the freshwater IJsselmeer of today). There it could unload, unobserved; the timber could be barged into the city and put straight into the construction job. It was cheap, fast, safe and efficient. Toll posts—time-consuming, costly and meddlesome—could be avoided at both ends. Today it seems incredible that three states renowned for their highly regulated commercial life could have allowed, even indirectly nurtured, this precedent of semi-anarchy.

These features also perpetuated developmental anomalies. Finished wood products, often in the form of Renaissance or church furniture, made its way back north from Holland to Scandinavia. Only later, well into the Golden Age, did much of this export come in exotic content like mahogany and nutwood; some was of local origin, returning in finished form.

Netherlanders exported other culture too, some of it directly to Norway but mostly indirectly and in grander form, via the Danish royal court and from Sweden too. Dutch Palladianism became a huge influence in Swedish artistic circles, while Dutch architects filled the court of King Christian IV, effectively bringing the Renaissance with them. Dutch architects designed such Copenhagen landmarks as the Boerse and the famous Round Tower. The Steenwinkel brothers designed the Stock Exchange, one of whom (Hans) also designed Rosenborg Palace. Pieter Isaacsz, yet another Hollander, is thought to have executed the first-ever landscape painting in Denmark, as a backdrop to a portrait of the young King Frederik III.

A crowning irony to all this came in 1917, when Norwegian explorer Roald Amundsen, failing to find suitable wood locally for his custom-built ship *Maud*, felt compelled (as he relates in his memoirs) to import "specially fine timbers" from none other than Holland. The expense was so high that it contributed to his late-life debt woes. What goes around can indeed come around.

For Norwegians, the Dutch opening was optimally timed. The national picture *circa* 1500 was one of double isolation. Many farms, abandoned since the Black Death, had reverted to natural forest cover. Underemployment was rife and economic autonomy under the Danes and Hansas ever more crimped. Rural districts were sparsely populated and impossible to monitor effectively, even if the Danes had wished to do so. Outward connections had great significance in such a time and place.

Developmentally the timing was equally providential. The water-saw, introduced in Sweden in the 1460s, came to Norway around 1503. Within a generation, they were operating by the hundreds in southern parts. These rudimentary sawmills operated nonstop in spring and autumn, when rains and snowmelt provided a steady energy source. As most farmers had some sort of running water supply, aiding their self-sufficiency, it was tailor-made for rural life and small-scale operation in a hilly land. Usefully, it extended the working season beyond the brief crop-growing norm of the high latitudes.

It also improved the terms of trade. Norwegian farmers became their own producers, or banded together as cooperatives. Rather than just dealing in raw timber, the water mill gave them a controlling hand in creating a semifinished product—in this case, by sawing logs into planks (up to eight per tree trunk) for further use and refinement elsewhere. This gave farmers extra bargaining leverage and a sense of engaging in a chain of production with a foreign angle. While extractive, the timber trade was not always blindly exploitative. It became more so after around 1650, when sagging prices caused farmers to cut more and higher. By then the negative effects were self-generated and not so easily blamed on foreigners.

The timber train to Holland eventually derailed, for some compelling reasons at both ends. On the supply side the most accessible fjordside forests were the first to go. Farmer-foresters then had to venture upcountry in search of new supply, adding complications and manpower costs. Trees were irregularly bunched in mountainside folds; they were harder to access, process and bring shipboard. The tighter hand of regulation and Christian IV's desperate tax hikes also drove costs up.

The demand side experienced even more structural upheaval. Ever-tightening English and French import and carry-trade controls were compounded by the cruel hand of nature. An outbreak of *Teredo Navalis*, a mollusk-like infestation commonly called pile-worm (or shipworm) in 1730, set the Dutch bureaucracy into a panic. Alarmist reports suggested that the entire dike system, reinforced by wood, was being eaten away from below. The receding of the Little Ice Age had brought warmer waters, and shipworm gravitated as far south as Holland. Mystically inclined observers posited the scourge as divine justice—colonial exploiters paying for their excesses—and it galvanized Dutch planners into action. New policies decreed that foundations should be shored up with inorganic stone. The panic receded within the decade, but the psychological damage was even worse than the physical. Once Norway began exporting rock in lieu of wood, the game was up.

By the late eighteenth century Dutch imports from Norway had dropped to 25,000 *last* per year, a small fraction of its heyday two centuries before. Overall Dutch trade suffered absolute declines by this time, but the relative drop in the timber trade was far bigger. Britain emerged as Norway's chief export market, prompted by the Anglo-French war of 1689–97, which effectively doubled the tonnage shipped from Norway. By 1700 England was a far bigger market for Norwegian timber and wood product, which in turn encouraged the building of ships in Norway. Seemingly at a stroke, but in reality after a century of quiet progress, the Norwegian export trade proved to be more diverse, resilient and flexible than anything imaginable even in 1650.

The Dutch connection derived its real importance from the exchange of people. Historians often speak of "push" and "pull" factors in describing migrations, and in this case both were prominent. Departing Norwegians left behind lives of isolation and seasonal-at-best employment. They flocked south—a timeless Scandinavian pattern—across the Skaggerak, lured by the milder winters and to-do Dutch imperial bustle, a case of "bright lights, big city" outshining humdrum farm life. The migration, in the tens of thousands, to Haarlem, Delft, Rotterdam, Amsterdam and other booming Dutch cities created an expatriate foreign community, a miniature *Noordsie Natie*, a Nordic nation, and within that a substantial Norwegian nation or *Norse Natie*.

They filled crucial if unheralded jobs. For men in the mobile maritime fraternity, this involved ships, on land as builders or at sea as sailors. They had expertise and worked willingly. Often they were recruited at home in Norway by Dutch interests facing manpower shortages. Countless other, stationary workers wove the ropes, swept the docks, tended the parlors and sewed the shoes that tread on every continent.

Historians have noted some surprising aspects to this flow. Most came from rural locales rather than cities. And many were girls and women, going as domestic servants before staying on. Like the timber they followed to Holland, much of this movement was unregistered, but two forms of paper trail—church and marriage registers—give some indication of numbers and trends. Between 1600 and 1800 nearly 12,000 marriages were recorded in Amsterdam involving Norwegians, over a third of whom were Norwegian women, often very young.

Still, sailors were the main migrants. Around 5 percent of the Dutch merchant marine was Norwegian, but much higher concentrations marked some sectors. The promise often outstripped the reality as sailors faced constant uncertainty and danger. The long-distance voyages aboard VOC vessels were by far the most perilous. Sailors spent many months in strange climes, facing enemies ranging from exotic diseases to pirates to sudden enemy engagement, with the additional, abundant possibility of falling overboard. An astonishing two-thirds never survived their first such voyage, a fact rarely mentioned in recruitment drives. Not surprisingly, the VOC represented the lowest of the low in terms of sailor status and had the highest percentage, often up to half the manpower, of foreigners—notably Norwegians—working the ropes.

Life was a little more stable for the "fixed" workers who remained on dry land. An expanding premodern economy, heavily dependent on imported labor, was unstable almost by definition. Holland sometimes set new standards in this regard. In the midst of the great boom, the famous Tulipmania of 1637 peaked, leaving such a destructive wake that it still serves as a cautionary tale by market economists. Nordic migrants lived in hovels and plied low-skill trades as dockhands, seamstresses, shopkeepers, market hawkers and other roustabout trades that we associate with rootless port-city life. While short of forced labor, it did not make for a pretty picture.

A lone statistic speaks volumes: of Norwegian immigrants in Holland, roughly 35 percent of the men could read and write—but just 7 percent of the women. Such numbers also leave social history impoverished, as so few were able (much less motivated) to leave firsthand accounts. Along with their lives, their legacies remain obscure.

Mortality rates were high; Dutch cities may have been swept clean, but they were periodically decimated by plague waves which, in true Hobbesian fashion, kept populations down and replacement demand buoyant. Even for illustrious natives, fortunes could sour quickly. Rembrandt van Rijn is a poignant example: famous while young, he bought a mansion on credit, lived beyond his means, then lost credibility (and paying clients) with the poor reception for what turned out to be his greatest masterpiece (*The Night Watch*) and went bankrupt. At the height of the Dutch Golden Age, its most illustrious artist was having his works auctioned to cover personal debts. Frans Hals, in Haarlem, met a similar fate, as did Jan Vermeer in Delft; even his widowed wife was pursued by creditors.

Nor was the Dutch labor market the mixing ground so commonly portrayed. Informal segregation was the norm. On one reading it consisted of an "internal" (indigenous) component and another, "external" one populated by immigrants and readily exploited. Others describe a triple-tiered market: a top one reserved for the titled (or self-titled) few, a middle stratum of emergent bourgeoisie and a big group of irregular workers, indigents, migrants and others for whom the modern term "working class" (or even Toynbee's sharper term "expatriate proletariat") doubtfully applied. This lower stratum, with its shifting opportunities, was the world to which such Norwegians flocked and which they typified.

Via Dutch opportunity, a more illustrious handful broke out of Norway to become transnational figures and empire builders. Some, notably Peter Bredal and Cornelius Cruys, used Dutch bases as a launching pad for fame as architects of the Russian imperial navy. Cort Adler was another, entering Danish service as an admiral.

The case of Cruys was easily the most spectacular. The man later claimed by four countries had obscure origins. Born in Stavanger with the eminently Danish name of Niels Olsen, his birth year is put at either 1655 or 1657, a disputed point that arose when he registered to be married in Amsterdam (1681), apparently claiming orphan status, under the name Cruijs. As a teen he was packed off to Holland to learn the seafaring trade.

It would probably have remained his adoptive base, had fate not intervened in a big way.

As a young migrant on the make in bustling Dutch shipyards, Cruys honed the trades of shipbuilder, ship salvager, naval captain and mapmaker while making forays into the Mediterranean. A remarkable break came his way at the fairly ripe age of 40 (or 42) when his path crossed with Peter the Great, Russia's westward-leaning leader seeking expertise in Holland. On the invitation of Russophile mayor Nicolaas Witsen, the itinerant czar set up shop at the great naval yard of Zaandam, on the North Sea, for four months.

Peter's time doubled as a recruitment drive, and the experienced Cruys made for a prize addition. Twenty years separated the two, but they shared a physical similarity, imposing height (Peter stood 2.03 meters or 6 feet eight inches tall, Cruys apparently near to that). A Cruys biographer, Torgrim Titlestad, postulates that Peter may have seen Cruys as a father figure and offered him a vice admiralty. Other foreign advisors were also pulled eastward, including a prominent Swiss, Franz Lefort, but Cruys outlasted him. In the process he left a big mark in the eastern Baltic: in Taganrog, where he served as mayor (1698–1702), he masterminded the building of Kronstadt fortress outside St. Petersburg and other works in Arkhangel in the far north.

Like many a career leap, this one led to professional skirmishes well documented in the maritime annals. No shrinking violet, Cruys clashed with many including rear admiral Botsis, yet another of the foreigners (he having Italian origin) who were angling for influence in Russia's royal court. Cruys served at a pivotal time: from 1705 he was a commander of the Russian fleet and served as a major czarist advisor during the drawn-out Great Northern War (1700–1721), which effectively ended Sweden's great power era at the expense of Russia.

Cruys played a key role in that protracted conflict. In July 1709 the Russian navy defeated the Swedes, under King Karl XII, at Poltava—one of the decisive losses in Swedish history, when Karl suffered a serious foot injury. The year after, Cruys was instrumental in the capture of Viborg fortress.

Cruys built a swashbuckling reputation as the "Tordenskiold of the East," after the celebrated Norwegian keystone of the Danish navy who was active at the time. In fact, the Tordenskiold family linked Cruys with one Johan Caspar de Cicignon, who came to Norway from Luxembourg and made his mark designing the strategic town of Fredrikstad. Cruys worked with Tordenskiold's brother, Henrik Wessel, who was actively helping the anti-Swedish campaign in the eastern Baltic, while Tordenskiold fortified Fredrikstad as a key naval base protecting Denmark's northern flank.

Cruys, like Cicignon, also left his mark on urban planning, helping lay the foundations for St. Petersburg, Peter's great planned city, where he was based. His home stood where the Winter Palace was later built. He even left an ecclesiastical legacy, being a keen Lutheran who helped build the first Norwegian-style church in St. Petersburg.

Life in the czarist inner circle was no insulation from trouble. Following a naval mishap in 1713, involving an attack against Finland during which a trapped enemy ship escaped, Cruys was sentenced to death. He evaded the charge and later returned to favor, reaching the rank of full admiral in 1721. He died in 1727, two years after Peter and into the reign of his successor, Catherine the Great. The Norwegian with the Danish name who built the Russian navy was buried in Amsterdam.

Most expat Norwegians, of course, led far more mundane lives, blending into the bustle. A few, however, were unknowingly immortalized. Rembrandt painted a second-generation immigrant from Oslo, Mennonite pastor Cornelis Claesz Anslo, with his customary blend of insight and luminosity. Two decades later, in his pious phase, one of Rembrandt's graphic brown-ink drawings starkly depicted a Danish immigrant, Elsie Christiaens, who had just been hanged in Volewijk for committing a grisly murder. Nor, for countless anonymous others, did their "Dutch time" pay dividends back home; labeled as *Hollændsker*, those Norwegians who returned home often faced reverse discrimination for their efforts and trials in having left at all.

There was a further, strategic dimension to the Norwegian migration. The Dutch frequently, and semi-officially, engaged in aggressive recruiting in southern Norway, luring sailors with promises of high pay and exciting opportunity. The result was a novel combination of draft dodging and international headhunting. But it came at the direct expense of Denmark, whose imperial dominance was increasingly under threat from the Swedes. The Danish crown could ill afford the drainage of able-bodied sailors into the Dutch service. The joint-stock companies were like sovereign entities that frequently pressed sailors in their pay into military action, so for the sailors themselves, the end result was not so different.

At the height of this human exodus, around 1675, Danish crown officials, short on manpower when the Skåne (Scania) war broke out, themselves conducted a military recruitment drive among Norwegian expatriates already in the Netherlands. It was a striking twist of fortune: what started out as a seemingly one-way dependency, of Norway on Holland (and Denmark), began to assume the opposite characteristic, namely a Dutch and Danish dependency on Norwegians as the strategic screws tightened on both.

The Dutch imperial age contained the seeds of its own downfall, which again worked to Norway's ultimate advantage. Their success provoked determined counterstrategies as early as 1614. James I of England and Scotland—who had wed in Oslo and was the Danish king's brother-in-law—issued the so-called Cocayne restrictions on trade in Dutch cloth. Far tougher were the above-mentioned Navigation Acts imposed by Cromwellian England from 1651—just three years after the Dutch triumph at Westphalia and its liberation from Spain—which effectively barred Dutch access to English ports. Three successive wars (in 1652–54, 1665–67 and 1672) followed, in the midst of which Louis XIV slapped similar restrictions on the Dutch. Meanwhile the Danes ramped up the Sound Tolls in a desperate bid for income, increasingly at Dutch expense. The freewheeling Dutch could not long thrive in a mercantilist world.

Yet Norwegians emerged as surreptitious winners from these clampdowns. *Skuder* trading vessels were built to order in Norway. That expertise brought contracts to construct Spanish vessels in Norwegian ports, sparking a shipbuilding industry and helping to diversify the economy. The fledgling merchant marine, boosted by the Dutch service, could step into the void left by the faltering Dutch carry trade and by Denmark's gradual eclipse by Sweden. This supposed time of national introversion was, in fact, one of striking opportunity for Norway's people and its budding commodity-based businesses. The result was not just temporary or tactical advantage but something strategic and fundamental in nature.

The *hollandertid* was an unheralded force for Norwegian modernization. It stimulated economic diversity, encouraged social and physical mobility and broke long-standing patterns of rural isolation. It also affirmed a latent sense of autonomy vis-à-vis Denmark and spawned renewed awareness of Norway's maritime destiny. And it sowed the seeds for a new cosmopolitanism, by opening a window onto continental Europe and a world beyond fjord and farm. The Dutch connection, in short, laid many of the foundations of modern Norway.

Much will remain anonymous. We will never know how many Norwegians traveled with Abel van Tasman, the Dutch explorer who circumnavigated Australia and discovered New Zealand in 1642. We will never know how many Norwegian sailors witnessed—or were compelled to participate in—the Spice Island atrocities of the 1620s. Much of that era was characterized by elements, from illicit trade to indigent human drift, which doubtfully qualify it as Norway's finest hour. It all unfolded in a relationship that might well be labeled neocolonial and exploitative, notwithstanding benefits at both ends.

At home, resource overexploitation left a melancholic legacy and sharp lesson in resource sustainability. For some the impression was vivid. King Christian IV railed against the brutal cutting methods of the itinerant Finns, who typically cleared land, burned the trees and grew rye in the ashes, a damaging process known as "burn-beating" that persisted until the nineteenth century.

Mary Wollstonecraft in 1795 not only noticed the effects of indiscriminate felling but anticipated its fallout. "The destruction, or gradual reduction, of their forests will probably meliorate the climate," she wrote with astonishing prescience, two centuries ahead of wider global warming awareness. Half a century later, Bayard Taylor lamented the sight. Norwegian forests, he said, were "very straight and beautiful, but there were none of more than middle age. All the fine old timber had been cut away; all Norway, in fact, has been despoiled [...] and the people are just awakening to the fact, that they are killing the goose which lays golden eggs." Yet the blame was not all local; in the nineteenth century British interests bought large tracts of northern forest and proceeded to exploit them as absentee owners are wont to do.

Long after the Dutch had sunk into postimperial torpor, the *idea* of Holland continued to color the Norwegian discourse. An intriguing instance was *Det Lærde Holland*, the "Learned Holland," a clutch of young intellectuals prominent in mid-nineteenth century Bergen who were trying to make an impact on the Norwegian scene. Two key members of this skeptical cohort were A. O. Vinje and Henrik Ibsen. Ibsen was "Gert," after a Ludwig Holberg character, and a shared sense of sarcasm and irony kept the group loosely in friendship until life took them in different directions. Vinje went on to advocate Landsmål (nowadays Nynorsk) as a Norwegian cultural countermovement, even editing the first publication devoted to the form, while a bitter Ibsen left Norway and stayed away for nearly three decades. The two traded barbs and satirical works, in their own ways personifying one of the great cultural divides of nineteenth-century Norway.

Some Dutch spirit had worked its way into the joints and sinews of Norwegian society. By such backdoor means did the humble tree, Norway's staple, become the *Yggdrasil*, the tree of life with branches encircling the globe.

7

The Union of Weights and Wings

The kingdom of Norway [...] as well as the dependencies belonging to it (Greenland, the Færoe Islands and Iceland not included)—shall in the future belong to HM the King of Sweden and constitute a kingdom, united with Sweden's realm.
Article 4, Treaty of Kiel, January 14, 1814

The Union with Sweden under one king is dissolved, the king having ceased to function as King of Norway.
Storting declaration, June 7, 1905

Kiel is one of those place-names that ring bells in the mind but are hard to find on a map. An aesthetically challenged port city on the south Baltic coast, it long served as home base for the German fleet and remains the outlet for the eponymous canal linking the North Sea with the Baltic. Kiel's historical *gravitas* has since given way to the baser pleasures of the Baltic leisure industry. For Norwegians it's mainly a turnaround-and-refueling place for hulking cruise ships that weigh anchor each day in Oslo at two o'clock and head for the *real* Europe that Denmark, for all its quirky charm and Sunday shopping, can't quite deliver. Even on a trip to the place, Kiel has become an afterthought to a booze cruise.

The city's past associations are lost in the sober sort of Baltic mist. A treaty signed there in early 1814 is now all but forgotten. Even for European historians it is a footnote (or less; David Thomson's exhaustive *Europe since Napoleon* does not mention it). But in its time the Kiel Treaty was catalytic. It rearranged the

Nordic political furniture, turning Sweden west and Finland east, while indirectly affecting France and Germany. It compromised Danish–Norwegian relations for more than a century. And it was the seed from which modern Norway emerged.

Kiel's legacy for each affected country has been radically different. For Norwegians with an eye on history, the name still reeks of pernicious intent that left them nursing a long-term distrust of European political designs. For Danes it capped an era of futility and calamitous choices. For Swedes it represented welcome payback, while for Finns it cemented a new, eastward orientation. And for France, the Kiel Treaty effectively ensured that Napoleon's successor would be a returning Bourbon king rather than his former marshal from Pau in the French south. That man, called Bernadotte, would instead become Swedish king—and chief determinant of Norway's nineteenth-century trajectory.

Much of the treaty's importance, and most of its historical oddity, derives from what it didn't do or failed to deliver on. In stripping Denmark of Norway it promised the Danes land compensation that never materialized. It saddled Norway with debts it had not racked up. It sparked an independence movement in Norway that few—least of all its authors—could have anticipated, making it a classic case of unintended consequences. Its biggest impact, in terms of space and time, came via a parenthetical afterthought. A textbook case of textual fuzziness, the Kiel Treaty demonstrates the ruthless imperatives of geopolitics and the staying power of treaties, however flawed or hastily conceived.

Along with Moss and Eidsvoll, Kiel is one of three placenames directly linked with Norway's "miracle year" of 1814, and the only one on foreign soil. Eidsvoll is the familiar, domestic name because of the constitution hammered out there, in circumstances superficially known to every Norwegian, thanks to Oscar Wergeland's famous painting of that crowded-room scene. In Moss a subsequent, bilateral deal was cut with Sweden establishing a dual monarchy that would survive for nearly a century. The treaty which preceded both jolted Norwegians into action at home. Kiel, where mutinous sailors launched an abortive revolution in late 1918, has an equal knack for sparking revolts outside Germany.

The Union of Weights and Wings   191

Kiel signaled a double emergence for Norway, as an independent presence on the Nordic scene and as an actionable piece on the European geopolitical chessboard. The chess metaphor is apt. Norwegians, who were scarcely unified to begin with, quickly plunged into a battle of wills with Sweden even as a second cat-and-mouse game played out between the two royal figures at its heart—a Danish prince turned Norwegian patriot and a nominally Swedish Frenchman—each of whom was further engaged in a double game of his own ambition. This was not merely high-stakes chess but a 3-D version of it. Within this political tangle, Norway's power position evolved from lowly pawn in early 1814 to middling bishop by midyear, to something closer to a rook over the coming decades: a lurking presence that can have an unpredictable impact on the game's outcome.

Two Norways effectively emerged in the long nineteenth century. One was the newly stamped polity that played a demoralizing second fiddle in a union with Sweden, whose successive kings indulged rather than enhanced Norwegian interests. The other was the preternaturally global Norway that blossomed even without the trappings of statehood. Norway became a novelty, a world-cultural presence in the shell of a political halfway house. This "other" Norway emerged in exploration, sport, shipping, the various arts and a surprising array of hard sciences. It had a direct hand in the birth of global society via mass emigration to America. And thanks to a guilt-prone Swedish entrepreneur called Alfred Nobel, it landed a designated role, by the century's end, as an arbiter of war and peace via his famous peace prize. The emergence of Norway as a global force, indeed as an *idea*, without the formal trappings of sovereignty, was nothing short of astonishing.

It is tempting to assign to this transformation the quality of sublimation—the Freudian tendency to compensate for deficiencies in one area of life with superhuman effort in another. Norway, by this reckoning, was making up for its political frustrations by channeling its energies elsewhere. Less extravagantly and perhaps more plausibly, there can be seen in all this something of the competitive notion that if Norway could not beat the Swedes directly, it could outdo them indirectly. Norway's independence thrust in 1814 was quickly cut down at the knees by the Swedish royal house, but the process had the effect of deepening propensities for perseverance, fortitude and ingenuity which had been cultivated during the Danish *eneveld*. Denmark had hindered the development of the Norwegian nation and Sweden stymied the emergence of a Norwegian state. The push to overcome both these damaging legacies, more or less simultaneously, was at the heart of Norway's uneven but extraordinary nineteenth century.

Barton's astute thesis, that Norway managed to outfox the Swedes and beat them at their own game, might well be taken a step further: Norway emerged as more self-consciously global, and more conspicuously democratic, than Sweden by 1905 substantially *because* of the strictures of the dual monarchy. Being anchored politically to the Swedes quickly became an irritant and a national drag, but it had a less obvious, liberating side for Norwegians. The same union that weighed them down inadvertently gave them wings, along with a usefully favorable foreign image.

A need for boldness, for pursuing nontraditional ways to make a mark, manifested in Norwegian pursuits across a broad front. Some misfired, like Ole Bull's Oleana colony in Pennsylvania and Hendrick Andersen's "world city" scheme, draining their personal resources while drawing quizzical commentary. In such ways did Norway emerge as a distinctly different sort of national entity, a buttoned-down country capable of extravagant surprise.

If Kiel represents the dark side of 1814 for Norway, the name Eidsvoll has the ring of subdued magic for Norwegians. Physically it is worlds away from industrial and seaside Kiel. Set in a copse of stately trees in rural upland north of Oslo, overlooking a water mill, a manor house owned by Carsten Anker hosted meetings and a constitutional convention that birthed modern Norway. There a cross-section of Norwegian society, 112 public officials, patricians and farmers, put together a document that, aside from amendments, has lasted. It is the oldest in Europe and second-oldest in the world after the proud-but-battered US constitution. The closest thing in Norway to a national shrine, the Eidsvoll manor seems hidden away among the plowed fields in a self-effacing and curiously Norwegian kind of gesture. Three months later, at fjordside Moss south of Christiania, the seemingly contradictory thrusts of Kiel and Eidsvoll were melded via an

THE UNION OF WEIGHTS AND WINGS   193

uneasy compromise formalized in November. The events linking these three events and towns unfolded in rapid sequence.

In February Christian Frederik, the Danish heir-apparent and chief royal representative in Norway, publicly converted to the Norwegian cause and embarked on a "talking tour" in the country's heartland. On February 17, exactly three months before his election as Norwegian king, he wrote of winning "a victory over myself: I had won more than a king's throne, I had won all Norwegians' hearts for all time." He began agitating for his *Kjære Norge*; in March this became a call for a patriotic pledge. The convention that elected him as their king finished its work in mid-May. Tensions then arose with the continental allies over the end-game against Napoleon. A brief summer war with Sweden quashed Norwegian aspirations. At Moss in mid-August, the Norwegians acquiesced to Swedish rule while keeping home autonomy. In October they revised the constitution, and early in November Sweden's aging king, Karl XIII, was "unanimously elected and acknowledged" as the Norwegians' rightful sovereign. The long union with Denmark thus came to an end, in Derry's choice words, in "a year of catastrophe, shock and improvisation." In another sense, though, the year described a circle: it opened with Sweden's Norway grab (on which more below) and ended with the Norwegians legally recognizing it.

On 6 August 1815 an Act of Union (*Riksakten*) formalized relations between Norway and Sweden while leaving some vital matters, like foreign policy, unaddressed. And almost immediately the Norwegian Parliament began chipping away at Swedish hopes for imposing either its military rule or its social system on Norway. A Norway with autonomy, but without formal independence, was the awkward reality for the next 90 years.

The world into which Norway was "born" in 1814 was profoundly unpromising for an upstart polity. In this there are distinct parallels with the situation as of 1905. Both years marked Norwegian end-phases as well as new chapters. Each phase was complicated by emergent nationalism next door, respectively in Denmark and Sweden, a factor underplayed in the Norwegian narrative. In the tense environments of both years, a shooting war with Sweden seemed the likeliest outcome. Both breakthroughs were followed by anticlimax, leaving the Norwegians frustrated over the lack of outside (primarily British) interest in their efforts. Anticipating the labors of Nansen and Count Wedel Jarlsberg after 1905 to secure London's recognition, Carsten Anker floundered in his post-Kiel push for the same aim. At both stages, global tensions crowded out the concerns of a peripheral country. Both eras were harsh and the lessons for Norway rude.

At Vienna and Paris, where the post-Napoleonic settlement was agreed in 1814–15, the big powers wove a thick net of compromise that reaffirmed the settlements reached to that point, including Kiel. The upshot was a new state of play in northern Europe, but fundamentally for Norway it amounted to a case of old wine in new bottles. It was a European power maneuver of the classic sort in an age before "consent of the governed" became a complicating irritant of the diplomatic game. Norway, like Belgium and Finland, was a political football in a Europe bent on stability at any cost: the victim, many grumbled, of a prison transfer or a *diktat*. For knowing insiders, though, acutely aware of Norway's limited capacities, Kiel smacked less of perfidy than of realism, opening a window of opportunity as opposed to slamming the door.

Kieltraktaten, signed just before midnight on January 14, was finalized between the British and Swedes on one side and Denmark–Norway on the other. It came in two parts, a terse Danish agreement with Britain and another, lengthier Danish accord with Sweden. Norway was a concern only of the latter. The Danish king and all successors renounced future rights to Norwegian territories and properties, excepting those excluded. Denmark was set to receive Swedish Pomerania as part-compensation for its loss. At the Vienna Congress a year later, Sweden was confirmed in its Norwegian possession, but Pomerania went to Prussia instead (with Denmark getting some minor compensation). Norway was the treaty's subject and object, but it was not a signatory and never accepted its legitimacy.

The treaty also addressed issues like prisoners of war and property rights of Danes in Norway. Importantly left aside was the fate of territories outside of Norway but linked historically to it, namely the Færoe Islands, Iceland and Greenland. Because of this exclusion, their official link to Norway was lost even as their fate was left hanging. Gradually they became reunited with Denmark. As mentioned in the first chapter, Norway was still grappling with Kiel's political legacy in the 1930s when it waged a legal, psychological and exploratory battle with Denmark for control over eastern parts of Greenland. (Iceland in 1944 became independent, Greenland achieved home rule in 2009 and the Færoes are now seeing agitation for autonomy.)

Among much else, Kiel's legacy shows the peculiarities of international treaty law. Treaties may make for dull reading, but their small print can be decisive, which lends them a surreptitious sort of power. Once negotiated politically, they require legal ratification; once ratified they become solemn interstate agreements just as surely as cement becomes concrete. They begin as contracts and evolve into common law through general assent. Once done, they cannot easily be undone. Those like Westphalia (1648) and Versailles (1919) achieve lasting notoriety.

The dealings at Kiel were soon overtaken by dramatic events to the south. In its wake came Napoleon's escape from Elba, his "hundred days" campaign back in France and, in June 1815, his defeat—a close-run thing—at Waterloo. This was contextually important twice over. It meant a world taken up by issues of infinitely greater urgency than the fate of Norway, and it meant a world far distant from any Enlightenment spirit. It was an age of Restoration and, if push came to shove, of counterrevolution. A newly hatching liberal state was inimical to prevailing sentiment. The Norwegians were swimming against a powerful tide.

Within two months of Kiel, in March 1814, the Treaty of Chaumont committed the British, Austrians, Prussians and Russians to extend their Quadruple Alliance against Napoleon for 20 years. Two months later, in May, the first Treaty of Paris restricted French boundaries; a second Paris Treaty, in November 1815, reduced them further, to those of 1790. Amidst it all came the Treaty of Vienna, signed in June 1815—the basis of the so-called Congress System.

The environment was dominated by the so-called great powers, orchestrated by Klemens von Metternich of Austria, a minor noble from Koblenz, and manipulated by Talleyrand of France, a rare survivor from the revolution. Its architects, including Czar Alexander I and Castlereagh of Britain, were preoccupied with matters extraneous to Nordic Europe: the division of Poland, restiveness in northern Italy, the Dutch border, the Swiss confederation and, above all, the fate of Napoleon.

None of the principals was willing to countenance an independent Norway. Even Britain, the great hope of many, was a poor candidate as a Norwegian savior after having blockaded Denmark–Norway in 1812–13. This reality was brought home in a crucial meeting, detailed in Christian Frederik's diary, with a British envoy in the first week of June. Britain had two overriding aims when it came to Norway: to prevent war in Scandinavia and to fulfill their promises to Sweden at Kiel. Not for the last time, Norway was sprung momentarily from its trap, only to find itself in political territory that was not so much hostile as indifferent to its concerns.

The Norwegian "switch" at Kiel that seemed, to outsiders, as another chapter in a long-running, faceless Nordic tug-of-war in fact marked the signature diplomatic triumph of a single, non-Scandinavian man. Its driving force was Sweden's imported crown prince, Jean-Baptiste Bernadotte, for whom Norway was a long-standing prize. A compact Frenchman (he stood 1.52 meters, roughly five feet) with outsized ambition, curly mane and prominent Gallic nose, Bernadotte had been one of France's 18 marshals (and 14 active) until being plucked, in summer 1810, from Napoleon's service to be Sweden's crown prince. He quickly set out to be Scandinavia's *eminence grise*, and Kiel represented his portal into that role.

That he represented Sweden at all was the product of separate upheaval. In 1808–09 Russia under Czar Alexander I, then still a Napoleonic ally after the Tilsit Treaty the year before, defeated Swedish forces and took control of Finland, a long-standing Swedish province. The loss sparked a bloodless coup in Stockholm that deposed Gustav IV, the hapless king, and brought a new, more modern constitution. A long twilight reign by Gustav's childless uncle, Karl XIII, was the prelude to a new royal bloodline.

Head of that line was not, initially, French but German. The first "new" Swedish crown prince was Christian August, a cousin of the careholder king, who was selected in summer 1809. A year later he died suddenly after a fall from a horse, possibly after a stroke. Another constitutional crisis loomed. After a summer of behind-the-scenes maneuverings a special diet at Örebro selected Bernadotte as Christian August's replacement. It was a dramatic statement of Sweden's distress under the Napoleonic blockade, but it also confirmed some long-standing Swedish–French ties. Napoleon claimed the choice was "an honorable monument to my reign and an extension of my glory." Seven generations on Bernadotte's descendants still reign, if that is the right word for a powerless constitutional monarchy, in today's Sweden.

Bernadotte, prince of Pontecorvo, took the very Swedish name of Karl Johan and was later to rule as Karl XIV. But that was after an eight-year period as crown prince. Seconded to Sweden under one set of circumstances, he quickly faced another. He had been the choice of a "French party" operating behind Swedish scenes that was determined to win back Finland from the Russians—while maintaining the goodwill of Napoleon, who as of 1810 was still shaping Europe's destiny. Military expertise, not Swedishness, was for them the crucial ingredient.

The north European tide turned during 1810–12 when Bernadotte (reluctantly) joined the continental alliance against his former commander and mentor. Events were precipitated by the emperor himself when he marched unannounced into Swedish Pomerania, in today's southern Baltic coast, in January 1812. This, the first of a series of Napoleonic missteps, drove Sweden into Russian arms on the cusp of the disastrous French invasion of Russia.

In defiance of his roots, his Swedish backers and general expectation, Bernadotte demanded Norway from Denmark—which was still allied with France—to compensate for the loss of Finland he could not fight for. More pointedly, it was his price of alliance against his former boss. Alexander I, who had the biggest stake in this switch, gave the first, crucial outside assent to his demand in April 1812. Britain under Foreign Minister Castlereagh assented indirectly, in July, and formally through an Anglo-Swedish Treaty in March 1813. With Prussian agreement in July, the essence of Kiel was set.

The Grand Army's calamitous retreat from the Russian winter allowed Bernadotte to press his demand. Following Napoleon's defeat at Leipzig in October, his position was stronger still, and he pounced. The pitiless politics at work are shown in the fate of Lübeck, the old Hanseatic capital (and stately backdrop for *Buddenbrooks*, Thomas Mann's intergenerational novel). As a French commander, Bernadotte had defeated Blücher's Prussian army, besieged the city and requisitioned its silver; in December 1813 he arrived as a liberator representing Sweden. He then marched into the Germanic territories of a now defenseless Denmark, waging his own little war. After a week of tense negotiations at Kiel, the Danish king grudgingly accepted his impossible position.

The treaty that changed Norway's outward trajectory also had the effect of transforming Norway's self-conception. As Weibull and others have related, its roots are found in the drafting stages of the treaty's crucial (fourth) article. Under the first reading, "the whole kingdom of Norway [...] will belong hereafter in all property and sovereignty to the kingdom of Sweden [...] and remain incorporated in it." Incorporation implied absorption. This provision was then altered (in longhand) by a Swedish negotiator for Bernadotte, Gustaf af Wetterstedt, to a specific designation of Norway as a kingdom (*un Royaume*) that would revert instead "to His Majesty the King of Sweden" and would thereafter form "a realm united with that of Sweden" (*et réuni a celui de Suede*). Norway, in other words, was both specified as a separate entity and assigned not to the Swedish crown (effectively its government) but specifically to the Swedish king, a far more personal and limited prospect.

Frederik VI may have done Norway the same favor. When an Austrian diplomat, Bombelles, proposed that Trøndelag be hived off and given to Sweden, he brusquely dismissed this halfway measure. In other words Norway, for the first time, was openly considered by *both* Denmark and Sweden as a unit with a political essence, not just as territory to be chopped up and shifted about.

Through this eleventh-hour change, a Swedish diplomat unintentionally lit a fire in Norway by officially referring to it as a separate kingdom with a more tenuous owner. Aside from its practical implications, it was a striking parallel with Denmark's ambiguous references to Norway after 1536. A scratch of a pencil altered the union's entire basis. At the very instant of winning Norway, Sweden's crown prince may have begun to lose it.

Interpretive disputes were hard-wired into a Scandinavian agreement negotiated in haste and written in French. They would erupt whenever Sweden's royal house underwent a change—which had occurred just five years before, as in 1792 and 1772. At any rate, Bernadotte's continental perspective failed to comprehend the conditions prevailing in Scandinavia. Ignorant of Færoese or Icelandic (much less Greenlandic) reality, he simply chose to keep his prize's center cut, contiguous Norway. (It was as if a purchaser of America, obsessed with the lower 48, discarded Hawaii and Alaska.) The same logic informed his airy promise of Swedish Pomerania to Denmark.

The period just after Kiel brought to the fore the year's other royal principal, Christian Frederik of Denmark. He embarked on a counterstrategy to encourage discontent in Norway and arouse opposition to the tie-up with Sweden. The "spirit of Eidsvoll" is not so much of a national foundation myth as a consequence—part natural and part fabricated—of a new and fluid international reality. Norway (or rather, its autonomy mongers, prominent in the country's south and west) quickly moved to nullify the provisions of Kiel by pushing for outright independence.

Christian Frederik, the Danish viceroy in Oslo who was also heir to the Danish throne, seems genuinely to have taken Norwegian interests to heart. His two-week winter trip to Trondheim and back to Eidsvoll took him through heartland regions where he found wide Norwegian antipathy to being "slaves to Sweden." His conversion seems nonetheless tempered by his scarcely disguised other (and perhaps main) interest in keeping the Danish link alive; perhaps he was earnestly juggling contradictory aims. The conspicuous reluctance of Denmark's King Frederik VI to facilitate the transfer of Norway to Sweden in the months after Kiel (and his efforts to ship them grain against express British policy) seems to affirm this dual aim and, perhaps, this double game. The relationship between Christian Frederik and Frederik VI seems purposefully opaque and calculated to enable a kind of plausible deniability as to their intentions, joint or individual.

Christian Frederik, elected at Eidsvoll as regent for a self-proclaimed kingdom, much later (1839) became a cautiously reformist king of Denmark. But he is a largely forgotten figure in Norway because of his failure to consolidate his position, his military incompetence in the short war against his French–Swedish rival (whom he dismissively called "Ponte Corvo"), his humiliating climb down at Moss and his subsequent banishment from Norway. Yet ambiguity was built into his situation, and for all his inexperience (he was just 26) he gave timely encouragement to those Norwegians agitating for autonomy. In his way he midwifed the more confident Norway that emerged after 1814.

Easily the most overlooked aspect of 1814 was Bernadotte himself. Hesitation, an unlikely hallmark for a military man, governed his actions in the months following Kiel. Even as Norway's independence advocates gained momentum, Bernadotte's position weakened. Having left Scandinavia in spring 1813 he remained on the continent until late May 1814. He stayed mostly in Paris, revisiting old acquaintances (including Napoleon and Louis XVIII) and spending time with his wife, Désirée, Napoleon's old flame. He was also ostensibly working the political ropes to ensure that his allies would back his Norwegian claim.

Seemingly in command, Bernadotte had to tread lightly. His discomfiture was not just situational but structural. He had not been first choice as crown prince (or indeed Karl XIII's first crown prince), and his position even in Sweden was tenuous. He was a Frenchman displaced to Scandinavia and a military man thrust into the world of politics, far from either comfort zone. He had disappointed backers agitating for a war with Russia over Finland. He was a designated Prince Royal and chief puller of strings but not yet king. He dawdled in France even as Norwegians were drawing up a constitution and choosing somebody else to warm their throne.

Bernadotte spoke little Swedish and, after some half-hearted attempts, never made a serious effort to master it—like his reluctant queen, who never took to Sweden but unlike his linguistically adept son and heir Oscar, who quickly learned Norwegian into the bargain. The language question went beyond protocol. It amplified his suspicions of palace intrigue, part of which involved lingering sympathy for Gustav, son of the deposed Gustav IV and one-time heir to the same throne. A seriously ugly political climate had prevailed in summer 1810: Count Axel Ferson, a Swedish diplomat and former intimate of Marie Antoinette, was attacked and beaten to death by a street mob during Christian August's funeral in Stockholm as police looked on.

Bernadotte's months in France were also spent nurturing a second personal ambition, succeeding Napoleon. As his biographer Alan Palmer puts it, this hope was a "will-o'-the-wisp" that had disintegrated by late spring. But it divided his attention and kept him behind the curve of Norwegian developments. Back in Sweden he found his aim and position seriously jeopardized. He felt under acute time pressure, with the powers due to convene in Vienna by year's end to effect a final settlement, and he needed a workable solution before then—especially as he was not much liked or trusted by the other European leaders, notably Metternich. As suspicion typically increases with ignorance, Bernadotte feared an insurrection that could cost him not just Norway but the crown and perhaps his life. The months after Eidsvoll were also marked by overweening Norwegian confidence, egged on by Christian Frederik and driven by righteous anger at "the assumption that they were chattel, up for barter."

Absence had sharpened Bernadotte's bellicosity, which spilled over in talks with a contingent of allied representatives engaging in some shuttle diplomacy. The tough talk masked a vulnerability that in turn forced him to curb his ambitions. It compelled a two-pronged strategy: demonstrating his authority in Norway while conciliating the Norwegians, a hard-cop/soft-cop role aimed at keeping Norway tethered to Sweden while loosening the rope.

In late July he waged a brief demonstration war with the unprepared Norwegians in which both sides suffered minimal casualties. His point made, the two sides met at Moss in mid-August to negotiate new terms. Those talks are generally seen as a capitulation by Christian Frederik, but they were no less a compromise by Bernadotte, who agreed that the Eidsvoll constitution, and Norwegian self-governance, could remain intact. He further agreed that Norwegian troops would not be sent into foreign wars, a substantial concession given that Sweden would still dictate the union's foreign policy.

And in a crucial move, mulled during that twilit summer, he agreed to give up the absolute Swedish veto (which he, acting increasingly for the king, already wielded in Swedish affairs) for a suspensive veto that could be overridden by the Norwegian parliament. Still, and crucially, this was a concession in the Gallic but not the Scandinavian mold. A product of the French

Revolution, Bernadotte was convinced that Norway's constitution was not holy writ but a political statement (a "practical expedient" to Palmer) that could be overturned as circumstances permitted. That was hardly the Norwegian interpretation of things.

His allowances were tactical and predicated on the notion of *contingency*: that his role, and Swedish rule over Norway, would be consolidated in due course. In fact, the opposite tended to happen. Meanwhile, in early November he visited Norway for the first time and saw the new Storting select Karl XIII as Norwegian king. Thereafter Bernadotte considered Norway's national day to be November 4. His later attempts to suppress May 17 celebrations were intended not to crush a national day as such but merely that particular one (which was also associated with his vanquished rival). Still, Bernadotte's skillful maneuverings in the latter half of 1814 compensated for his blunders in the first half. Overplaying or underplaying his hand would likely have lost him the support of the other four European powers on which, in the end, his entire position hinged.

For three decades after 1814, Norwegians' effective ruler was a Frenchman who regarded them as property, rattled the occasional sword at them and rarely paid a visit. It is an unremarked act of historical generosity that Oslo continues to call its main drag, Karl Johans Gate, after him. But it's also a grudging nod of admiration, for the same ruthless realism that won him title to Norway compelled him to bend to the Norwegians' stifled will—unhappily but ineluctably—once he took the throne, at age 55, in 1818. Bernadotte never squared with the idea of Norwegian autonomy, but was more or less compelled to accept it by 1830, by which time he was too tired to fight the trend. Toward the end he became more popular in Norway, which he had forcibly captured, invaded and waged war against, than in Sweden, where he had been brought in as a savior.

If a game of attrition was built into the union, Norwegians were predisposed by circumstances to win it. For Norway, having experienced a false dawn, assertions of self-determination took an embittered but also more determined aspect. Modern Norway has had three bona fide rebirths, in 1814, 1905 and 1945, which means recoveries from triple setbacks.

The omens were scarcely positive in 1814. The country had just been through the shattering experience of forced alignment with Napoleon, a British blockade and consequent hunger. Norwegians confronted the conjoined problems of state- and nation-building in the face of a national economic emergency and a covetous royal house in Stockholm. Christiania, the once-and-future capital, was an eighth the size of Stockholm, which counted roughly 80,000 inhabitants, and had no official standing. All told, Norwegians numbered under a million, nine-tenths of them living rurally. The spirit of Eidsvoll was dead. As Michael Drake's work emphasizes, there was no state to speak of. The Lutheran clergy performed basic public functions from census-taking to child vaccinations to the introduction of potatoes, a major breakthrough. Few would have given Norway a chance. (Even in the 1880s, few observant outsiders rated an independent Norway a good survival prospect.)

Norwegians found themselves in an exceedingly strange position after 1814. They were politically subservient to Sweden yet constitutionally empowered to chart their own course. While liberated from Denmark, they remained vulnerable to its cultural domination. And this being Scandinavia, total separation from either one was never on the cards. While the political transition was abrupt, the social one was subtle and the economic challenges intractable. Norwegians were fighting battles on three fronts. It's no surprise that the themes arising from that era can sound to us oppositional and melodramatic.

A concerted post-1814 effort, urged by some in the literary set, was made to "move beyond" Denmark, which implied conscious acts of cultural separation. Norwegian nationalism proceeded along an exceptionally broad front, prompted by the perceived need for a kind of national great leap forward. The resulting cultural output took the world by surprise and, eventually, by storm. It also sparked ill-tempered culture wars inside Norway. All this suggests that Norway's Danish "tutelage" took on greater significance *after* it was over. Powerful legacies have to be grappled with and reconciled. As late as the mid-nineteenth century Norwegians were still dying in the Danish service; Norway-born general Olaf Rye (whose name now adorns a central Oslo square) was killed on a battlefield in the first Dano-Prussian war in July 1849.

Language was both a help and a hindrance. A full half-century into home rule, Norwegians were being admonished by Aasmund Vinje not to "kiss the slave chains" of Danish but to cultivate their own linguistic identity. He was an outspoken advocate of Ivar Aasen's peculiar creation of *Landsmål*, a new-old alternative language built on elements of dialect and Old Norse and put in written form. Hulda Garborg's efforts to refashion the *bunad* as a national symbol became another part of this cultural push, as did her husband's novels, amounting to a double-barreled folk-revival under a single roof. The great Norwegian figures chose sides; while Grieg approved of Landsmål, Ibsen and Bjørnson demurred.

Such debates mattered because Denmark remained a literary clearinghouse and place of learning. Take Ibsen: the dramatist relied on Danish publishers (Gyldendal and Frederik Hegel), got his biggest boost from Georg Brandes, a Danish friend and publicist, and found his worst nemesis in another Danish critic, Clemens Petersen. It was Brandes who in the 1870s first urged a leap toward Scandinavian modernism. Not until 1895 was a Norwegian Publishers Association founded and Aschehoug emerged, under William Martin Nygaard, as Norway's first home-grown publishing outlet. For a vigorously literate society that, as much as Nansen's exploratory feats or parliamentary rule, was an essential step toward true autonomy.

Another urgent issue was physical health or its lack. For nineteenth-century Norway "the key words," wrote medical historian Øivind Larsen, "are overpopulation, poverty, poor nutrition, poor quality of drinking water and sanitation, poor housing conditions" along with "an abundance of diseases and misery, measured by any standards." Medical infrastructure was rudimentary at best.

Apart from improving life's basics, Norway's prospects for autonomy hinged on its ability to drive a wedge between the Swedish crown and the Swedish state—much as Norway gained leeway under Denmark whenever it complicated Danish court politics. The peculiar administrative structure of the dual monarchy may have helped, insofar as Norwegian officials resided in Stockholm as well as Christiania/Oslo, and had difficulty communicating in a horse-and-buggy age.

More subtly, the opposite dynamic was also needed. Norway's prospects would be improved by fostering greater democratization. That in turn presupposed not unity but division at home, expressed through the usual vehicles of factions and parties, opposition and argument. And the international image of a democratizing Norway would be buffed by Swedish resistance to it. The internal doings of dual monarchies are very situation-specific, but Norway's bind exemplified how domestic politics can have outside reverberations.

The years 1815–30 set a pattern of resistance. The monarchy grudgingly accepted the constitution while objecting to events marking its date. Some provisions, notably insistence on a Lutheran king, took direct aim at Bernadotte, who was raised a Catholic. Its continuation involved a quid pro quo: Norwegian institutions—essentially, the Storting—were allowed to function so long as there was no danger of insurrection. Rumors of an impending Swedish coup swirled in 1821, when Karl Johan visited Norway and publicly reviewed troops. The fears reemerged in 1829, when his soldiers scattered a mass celebration in the capital. The Storting was a perennial bee in the Swedish bonnet—starting with its first major move, the elimination (in three successive votes, over royal vetoes) to eliminate aristocratic titles. More important symbolically than practically, it sent a double message of defiance of Sweden's crown and its still-powerful aristocracy.

Still, the unhappy union was characterized by a fluidity that probably extended its lifetime. Bernadotte's aims may have been scurrilous, but the union he wrought had a constructive side in buying the Norwegians valuable time that helped to make Norway more Norwegian, by focusing on unmet needs and pushing the national project by nontraditional means. If Swedish rule could not be challenged directly, it could be done by stealth. Opponents who could not be defeated could be won over. If diplomacy was denied to Norway, other channels would be found. It helped that Norway's first *statsminister* in Stockholm was Peder Anker, Wedel's father-in-law, who spoke French. Relations were frequently strained but never broken.

Debates took up issues that might appear petty (symbols, commemorative days) or generated pseudo-conflicts grandly named, from the Battle of the Marketplace to the Battle of the

Governors to the Battle of Trollfjord in Lofoten. Norway–Sweden's 91-year marriage sounds to the uninitiated like one riddled with tumult, rather than a codependency addicted to the language of confrontation. It is easy to dismiss the haggling over symbolism as damp squib politics, yet the issues revolved around matters of principle, namely the king's right to impose in Norwegian life. The cumulative effect was to erode, from the earliest years, the union's legitimacy. Norwegians chafed, but the whole arrangement—conducted for some three decades in French—was awkward for Sweden too.

Along with patrician unionist figures like Severin Løvenskiold, a key figure was Herman Wedel Jarlsberg. Count Wedel, at the crux of an aristocratic network based in Bogstad, had worked to secure a smooth transition to Swedish rule leading to independence. Successful in the first aim, his second fell short. As the dominant political figure based in Norway from 1814 to 1822, Wedel waged an enervating power struggle with Bernadotte, who distrusted Wedel's motives, fancied himself an economic expert and tied Norwegians' hopes for independence to their willingness to pay off old debts to Denmark—another irritating holdover from the Kiel Treaty (Article 6).

Strengthening the Norwegian economy was essential to its political independence and sense of self. Some of Wedel's measures amounted to executive orders, skirting parliament, which earned him domestic enemies as well. It did not help that the economy crashed in 1817–19, that patrician family fortunes were collapsing and that the currency was crumbling even as taxes were going up. Outside factors were again partly responsible (in this case, British policy favoring timber imports from Canada).

Norwegian hopes after 1814 lay less in principles than in practicalities: righting a moribund economy, establishing a university and building a civil service that would become the de facto aristocracy. Wedel was central to it all. As finance minister he helped to secure Norway's creditworthiness by putting a new currency of *specie*-dollars on a solid (silver) basis, raising foreign loans, taming inflation and shoring up the Bank of Norway. The debt question too lingered but never fully erupted.

Within this crisis a small miracle emerged in the telling shape of early social reform. In the midst of the English blockade in 1810,

Norwegian midwives were granted legal protection; eight years later, a midwifery training school was established. Two years before that came a parliamentary initiative to subsidize doctors working in remote provinces. All this prefigured the landmark Health Act of 1860. "With this act," writes Schønsby, "the government turned away from the passive role, characteristic of a liberalist state [...] to a more active role. The government took on responsibility for public health." It marked the tentative beginning of a Norwegian welfare state, while the systematic education of medical personnel actually predated Victorian Britain, a leader of the "sanitary movement" and the preeminent world power, by decades.

Since the Norwegian *state* was a muffled entity, the Norwegian *nation* would be the increasing focus and outlet for hurt pride. This widened the scope for Norwegian collective expression, which became a matter of broadly construed patriotism rather than militaristic nationalism. If the aims were high, much of the digging was deep. Poverty and infectious diseases like typhoid fever were rife. Wretched housing and seasonal migrational patterns made Bergen the "hole of plague" to area peasants, susceptible to infection because of shockingly unsanitary conditions. Physicians' reports of West Coast conditions would not have been out of place in Calcutta a century later. Annual gatherings of fishermen for the catch created special problems; many were forced, Hogne Sandvik notes, "to sleep in an upright position in drenched clothes" in crammed fishermen's cabins. Statistics were increasingly reliable but the challenge to medical personnel, due to weather and access problems, was unrelenting. "Being a doctor in North Norway," Anders Forsdahl understates, "was a hard and toilsome life."

Yet infectious diseases were tamed and medical professionals able to keep abreast of developments. The treatment for diphtheria, discovered in Germany in 1891, made its way as a serum to northern Norway within three years. Mortality rates dropped sharply after 1815, but the birth rate only fell by the century's end, which made for a fast-rising population despite the growing exodus.

Norway's chief outward expression was broadly cultural—painting, literature, theater, poetry, history, technology and science, exploration and sport—rather than narrowly political, although the distinction grew muddled over time. This is the backcloth against which Norway produced the likes of Ibsen, a revolutionary of the theater, and Munch, rattler of the art world, rather than ideological firebrands in the mold of Bakunin or abstract theorists like Engels and Marx. And it is one reason why Norwegian national expression took its animus from otherwise wildly dissimilar personalities like Nansen, Grieg, Bjørnson, Werenskiold and Krohg than it did from politicians like Johan Sverdrup and Christian Michelsen, who were key figures in the breakup yet practically unknown outside Norway even in their own time.

Norway would become for many in Europe, including sympathizers in Sweden, a symbol of defiance and liberty in the face of long odds. By the century's end it came to be seen, almost incredibly, as a fount of civilization in what had long been thought of, when at all, as an artistically barren land. Painters (Dahl, Tidemand, Gude) and poets (Wergeland, Welhaven), musicians (Bull, Grieg) and dramatists (Bjørnson, Ibsen), linguistic reformers (Aasen, Garborg, Vinje) and folk-tradition advocates (Hulda Garborg), sportsmen (Oscar Mathisen) and scientists (Kristian Birkeland, Armaur Hansen) became insistent instruments of national expression—or, more to the point, they emerged to impose their own views about what that expression should entail. Even its explorers' feats, Norway's splashiest mark on the physical world, became a kind of performance art on behalf of a reawakened nation, one that confronted conventional wisdom while pushing global expansion of the noncolonial sort.

Politically Swedes felt bound to, but not limited by, the specifics of the *Riksakt* of 1815. Prompted by the king's lead, they assumed substantial interpretive leeway. The Swedes—specifically the nobility—regarded Norwegian independence as symbolic and mutable, and assumed that the two would grow closer together rather than estranged. Norwegians, too, felt free to consolidate politically without Swedish interference. Chained together, they were looking and trending in opposite directions.

Karl XIV's death in 1844 sparked uncertainty that prompted demands for change. For a time these differences remained latent; but from 1859, when Bernadotte's son and successor, Oskar I, died after a 15-year reign, tensions built steadily until the final break in 1905. We tend to look on that long unfolding as historically inevitable, but it actually took two generations, half a century and a great deal of tension tempered by forbearance to bring about peacefully.

The 1837 Municipalities Act, setting up new forms of local government, was an example of Norwegians going their own way while confirming the decentralized nature of Norway itself. This followed the naming (once again, of Wedel) in 1836 as the first "native" Norwegian to the post of *stattholder*, marking another step toward Norwegian own-governance.

It was not an unbroken time of stress; the failure of the 1848 "liberal revolutions" in Europe elicited little reaction in Norway–Sweden, apart from an early unionist movement spearheaded by Marcus Thrane. The mid-century upsurge in pan-Scandinavianism, mainly among the intelligentsia and the young, left Norwegians broadly cooler than Henrik Ibsen's outbursts would imply.

Over time the Swedish nobility, under reformist pressures, began attacking King Oscar I, a Norwegian speaker, for his "pro-Norwegian" leanings. Worries about Denmark (now threatened by war from Prussia) and pressures for domestic political reform also challenged the creaking status quo. The Swedish system was still based on the hidebound four estates (nobility, church, tradesmen and farmers). Finally by 1866–67 the switch was made to a two-chamber Riksdag. Yet far fewer Swedes could vote, percentage-wise, than the Norwegians of 1814. And soon another "helpful complication" arose, namely Swedish laborers who were given to cite Norway as a weapon in their own struggles against the establishment. Once again a quarrelling mother country came to Norwegians' aid.

In December 1859 a seemingly innocuous issue, the appointment of a Swedish governor (now termed "viceroy") for Norway, produced a backlash in the Swedish *Riddarhus*, the old house of the nobility. The Swedish upper classes sniffed a softening in the new king's attitude as Karl XV, son of Oscar I, had served as a viceroy only to bend to Storting pressure to abolish the office. He, the king, was rebuffed by the Swedish government and J. A. Gripenstedt, its powerful finance minister.

This was reform, not revolution; governance still reflected interests concentrated in the new upper house (*första kammeren*), with a lower house, though now dominated by farmers, having only theoretical power. Parliamentary life in Sweden splintered, with upper and lower houses vigorously disputing each one's authority. Liberal revisionists in Sweden pushed for faster moves down the democratic road. In time, Norway became a powerful if unlikely vehicle for political modernization in Sweden itself, a kind of symbolic ally for those pushing for democracy.

Much was coming to a head outside Europe as well. In 1861 Czar Alexander II of Russia issued his proclamation liberating the serfs while, in April, the US Civil War broke out at Fort Sumter. That year is less known for a shot across another bow, namely a proposal by Sweden's Louis de Geer for a new *Riksakt* that would eliminate the old presumption of Norwegian–Swedish parity and replace it with a proportional system based on population—which, given Sweden's size, would reduce Norway's say from half to a third. The idea was quickly dropped, but it left a stain. It was controversially resurrected in the tense decade from 1895, amid dark Norwegian mutterings about Sweden's "compulsory revision" of the union that could spark a war.

Over these four decades from 1860, the central question became how to differentiate between strictly Norwegian matters and broadly union affairs; where, how and when to draw the line. These questions became urgent because Norway was, in many ways, changing faster than Sweden. It was democratizing more vigorously from a more egalitarian basis, while its economic growth (from a lower level) boosted its shipping sector in a way that exacerbated tensions. The ostensible issue was consular, but the fundamental question of who spoke for Norway turned it increasingly into a matter of basic sovereignty.

Astute as ever, Nansen—an explorer caught up in independence fever—took care, later on, to blame the breakdown not on "Sweden" but rather on its ruling aristocracy which "had a tendency to look with a certain disdain on the Norwegian people." Baser feelings of being lorded over provided the emotional subtext to a union born in war, forged in cold print and haggled over with legalisms.

Rising Swedish nationalism was muddying the waters in other ways. As in Norway the symptoms could emerge unexpectedly, and through art. In 1868 the erection of a statue to Karl XII, Sweden's last warrior king who had died (on Norwegian soil) 150 years before, brought protests in Stockholm's Kungsträdgården. Swedish nationalists, like the Asian explorer Sven Hedin, regarded Karl XII not just as a Swedish patriot but as a putative guardian of Western civilization (as against, in large measure, Russia), while unchained modernists like August Strindberg ridiculed the blinkered sort of native nationalism. Norway was swept into such arguments because the union was so closely bound up with monarchy past as well as present.

As attitudes stiffened, a competitive dynamic reemerged. Barton, for one, sees in this process a remarkable turnabout in the Norwegians' favor. Norway, nominally inferior in most respects to Sweden after 1814, eventually "came to exercise a greater influence upon Sweden during the Union than Sweden did upon Norway." Half a century on, even as both countries drained emigrants, Norway had more equality of opportunity, momentum, collective self-belief, a righteous cause, a global seafaring presence and artistic notoriety in Europe. Far from least, Norway attracted a surge of international fascination it tried to leverage into politically useful goodwill. Young radical thinkers, like the writer Alexander Kielland, were admired among their Swedish peers as inspirations. By the 1870s Sweden was experiencing a paroxysm of *norvegomania* in which figures like Bjørnson, Ibsen, Bull and Grieg became the toast of (liberal) Stockholm.

In a way, the fierce Norwegian debate over cultural priorities became externalized, interpreted as dynamism and turned to its benefit internationally. In turn, widening interest in all things Nordic (seen from Britain to Germany) drew attention increasingly to Norway, with its Norse symbols from stave churches to unearthed Viking ships and mythic sagas given dramatic impetus through Richard Wagner's grand operas.

Again such an outcome was hardly prefigured. In 1814, as Kent notes, Queen Hedvig Elisabet Charlotta wrote in her diary that Norway "lacks all civilization" while "every Norwegian devotes himself to commerce and strives to become rich." Yet out of this supposedly grasping, untutored culture, this artistic wasteland unrelieved by glittering salon or upholstered opera house, marched a procession of musical, artistic and literary genius that seems inexplicable. Homilies about "cultural construction" and catch-up nation-building fall short. It was a northern echo, and not a particularly faint one, of the Italian Renaissance of Brunelleschi, Leonardo and Michelangelo that still stands as a pinnacle of Western achievement. Yet the question looms. How and why did it happen—with minimal state support—and have the extraordinary impact it did? At the risk of generalization, at least seven interwoven factors might be cited.

One was Norway's growing physical accessibility and a related sense of Grand Tour fatigue. The traditional obsession among the learned set with southern Europe, especially Italy, gave way to interest in places further north as the rail age progressed. Alpine saturation in turn set in by the 1860s, which made Norway interesting from a sporting as well as an artistic perspective. A trickle of visitors to Norway became a flood. Among Norwegians too there was a shift of the mental gravity as the north's grandeur and separate character came to the general attention.

A second reason was the emergence of multiple and competing centers of art in Europe. Norwegians were not just pulled southward for opportunity; they had a range of choices and, with it, multiple possibilities for influence. In Germany alone Düsseldorf, Leipzig and Munich attracted young talent in the decentralized pre-1870 German confederation, different names from the Frankfurts and Bonns and Berlins that shaped twentieth-century Germany. The modernist allure of Dieppe and Paris grew with the Impressionists and post-Impressionists, while Italy kept its timeless appeal for writers.

Third was the national consequence of 1814, when Norway found itself with the trappings of a state but without a definable home culture (or foreign policy apparatus). A conscious effort was made by succeeding generations of artists, a term used broadly, to establish a bona fide cultural underlay, to define as well as refine its parameters. It was a massive push to establish as well as to reestablish, to build and not just rebuild, to write history even while making it.

Fourth and closely related was the sense of urgency that animated this process. Norway was trying to catch up to itself, not just to Sweden, Denmark or Europe. Its new capital, Christiania, was also its one-time capital of Oslo. In this way the fractured timeline that so marked the Norwegian narrative came to Norway's rescue. The sense of a lapsed and half-forgotten cultural essence was real, as if Norwegians had been raking over their own, neglected and weed-filled garden. Like Finland through its *Kalevala, Gamle Norge* was an unfinished and open-ended project that assumed urgency in an age defined by headlong change.

A fifth reason, again related to the Long Night, was a flexibility made possible by that same lack of a burdensome national tradition. Norwegian artists could reimagine Norway itself: to paint vivid fjord scenes while sitting in German ateliers (as Dahl, Gude and others managed), to experiment with different forms and mediums, to keep or discard them at will with little to lose. This made them, in an important sense, artistic entrepreneurs. The upsurge in Norwegian art was equally marked by its plasticity, from its Düsseldorf-schooled National Romantics to Ibsen's realism to Grieg's outpourings of song and incidental music to the politicized social realism of Krohg's paintings and writings.

Thus Erik Werenskiold, an underrated artist whose career stretched some 60 years, could experiment in paint with portraits, nudes and landscapes while also dabbling in draftsmanship. Much the same was true for Theodore Kittelsen, while Munch too experimented in drawing and woodcuts alongside his more famous works on canvas. A German Romantic composer like Schumann labored in the shadow of Beethoven and Schubert; Norwegian composer Grieg, despite a difficult life, was freer from historical wrestling matches and unhaunted by dead giants. This flexibility allowed Norwegians to ride successive waves of change; Romantic painters segued into Realism and Modernism as the century wore on. Norwegians helped to shape the wheel as well as push it along.

A sixth reason might be called a compounding effect, one in which a small and peripheral country could only be heard by making itself heard: by combining forces to issue a collective statement bigger than the sum of its parts. For all the anguished talk of cultural clashes, Norway was truly remarkable—and seemingly unique—in fostering a symbiosis among highly original artists who themselves experimented. This process went beyond the gradual and arithmetical to become a geometric leap in output and influence. The idea of Norwegians pitching in with their countrymen is nothing special, but this suggests a qualitatively different notion. It was a will to fuse, a collective incubation of Norwegianness. Bit by bit a Norwegian mosaic was taking shape.

This art was *discretely collective*, a notion that might well be seen by outsiders as a contradiction in terms. It was also purposeful, it was synthesized, it was chain-linked, it was intergenerational and it was—broadly and not always knowingly—political.

Thus the great violinist Ole Bull "discovered" a young writer, Henrik Ibsen. Ibsen later contracted Edvard Grieg to write the incidental music to *Peer Gynt* that came, for many, to be more closely associated with it than the work's literary author. Grieg had already collaborated (if none too happily) with Bjørnstjerne Bjørnson on a play, *Sigurd Jorsalfar*. Ibsen, in turn, from their first meeting in 1895 deeply inspired Edvard Munch, who in his later years often returned to Ibsenesque imagery. (Perhaps we can now dispense with the old truism about Ibsen the sphinx and antisocial loner!). Grieg also put poetry by A. O. Vinje into music, while his Holberg Suites paid homage to a dramatic satirist of the past.

Such sliding partnerships were nurtured by the common experience of European exile and the often painful awareness of discrepancies between thickly layered European culture and Norway's blank-slate opposite. Painters Kittelsen and Skredsvig came together in the valley of Soria Moria. Werenskiold created scenes based on Jonas Lie's novels and imagined from Snorri Sturleson's sagas. Childhood friends Asbjørnson and Moe—one a priest, the other a folklorist—compiled Norway's folk tales. And this is hardly an exhaustive list. The so-called Lysaker Group, which coalesced at century's end around Nansen and friends, aimed at strengthening the national artistic standing, but it equally expressed a process already underway. Over time it was also political in the sharper sense; Werenskiold and Krohg were committed to the radical left as the initial umbrella grouping behind Venstre began to fragment late in the nineteenth century.

The emergent realism at century's end also worked in Norwegian favor, because it placed a greater emphasis on the "aware" artist, in touch with his times. Norwegian artists were not just being creative, they were engaging. This had a grounding element, Bjørnson being a case in point. The great inspirational patriot of preindependence Norway came to be a voice of pragmatism not radicalism, an expression of a boldly independent Norwegian spirit leavened with caution, rather than the "independence now!" firebrand many preferred or expected to see.

Finally, a seventh identifiable factor was a language issue that became a touchstone for a wider debate. Art is expression, and the way Norwegians expressed themselves orally and in writing opened up questions about the medium as well as the message. Writerly associates bitterly argued over the relative virtues of Landsmål and Riksmål (notably Vinje and Ibsen).

The same qualities that forced so many Norwegians away from Norway—isolation, lack of opportunity, absence of facilities, attitudes of diminishment—also came to the country's rescue, chickens of a sort coming home to roost. Passion for travel, and a Norwegian propensity for relocation, shaped a possible eighth explanation. The transformation of Norway, indeed the birth of the idea of modern Norway, happened very largely *outside* of Norway. The whole process was externally fueled, not unlike the resurrection of the Greek Idea in the late-eighteenth century Black Sea region. Right at the time of Sweden's 1866–67 parliamentary reforms, Rome, Ischia and Sorrento became unlikely centers for Norwegian culture, for that is where Ibsen wrote his great verse drama *Peer Gynt* in some feverish and fittingly peripatetic months.

So much indeed returns to Ibsen, who emerges as a pivotal figure even in a geographical sense. While his reputation stems from his ability to articulate wider social concerns and moral conundrums, Ibsen—the famously apolitical dramatist, the famous dramatist who called himself a poet—helped to mark a mid-century cognitive shift: from a Norway influenced by Europe to a Norway increasingly sensitized by the transatlantic link, as multitudes of Norwegians scratched out livings in the New World and relayed their impressions back home. And again, the mid-1860s was a pivot point. In 1864 Ibsen left Norway in a huff over Denmark, but once in Rome he heard the news, in April 1865, of Abraham Lincoln's assassination. It brought a bitter poetic outburst.

"A shot was fired over there in the West," he began (as rendered by Robert Bly), "and Europe was shaken." A killing of a prominent American by a disgruntled compatriot (or Southerner, which at the time was not the same thing) was occasion to rail against "Antique Europe" and "Germany, the home of lies." By now Norway was a catchment area for impulses emanating from three directions: Europe, America and itself.

It is easy to describe these as developmental waves but risky to assign them a narrowly political essence. An artist is not necessarily writing, drawing or composing for the nation, much less the guild, the village, the social class or anyone else. Still, a broader Norwegian project, built on powerful intangibles, was unquestionably bound up in this explosion of paint and print. It was a collective expression, in the abstract, of some concrete issues playing out internationally. In some respects they even dampened the politics down; in Sweden, they helped to disarm Norway's critics while winning some over. Norwegians became path-breakers for a non-national modernity even as they helped to forge their own nation. This thrust, conscious or semiconscious, gained for Norway a wide basis of sympathy and not a little awe.

In all the attention given to art and politics, the economic element is the unheralded third (or after science and medicine, fourth) leg of Norway's emergence. Trade-based liberalism, not wealth as such, was the main impetus. Norway's economic transformation was scarcely less dramatic, no less full of *sturm und drang* than other fields, considering the dismal baseline of 1820, let alone 1814 or 1800. Exports rose sharply, helped by the free trade movement that was sparked in Britain with the 1832 reforms, the repeal in 1846 of the restrictive Corn Laws and, most importantly for Norway, repeal of the seventeenth-century Navigation Acts.

These liberal waves came to Scandinavia under Oscar I (1844–59) and sparked industrialization. In Norway's case it came abruptly and late, from the 1860s. As with the decades before 1814, those before 1905 were marked by an upsurge in Norwegian shipping that signified newfound confidence while building more of it. A third "golden age" from 1850 to 1880 revolutionized this sector both in quality and in numbers. At mid-century, leaky tramp boats typically still carried timber by sail; by 1880 Norway's mechanized merchant fleet was third-largest in the world after the United States and the UK. A fitting finale to a heady half-century came in 1899 with the founding of a Norwegian shipbrokers' association, bringing together two Norwegian characteristics—a seagoing culture and a niche mentality—with a new and modern one, built around finance and global connections.

Liberalization wound up benefiting Norway more than Sweden, whose maritime world revolved around the Baltic. Norway's absolute advances were seconded by relative ones. The consular issue that came to poison relations with Sweden was directly grounded in shipping, even if it played out as a question of political control. Sweden's abrogation, in 1897, of the free trade arrangement that underpinned the union richly symptomized the political tensions.

A countervailing element that released some of the pressures of economic divergence came in the form of monetary cooperation. A Scandinavian currency union, backed by gold, was *established* in the 1870s—in May 1873 between Denmark and Sweden, Norway then joining two years later—and it actually survived the political breakup of 1905. The availability of cross-border capital was another mitigating factor. Individual figures like Marcus Wallenberg, a well-connected Swedish banker engaged in industry (who sat on the board of Norsk Hydro for 37 years), ensured that a breakup of the political union would not bring on a socioeconomic bust-up.

Yet heartland Norway at mid-century still seemed, to visitors, an uncomplicated place, the "unsophisticated country" that Emily Lowe and her mother passed through, displaying ways "still as simple as in patriarchal times," reflecting some misty past. In one unadorned rural hut she ate porridge and found diversion in the sole book in the house, a Bible. However prosaic or restrictive life might have been—and the increasingly mass migration must always be kept in mind—Norway nonetheless began to attract plaudits in print for its open-ended progress mixed with rustic ways.

It was in a reputational sense doubly fortunate; Norway, having gained a reformist gloss politically vis-à-vis Sweden, captured the cultural upper hand too. Seen as willing to challenge their own limitations while trapped in a situation not of their making—a perceived, ongoing case of transcending, not just overcoming their conditions—Norwegians embodied an age of seemingly endless potential. The dazzled Swedes were finally and deliberately brought down a notch by August Strindberg, the brilliant but troubled writer, who decided that the veneration of all things Norwegian was getting out of hand.

The union's final break came about in decidedly Norwegian fashion: gradually, with selective boldness and stubborn logic wrapped in heroic cloth. It was spurred by an unorthodox coalition of liberalizing forces. As early as 1874 the modern terms *Høyre* and *Venstre*, right and left, emerged in the public parlance; a decade later they had formed the main opposing political groupings. The tense years to 1884 brought the great breakthrough: impeachment of an unrepresentative government run by non-Norwegian civil servants and establishment of the principle of ministerial responsibility, making officials answerable to the Norwegian parliament rather than to the Swedish crown. This breakthrough is still cited as a benchmark by democratic comparativists. It was prompted by the Swedish king's decision to take a stand, followed by the same monarch's decision not to intervene.

The dispute to that point had divided Norwegian farmers and bourgeoisie—the heart of the *Venstre* coalition—from the Swedish upper house while aligning them with forces in its lower house. But the crux was the king's role. From 1872 this was the cranky but basically benevolent figure of Oscar II, who had a soft spot for his Norwegian kinsmen that was not always reciprocated.

Stung by defeat in 1884, Sweden the following year altered its executive power structure. This was partly a consequence of earlier parliamentary reforms. But this change, unlike that of 1866, directly affected Norway, since the foreign minister became responsible to the (Swedish) Riksdag rather than to the king. For the Swedes this amounted to a (still-limited) step toward cabinet government. To Norwegians of increasingly nationalist bent, this shifted the entire union calculus.

Even more disconcerting for Norwegians was the unilateral Swedish decision to expand the Council on Foreign Affairs, which advised the crown, from one to three Swedes while keeping a single, token Norwegian. Beyond the numbers, this shift had wider implications because it also dragged Norway in a new and unwelcome policy direction. In Norway the main nationalists were liberal and British-oriented, whereas in Sweden it had become the opposite: conservative forces, aligned with the king, the aristocracy and the military establishment, tended to be more nationalist, openly German-oriented and more agitated by imperial Russian designs than their restive Norwegian brethren.

Foreign relations were really the crux of union tension and cause of the split. Before 1884 the essential question was who *ruled* Norway from within; after that it became one of who *represented* Norway to the world. In both periods representative democracy, Norwegian style came to be seen as a symbol of resistance against Sweden, a country which by nature and tradition was more centralized, bureaucratized and slower to reform. By 1898 all adult Norwegian men could vote; by 1913, women could as well, securing adult universal franchise already on the eve of World War I. Sweden's great breakthroughs—first in 1907–9, then with full suffrage in 1921—all came years after Norway's, but the knock-on effect was evident. Finland beat them all to the punch, granting women the vote in 1906, in a move that reflected tensions in its own troubled union with a nondemocratic Russia.

Firebombs, pitched battles, assassination plots, ratcheting rhetoric, mass demonstrations, cross-border sabotage: these, the usual symptoms of unhappy political breakup, never happened in, or to, Sweden–Norway. If the union was an unusual concoction, its unwinding defied the standard noisy complement of revolution. Still, the endgame—the chess metaphor once again applies—was a drawn-out affair shadowed by bilateral tensions bubbling within a wider world crisis. Nationalism was part of both Nordic and European landscapes, but each country had a different take on it and other factors were also at play.

The representational issue that decided the union's fate was a complicated and delicate question, in triplicate. The final tripwire was also the first one, namely the question of a separate Norwegian consular service. But in fact it touched on three different levels of representation: consulates, diplomats and the role of foreign minister. In the early 1890s some were agitating to open up the job of foreign minister to Norwegians, a nominally simple but more fundamental, even constitutional matter.

Between the two lay a third problem-stratum, diplomatic representation, since consulates in some areas (notably South America) doubled as diplomats. And if the issues were muddled, the way they were dealt with could be ludicrous. In one case, top Swedish figures traveled to Kristiania—then still 17 train-hours from Stockholm in summer, 23 hours in winter—to hold a Swedish Council of State meeting, followed by a separate meeting of the

Norwegian-Swedish Council of State. Then they returned home the same night.

The 1890s present a confused spectacle: mutual distrust mixed with soothing words; a gauntlet thrown down by the Storting, which voted for a separate consular service it couldn't create; the first mention of resort to arms, by Norwegian Prime Minister Johannes Steen; an about-face by Bjørnson, the poet-politician and patron saint of the radical-republican persuasion who suddenly emerged as a prounion moderate; and the constant Swedish need to walk on eggshells when it came to Norwegian sensibilities. The man of the hour was Wedel Jarlsberg, family scion of the 1814 engineer who was an envoy in Spain; Nansen was trying to stay alive in the Arctic. "Here in Stockholm," wrote the British minister, Plunkett, mixing his metaphors, "Bjørnson's letter fell as a flash of lightning in a hard frost." It was symptomatic of a fluid situation that had even the boldest Norwegians getting cold feet.

Representation was driven by the practicalities of commerce but the fundaments of power. The Norwegians wanted equality (equal access to key diplomatic posts) while the Swedes regarded their controlling foreign policy role as a given. That the issue became decisive boiled down to the headlong growth in Norwegian shipping. And its practice boiled down to a practical absurdity, a seafaring nation that was irritatingly reliant on Swedish consular officials who were ill-inclined to pitch for Norwegian interests.

Macroeconomic policy differences were also widening, for Sweden was waxing protectionist even as Norway was going in a free trade direction. The currency union was no panacea; as the 2008–10 Eurozone crisis later showed, common money has a way of exacerbating tensions among countries maintaining separate fiscal policies and budgets. All this hardened attitudes while lessening any inclination to understand the other side.

Amidst these complications, an unrelated circumstance landed an unusual institution in Norway's lap: the Nobel Peace Prize. Nobel, who died in late 1896, privately willed his fortune to cover annual awards to be handed out by Sweden and Norway, with the Norwegians allotted one, for peace advocacy. Its timing was fortuitous and its impact on the union unclear. The tensions over the bequest (see Chapter 11) were probably worsened by the context of the times. It's not hard to see why: a Swede put a politically sensitive prize in Norwegian hands at a politically sensitive time for Sweden–Norway. The prize quickly became intertwined with the Norwegian national narrative, giving Norway sudden global visibility even as Sweden was hindering its official expression.

The union flag was an even more obvious "visibility" issue. The flag that Norway was long compelled to display featured, in its top-left corner, a union symbol that was a confusing (and aesthetically unappealing) mix of Swedish and Norwegian colors that pointedly sullied Norwegian self-standing. For the Norwegians it was the worst kind of double-binding; ridding their ships of it would be purifying, beautifying and above all liberating. The flag issue first arose in the 1870s and persisted until 1898, when Norway won the right to its own (present) flag. The issue was, to Norwegians, elementary: each country deserved its own standard, purged of irritating complications and complicating irritants. Each country, the Norwegians asserted, was just that: a country.

There is something of a "catching up to reality" about pre-1905 Norway that gives the whole independence breakthrough an anticlimactic feel to it. The final chapter unfolded in Ibsenesque, life-imitating-art fashion, a tightly wound drama from which any number of options was possible. In a masterstroke the Norwegians forced Sweden's hand while making it look as if they were forced into it. The issue was again consular, but in the confusing back-and-forth, this was almost not an issue; in March 1903 the Swedes in a communiqué (from the Boström government) appeared to dissolve the old consular partnership but then backtracked, apparently thinking the Norwegians would, as before, squabble among themselves. This pullback, in turn, was taken by the Norwegians as a breach of faith.

The Storting in March 1905 passed an "enabling bill" that would create a system of Norwegian consuls; predictably, King Oscar refused to sanction it. The Norwegian government, now headed by Christian Michelson (who, usefully, was a shipping magnate), then resigned, knowing the king would find no workable alternative. The king then proved the Norwegians right (all this transpiring in May). The Norwegians concluded, officially, that the king was powerless to govern in Norway and summarily declared the union null and void by virtue of circumstance. They even had the good grace (and political wherewithal) to so declare on the day *after* Sweden's national day of June 6. Thus June 7 became the Norwegian independence day of record. Claimants to sovereignty on principle, Norway won it on a technicality. Six centuries of foreign rule ended not by force of arms but on the force of an argument. A century of dazzling Norwegian art was capped by a flourish of lawyers.

The Swedes were thus stripped of Norway and outmaneuvered in the process, looking both guilty and guileless in the aftermath. Soon the Norwegians also withdrew their main concessionary offer, for a descendant of the Bernadotte monarchy to take over the Norwegian throne so as to ensure a modicum of political continuity. Eventually a Dane, Prince Carl, was chosen instead.

From there events unfolded quickly. A Norwegian referendum on August 13 famously generated just 184 votes to keep the union alive, against 368,208 to terminate it, a ratio of 2000:1 in favor of independence whose one-sidedness stands alone in the annals of the closed ballot box. This was followed by tense negotiations at Karlstad, in central Sweden, which tottered on breakup amid some half-hearted saber-rattling on both sides. Soothing words from the great powers helped, and a renunciation (October 26) by King Oscar II of Swedish claims on the Norwegian throne marked another end. A second plebiscite (November 13) then confirmed the new Norway would be a monarchy—but it was not, as is sometimes thought, a vote of confidence in the new king himself.

The process wound up encouraging democratization in both countries. It demonstrated a consummate Norwegian political skill, not just in shaping the outcome but in dictating the means by which it was reached. These events also proved traumatic to Sweden; no less than four men passed through the office of prime minister in 1905 alone (Eric Boström, Johan Ramstedt, Christian Lundeberg and finally Karl Staaff, a Liberal and the first identifiably party-political prime minister in modern Swedish history). Denmark suffered similarly wrenching adjustments after losing Norway in 1814 that few observers (apart from Glenthøj and Ottosen) have remarked on.

Yet despite all—the breakup, the European fascination with Munch and Ibsen, the democratic breakthrough, the polar achievements of Amundsen and Nansen—Norway retained, for many, the reputation of a Nordic backwater. Like Norway, Sweden had a rocky path in its domestic politics, with minority governments dominating up to the 1930s. But it also emerged by the 1930s as a founder of the cooperative movement, whose praises were being sung by Marquis Childs in *Sweden: The Middle Way*, published in 1936.

A reminder of Norway's undifferentiated reputation came from John Gunther, a well-traveled observer who spent some time in Scandinavia in the late 1930s. "Sweden, together with Denmark," he wrote, "may be said to represent the highest type of state paternalism yet seen in the world" by which they maintain "the highest standards of living in Europe." Norway in contrast is "less rich [...] the people are mostly of peasant stock, their chief exports are timber, paper, pulp," the ingredients of "little Norway" in the choicest journalese.

He notes, in a brighter aside, their shared ideals of solidarity and peace that befitted a poor man's internationalist. His brief account, while not condescending, is scarcely uplifting. Prime Minister Johan Nygaardsvold comes off as a hardscrabble socialist beholden to the Farmer's Party. The contrast with Denmark's Thorvald Stauning, "a modern Viking" who was also a playwright, is unmistakable. On the cusp of World War II, a stage was set for a descent into Norway's briefest but deepest night, Nazi occupation coupled with a home-grown dictatorship—a coming trial that would prove the making of contemporary Norway.

8

A Sporting Start

When life has succeeded [...] in conquering the enemies around it—natural forces, wild beasts, hunger, thirst, sickness— sometimes it is lucky enough to have abundant strength left over. This strength it seeks to squander in sport. Civilization begins at the moment sport begins.
                              Nikos Kazantzakis, *Report to Greco*

The loss of Norway is a stain on the national consciousness.
                              Viktor Balck, Swedish IOC member

Midsummer in Scandinavia is a moment to savor, its profusion of wildflowers and greenery enhanced by the magical absence of night. Midsummer 1906 was even more scintillating than usual for Norwegians. That year this ageless pagan festival, which marks the sun's annual zenith, coincided with the first Norwegian state affair staged for nearly 600 years. On June 22 a Danish prince and his English-born wife were crowned king and queen of Norway at Nidaros Cathedral. As one era dawned, another was ending: a month before, on May 23, pioneering playwright Henrik Ibsen passed away in Oslo. And in early August the wheels of national politics would start to turn with the opening of a two-round parliamentary election that would grind on, exasperatingly, until October.

First elections, enthronements, greats passing: such events carry vast meaning for a newly minted country. These were solemn, momentous events that did not much stir the popular blood. But they, too, had a precedent, and a far more festive one. Precisely

225

two months before the coronation, at mid-afternoon on April 22 (by the Western calendar) a clutch of Norwegian athletes, hearts in their throats, marched into an ancient stadium at an Olympic Games opening ceremony. It was sovereign Norway's public debut on the world stage. Norway's first, unofficial diplomats were its sportsmen, and for a sporting nation long denied its own diplomatic corps, what could be more fitting?

And it was quite a venue, decked out with flags and finery and packed with 60,000 cheering spectators, among them a smattering of European royalty. The Greeks were making a national statement of their own. Wiser for the experience of 1896, when Athens hosted the inaugural modern Olympics, the organizers—prominently led by a future king (Crown Prince Constantine) and a future prime minister (Spyros Lambros)—staged a happening that resonated far beyond sport. And the Norwegians, absent in 1896, certainly made their presence felt, decked out, wrote Alexander Powell, in their "jaunty upturned sombreros that made them look like troopers of the African Light Horse."

Powell's account, published later that year, laced those games in superlatives, calling them "undoubtedly the greatest international athletic contest that has ever taken place." With 20 countries and over 800 athletes competing, his claim is less extravagant than it seems. He paints a scene of magnificence. "No athletic meeting in the history of modern sport," he wrote, "ever had so glorious a setting [...] imagine, if you can, a magnet-shaped amphitheatre, larger than the Colosseum at Rome, more dazzling in its whiteness than the Grand Palais in Paris, its only roof the blue Aegean sky. Imagine a gathering of spectators [...] displaying in their apparel that brilliancy of colouring which is found only beneath a southern sun."

Weeks before, in the snowy depths of winter, 32 Norwegian athletes along with sundry organizers and trainers—having official imprimatur and underwritten by 5,000 crowns' worth of public funds—had set off from Oslo/Kristiania for the Mediterranean. Their journey had all the trappings of adventure, and it lent a touch of eastern exoticism to an exploratory age otherwise focused on the polar wastes. The voyage took weeks. Once there they were caught, literally, in a time warp. Greece still used the old Julian calendar dating from 46 BC, which had slipped 13 days behind the newer "Western" Gregorian system that Norway, via Denmark, had adopted in the curiously elongated year of 1700.

The destination was saturated with ancient associations, which in turn resonated deeply in a Norway busily reconnecting with its own past. Greece, Classicism's epicenter, was the ancient homeland of Olympia, where games were held for 1,200 virtually uninterrupted years. The evocative linkages captured the public imagination for what became known as *athenerfærden*, the "Athenian expedition." The Swedes were just as enthused about what one of theirs, Gustav Uggla, called the *vikingafärden till Hellas*.

Both appellations rang of Xenophon and King Leonidas, of Sigurd the Crusader and the Norse Vikings who had served Byzantium with fearsome distinction. For the Swedish contingent, led by Sigfrid Edström, a future president of the International Olympic Committee (IOC), the Athens experience left such a deep impression that it would be commemorated at a black-tie reunion dinner in Stockholm in 1956, half a century later. As we'll see, it also marked a sensitive new angle on Norwegian–Swedish relations following the union's acrimonious breakup just months before.

In his book *Olympia och Valhalla*, which explores the rise of modern sport in Scandinavia, Henrik Sandblad singles out two forces deriving from the deep past. One was the resurgence of neo-Classicist thought, paralleling the Enlightenment as an artistic ideal from the eighteenth century. The influence came via Germany and the writings of J. J. Winckelmann. It was stimulated by the Greek nationalist revolution of 1821 which had captured the European imagination via Lord Byron (in *Childe Harold*) and, in Norway, from Johan Welhaven's less exuberant pen. It was deepened by the trove of nineteenth-century discovery at long-buried sites like Delphi (excavated by the French) and Ancient Olympia, a German endeavor. The other influence was the renewed fascination with Norway's Viking roots, via a "Gotian revival" that emphasized the competitive martial virtues of a long-lost culture. These powerful but abstract notions came uncannily real in 1906.

The games, which ran for 10 days, headlined a city-wide extravaganza that included torch-lit parades, public concerts, flood-lit monuments, lavish decorations in every square, a Venetian-themed festival, public readings, learned conferences, classical concerts, fireworks in Faliron Bay and live theatre including Sophocles' *Oedipus Rex* staged (after competition hours) in the main stadium. Winning athletes received laurels grown on the banks of the Alpheus River and were crowned with olive wreaths fashioned, like in antiquity, from a tree growing in Olympia's once-sacred *Altis*. A range of events drew on ancient competitions or imaginings thereof. Gloriously over the top it may have been, but there was plenty of historical heft behind the spectacle that would be inconceivable today.

The city's mayor, Spyros Merkouris, brought a flamboyant touch later displayed by his granddaughter, actress Melina Mercouri, who as culture minister in the 1980s launched the campaign to repatriate the "Elgin Marbles" back to Greece. And no Greek public event would be complete without political spice, in this case a local election campaign that erupted, at one point, in fatal shootings at central Syntagma Square, leaving the nonplussed visiting athletes scurrying for cover and wondering what they had got themselves into.

The Panathenaic Stadium (*Kallimarmaro*) was cradled in the green folds of Arditos hill with the Acropolis and its cluster of temples, crowned by the Parthenon, forming a magnificent backdrop to the northwest. The original venue dated from 330 BC, and it remains the world's oldest stadium still in active use (archery was competed there at the 2004 Olympics). It was a prestige project of Lycurgos, a leading statesman in a post-Classical Athens desperate to regain its prestige after its defeat by Philip of Macedon at Chaeronia eight years before. For all its politicocultural heft, ancient Athens was never part of "the Circuit," the Big Four athletics contests held quadrennially at Olympia and Delphi and biennially at Nemea and Corinth. Lycurgus's project may have been a bid to crack that prestigious foursome.

Renovated by Herodes Atticus in the second century AD, the site had moldered under the Ottomans before being excavated by Ernst Ziller in 1870 and used for the "Zappas Games" that year. After rushed renovations ahead of 1896, the work was finally done by 1906, fully clad in Pentelic marble and flaring white in the spring sunshine. Athens wasn't Olympia, but for Norwegians alighting in such a setting, what did it matter?

The royalty present in Athens linked Norway, Denmark, England and Greece in a complex intermingling of blue blood. The ample centerpiece was Britain's King Edward VII, whose sister-in-law was Olga, the Greek queen. He was accompanied by his Danish-born wife, Queen Alexandra, and his son George, Prince of Wales. The panoply of Greek royals included King George—born Danish, and the brother of Alexandra—and one Prince Andrew, the (Greek) father of Philip, the same Duke of Edinburgh who later became the royal consort of Queen Elizabeth II. This titled interbreeding now roped in Norway too. King Edward's daughter, Maud, was to-be queen to the still-uncrowned Norwegian king, Haakon VII, who of course had been raised a Danish prince.

In Athens the meeting of place, occasion and association was intensely evocative. By all accounts—and there are many—it left the visiting Scandinavians gushing. Even Sweden's Colonel Viktor Balck, a hard-bit champion of sport for the fatherland, was moved by the scene. Norwegian team leader Johann Sverre and a team athlete K. A. Haagensen, along with a Swede, Balthazar Roosval, and Balck himself, all left diaries. Sverre's account, published the following year, betrays an almost childlike fascination with the sight of the Norwegian flag, with its own checkered history, fluttering on the stadium's upper tiers along with the rest. Norway's long-sought place among nations had been realized in the giddiest of circumstances.

The whole episode is a sharp reminder of the importance of context. The Olympic Games, revived as an idea in 1894, mixed inspiration from a vaguely understood past with ambition to use sport to advance humanity. They were more of a reconstruction than a true revival, while the founding body, the IOC, was an odd bird of the pre–World War I world. It was the brainchild of Pierre de Coubertin, a minor French noble who nursed grand, if fuzzy, ideas about linking sport, culture and education that borrowed liberally from others of like mind. The IOC operated out of his Paris home (moving to Lausanne, in neutral Switzerland, in 1915). De Coubertin had a proprietary attitude that might today attract the label of control freak. But he was passionately dedicated to his cause, giving his life and family fortune over to his grand project before his death in 1937.

His Olympic movement collected a range of sports that were jealous of their rules and ill-inclined to share a stage. For an activist nation the appeal was obvious. But the IOC additionally had a political allure for Norway. Hard as it is to imagine in a world awash in NGOs, the IOC before 1914 was one of but a handful of international organizations worthy of the name. It played a niche role in international life, regularizing competitions and laying a tentative foundation for global society while providing an outlet for nationalist tensions.

The Olympics provided a forum for visibility while the IOC acted as a sort of antechamber of first recognition, just as it does today. Norway was a beneficiary in 1900 when its first, tentative Olympic participation (at Paris) produced an outsized result that was tabulated separately from Sweden's. The Olympics provided a ready-made source of symbolic, political and visual recognition. On the other hand, the early Olympics were elitist and racially tinged, so Norway became deeply split between those advocating participation and those skeptical of the whole idea.

The 1906 games were an oddity in themselves. After the surprise success of 1896, Greek officials had pushed hard to bring the Olympics permanently to Greece, which flew against Coubertin's conception of rotating the games among cities. After poor efforts at Paris (1900) and St. Louis (1904) the IOC reluctantly agreed to a compromise; a separate, four-year cycle of Olympic Games to be held in Athens, starting in 1906. Extraneous pressures later halted the series at one. Because of that, those "intercalated" games became a one-off event that was subsequently airbrushed from the Olympic record, to the chagrin of Olympic historians.

The remarkable upshot is that these games—which marked independent Norway's first appearance since the Middle Ages and which helped save the Olympic movement from ignominy—officially never happened. Yet *at the time* they glowed with significance for Norway and the other Nordics, all of which fielded teams and scored some notable results. The games even marked a gender first, with a fittingly Nordic stamp. After the opening ceremony, a girls' gymnastics contingent from Denmark performed a group exhibition—making them the first female athletes, ever, to perform in that ancient arena. According to a report (April 13) in *Empros* newspaper, the Danish women's appearance caused a sensation. An "obsession has seized (Greek) females, who have lost their sleep after [seeing] the Danish women's team [...] Greek women began seriously considering the propagation of sportive exercise among their sex and their participation at future games."

According to Greek press accounts, the local population genuinely warmed to the Nordic visitors. "Zito Souidie!" (Long live the Swedes!) was heard on the streets, although the greeting may have been meant for all the northerners who, after all, looked alike. A prominent organizer, Ioannis Chrysafis, admired the Ling gymnastics system then in Scandinavian vogue and had specifically petitioned for the Swedes to send a big team, going so far as sending a subsidy.

The heady atmosphere of 1906 nonetheless had a troubling subcurrent of nationalism that had been refreshingly absent in 1896. According to Vassilis Kardasis, who compared the two events' atmospheres, "The spirit of solidarity and of friendly competition [...] had been forgotten. National competition was now to the forefront." In Greece these trends were especially marked. The so-called Great Idea was a national reawakening (εθνικη αναγεννησησς) in Greek political life. Stimulated by the Olympic stirrings and the two Balkan wars (1912–13), it later became supercharged with emotion that in turn fueled grandiose claims for territorial expansion into Asia Minor, not excluding the recapture of Constantinople (Istanbul), the old Byzantine capital. It all came to a shattering defeat in 1922 with the Asia Minor catastrophe. Nansen was a pivotal player in hammering out the controversial refugee exchange between Turkey and Greece that so indelibly marked both countries and the wider region.

The entire era marked a north-and-south meeting of opposites that registered keenly on both sides. The old Nordic–Mediterranean connection established by the Varangians had been deepened by modern developments. In 1709 King Karl XII of Sweden escaped to Turkey following the disastrous defeat at Poltava, and after five years of Ottoman exile brought back the recipe for *koldomar*, ground spicy meat wrapped in cabbage leaves, which remains a staple Nordic dish. Later that century, Swedish King Gustav III nursed a fascination with Greek antiquities, traveled in Sicily and even played a role in the rediscovery of Greek temples at Agrigento. In the nineteenth century, two influential Danes (the brothers Hansen) had given Athens the grand, neoclassical touch they believed a reborn capital deserved. Swedish writer Fredrika Bremer mingled with its (imported, Bavarian) royalty, noting her impressions as she traveled the country on horseback in her fifties.

Norway, too, was caught up in the Greek wave. Ingvald Undset was an archaeologist who specialized in the southeastern Mediterranean and its northern Iron Age connections. As recounted by biographer Liv Bliksrud, Undset, on his deathbed in 1893, aged just 40, dictated his last book, *Fra Akershus til Akropolis*, which details his life link between Norway and ancient Greece. His daughter Sigrid, a future Norwegian literary Nobelist, then aged 10, assisted.

A theme was emerging, a civilizational link stretching between two corners of Europe. Inklings of common purpose arose from feelings of kinship—indefinable yet persistent—that flowed from their shared centrality as formative European influences not in spite of their peripherality but because of it. Old states reborn, they fired wider imaginations. Robert Byron was to argue some decades later (in *The Byzantine Achievement*) that Greece, and Byzantine Greece, was a useful prism on which to view the European Renaissance. Norway in 1906 had similar cause to regard itself as an inspiration from the European edge.

Since the mid-nineteenth century, Swedes and (by extension) Norwegians had sponsored digs throughout Greece including, from 1863, at the pre-Olympian cult site of Samothrace. At Asine, on the Argolid coast, Sweden's future king Gustav VI, who trained in this field, worked on site for four years. The link was deepened by Carl Blegen, a tenacious Norwegian–American who excavated at Troy and Pylos and found evidence, on the mainland, of the Linear-B language dating back to the Minoan age. All this literal digging into the past enriched the symbolism of the Olympic rebirth, strengthened the Nordic angle and gave 1906 a unique character.

But for Norway alone, Athens 1906 also marked a national first. On April 23, in the very first competition which had spilled over to a second day, the 20-strong Norwegian gymnastics team performed their rounds. They narrowly outpointed the Danes to win Olympic gold, marking the first-ever Norwegian victory in international competition, and a collective win at that. It even brought some domestic payback, given that the gymnasts had been denied public funding by a niggardly Storting in 1900 to compete in Paris. With Norway's team gold in an ancient arena, the expression *Alt for Norge* first coalesced in the cradle of democracy and the homeland of sport.

Sport has played a wide-ranging role in Norway's national emergence and marks an important thread to the past. Yet it's unconscionably overlooked as a developmental factor. A forged written language, resurrected dialects, poetry, prose dramas, grand histories, folktales: these were the instruments by which Norway broke the Danish cultural stranglehold, swept through Sweden and wrote its way into the modern world. They animated the cultural skirmishes and molded Norway's external image.

But if the story ended there, modern Norway would resemble a disembodied intellectual construct. The printed word informed the modern Norwegian mind and gave it cultural cachet, but *actions* shaped the modern Norwegian heart and gave the country its mojo. Words expressed Norwegianness, but physical exploits heightened its sense of purpose. In the process Norway was reawakened as a country of doers as well as thinkers, or better still, a country that deftly combined the two.

This characteristic runs like a rich vein through the lives of Norway's modern explorers. Famous for their exploits, they became equally famed for their writings about them. Their cumulative works could fill a small library, while their authors vary enormously in style. Nansen churned out sober scientific studies, speeches and political tracts alongside the popular accounts that infuse his Greenland and *Fram* bestsellers with slow-burn drama. His enormous output, it is reliably said, forms the biggest single holding in the archives of Norway's national library. The main beneficiary of his multiple talents and easily diverted attention was the goal-focused Roald Amundsen. His score-settling memoirs reveal a complex man who mixed inscrutability, modesty and bottomless drive and displayed a conspicuous talent for making enemies and alienating people.

Helge Ingstad, perhaps the best pure writer of them all, documented a remarkable life trajectory of 101 years, which began in the nineteenth century and ended in the twenty-first. His progression from escapist trapper in Canada to Greenland hut-builder to Svalbard governor to Viking excavator to champion of indigenous peoples has no equal. It is Ingstad, and his wife Anne Stine, who get the credit for turning the Norse sagas about Vinland into a documented episode of history, and their daughter, Benedikte, who authored biographies of both.

This group also includes Tryggve Gran, the conflicted Norwegian ski instructor in Scott's ill-fated British Antarctic party of 1910–12 and a discoverer of the tent site where Scott and his party perished. The Gran diaries later fetched 150,000 pounds sterling at auction in London. It was a testament to fascination with his role in the Scott tragedy—and an astonishing footnote to a post-polar life that had veered into poverty and Nazi sympathy, and which left him *persona non grata* at home in his own lifetime. Together this diverse foursome established Norway as a country of complex explorer-writers with strikingly individual personalities, not rash adventurers of identical Scandinavian stripe. Even the heroic Nansen later owned up to the escapism and dissolute leanings that he called his "master irresponsible."

They, in turn, underscored Norway's self-identity as a physical nation. Sport now forms "a central part of official cultural policy" and even, in one thoughtful reckoning (in the volume *Norsk Idehistorie*) as "the most important expression of national purpose." Participation in international sporting events became, as Matti Goksøyr puts it, "an implicit, indirect form of nation-building" for Norway in particular. No account of modern Norway is complete if it leaves this element aside.

Historians of sport proliferate in northern Europe and in Norway, but many general historians won't touch the subject, prejudicially considering it the stuff of entertainment. Only with time and distance does it seem to matter. Yet even for classicists it can be a problem. Stephen Miller, who has excavated at Nemea and written copiously about the societal role of ancient sport, complains of "an artificial division by which the study of athletics has become divorced from the remainder of the ancient world," despite overwhelming evidence of its importance through painted vases, statues and Pindar's epic poems—not to mention an ancient calendar system built around the quadrennial Olympiad cycle. This was confirmed spectacularly with the chance discovery of the ancient Kythira mechanism on the Greek seabed.

Similar prejudices attend treatment of the Viking period. Historians' neglect of athleticism has extended to ancient Norse as well as modern Nordic (and classical Greek) history. An authority on Viking martial arts, Lars Magnar Enoksen, regards it as a missing third element of the Viking miracle. Whereas attention has been lavished on maritime exploits and shipbuilding innovations of the Norsemen, "almost none" has focused on an equally vital aspect of Norse life, namely robust physical fitness. It was the product of organized training and it made possible the lifestyle they led in the places they lived.

Fitness was a point of pride for kings; Snorri cites Harald Hardråde's boasts that he "could ride, swim, run on skis, shoot [and] throw javelins," as well as write poetry and play the harp. Such talents were not just valued but evidently respected as worthy attributes of a great leader. Olav Tryggvason, Norwegian king from approximately 995 to 1000, was reputedly the strongest man in Norway and its best skier. His ally, Erling Skjalgsson, was considered a close second; their physical renown shines through Snorri's sagas, penned centuries later.

A modern scholar of medieval Norway, Torgrim Titlestad, points to a fitness premium in the Viking peacetime no less than in war. He cites evidence of athletic preparation and testing, including regular and punishing competitions. "Scandinavians both at home and abroad," he writes, "greatly enjoyed sporting performances and contests among themselves." The range of activity was astonishing; it went beyond the expected (e.g., wrestling) to include swimming, rowing, spear target-throwing, weightlifting, tug of war, swordplay, ball games and horse racing. They employed techniques and coaches, and training was unsurprisingly intense. Great store was placed on complete fitness, and social prestige accrued to individuals who excelled.

The Viking martial art, known as *Glima*, came in several variations basic to warrior preparation. Narrowly, it was used to train soldiers for hand-to-hand combat; more broadly, it provided an overarching set of guidelines for how to act. It was built around a strict system of rules and was woven into the warrior code of honor. It also put a premium on agility, bodily balance, versatility and endurance as well as brute strength. These qualities were valuable in peacetime as well as in combat, helping, for example, sailors to endure long voyages while cooped up on ships, and speeding recovery from injuries. Not least, it helped to ward off the cold.

There is also evidence that spectator sport was important in the Viking and post-Viking exogenous world. Snorre's saga of Sigurd, who traveled extensively and extravagantly early in the twelfth century, relates how he, Sigurd, chose a pageantry of games in Miklagård over a haul of treasure. The emperor, one Kyriolax, offered him the option of "six ship-pounds in weight of gold or should order all his favorite games to be played at the *Padreimr* (hippodrome)," an event that, while evanescent, was considered equally costly. Sigurd's choice of games over gold made a powerful statement. Moreover the king's success betting on individual events (at his queen's expense) were said by the Greeks to presage his victory in a coming war.

Viking superiority in hand-to-hand combat is well known yet not always explained. Often it is passed off, improbably, as the result of enraged madness that was possibly drug-aided. It is often attributed by name to Berserkers, the warrior-sect with a no-holds-barred approach to battle that may have been associated with a hyper-animated subgroup known as the Jomsvikings. Yet systematic hard training—and advance knowledge of it by potential opponents—is surely the better explanation. This cultivated quality lent Viking raiders a fearsome reputation all over Europe, despite being frequently outnumbered. This also gave them a huge psychological edge in anticipation of battle. It was akin to the reputation that preceded the superfit Spartans of ancient Greece, who won some notable victories without actually having to fight.

The Norse fitness premium was a boon to societies having to survive in harsh environments. A sailing culture needed men with dexterity and strength to haul boats across land bridges. More widely—and this element informs much contemporary Viking research—fitness helped consistently to insulate Viking Scandinavia from outside attack by far larger expansionist powers, notably the Franks. For it is an astonishing fact that the chronically outnumbered Scandinavians were never (apart from Knut's eleventh-century raids from England) attacked or occupied from outside during their centuries-long heyday. Fast ships and distance alone cannot explain it.

In the nineteenth century, polar exploration and mass westward migration were the two main manifestations of Norway's active outward thrust. Both had ample precedents. Even Nansen, the exploratory pioneer, was following footsteps, in his case those of Hans Nansen, an ancestor and Arctic explorer, who 200 years before served as mayor of Copenhagen.

Nansen's physical feats grew in renown and audacity. While publicly disdaining competitive sport, he made his early mark precisely in that area. From being "merely" a champion skier (and skater too) in his youth, he was first person to ski from west to east across the forbidding Hardangervidda, in 1884, in order to participate in the Huseby ski jump competition that was finally canceled. In a little-known sequel, detailed in a later compilation (*Friluftsliv*) he turned around and repeated the feat in the other direction. His Greenland crossing and North Pole dash from the *Fram* would not have been possible without such rigorous training.

Over time Nansen wove those feats into a cultural narrative linking activity and wellness, the individual and the collective, athleticism and Norway. He disliked the term "sport" because of its implications for winning prizes. *Idræt* or "real" sport, he insisted, "was supposed to educate and strengthen the body and soul and take us out into nature," a sort of life-affirming self-challenge. "Practice *idræt*, but stay away from sport!" typified his thinking. He was effectively channeling ancient Greek notions of *kalos k'agathos*, akin to our link between a healthy body and a healthy mind.

To Nansen skiing was a means to completion and preparedness which could produce outsized achievement with social and broadly national purpose. In his telegram congratulating Roald Amundsen for making it through the North-West Passage, Nansen emphasized the feat's national side. And when Amundsen reached the South Pole in December 1911—with dogs and on skis, in contrast to Scott's dismissiveness of skiing in favor of man-hauling his heavy sledges—and returned safely, it was not just a (somewhat tainted) personal win or even a Norwegian triumph but a world athletic first that Norway would forever and collectively own.

These expeditions turned both poles into perceived Norwegian backyards and brought Norway renown as a homeland of athletes who explored (and wrote). This also helped incubate, as we saw in Chapter 2, a knack for the sort of imaginative but calibrated risk-taking that is only possible by combining mental and physical attributes into a singular, potent package.

Sport for purpose played a little-known role in the long Norwegian independence push that complements the artistic, economic and political factors noted in the last chapter. In 1861, Norwegians formed one of the world's first bodies to promote sport, *Centralføreningen for Utbredelse af Idræt,* for "the promotion of physical exercise and marksmanship." Norwegians perceived a need for mobile, territorial-defense forces should war break out with Sweden—still not likely but no longer unthinkable. Shooting became the focal point for the first, preindependence sports organizations in Norway, and practically the only one prior to 1893. To this day, shooting and sailing account for the bulk of Norway's (summer) Olympic medals haul, much of it coming in the first two decades of the modern Olympic era. Norway's first undisputed individual gold medal in international competition came in 1906, at Athens, in shooting. Later (1928) King Olav V, as Norwegian crown prince, won an Olympic gold in sailing.

In 1893 the *Centralforening* was widened and renamed to encompass gymnastics and a few other sports, which combined shooting, athletics and gymnastics federations. In 1900, the germ of a national Olympic committee was formed under Asbjørn Bjerke, before the other Nordic countries. Yet riven by doctrinal conflict, the central sporting body was badly split in 1910 and fractured anew in 1924.

If fitness and sport are important to Norway, its skiing component is off the charts. A Martian arriving in twenty-first century Norway would find a national obsession bordering on pathology. Among much else, she would find a nation that has lapped the competition. The Norwegian team at the 2018 Winter Olympics at PyeongChang took home more winter games medals (39) than any other national team, ever. Still hungry, Norway at the following year's Nordic world championships, in Austria, won 25 medals; the next best team, Germany, took nine.

The historical trail behind it is equally comprehensive. In the Norse cosmology, Ull was god of skiing, Skade his wife and a ski goddess. Prehistoric rock carvings near Alta show images of hunters on skis. Birkebeiner legends of the thirteenth century birthed a uniquely Norwegian narrative, the deliverance of the infant king, Håkon Håkonsson, to safety, and on skis—a national identity at once defined, reinforced and secured by wintertime mobility.

Skiing is equally territorial in a local sense. The modern sport's attributed birthplace is Morgedal in Telemark, the home of ski jump pioneer Sondre Norheim. Oslo was the world's first (and until Beijing 2022 the only) national capital to host a winter Olympics. Lillehammer became modern Norway's face to the world with a rousing 1994 Olympics success. Holmenkollen ski jump is a familiar backdrop to the Oslo cityscape, while the world's best ski museum operates at its base. Norway produced, in Norheim and later Stein Eriksen, skiing's global ambassadors. The sport's terminology, including slalom and ski itself, derives from Norwegian. The connection extends to art: A tradition of winter landscape painting has enriched the Norwegian visual image of itself. Harald Sohlberg's *Winter Night in the Mountains* was once voted the country's favorite painting. Norway has cornered the market in ski wax.

From the start in 1924, Norway has been a dominant force at the Winter Olympics. It is not only the world's leading medal winner on a per capita basis but also holds (depending on how the old Soviet results are tabulated) the *absolute* winning record, with more overall medals than Canada or the United States. It generated the earliest Winter Olympic legends, including its first humble-origin winner (Thorleif Haug), its first rock star (Birger Ruud) and the perennial queen of the ice, Sonja Henie, still the only triple gold medalist in figure skating, later a Hollywood film star and still later a noted art collector.

Skiing has also been a force for gender equality. "In Norway," ventures Roland Huntford, "the emancipation of women owed as much to skiing as to the plays of Ibsen and the feminist movement proper." Fittingly, Nansen met his first wife, Eva, on the ski trails above Oslo. A competition sport once restricted to men has produced, in Norwegian star Marit Bjørgen, the top Winter Olympic medal winner of all time, with 15—displacing a compatriot (male) skier, Ole Einer Bjørndalen who, in turn, had replaced another Norwegian, Bjørn Dæhlie, atop the all-time Olympic list.

The top downhill skiers, Lasse Kjus and Kjetil André Aamodt, are also Norwegian, who along the way displayed an impressively Norwegian versatility. At the 1999 world championships, Kjus medaled in all five downhill disciplines, a feat never equaled before or since.

The soft-power impact of ski success was indicated by the Norwegian anthem being played 14 times—nearly once a day during the 2018 Winter Olympics—before a vast world viewership. The pervasiveness of skiing in Norway itself is unrelenting. Any given winter weekend will deliver four simultaneous TV broadcasts of four types of ski competition from different countries.

The obsessive attention can also veer in other directions. It delivered up the deeply fraught spectacle of a popular skier, Therese Johaug, caught in a doping infraction in October 2017. Her case was splayed so unceasingly before the national media that it crowded out a legal hearing by Anders Breivik, a convicted mass murderer, the week before. The saturation coverage can reach the limits of human endurance, not just for athletes in the grueling 50-kilometer cross-country race but for couch potatoes.

It is precisely the grounding role of skiing that made Norway a reluctant entrant into the world of global sport. While the early Olympics provided a vehicle for flying the Norwegian colors, proprietary attitudes about the value of skiing made the Norwegians reluctant to share the wealth. "On the ski slopes," writes Huntford in his acclaimed biography of Nansen, is found "one of the few settings in which Norwegians come fully to life and present to each other the best aspects of their divided selves."

Here we have yet another Norwegian paradox. Sport, and specifically skiing, would seem to represent the essence of the Norwegian synthesis. It suggests a symbolic wholeness in a country marked deeply by fragmentation. Dominance of skiing is open shorthand for being the best in the world at the most complete of sports. But as Thor Gotaas cautions, the cult of skiing arose as something of an artifice in which "Kristiania's social elite used skis and skiing to fashion a Norwegian self-image," an effort solidified by "a handful of contemporary writers."

This subject too is full of surprise. For decades Norway put itself through the ringer of agonized debate over what sport was and should represent. The seeming unity of today's Norwegian sporting personality, the fearsome phalanx of its confident ski conquerors, was a long time coming. For decades sport was a force for dissensus, not consensus in Norway, and the symptoms go back to those same early Olympics that opened this chapter.

It manifested in two countervailing impulses, competition and idræt. Nansen was the most vocal proponent of the latter; in fact he spearheaded Norway's last-minute boycott of *Nordisk spelet*, the Nordic (ski) games of March 1905, held on the brink of the union breakup. It was an act that made Norway an unlikely pioneer in the use of sports boycotts for political purposes. Norway long opposed a separate Winter Olympic Games and succeeded in delaying it until 1924. For decades, a rancorous sporting debate pit nationalists against internationalists, skiers against summer sport proponents, pro- and anti-Olympians, competition-oriented mind-sets against *idræt* advocates, and privileged sportsmen versus populist proponents of "worker Olympics" that emerged in the 1920s under an influential figure, Rolf Hofmo.

Norwegians had first competed at an Olympic Games in 1900, sending a rifle club and a lone runner to Paris. It was not a full-fledged national squad (the *Turnforbundet* had been denied funding), but it still made some unusual history. Every athlete eventually wound up with Olympic medals (one of them, sprinter Yngve Bryn, won his in 1920 as an ice skater)—a 100 percent success rate that is unsurpassable and historically is Norway's record alone. More importantly, the Norwegians outshone the Swedes, the troubled union's dominant half, with five medals overall to a single Swedish medal (a bronze in the marathon, by a runner uncannily named Ernst Fast). It marked the first—and until Beijing 2008, the only—time that Norway has bested Sweden at a summer Olympics.

That result rankled in Sweden and prompted a drive to become a global sporting power. Vast resources were lavished on a Swedish athletics push during 1900–10, helped by a crown prince (Gustav) who was an avid tennis player. It proved to be a turning point for Swedish and international sport—and its origins are partly traceable to the Norwegian insurgency, the athletic sting of 1900 and the union breakup in 1905, all of which caught Sweden wrong-footed. The same developments that galvanized the Swedes tied the Norwegians up in knots. Remarkably, ahead of the 1912

Olympics scheduled for Stockholm—a golden opportunity for Norway—one-third of the Norwegian parliament voted *against* the 15,000 kronor support fund for the Norwegian team, which they thought extravagant for lean times.

Sweden meanwhile achieved breakthroughs at the 1906 and 1908 Olympics. It brilliantly culminated in 1912, when it hosted the "sunshine games" while topping the overall medals table with an astounding 65 medals, 23 of them gold. Sandblad's study suggests this as a wider example of how the biggest sporting strides come after a traumatic national crisis, as a way of compensating. Sweden's "loss" of Norway sparked a revenge factor for Sweden and for Balck, a died-in-the-wool nationalist and staunch believer in pushing sport for national defense purposes. Balck fumed over the Norwegians and their insubordination in 1905, worsened by Sweden's inability to do anything to stop it, considering it a "stain" (*skamfläck*) on Sweden's honor that could only be washed away by a triumphant wave of national athleticism.

Sport became a nationalist vehicle—for both countries—to pursue politics by other means in the years after the *unionsoppløsning*. Their occasionally ill-tempered rivalry spilled into the 1906 games in Athens, while in 1908 in London, Sweden became the first country to boycott an opening ceremony (after their flag had been mistakenly left out of the stadium). The first Norwegian football international, against Sweden in Gothenburg in 1909, was called before time because of rowdy behavior. The rivalry complicated the bilateral relationship after 1905 and formed a fascinating subplot to the 1912 Summer Olympic Games—hosted by none other than Sweden.

For the Norwegians, the problems of committing to an international athletic push were compensated for by other qualities. Versatility again came to be a hallmark of their lesser success, and it remains so. In summer sport, Carl "Flisa" Andersen became in 1908 the first multisport medalist in Olympic history, adding a gymnastics medal to his earlier silver in the pole vault. Endurance, a related quality, is personified by Norway's Magnus Konow, a sailor who debuted at the London Olympics in 1908 and ended his storied career 40 years later, at the next London Games in 1948—a feat of longevity since matched but never surpassed. Of the totality of Olympic athletes (now numbering into the six figures), a mere five have medaled at both a summer and a winter Games; almost predictably, one was Norwegian (Jacob Tullin Thams, a ski jumper-turned-yachtsman).

All told, sport was a complicated factor and a very big deal in Norway's breakout era. Domestically it stoked organizational and social disputes; bilaterally it became a charged channel to compete with Swedes; and internationally, it provided a competitive visibility that not everyone—especially in the skiing community—thought a good thing. It does seem apt that Norway, and perhaps only Norway, could manage to turn a debate over something benign like sport into a doctrinal battle touching on philosophies, principles and the country's political standing. Decades passed before the cross-pressures could resolve themselves.

Until that time, gamesmanship and boycotts marked the country's tortuous road to making its Olympic peace and becoming a standard bearer for global sport. They might in this sense be slotted into the foundation myths over the soul of Norway. Sport remains a keen and sometimes politicized national concern, if in very different ways from a hundred years ago—but in keeping with traditions dating back a thousand.

One final and perhaps unsurprising offshoot of Norwegian sport was the export of talent in the wave of westward migration. The United States was the main beneficiary. An array of Norwegian expatriate talent set some unassailable records even as they slotted into the cultural fabric of a new land. Penniless migrants from one became hall-of-famers in another. And again, the counterfactuals are intriguing: how many athletic (or other) careers never blossomed because of the call of the family farm?

Nearly a century after his untimely death in a 1931 plane crash, Knute Rockne remains the unsurpassed legend of American football and a bedrock archetype of Americana. He almost single-handedly transformed the twentieth-century game that replaced baseball as the national pastime. The annual frenzy over the Super Bowl—a single-day event so watched and scrutinized that it spawns its own advertising subculture—was something he never saw but was largely responsible for. That he was born Norwegian is a fact almost unknown. This makes Rockne's role all the more extraordinary, since the game he catapulted into the modern age, and into the American heartland, is neither an Olympic sport nor (until very recently) played at all in Norway, from which his family emigrated in 1893 when he was a child of 5.

First as a player and then as head coach, Rockne turned Notre Dame into a gridiron powerhouse. For many decades it was the figurative gold standard of the college game, the closest thing to America's national team, long too proudly independent to join an athletic conference. ND's famous gold helmets are still recognizable on sight. He revolutionized strategy, establishing the forward pass as the game's main offensive weapon. That strategic twist turned a brutal running game of attrition, long dominated by the "flying wedge," where players could get killed on the field, into the high-scoring aerial circus it eventually became.

His renown extended to mind as well as body. He parlayed early training in psychology, his university degree, into mind games to pump up his teams and psyche out opponents, presaging today's multi-billion-dollar global industry of sports psychology. Not for nothing did *Life* magazine name Rockne, along with Andrew Carnegie and Albert Einstein, as the three most influential immigrants to America, ever.

Rockne's fate was sealed and his legend launched with the plane crash that killed him at 43. He was at the top of his game, coming off two straight undefeated seasons and national championships. And his immortality was later ensured by the film that made Ronald Reagan a household name, playing a dying George Gipp. Extrapolating furiously, we could credit (or blame) the rise of neoconservatism itself on Knute Rockne, a Norwegian mountain boy from Voss who helped elect a president from the grave. Yet at the time of his death *Aftenposten*, in a rare blunder that became a classic howler, announced the death of a Norwegian-American "football trainer."

In the summer of 1896, two Norway-born emigrants made sporting history that is almost unknown. It was a record that was set neither at the first modern Olympics in Athens a few months earlier nor in the Arctic wastes, from which the *Fram* emerged a few months later. It was and still is an athletic standard, and a testament to durability that was not even set by conventional athletes. Two itinerant clam diggers, George Harbo (born in Sandefjord) and Frank Samuelsen (born outside Farsund), rowed across the Atlantic and set a world record in a quixotic bid to win immortality and riches.

Alternating at the oars, the friends took their rudderless boat from the tip of Manhattan to the Scilly Isles of Britain. They managed the feat in 55 days, despite being swamped at one stage, when much of their food (and worse, coffee) was lost. Their stirring feat, described in David Shaw's *Daring the Sea*, remains the all-time record for a two-man crew on the transatlantic route; only in 2010 was the speed record bettered, and that involved a four-man British crew. Few world records last a decade, let alone a century: here we have a nineteenth-century sporting record, set in a phantom competition, which survived into the twenty-first. What Shaw did not emphasize, being more knowledgeable of the sea than of Norway, is the degree to which his protagonists channeled some cultivated Norwegian qualities like fortitude, public humility and naivety that ultimately denied them the pecuniary award (offered by a prevaricating publisher) they regarded as their due.

Two other pivotal names in this context, equally "lost" Norwegians, are female. One, Mildred "Babe" Didrickson, later Zaharias, became the first woman athletic superstar and, to many minds, the most accomplished female athlete of the modern era. Only on a technicality was she American by birth; both her parents were native Norwegians and her three older siblings were all born there, just before the family migrated to the United States, eventually landing in Texas. (Her name was once spelled wrongly and she retained the mistake, as happened with Knut Hamsun.) A multisports star with the effortless versatility of Jim Thorpe—but without his sense of humility—she made all-American in women's basketball before turning to the track and, still later, the golf course.

At the Olympics of Los Angeles in 1932 she won two golds and was forced to settle for high jump silver after being denied the win because of an improper technique. She later took up golf, winning three US Opens—one of them in the year following cancer treatment—and a total of ten women's majors and 82 professional tournaments. She is still the only woman, ever, to make the halfway cut in a men's tournament. In a 1999 vote, The Associated Press named her the most outstanding female athlete of the twentieth century, the "most devastating all-rounder of all time" as David Miller describes her. Again, her Norwegian provenance is almost completely unknown.

Exodus also took Molla Bjurstedt, Norway's top tennis player ever—and intriguingly, its first champion black athlete, as an adoptee from Africa—to the United States. In 1912 she also made a gender breakthrough as the first Norwegian woman athlete to win an Olympic medal, a bronze in Stockholm. During and after the war, competing under her marital name of Mallory, she won a total of eight US Open championships—still the all-time record in singles, men or women—and five more in doubles and mixed doubles, an unsurpassed total of 13 trophies. Along with Helen Wills (Moody) and France's Suzanne Lenglen, she was one of the "big three" in the first tennis heyday of long skirts. She was also the prototypical power hitter in an era of soft lobs, a pioneer also in her style of play.

Loss by migration has also deprived Norway of some Olympic history. Two Norway-born wrestlers competed for the United States at St. Louis in 1904, both winning gold medals. This was still a time before formal national squads and cross-checked credentials. The pair, Charles Erickson (a welterweight) and heavyweight Bernhuff Hansen, were openly sponsored by the Norwegian *Turnverein* of Brooklyn. Archival research by Tom Schanke and Arild Gjerde has revealed that both athletes were still Norwegian nationals when they competed and won.

The researchers unearthed a naturalization form dated March 22, 1905 (the year *after* the games) showing the apparent day that Erickson took American nationality; Hansen, an alien as late as 1925, may never have taken American citizenship at all. The Norwegian Olympic Committee has petitioned the International Olympic Committee to adjust the record books, a task best assigned to Sisyphus.

This has also had the frustrating impact of delaying Norway's officially recognized first Olympic gold medal, a matter of deep Norwegian pride for evident reasons. In 1900 Norway scored two silvers but no wins; in 1904 it was denied two legitimate victories; and its four gold medals at Athens 1906 (three by Gulbrand Skatteboe) remain unofficial. Only in 1908 at London did Norway, officially and finally, score its first Olympic wins.

Part III

Perennials and Currents

9

The Reluctant Unionists

We are so similar—a non-Nordic foreigner couldn't tell the difference between us. But to us, we are so different.
                                                            Harald Gustafsson

Cross-border thinking is part of the Nordic DNA.
                                                            Ruth Hemstad

In spite of the pious aspirations[...] Norden does not yet exist.
                                                            Richard Vaughn

There is a built-in duality about Nordic identity, nicely captured in the snippet from Gustafsson. For every demonstration of unity is a pointed divergence; every claim to common cause faces its doubting opposite. The entire notion—"we're alike except where we're different"—can be reductionist and tiresome for those not professionally devoted to it. It's easy to understand the outsider frustration that Vaughn lays bare. The subject broaches one of those perennially obtuse questions of European subregional identity, debated by the earnest only to be left hanging by the same, another can kicked down a scholarly road.

Yet it matters in a world seemingly fixated on identity issues and unsure about where to draw the mental lines. For as Ruth Hemstad suggests, there is something unusual and forward-looking about a Nordic mentality that entails a worldview predicated on diffusing boundaries. There are plenty of centripetal forces operating in Scandinavia despite the obviously divergent ones that long ago forged separate countries. These reflect shared roots that, in turn, nudge their world perspectives in broadly similar directions.

A house requires a setting, and the idea of a common Nordic home or *folkhemmet* has persisted, not just in abstraction but as a basis for social policy and a term of common use. Some of this reflects the historical consequences of geography, since the Nordic states—off the beaten track, unconquered by Rome, Christianized late—are bunched together at the top of Europe and physically separated from it by open water. The only exception is Denmark's Jutland peninsula, and even there the Eider River long served as a recognized boundary. Because they occupy northern Europe physically, they define its qualities in the minds of most.

Still, the Nordic "home" historically is a ramshackle structure housing peoples with a penchant for squabbling in the frequent form, as we've seen, of war. In our context there are two significant questions within. One is whether there is such a thing as a Nordic or Scandinavian identity that meaningfully encompasses a Norwegian one; the other is whether Norway's self-perception and world role derive primarily from it or reflect other, wider circumstances.

For a distinctive subregion consisting of a handful of countries, the collective appellation is surprisingly loose. Traditionally "Scandinavia" referred to the triad of Denmark, Norway and Sweden, because of their linguistic, ethnic and racial similarities—although the latter is fading because of intercultural mixing since the 1960s and 1970s. Technically the number is two: only Norway and Sweden qualify as Scandinavian in the geophysical sense. The term Fenno-Scandinavia extends the orientation further east, as Finland was Swedish property for centuries until 1809.

The term "Nordic" expands the number to five (or five plus, including Iceland and Danish dependencies like the Færoe Islands and Greenland, and the Åland Islands, a Swedish-speaking archipelago that's part of Finland). Common practice settles on four. Nordic discussion typically includes Finland but leaves Iceland aside—a special discourtesy to the island nation that long held the Nordic torch by writing its medieval history in the world's oldest continuous language. Perhaps settling at a number like four and a half would serve the dual Nordic need for exactitude and whimsy when it comes to this slippery subject.

Whatever the number, they are all assuredly different countries with interests that converge and diverge on a sliding scale. Yet outside the region, the notion of a Scandinavian collective has hung on tenaciously. Knowledgeable observers tend to think them into the same box. While this reveals more than it excuses, it attests to similarities so broad, basic and persistent that they seem to exist of their own accord.

Typical of social science textbooks on Europe is a separate chapter—earnestly informative, full of vaguely comforting statistics—about the similarities, fraternal links and low-level but dense ties that amounted, in Nils Andrén's memorable term from the 1960s, to "cobweb integration." Pan-Scandinavian professional journals and popular publications proliferate in literature, history, politics and other fields. It seems natural to lump them together, and the tendency becomes self-reinforcing.

It's the tendency to extrapolate loosely that becomes the problem, and a reason why the shades of Scandinavian distinction often fail to register with outsiders. Within the proverbial Nordic cosmos, their heightened sensitivity to the minor cross-border distinctions may be a factor behind the suspiciously high regard in which Scandinavians tend to hold themselves, their national cultures and their region. It is a creeping form of hubris that is partly hidden by the public modesty dictated by the *jantelov* but which is sustained by generous exposure to cultural nuances that others miss. Running successful countries doesn't hurt either. The arrogant quality that off-puttingly attaches to the world of academia, sustained by the amorphous jargon that pervades professional journals and keeps the general public away, flows from a similar well.

There are also telling cultural twists—unmentioned in any textbook but obvious to the casual traveler from the get-go—that mark "the Nordics" off from (the rest of) civilization. These range from caviar sold in toothpaste tubes to *snus* (wet spiced tobacco pinched in the upper lip) to a craze for ice hotels that melt each spring to a mortal fear of the salt shaker to the curtainless windows that leave visitors sleepless and aghast when the sun streams in at four o'clock on summer mornings. But real understanding of this region requires deeper probes than fish eggs and drapery notable for its absence.

Scandinavia is often compared with another subregional grouping, the Low Countries of Luxembourg, Belgium and the Netherlands. The three are continental countries that are more closely bound geographically (sharing land borders) and via politics (forming a single political unit until Belgium was hived off in 1830).

In modern times they have pursued the "hard stuff" of political unity more persistently. "Benelux" provided the seed for postwar European integration. In 1944, in the midst of war, the three governments, exiled in London, signed a customs convention that sparked a wider idea. In February 1958 this expanded to an economic union. But it was quickly overwhelmed by the far bigger European Economic Community (EEC) project launched at the same time. Two of them (Belgium and Luxembourg) had been linked, as "Belux," in a currency union dating back to March 1922 and which persisted until the euro was introduced (at the consumer level) in January 2002. In politics, trade and money, Benelux has outpointed Scandinavia in formalizing a semblance of union. Yet it is the Scandinavians who are still perceived as more of a unit, which is impressive in its way.

This probably reflects broadly cultural attributes. The Nordic countries all imported Lutheranism, but the same Reformation divided Benelux, splitting mostly Catholic Belgium from the Netherlands and some Dutch republics from others where the Reformed Church failed to eviscerate the old faith. Foreign rule also had a hand; the Spanish Bourbons' clampdown on their Flemish property helped spark the Dutch revolt in the sixteenth century.

Language is trickier. Benelux is split between French and Flemish speakers (Luxembourgers have their own distinctive *patois*), whereas Scandinavians boast of their mutual comprehensibility. Yet Danish is the standard butt of regional humor, while Finns speak a radically different, non-Indo-European tongue; even Icelanders, settled from Norway, have to speak in English with the others. Language has also been a politically sensitive theme in the wider region. Finland's ruling elite (and its national poet Johan Runeberg) long wrote in Swedish, so there's a quasi-colonialist linguistic overhang for the Finns as there has been in Norway.

All this has fostered intercultural ventures and literary ties. It has also encouraged regional intermixing of peoples all the way up to their royal houses. From (Norway's) Princess Ingebjorg's marriage to Swedish Duke Eirik in 1312 to today's Queen Margrethe II of Denmark, whose mother was Swedish, the mixing of royalty in Scandinavia has been a frequent fact and, sometimes, a deliberate strategy to encourage common purpose.

Perhaps the main point of similarity, and cause of outside confusion, concerns the Scandinavians' social sides, their ways of behaving and doing, especially those much-remarked Nordic traits like a hankering for order, outward modesty and that elusive classic, Nordic cool. Even in informal matters like dress sense, a certain Nordic style can be detected (notably, the decline of neckties). Yet cultural crossovers don't always translate into coordinated policies, and the Nordic states have learned this the hard way. Peoples may be similar but their countries different.

But in this case, not too different: the postwar years brought multiple efforts to deepen ties along social policy lines. Many were successful, and a few emerged effortlessly. Building on prewar beginnings, they established transnational links that preceded the EEC. A raft of common measures gave Nordic peoples reciprocal rights in healthcare, pensions, consular support and other aspects of everyday life. Gradually and deftly, postwar Finland adhered to these conventions too, helping to counter the pressures from a menacing Soviet Union next door.

Corporate ties too have flourished. In the mushrooming world of postwar air travel, SAS, the Scandinavian Airlines System, jointly owned by the three Scandinavian countries, gave uniquely multinational expression to an industry otherwise dominated by national flag carriers. When Scandinavians speak of giving a collective lead it's not all pious rhetoric, nor only about governments and officialdom.

The *essence* of a Nordic home dates back more than a millennium, with the post-Roman blending of north German tribes that spoke in a similar Norse tongue, out of which Swedish, Danish and Norwegian identities grew in the late Middle Ages. But the *notion* of one—the conscious cultivation of Nordism—is much more recent, mostly post-1815. The Napoleonic era marked a turning point: apart from Finland's dreadful dilemmas in World

War II, the Nordic states since 1815 have never been caught on opposite sides of a great power conflict. In this sense it is a modern notion. Yet the term "Nordic," believes Pauli Kettunen, "is primarily a term of nostalgia, relating to history rather than to our time, built around the familiar figure of the 'free Nordic peasant'."

Efforts to keep it collectively alive have proliferated. Time after time Nordic quasi-unions have been attempted, only to be rejected, aborted or deliberated into the dust. Nordic political unity in the strictly formal sense was tested, found wanting and essentially abandoned five centuries ago, after the bloodbath of Stockholm and the Vasa royal line was established in Sweden.

When it comes to spinning history, the Nordics can be just as nationalistic as anyone. A prime example is Denmark's Christian II, who put to death over 80 Swedish nobles and hundreds of their followers in November 1520. The midnight massacre earned him the epithet of *Kristian Tyrann* (the tyrant) in Sweden. In Denmark, where he was deposed in 1523, he is more known for his reforms and progressivism and a personal style considered excessive or brilliantly erratic rather than the face of evil. It is hard to avoid some cynicism about notions of deeper Nordic unity if even murderous rampages generate such dissimilar conventional readings.

An eloquent statement of this tendency could only come from an outside observer, in this case a German historian, Stefan Berger. "I was surprised to realize," he writes, "how nationalized the work on [Nordic] historiography was [...] even in a region often talked about as if it were one large unified part of Europe." Unitary national tales, not others' domestic quarrels, typically dominate such efforts. The surprising upshot is that while Scandinavians may feel an abstract kinship, it doesn't always translate into a common pool of knowledge (or prompt efforts to acquire one). Nor is the Norwegian-on-the-street notably conversant in Danish or Swedish affairs, much less doings in far-away Helsinki or distant Riga.

The Nordic area, lacking the characteristics of either a nation or a state or even (unlike Benelux) a modern quasi-political identity, has nonetheless sustained a sense of common purpose. A softer, informal kind of unity—warranting synonyms like sustained cooperation, ideas convergence, regional amity or Nordic solidarity—continues to percolate.

Some of it comes across as rhetoric nurtured by politicians, but a lot is earnest and comes naturally. It is a quality that is more easily sensed than seen. Even in the political world it often takes informal shape. One example is the Scandinavian caucus in the UN (birthed, as mentioned in Chapter 1, in the 1950s), where their representatives meet regularly, share an easy commonality and (apart from Finns) can speak their own language and be understood. Naturally this eases the way to coordinating positions, even as it brings insinuations of a benevolent Scandinavian mafia. It did not hurt that the UN was headed by a pair of Scandinavians for its first 16 years.

Karl Deutsch, writing in the 1950s, employed the term "we-feeling" to describe the intricate pattern of communications, culture of responsiveness and shared sameness that produce what he called an "amalgamated security community" such as (his examples) that between the United States and Canada, or between Norway and Sweden: like-minded pairings that are willing to diverge without fully parting ways. "Firm friends" would be a simpler way of putting it.

Deutsch's reference points to a shared foreign policy element that has a long history but often gets overlooked. Notions of neutrality, aimed at avoiding great-power conflicts, united their outlooks increasingly from the late eighteenth century. So-called Leagues of Armed Neutrality were formed in 1780 and again briefly in 1800, with varying Nordic enthusiasm but driven by the urgency of keeping their economies afloat in times of war. "Free ships, free goods" was the refrain then. A relatively quiescent nineteenth century allowed those connections to expand beyond trade. Norway instinctively chose a neutral posture after 1905, finding solace if not strength in quiet isolation. Would-be Nordic unions based on small-state solidarity (1914), on "differential neutrality" as members of the League of Nations (after 1918) and on neutral isolationism (from 1936) all emanated from this thrust.

Much changed with World War II, after which attempts at regional defense cooperation (1948–49) proved unworkable. Norway and Denmark propounded no-nuclear doctrines but from the start were active members of NATO. Sweden stayed out, based on its war experience and worries over what might happen to Finland, its neighbor and onetime colony. Yet vestiges of common cause remained, as a "Nordic balance" was said to ameliorate pressures in the north. It is a matter of cautiously watching out for each other.

Their economies show many similarities, but cooperative efforts in foreign economic policy have likewise languished. The little-known 1931 Oslo Trade Convention helped promote economic coordination among the small-state members (the three Low Countries and the three Scandinavian states, Finland later) in the post-1929 economic downturn, but deeper coordination was beyond its scope. This has been amply proven during decades of debates over a Nordic free trade area and seen in their paths from common memberships in the European Free Trade Association (EFTA) to their divergencies over the EEC and later the EU.

Norway's geography and culture make it Scandinavian, but its history and orientation have long kept it a step apart. The Kalmar experiment that floundered in the fifteenth century, while long past, has played significantly on Norwegian attitudes. Kalmar—based in Sweden and effectively ruled from Copenhagen—is historically (if loosely) associated with the obliteration of Norwegian autonomy and the end of *Gamle Norge*. What for Swedes and especially Danes marked the beginning of great powerdom and consolidated national states became, for Norway, the progenitor of a very long night.

But while *complete* political union in Scandinavia has proved elusive, *partial* union, often in the form of dual monarchy, was the rule, not the exception, from the fourteenth until the twentieth centuries. In their times Denmark–Norway, Denmark–Iceland, Sweden–Finland and Sweden–Norway were all manifestations of it. This produces a sub-sub-factor of regional identity with still other complicating spin-offs. One noted example was the Danish–Norwegian union that ended officially in 1814 but which clouded the relationship for another century and shifted into yet another gear after 1905—prompted by Norway's break with Sweden.

For centuries the notion of "something Nordic" and thus interconnected has been egged along. There is a visual component in the common flag designs, in each case a cross on brightly colored background. Sometimes it has morphed into a kind of meta-nationalism and sounded as a clarion call for action. The outstanding example of this was the mid-nineteenth century pan-Scandinavian movement that was "intellectual" as well as emotive and political. It flared then faded just as quickly.

Historically any talk of political unity has to be set against an awkward backdrop, the numbingly endless wars that ravaged the region for centuries—conflicts that may actually have reinforced the sense of commonality, precisely because few people could fathom why they were being fought at all or could grasp their quasi-incestuous underpinnings. Even a dedicated Nordic specialist has a fine time keeping the region's conflicts apart in name, let alone their aims or outcomes.

Even limited to fairly modern times, the list is impressive: the Sten Sture Wars of Christians I and II (1471, 1520); the Northern Seven Years' War (1563–70); the Kalmar War (1611–13); the Emperors' War (1625–29); the Torstensson War (1643–45); the Karl Gustav Wars (1657–60); the Scanian War (1675–79); and the dragged-out Great Northern War (1700–21). Wider European conflicts from the Thirty Years' War (1618–48) to the Napoleonic Wars (1798–1815) and the Prussian-Danish War (1864, with a preview in 1848–51) also impinged directly on the region. Generally overlooked are all the wars that nearly were—Sweden's with Norway in 1788 and 1905 for instance—or conflicts so brief that it's hard to label them wars (e.g., Bernadotte's Norwegian campaign of summer 1814). A skeptical outsider might well conclude that with friends like these, who needs enemies?

Most were fought for territorial adjustment, revenge or dynastic muscle-flexing. Some were continuations of other wars, after a pause. Many were "spill-up" conflicts, power plays between groups jostling for influence: aristocracies and monarchies, church and state authorities, commercial and landed interests. Few were decisive. Some were lusts for wider tax bases, ruinous new wars launched to pay for previous ones, perpetuating cycles of violence. Killing each other was an oddly Scandinavian form of nation-building. The domestic origins of many of the conflicts also make them hard to grasp by outsiders who only see, for example, what "Denmark" did, as opposed to what the Danish (or Swedish) crown—in both cases an elective institution—was doing. Yet these elements often get overlooked, even in Scandinavia, because of the tendency, among Nordic historians, to elevate their own national stories and subtly underplay their neighbors'.

A great deal of history, hopes and hype underpin the Nordic-unity theme, outstripping the fairly meager high-policy results in modern times. By this logic we see agreement on the margins and disagreement on the essentials, which is manna for the cynics. Another interpretive problem may be that agreement tends to focus on abstractions and shared general sentiments—like support for basic welfare or environmentalism—while differences tend to revolve around measurable or concrete issues, like NATO or EU membership. What we see depends on what we value. Whereas a political scientist might see divergences over Europe as a symptom of failure, a sociologist might regard their common commitment to subsidized child care as evidence of bedrock similarity. Ruth Hemstad's fetching notion that deep-seated (Protestant) guilt is a shared—but unmeasurable—modern Nordic trait exemplifies this conceptual split.

Pointedly, too, most cooperative initiatives have emanated from Sweden or Denmark. All too frequently, Norwegians have opted out or looked in a different direction. Sweden, at the geographical center of Scandinavia and the biggest of the lot, is a natural proponent of Nordic identity. So are Danes, given their pivotal Baltic role for centuries. It was Danish figures like N. F. S. Grundtvig, an educational reformer, and Adam Oehlenschlæger, a dramatist, who forcefully articulated the pan-Scandinavian vision, and more recently a Danish prime minister, Hans Hedtoft, who tabled the Nordic Council idea. The veneer of sameness among members may be important in a region sharing deep democratic roots, but it will always have some rough edges and be jaundiced by historical hurts not entirely forgotten.

The Nordic unity theme usually resurfaces at turning points or crises such as the 1840s, World War I, the 1930s, the late 1940s, late 1960s and early 1990s. And generally, it has not been seen as an alternative to the national path but as a corollary to it. As Louis Tissot's study of 1848 and its Scandinavian effects indicated, the "Nordic renaissance" paralleled the strengthening, not weakening, of nationalism in the region. In the 1870s a little-known Scandinavian currency union was established at the very time Norway and Sweden were bickering politically: a neat and perplexing counter-example of hard interests trumping sentiment and a robust indication that Scandinavians are not utopians.

Regional common interests, prompted by fears of German imperialism, led to meetings of the three Scandinavian kings early in the twentieth century. This took on urgent political significance in 1914, when World War I threatened countries trying to stay out. Having managed that feat for four years, the idea of deeper cooperation led to common position-taking within the League of Nations after 1918. In the 1930s it brought regular meetings of their foreign ministers. In the 1940s as the Cold War developed, it brought efforts to forge a Scandinavian defense pact. A once-royal matter had segued into a governmental one.

In turn, a straight strategic and political matter widened into economics. An attempt to forge a Nordic common market in the 1950s reached the exploratory stage, before they settled on membership in the EFTA, formed in 1959–60, with Britain in the lead, as an alternative to the EEC. In the late 1960s, they fruitlessly negotiated a Nordic customs union (Nordek) as a halfway house between the limited EFTA and the ambitious EEC. In the early 1990s they tried valiantly to coordinate a common entry into the EU.

It sounds flippant to say that each of these efforts flailed and ultimately failed, though fail they did in an important sense. It sounds even harsher to suggest that they were willed failures, deliberate (collective) steps backward in order to take two steps ahead individually. And it's easy to dismiss such efforts to coordinate Nordic policy as halting, process-driven "steps toward steps" fated not to work out because their hard interests were too diverse and their collective heft too limited. Still, their dogged persistence in probing possibilities is noteworthy in itself. There is much truth in Henrik Nissen's point about the Nordics being "united on the march, separated in battle," which speaks to the half-full versus half-empty crux of the Nordic paradox. Yet the Scandinavians always manage to give voice to pragmatism: that their convergent outlooks make joint policy seem unnecessarily formalized. Why shackle yourself to your neighbor when you agree with her?

If the Scandinavians have often overreached in their aspirations for unity, outsiders have made the same mistake. Early in World War II, British efforts to pull the Nordic region into the war foundered partly on overblown hopes of linking the Finnish Winter War (in 1939–40 against the Soviet Union) with the fight against Germany. Memoirs by Winston Churchill and his diplomatic aide John (Jock) Colville make it clear how closely, and disastrously, British strategic thinking regarded Scandinavia as a malleable unit. Specifically, a desire to help the Finns fight the Soviets led to plans for landing "volunteers" in Norway and Sweden; these would become an occupying force that would drag both Norway and Sweden into the war against Hitler.

The idea met (writes Colville) with "unexpectedly severe" Swedish and Norwegian opposition and was dropped when the Finns sued for peace in March; only Hitler's invasion of Norway (and Denmark) turned the Norwegians decisively westward. That invasion, in early April 1940, marked a point of no return for Scandinavia, terminating their common positions and forcing them in different strategic directions. The similarities that later marked their developmental aid policies ameliorated these differences without eliminating them. NATO member Norway was never in a position to criticize US policy the way the government of neutral Sweden did, for example, over Vietnam, even if many of its citizens and some of its leading figures tacked that way.

Only at the broadly cultural level have intra-Nordic ties really flourished, drawing on their deepest common roots while plying the path of least resistance. The litany reads like a worthy but dull roll call of common endeavor. First off was the Nordic Inter-Parliamentary Union of 1907, a high-minded initiative whose purpose dissipated over time. The Norden Society was started in 1919 along different lines, as a private, membership-driven effort with national chapters and broadly educational aims. (Anecdotal indications are that it appeals to younger enthusiasts and not just retirees with time on their hands.) In 1952 the Nordic Council began its annual, week-long deliberations that still continue, if again in an advisory capacity and with limited goals.

But similar aims and willingness to confer is very different from staking out identical positions, much less pooling national resources, and such efforts rank as fairly small potatoes in policy terms. The results—annual literary and film prizes, consultative bodies, learned deliberations—scarcely impinge on the hard stuff, matters of government direction, priority or budget. But they do soften the edges of the hard stuff in a way that renders real conflict unthinkable.

A common cultural milieu is deepening through the growth of TV shows, like *Bron* (or *Broen*), The Bridge, which features mixed casts and dialogues that switch languages along with the characters. The popular talk show *Skavlan*, with its "Svorsk" mixing of Swedish and Norwegian encouraged by its genial host, is another good example. Centuries of interbreeding is reflected in TV programs like *Hvem tror at du er?* (Who do you think you are?), which traces well-known individuals' backgrounds and often their roots in neighboring lands. Between effortless regional travel, social media and broadcast productions like these, any 8-year-old can grasp something alive, kicking and common in today's Scandinavia.

These doings also reflect a long-standing tendency to look on their neighbors as kindred peoples and not just regard each other coldly as buffer territories against the Germanies and Russias of the world. It indicates a sense of shared values that goes beyond playing good, while falling well short of playing God. The very fact that Scandinavians keep trying to coordinate efforts in so many different fields is a sign of *something*, apart from stubbornness or mildly heroic stoicism. The image we are left with is one of a sprawling Nordic family, rather than a close-knit nuclear one, chains of cousins rather than siblings.

What this tendency shows is this: the notion of a "Nordic essence" is *not* to be seen in formal terms, as a structure or even—to use a beloved term of social science—as a "framework" but rather in plasticized or fluid ones. Less solid than liquid, it is an impulse that is bendable to circumstance. It has a way of seeping into fissures in the world's power structure. Instead of wedging those cracks open, the Nordic "presence" serves as a sort of glue to shore up international weak points. The Nordic states often stand accused of sanctimony on issues like development aid and climate change, but much of the Scandinavian involvement in world affairs is in fact pragmatic, unofficial, nongovernmental and quiet to the point of unseen.

The evidence of informal networking pops up in places both expected and unexpected. Its practitioners may be anything from aid personnel in Palestinian refugee camps to diplomats at Arctic Council meetings to athletes at Nordic ski championships to scholars at regional academic conferences to package holidayers at Mediterranean beach resorts, where only Scandinavians seem sufficiently brave, daft or sun-deprived to roast in the midday sun.

Close Nordic proximity can also work the other way around, by exacerbating differences at sensitive moments. The revelations in 2018 that Erik Solheim, a Norwegian politician who briefly headed the UN's environmental organ, had spent huge sums jetting around the world with various family members, ostensibly on fact-finding missions, provoked regional uproar—though less in Norway than in Sweden and Denmark, which actually suspended their payments to the body in angry retaliation. In their eyes his sins were triple: a Nordic public servant flouting public probity, an oil-rich Norwegian taking economic liberties in a cash-strapped global body and a would-be environmental activist leaving a frightful carbon footprint unbecoming of ecology-minded Scandinavians.

Even in their ostensible inability to unite, the Nordic peoples are linked by shared values and a general impulse toward collective decision-making that prioritizes *coordinated activity* as opposed to *joint action*. Scandinavians short on backslapping bonhomie still do a lot of bonding among themselves and much good toward others in a hard-to-measure sense, filling voids and providing assistance, expertise and relief. Their unheralded efforts are generally informed by good intentions and are worked into policy thanks to persistence and pragmatism. They may not bake the world's cake, but they represent the egg yolks that help the ingredients hang together.

Still, their lack of success in creating organizations that matter has been repeated and conspicuous. Hopes for formal unity have taken multiple blows since World War II. Two of the most significant postwar developments—the Cold War and European integration—more or less forced them to define their own interests separately and go their own ways, the former in the late

1940s (with the creation of NATO) and the latter in the 1970s and again in the early 1990s.

January 1995 marked a decisive break in the old Nordic free trade front that began to crack in 1973, when Denmark joined the then-EEC. Sweden and Finland entered the EU in 1995 in little-noticed defiance of their stated longtime outlooks based on principles of neutrality. Norway stayed out: now it was oil rather than fish to blame (or, perhaps, to thank), and now Norway was the odd one out. Norway had been knocking on the door since 1961 and had a history of establishment efforts to join Europe that either fell apart at the negotiating stage or were (twice) taken to a vote and rejected by the people. At a deeper level it was clear the Norwegians could not and did not countenance joining any outside body that smacked of continuous or permanent political union to which they would have to answer. Here we find the real crux of Norway's sense of difference.

The Scandinavian front was equally fragile when it came to European monetary union. Finland abandoned its currency, the *markka*, and joined the Eurozone (without a vote), taking it into some acrimonious debates in Brussels over budgetary politics in 2007–8 and beyond. The Danes however opted out, and the Swedes rejected the euro in a 1998 referendum. Iceland, so easily left aside from such discussions, never joined the EU but, after the 2008 financial crisis hit, the country began sending out feelers.

The notion of Nordic unity has taken an equally severe hit intellectually. Regional histories focusing on Scandinavia have elicited much "thinkers' doubt" over whether it exists in any meaningful sense. *The Cultural Construction of Norden*, a collection in the late 1990s, typified this new interest and deepening skepticism. "One cannot defend the hypothesis," writes Henrik Stenius, "that a common Nordic heritage is rooted in a feeling of belonging to a common, specific Nordic culture." Perhaps it never was. "Even in 1721," Øystein Rian adds mischievously, "one would have to climb to the moon to see a Scandinavia characterized by uniformity."

It is remarkable, as Henningsen notes, that Nordism has been such a tenacious cultural touchstone given that it has rarely been spelled out or formalized. It can amount, as Uffe Østergård dismissively notes in the same volume, to "Nordic myths and caustic outpourings of yesteryear." As if to repudiate past, pious hopes of Nordic unity (or even banish all optimism from the discussion), recent Scandinavian scholarship has bought heavily into Benedict Anderson's notion of "imagined communities," arguing that much of the supposed Nordic identity is actually artificial and concocted. Similar arguments, of course, have been thrown at Norwegian attempts to build a cultural nation in the nineteenth century. Some of this is academic fad-following, some is hair-splitting, and some is bandwagoning skepticism following the 1995 divergence; indeed at some level it is a rhetorical exercise, interesting but inconsequential.

It is also possible the pendulum has swung too far in the other direction, given the (noted) penchants for mutual Nordic ease, shared *jante* attitudes and fellow-traveling, along with like-minded policies. When the Nordic governments created a passport-free zone in the early 1950s, it was a reflection of the past as much as a step into the future. The result is an interesting twist: the overt expression of Scandinavian unity is far more prevalent at the elite than the popular level, while in practical terms it is more evident at the level of civil society. Officials may do the talking, but their societies do the walking.

A minor example is the annual "artist of the year" prizes given late each year by the *Nordiska Råd* (Nordic Council), an event that rotates among the Nordic countries. It is pleasantly earnest, high-minded and low-key, very Scandinavian in style as well as in content (which means that it never, ever runs over time). It's a sort of restrained love-in; few, apart from the prize winners, would call the event exciting. The Nordic prime ministers dutifully appear; award-winners gush that *Norden*, acting in concert, is alive and well and showing the world a better way. Yet there is something slightly complaisant about it, a touch nostalgic, faintly pro forma. It is not negative or misleading but a sentiment nonetheless.

Such happenings reinforce the notion that a single Nordic approach is an idea that represents, as per Thornton Wilder, the triumph of hope over experience. Whatever clunky label is applied—"Nordism," "Nordicity," or even worse, "Norskism"—and whatever unit is involved (the Nordics or plain-vanilla Scandinavia), the idea that it is, historically, more fake than real may be jarring, but it is quite widespread. This is not, of course, a universal view; some scholars, notably Christine Ingebritsen, a longtime observer of the region, cite plenty of commonality in their foreign policy postures and public superegos as "norm entrepreneurs." "Scandinavia has emerged as a moral superpower," she also holds, an assertion referencing both their outsized influence in the world and the openly ethical component of their general approach; no less intriguing is her use of the singular.

The very notion of union remains exceptionally vexed for Norway, in ways very unlike for Sweden or Denmark or even Finland. Six centuries of domination by its neighbors have left an indelible mark and, perhaps, a wild-card tendency to differ. Thus to regard Norway only, or even chiefly, via the prism of its Nordic setting—what we might call the "embedded nation" view of Norway—creates a host of misconceptions.

Probably the main one has to do with that endlessly touted Nordic standard, equality, which is of course a powerful basis for democracy and the rule of law; but as a principle of foreign policy sameness it has long been conspicuously absent. The regional power fluctuations have been, until the nineteenth century, unrelenting. The Napoleonic period was the harbinger of a more permanent sense of balance among them—but even then, Norwegian history remains colored by the fact that Sweden's last aggressive war was fought on their soil. Such elements seem negligible to most outsiders who typecast them as similarly compact welfare states where social democratic parties rule and neutralist tendencies lurk below the surface. But to the Nordics themselves, the gradations get magnified and take on outsized importance.

In terms of national economy, equality is again a rough not an absolute metric, and there are striking divergences in, for example, the Swedish and the Norwegian approaches. Both are market-oriented players in the global economy, yet their niches (even before oil) have differed. Sweden was long more offensively oriented in its national champion strategies, while Norwegians plied a very different, mainly defensive strategy, aimed at marshaling their national assets. Whereas Sweden has had a big-name presence via companies like ASEA, Volvo and Ikea, Norway hasn't (and in an interesting recent twist, an eponymous entity, Moods of Norway, went bankrupt).

Norway traditionally languished in a double regional shadow: a collective one cast by an obtuse Nordic construct and individual ones cast by grasping neighbors. However defined, Scandinavia is Norway's cultural nesting place. But it's hardly the only frame of reference, and arguably less decisive than ever. After 1995 especially, the divergent trend reinforced the Norwegian reflex against outside political union in any form. The result can be interpreted as weakness; Norway's relationship with the EU—a dues-paying nonmember, a nonvoting part of the single market—is often derided as humiliatingly one-sided. But it has also been a source of liberation for Norway, which is paying for its relative freedom. It is no coincidence that Norway's boldest steps toward defining its own world identity have come since 1995 and unsurprising that Norway has been hailed by anti-Brexit Remainers as well as Brexiters as an example to consider.

Norway's increasing northern focus was for a time obscured by a broader regional focus on the post–Cold War Baltic region. Norway signed on to the Council of Baltic Sea States, a loose body formed with high intentions in 1992, but its membership was *pro forma* (even distant Iceland joined). And with Sweden's and Finland's EU entry, Baltic and Nordic identity became even more diffuse. What was intended as a moment of orchestrated unity for the wider region instead fizzled and in some senses backtracked. With the EU's dramatic expansion in 2004 the contrast was deepened, as the Baltic Republics of Lithuania, Estonia and Latvia joined the EU, leaving Norway (and Iceland) alone in all of northern Europe as national free agents.

For decades, Europe was a focus of common Nordic activity; 1995 all but removed it from the agenda. The difference can be discerned in news coverage. In Denmark and Sweden, European coverage is prominent, almost an extension of the domestic environment, while in Norway it can seem like a passing, foreign concern. And since 2000 the most emotive of European issues, immigration, has also been the one that has most profoundly divided even those Scandinavian states that are EU members—notably accommodative Sweden as against far more restrictive Denmark.

For equally persistent and more root-historical reasons, Euroskeptical Norwegians also warrant the label of reluctant Scandinavians. Their reluctance to join forces is often best interpreted as a determination not to be pushed, or taken for granted. "When writing about pan-Scandinavianism in general, and on political Scandinavianism in particular," write Glenthøj and Ottosen, "historians often focus on the relationship between Denmark and Sweden, leaving Norway to some extent as the odd one out." Norway has long been forced by circumstances to define itself as *not* its neighbors, the quietly insistent rebel that knows it's different and that those differences matter quite a lot.

Finland is set off by language and less obviously by geopolitical circumstance; Norway's differences reflect posture and attitude, drawn from development patterns and historical memory. Westerners often look askance at the Balkans as a hopeless quagmire of never-forgotten local hatreds, but a similar, if far milder, national-historical slate of slights animates the collective Norwegian mind. These often slip the attention of outsiders because of complicating specifics in the Norwegian experience.

We find revealing glimpses in a trio of general works by journalists taking a comparative glance at Scandinavia at three different periods: John Gunther in the 1930s, Guido Piovene in the 1970s and, in a recent volume, Michael Booth. Each work is noticeably poorer on the Norwegian side. Piovene's chapter features Norwegians grumbling about Sweden, while Booth's is animated by the still-fresh Anders Breivik terrorist attacks. Gunther's survey, mentioned in Chapter 7, unflatteringly compares Norway with its neighbors in its culture and leadership.

In such works Finland often gets the best treatment, because the writers must try harder to understand it while lending it the sympathy of the gallant underdog. Norway typically is assigned a reflective profile. In Piovene's (briefer but more penetrating) treatment, Norway comes out as "an imperfect Sweden," unfairly measured via its neighbor much as Canada gets seen through the American filter. Gunther is surprised that a common laborer could head up an interwar European government and still be so well read. Booth's admiration is evident, but his analysis is colored by the singular nature of Utøya.

Such treatments have reinforced traditional views that Norway is the younger sibling in a Scandinavian family, subject to informal rules set by others. Presumed to share the same qualities, it is underexplored because those traits are covered elsewhere. When Norway's regional complexities start to impinge, interest begins to pall. There's a common pattern in outsider treatment: Denmark first, Sweden the main attraction, Finland the intriguing other; once in Norway, the tendency is to relax and enjoy the view. Longtime inattention by most observers to the far north reinforces the problem, since along with oil and the EU the Arctic distances Norway from its Nordic neighbors.

Modern Norwegians have shown a marked reluctance to jump into Nordic cooperation. In the 1920s notions of "political Scandinavianism" were floated—especially in the active press debate that Herbert Tingsten, a prominent Swedish editor and analyst, wrote copiously about—but never took root because the Norwegians in particular were critical. Norway's Greenland claims in the early 1930s aroused strong antipathy in Sweden. So, surprisingly, did Norway's seeming reluctance to accept compulsory conciliation procedures it had once championed and which were long considered basic to a common Scandinavian foreign policy.

Fraternal Norwegian resistance was equally strong in 1994, when Finland, Sweden and Norway, the three EU hopefuls—or rather, their governments—carefully arranged their national referendums in that order, perhaps naively anticipating that Norwegians might be inclined to follow suit (the Finns were thought to be most likely to vote yes). The Nordic dominos refused to fall; Finns and (more narrowly) Swedes opted to join, only for Norwegians to say No a few weeks later.

One institutional facilitator of the new agenda, founded just a year later, is the Arctic Council. It is in some senses a very Nordic kind of body: small, low-key, limited in its aims, consensus oriented, scientifically focused. Its membership has a Nordic majority: of the eight permanent members, five are Nordic. Norway's leading role has already been touched on. Its effective control over chunks of the Arctic seabed is obviously crucial for strategic, energy and environmental considerations that are extraneous to Sweden or Finland. The far north, like the EU, is a test of Nordic cooperation, and one area in which Norway leads rather than lags. Norway's role compared with the past is less Nordic and European, minimally Baltic, palpably Atlantic and emphatically northern. The broad result has turned some powerful historical tables.

A community of Nordic values remains intuitively valid at street level and close to the hearts of its leaders, but it is challenged by realities on the wider stage. More than a convenient fiction, it falls short of hard fact. Nordicity never attained take-off velocity as a basis for hard policy, and it never built the critical mass to be an actionable unit on the world stage. Its impact is primarily seen on the soft-power side: not unimportant but rarely central, and just as usually unseen.

And yet, the Nordic countries have a mischievous way of wrong-footing the doubters. A huge joint NATO military exercise in Norway in fall 2018, called Trident Juncture, for the first time involved the participation of Swedes and Finns, despite their neutrality. Just when it looked like Nordic security policy was diverging ineluctably, a sense of common purpose reemerged.

Scandinavia remains Norway's chief point of public reference, yet much perspective is lost if we posit Norwegian history and society solely in terms of the Danes and Swedes who dominated them for so long. To truly understand Norway's outlook on the world we need to look beyond Scandinavia for perspective.

A range of intriguing civilizational and historical parallels with Greece, broached in Chapter 8, tempt a wider analysis that is better left for another context. The same goes for Portugal, another periphery of a periphery (Iberia being its Scandinavia) that developed a similar maritime-based culture, exploratory tendencies, Atlanticist orientations, close British ties and, perhaps, an inbuilt tendency toward understatement deriving from centuries of being overshadowed by Spain.

In terms of political nationalism, Finland is Norway's regional alter ego. Latecomers to statehood, they each endured long stretches of Swedish rule. In the nineteenth century both countries were nominally ruled by neighboring countries via personal royal unions—loose arrangements that encouraged grassroots nationalism. Both countries constructed cultures on top of older folk bases, with an ear to the past. If anything Finland's *Kalevala*, the national epic poem, resounds more deeply for Finns than *Norwegian Folk Tales* does for Norwegians. Each country is officially bilingual, and both language histories touch on sensitive power relations. Swedish is to Finns as Bokmål is for many Norwegians, vital but full of cultural baggage.

Such overlaps have been emphasized by historians like Stefan Berger and Øystein Rian. Another, Barton, gives a nuanced parallel; Finland, he points out, could not draw on a Viking past, so its history was even more "imagined" than was Norway's. The Dutch ties elaborated in Chapter 6 corroborate the convergent similarities outlined by Johan Huizinga, a Dutch cultural historian, while Scotland—another small country overshadowed by a bigger, bordering neighbor—shares a generous political parallel with Norway to match their shared history.

Rian has drawn a different and intriguing similarity between preindependent Norway and nineteenth-century Hungary. Both languished as the lesser half of a dual monarchy, in Hungary's case as a supplicant to the Vienna-based Habsburg line. Only in 1867 did Austria–Hungary become a genuine binational arrangement, and it was never an equal one.

Still another parallel of the time concerned Ireland, which made Sweden–Norway a powerful Gladstonian reference point. The longtime British prime minister was struck by the Norwegian desire for full equality with Sweden within the dual kingdom and used it as a selling point for his late-career crusade to secure Home Rule for Ireland. "Freedom and voluntaryism" were his catchwords, with Norway inspiring his search for a viable Anglo-Irish relationship.

When it comes to four key national characteristics—wealth, landform, grassroots democracy and dealings with Europe—Norway's most obvious counterpoint is Switzerland. Here again, not all is as it seems. Norway is geographically remote, Switzerland central; Norway is seascaped, Switzerland landlocked. Yet politically they are both European outliers. Their topographical essence is similar: mountainous, cut by long valleys and boiling rivers, unforgiving landscapes that are a hiker's dream and a roadbuilder's conundrum. That dictated similar development patterns—isolated communities, scattered cities, revered rural traditions, much-traveled valley routes—which, in turn, nurtured a suspicion of foreign designs that dampened their otherwise very exposed cultures and economies. Their atomized societies became distinctive, mosaic-like forms of nationhood, mostly devoid of aristocracy. It follows that no other countries have so stoutly resisted the notion of a European superstate to the point of avoiding political Europe as such.

Both are driven by hard-nosed, modern self-interest. Norway is in the European Economic Area, a halfway house vis-à-vis the EU, while the Swiss have a looser, bilateral arrangement with Brussels that keeps them (unlike Norway) outside the customs union. Each country, too, has had an economic ace in the hole that vaulted it from poverty to the pinnacle of world wealth—the Swiss with banks, the Norwegians with oil—that poses ready-made caricatures about gnomes of Zürich meeting blue-eyed Arabs. A history-driven need to differentiate kept them out of the EU; zealously protected wealth will almost certainly keep them there.

In terms of socioeconomic development, Norway has been paired with Austria. Traditions of "social corporatism"—decision-making based on agreements hammered out by big interest groups—have marked both countries, Sweden to a lesser degree. Peter Katzenstein contrasted them with countries practicing forms of "liberal corporatism," like Belgium and the Netherlands.

And when it comes to manifesting its northern identity, Norway has more in common with Canada than with its neighbors. Both have Arctic Ocean frontage, access to northern shipping routes to Asia and copious continental shelf oil and gas. Both are cold weather oil states that require special resource management. Science policy networks link the two closely in the search for creative solutions.

Comparison is tricky business, and none of these discursive points explains everything. Contrasts too must be considered and accounted for. Each case, however, offers clues to a wider reality, including those of differentiation. Together they offer a more nuanced, three-dimensional and most crucially, *non-Nordic* back-cloth to Norway's orientation. They suggest that Norway sorely needs, and richly deserves, to be regarded with a wider angle lens than the purely Scandinavian one it is accustomed to.

10

Well and Truly Oiled

It is relative wealth—keeping ahead of the Joneses—and not absolute wealth, that contributes to happiness.
Anthony Gottlieb, Preface to Bertrand Russell's *In Praise of Idleness*

Votes count, but resources decide.
Stein Rokkan, "Numerical Democracy and Corporate Pluralism"

In late summer 2013, still finding my feet in Norway, I frequently passed through *jernbanetorget*, the square fronting Oslo's main railway station. It's a functional, workaday place that falls short of picturesque, while its centrality makes it hard to avoid for commuters or tourists. It has two entry points into the station which, in a Norwegian kind of way, is a mix of levels and styles.

The square outside the lower-level entrance—the older but recently overhauled Østbanehallen, which also makes it Norwegian-newer—is a convenient open-air venue for anything from candlelight vigils to beach volleyball tournaments. On the upper level is a mostly unnoticed "art space," a *Rom for Kunst*. (Or was: it seems to have disappeared.) Here's another Norwegian touch, legally mandated artwork on all public buildings, a policy with its own backstory (artists despairing of kronor-pinching philistinism by official Norway). It's surprising what you can learn about a country through how it treats its public spaces—and how that relationship can affect you.

273

One day an oversized sign appeared there, hand-drawn in bright, primary colors, affixed to the station wall. *Life Is Fantastic* was the only message, like a sign hanging from a college dorm room after a football win. It was no advertisement, much less a work of modern art, even stretching that elastic term. For unflattering reasons, its airy sentiment grated (being temporarily homeless as well as jobless, I took it as mockery). Then one day it was gone, replaced by a less baffling work. And soon, remarkably soon it seemed, life took a turn for the better.

The message stuck because it seemed so apt for its Norwegian context. Neither boastful nor overtly patriotic, it simply articulated circumstance. The composite reality—for public Norway, enhanced global clout and flush budgets, for private citizens a dizzying range of travel options, sports, educational subsidies, childcare, job leave schemes and deeply elastic notions of the "working Friday"—is not all due to the oil economy. But much is. Some effects percolate up, others filter down; lives get enhanced.

For the bulk of Norwegians who are basically healthy and gainfully employed, life does appear to be uncommonly benign. The message of *expansive possibility* reflects the huge all-around impact of the fossil fuel economy. Most powerfully, it buys Norwegians time. The discreetly subsidized society and a system of (seemingly) guaranteed future pensions—not just for one but for several generations to come—are liberators in a quite personal sense.

The combination provides both a soft cushion and a springboard for its people. It lets them plan their lives better, yet partly frees them from the time-consuming task of doing it. Many of those lives can be turned into ongoing personal experiments backed, effectively, by the state. It removes some—though certainly not all—of the medium-term anxiety and long-term uncertainty that routinely grips the rest of the world. Collective self-regard, and the lives of Norwegians, received a huge injection of attitude. The old, stern country of seeming joykillers and moralizers is hiding away. The mood effect, like the smiling society, is pervasive even if, as I found, it's not automatically catching.

A lot has been written about what oil has done *for* Norway. Thoughtful types increasingly ask what it's doing *to* Norway: whether it's draining the country of its mojo, turning people soft or selfish or greedy, eroding trust while creating an unshakable if semi-tangible dependency. Job absenteeism and sick-leave days are suspiciously high for a sporting land. Naturally, much fretting concerns Norwegian youth. It is a drumbeat of increasing urgency for a country now into its second generation in a preternaturally flush economy. It's only natural that some of its effects will be lamentable and lamented.

Oil's role in Norway is easy to intuit but hard to assess. The oil age, which officially reached its half-century point in 2019, has indelibly *changed* Norway. Economically, it's been a transformative agent of the first order. Whether it has *revolutionized* Norway is a far trickier question to answer, partly as it correlates with Norwegian leaps into the digital world and, in terms of women's rights, parallels a path from Nordic laggard to leader. It is easy to make the fatal logical leap to assuming that Norway's successes are "all because of oil": not just a factor but the sole cause, based on some lucky breaks.

It is easy to slip into such thinking because historically, Norway's self-image and outside reputation were built largely on the theme of overcoming deprivation. Norway has transcended the ranks of the poor without quite obliterating its long-term psychological effects, so as a perceptual revolution it is incomplete. A country long identified with want has left that feature, that mark of Cain, in the dust but not quite buried. A collective memory of poverty still nips at Norwegian heels. Norway's signature novel of the late nineteenth century, Knut Hamsun's *Sult* (Hunger), remains the indelible symbol of *that* Norway. An indictment of reality unencumbered by finger pointing, it is seared into the psyche yet remote in the profoundest contemporary sense.

There is, in fact, a solid case for arguing that oil has produced the antithesis of revolution: that it has been an agent of retrenchment and conservatism—the "small c," nonpolitical sort—allowing Norway to avoid the wrenching social changes that, for example, Sweden has undergone in the past quarter-century. There is evidence of poverty at the fringes that was not present in the 1960s, although some is attributable to rapid immigration. Rising economic inequality, now a growing worldwide concern, finds some sharp Norwegian echoes while social subcultures, as Hellevik noted, haven't disappeared.

And while oil is the commonly attributed factor behind Norway's new globalism, much of the wealth has been channeled nationally. It has invigorated a long-standing policy of decentralization and took modern infrastructure and services to far-flung corners of an already far-flung country. This means the effects and the evidence are liberally and literally scattered, and hard to tally.

In other ways too, oil has made Norway less overtly global. For example, the Norway of the 1960s and 1970s, still anxious to advertise its virtues, churned out books and magazines in English. These have disappeared; nearly all serious print publishing in Norway is in Norwegian (and surprising amounts in Nynorsk or "new" Norwegian). This trend not only reflects the pitiless economics of a devastated industry but also seems as though Norway no longer needs or wants the attention.

Much of the change is thus behavioral, and it has disrupted the ingrained pattern of national modesty that long underpinned attitudes and social patterns. Oil, in tandem with social media that touts its own power to "empower," is making Norway big for its boots and some Norwegians big for theirs. One sign is a certain entry-level arrogance that ties into the digital universe. Autobiographies fly off the presses, featuring self-satisfied postadolescent faces and carrying subtitles like "World's most seen on YouTube in Norwegian" and "The news site that changed Norway" or, in biographical form, "The Norwegian who made Norway bigger." The money economy feeds the tendency (and capability) to tout individual reputations online and fosters a showbiz mentality that gives Norway a flashy and unaccustomed new face. The resulting fit can get awkward because it seems to go against the grain, to be contrary to the natural order. Norwegians don't generally make for convincing sybarites and braggarts.

Part of this upsetting of the apple cart is regional. Norwegians have turned the tables on Sweden, the old *storsvenskar*, in a largely unspoken comeuppance. Just as important for Norway as becoming rich and secure is that it has become *richer*, not just compared to its own past but compared with Sweden's (and Denmark's) present. A recent study of vacationing habits, related by Hjalager and two co-writers, confirms that Norwegians typically spend more *per diem* on holiday than do Swedes and Danes. Even in modern lifespans this is a striking turnabout from the early 1970s when Sweden occupied the top rung on indices of world *per capita* income. The heady Norwegian experience of dining out while being served by Swedish waiters represents, in this regard, the sweetest possible revenge. But that, too, has a touch of the evanescent about it, something that can't possibly last.

Neighboring Finland offers a cautionary example. In the heyday of Nokia, the first mobile telephone multinational, the Finns briefly tasted life in the economic stratosphere. I happened to live in Tampere, close to Nokia, in the mid-1990s, just as the turn was underway—present at the creation, so to say, when bulky handsets suddenly appeared on sidewalks (and famously silent Finns started jabbering *in public*). But Norway's wealth effect is far more dramatic and sustained than was Finland's, since it's underpinned by a ready-for-sale commodity crucial to industry and transport, not just a global company facing competitors and feeding a social trend. Oil prices may gyrate, but demand is unceasing.

The "symptoms of oil" vary and proliferate even if, like attitudes, they are hard to measure. Betting shops, online gambling and Internet banks proliferate in the Norwegian retail market, which is quickly going cashless. The vanity trade is barging, not just edging, into a Norwegian lifestyle still, bravely, being touted for its naturalness. Comedy routines poke fun at the growing obsession with self—one rather caustic sketch is called, appropriately, *Ego*—to a plastic surgery subculture to breathtaking prices in cafes combined with a curious and possibly cynical shrinkage of portions. In a suburban mall I occasionally visit, a change recently occurred near the entrance. Narvesen, a ubiquitous shop selling snacks and magazines, had been replaced—by a Porsche dealership.

It can even be heard in the use of language. Listen carefully to the Norwegian spoken now compared to newsreels from 50 years ago: today it is far more bombastic, more sharply intoned, more like the Swedish way of speaking. Is this a coincidence?

Freer spending habits are part of the package. There is a buy-and-toss element, a constant sense of a need for renewal (whether of bathroom tiles or ski clothing) that rests uneasily beside the sustainability-minded (and equally strong) side of the culture. Yet carefree consumerism is possible because of its opposite: public Norway's remarkable self-discipline in *not* spending its oil incomes. The authorities have not just taken away the punch bowl, they've removed it from the house.

In order to understand the Norwegian oil economy, you could always travel to Stavanger, in the southwest, which has its own peculiar conditions (a prohibitionist, Bible-thumping past), a museum tracing the oil odyssey, American radio DJs and housing prices higher than the sky. Search in vain for an air ticket to or from Oslo, at any price, on a Sunday. Stavanger is Norway's emphatic answer to Aberdeen, its Scottish equivalent; both have giant oil rigs out to sea and a local economy dependent on them. Yet Stavanger is remarkably unblighted. It has a picturesque old town with white clapboard houses on winding lanes, an even more picturesque version of Bergen, minus the mountains (and forgetting the wind).

A better destination would be the Telemark region. In this rugged, wooded expanse, cut by a famous canal, old-style skiing is renowned and traditions are kept alive. Telemark is also the home of the *stabbur*. One of the most distinctive architectural features of old Norway, it is a set piece for any self-respecting open-air museum. The stabbur was the storehouse of the farmstead, a separate, upright, stained-wood structure, its base set well above ground. It was designed to hold quantities of grain and other foodstuffs, keeping it dry and safe from mice and other foragers.

It served as insurance for the lean years nearly certain to come. The stabbur represented a proclivity to save for the future. It was a solid, practical place to squirrel assets away—much as a dog will bury a bone, only in this case up in the air and housed in a curious structure hard to overlook. It was also physically separate, and unheated, which made it a destination of necessity not of choice, hardly the tempting cookie jar. Along with its architectural cousin the stave church, the stabbur is as authentically Norwegian as any man-made sight. And it's authentic not just structurally but also symbolically.

It may be a relic of the rural past, but it still resonates powerfully today. It's a sign of sturdy design, of planning ahead, of scrimping and discipline that still makes room for style, with walls often brightly decorated with *rosemaling* designs. It was the ultimate solution to known problems, the boom-and-bust nature of crop-growing and the need to manage seasonal excess, not just cope with shortfall. The stabbur is a sterling metaphor for Norway's saving-based and long-sighted approach to its oil wealth. If Norwegians are chronically underestimated, their management of their remarkable bounty exemplifies this trait. So does the country's unofficial niche-player status among the big producers.

Few could have predicted the transformative effect that oil would have even when, by the 1970s, it dawned on experts just how huge it would be. But even then it was a hesitant dawn. I began studying the Nordic region in 1980 but long had little inkling of it. I wasn't alone. In the mid-1980s, one of the brightest analysts of small-state behavior, Peter Katzenstein of Cornell University, wrote disarmingly that Norway (along with the Netherlands) was "temporarily cushioned" by North Sea oil and gas. Dizzying decades and hundreds of billions in global sales and petrodollar-funded long-term investments later, with more being discovered each year by an army of engineers, Norway is looking rather different.

Oil and its fast-growing offshoot natural gas are the elephants in the Norwegian room: a big and awkward reality that is almost too intimidating to inspect closely. Its "presence" is ubiquitous yet slippery as an oil slick. It does get discussed, notwithstanding Sanna Sarromaa's characterization of oil, in her book *Norske Tabuer*, as one of Norway's great taboos. There is a glimmer of truth in her view, insofar as oil's importance is not questioned in the mainstream debate. But it does arouse dissension, and the oil debate tends to erupt when especially sensitive regions of the country are proposed for development. Given Nordic outspokenness on climate change, the potential for Norwegian hypocrisy is abundant.

The stream of revenue is managed discreetly, shrewdly and, by all appearances, professionally and with a distinct nod in the direction of ethics. This being Norway, it has also produced a hit TV comedy show, *Lykkeland* (happy country), lampooning an outfit trying to cut shady deals with oligarchs. But the real-life version that does business also means business. It has divested from influential companies, like WalMart, accused of dubious labor practices. It won't go near a lot of "sin industries"; it is even divesting in fossil fuel projects. Its ethical element also works as a conditioning factor; companies know they need to behave in order to get the magic nod on a new investment from Norway. It has extraordinary leverage via a reputation that precedes it.

By law, and for largely macroeconomic reasons, most of it is parked "offshore," that is outside Norway. Oil wealth is a management and investment problem, and an ethical conundrum but not an existential one. All but the most militant environmentalists accept it as an ingrained feature of Norway and at least grudgingly acknowledge it as the key to their national affluence and the wellspring of their own substantial future pensions. All this has a dampening effect on any criticism and serves a residual source of pride.

Oil revenues are so vast that the little of it spent each year is enough to keep the public budget well in the black, a rare enough phenomenon in a debt-fueled world. The figures speak for themselves. At the end of 2017 Norway's budget surplus, as a percentage of gross domestic product (GDP), stood at 5.2 percent. This was not just the highest among the world's 42 biggest economies (as compiled in *The Economist*), it was in a category all to itself. Next highest on the list was Hong Kong (at 1.7 percent), while the nearest in Europe was next-door Sweden, at 1 percent; Germany, Europe's powerhouse economy (and frequently criticized for not spending enough), stood at just 0.6 percent. By May 2019 Norway's budget surplus had risen to 6.4 percent; next highest was 2 percent (Russia). Most other countries had figures well into the red, some deeply so.

Statens Pensjonsfond Utland, colloquially known as *fondet,* "the fund," is the discreet behemoth at the center of it all. It was created in 1995 as a long-term investment vehicle for Norway's future generations, a sort of national piggy bank. It quickly became an economic game changer, controlled by, and for the benefit of, a country of fewer than six million people. Its managers (led in recent times by Yngve Slyngstad) are among the world's most influential people you've never heard of. It has a stake in some 9,000 companies worldwide and controls around 1.5 percent of world stock market capitalizations. It can't be easily moved around although size brings its own rewards, as the managers can negotiate more favorable deals. Many of those holdings are now in physical form, notably prime central London real estate. Norway, which supplies the annual Christmas tree for Trafalgar Square, now owns much of nearby Regent's Street.

In an age that has spawned populist fist-shaking at an *uber*-rich and out-of-touch "One Percent," its uniqueness is found in this fact: the fund is the best example anywhere of popular capitalism, since the ultimate owners of the fund are the Norwegian people. Its holdings are public knowledge and regularly scrutinized by an ethics panel. While its main focus is financial return and only secondarily good corporate behavior, it also tries to nudge the world economy and its private-sector companies in a better, or at least less compromised direction. Whoever and wherever you are, Norway is having a say in your financial and ethical future.

In spring 2017 the Solberg government announced that, thanks to solid finances, the government would be tapping 2.9 percent of the fund that fiscal year for government spending purposes—a useful shade below the 3 percent maximum it had already proposed, and well under the 4 percent traditional figure. More interesting than the numbers was the timing, for it came just months before a national election. Most governments facing the voters are tempted to prime the pump. Norway's could afford to do just the opposite, to boast about *not* spending it. In an election year, that amounted to chest-thumping statements of confidence and competence by an openly chuffed prime minister who, together with her ebullient finance minister and coalition partner, Siv Jensen, was coasting to a second successive term, making an equally robust gender statement almost in passing.

Norway is applying a buzzword that a Norwegian (former Prime Minister Brundtland) helped coin in the 1970s, namely sustainability, in a highly unlikely context, the management of wealth that came, with equal improbability, from fossil fuel. Oil from the ground, sold in spot markets, has been parlayed into a pillar of the tertiary economy for the long term. Effectively the Norwegians are spending the interest while preserving the capital for the remote future. (As indicated in the next chapter, the same principle underlies the Nobel Prize monies.) It amounts to thrift on a heroic scale, an epic example of national saving—and a case of perpetually delayed gratification with an unmistakable Norwegian stamp.

In 2017 a combination of buoyant world markets, shrewd investments, guaranteed rental income and sheer momentum pushed the oil fund past the 8 trillion kronor level, which corresponded roughly to the 1-trillion-dollar (US) mark. This averaged out, at the time, to about 1.6 million kronor per Norwegian: a state-guaranteed nest egg that was fast approaching a quarter of a million dollars per citizen. "A billion here, a billion there, and pretty soon you're talking about real money"; such was the trenchant observation of Senator Everett Dirksen during a 1960s US budget battle over sums few mortals can relate to. The same applies to the oil fund, which is now so huge that monthly and even weekly gains or losses in the total constitute breathtaking, yet oddly disembodied, figures in themselves. There is a strange, phantom-like quality about it all.

Still another anomaly is at work; oil production is dropping while oil-based wealth is expanding. That also means that sharp drops in the oil price, like the one in 2014–15, barely disturb the broader society; job losses in the oil sector mainly impact Stavanger's local economy or cause brief wobbles in the real estate market. It is remarkable in some ways; Norway's oil fund is shielded from the oil price. *Insulation* does seem like a potent image for oil's role in Norway: like the inner lining of a winter coat, it invisibly protects the people from some of the harsh buffeting of life. Increasingly it is also protection against uncertainties of the future.

Black-figured budgets suggest that the country's well-being no longer depends on everyday oil production, but that would be a false view, since it still accounts for roughly half of Norway's total exports. It's just as important for today's current account as it is for tomorrow's grandparents. Many observers are convinced of its dampening, and damaging, effect on Norwegian initiative and competitiveness, not least by lessening the sense of urgency that drives a capitalist economy.

In many intangible respects this seems indisputable. But goodly amounts are funneled into high-tech research and initiatives like SINTEF, a sort of Norwegian Silicon Valley that feeds off the university at Trondheim, NTNU, now the country's biggest. And in many ways oil has lit more fires than it has extinguished, by whetting appetites for big gains, creating a growing army of semi-employed people on the make, restlessly seeking out niche opportunities by smartphone, or creating new ones, and turning Norway into a country it never was, one of lucrative gains, high-powered deals and rampant consumerism.

The year 1969, when drills hit a Christmastime gusher, stands out as a red-letter date in Norwegian history. The industry's evolution is briefly as follows. The immense Ekofisk field, in the Norwegian sector of the North Sea, started producing in 1971. Full-scale operations were underway within a few years. In the mid-1980s an oil price collapse caught Norway unawares, toppling the conservative government led by Kåre Willoch as a part-result. Lessons were learned. In the 1990s the famous oil fund was launched. Already by that time the sector qualified as a "mature industry" with production no longer rising. Having peaked at 3.3 million barrels a day in 2001 it had dropped to around 2 million daily by 2017. New sources were being sought and the cold expanses of the Arctic were being identified as the future of Norwegian oil and thus of the nation's future wealth and thus of the nation's future. The beginning of the end of production is in sight. But in terms of generational wealth impact, they are still closer to the end of the beginning.

Good timing, that wild-card ingredient of any success, may continue at Norway's side. There is a feeling among many—presumptuous and even smug perhaps but also realistically rooted—that Norway's oil and gas bounty will peter out in convenient tandem with the world's switch to a fossil-free economy. It is one thing to acknowledge good fortune in the past but another, riskier thing to assume that the fairy dust will blow into the distant future. That, too, may be another of oil's countless psychological benefits for Norway: a widely presumed grace factor.

Norway was hardly an empty vessel before oil arrived. It was a well-functioning society in the democratic, capitalist, high-export mold. Solid foundations for handling the new bounty were in place, about which more below. The whole oil chapter is a function of overlapping elements that make for a prime-time mix of luck and skill—if, that is, we discount the many lives lost in the wildcat speculation of the early days.

Like those waters, the early years are murky. To say the oil age began in 1969 is at best formally accurate, like dating a book by its year of publication. Extraordinary finds in Norwegian waters presupposed three major developments during the decade preceding it.

One was the big natural gas discoveries in 1959 off Groeningen, a Dutch coastal city. On the principle of "where there's smoke, there's fire," these sparked rumors of a much wider fossil fuel bonanza that were brusquely dismissed in public. A second factor was political: the North Sea was divided up in the mid-1960s via national negotiations—a largely untold story that worked, or was made to work, greatly to Norway's advantage especially compared to Denmark. This process brought a clear, legal delineation of who owned what and where. A third was the establishment, the same year (1965), of exploratory rights. Drilling began the following year and the first finds (in the Balder field) emerged in 1967. And this, in turn, was only possible because of recent advances in deep-sea drilling and well-testing technology. It all came to a head on December 23, 1969 with a massive gusher at Ekofisk, courtesy of Phillips Petroleum (now Conoco-Phillips).

But finds alone would make Norway another Venezuela or Nigeria, oil states flirting with the ignominious title of failed state. What then really matters is an array of other, enabling factors that turned a dependent oil pumper into an independent fuel producer, and thus increasingly a captain of its own destiny rather than a slave to fickle markets. It's important to understand that the oil economy sidled into a Norwegian society that was highly organized and effective—and into a Norwegian economy that was not just industrial but built substantially on the energy sector. Its timing and context were practically ideal, and so in that sense oil was a matter of luck, but it drew upon hard-won capabilities and past progress.

These, in staccato, are as follows. Postwar Norway had a strong manufacturing base and diversified economy. By the mid-1960s it was coming off two long, postwar decades of state-imposed austerity (private cars were actually rationed until 1960) and was more than ready, like South Korea in the 1980s, to get a belated taste of consumerism. The political climate at home was mostly calm, apart from periodic grumbling over NATO that spiked during Vietnam, while the divisions over Europe had not yet erupted. The North Sea continental shelf had been removed as a source of dispute, and at any rate Norway neighbored friendly states, notably Britain and Denmark, in the oil regions.

The micro-level was just as promising. There was plenty of electrochemical expertise around that could be transferred to the new industry. The domestic energy sector, especially in hydroelectric power, was maxed out and ripe for a new chapter. The coal industry had taken a huge hit early in the decade with the King's Bay mining disaster in Ny Ålesund. Shipping modernization had taken Norway into a leading position in tankers; by the 1960s a quarter of all oil transported worldwide was carried in Norwegian-owned ships, which was a stroke of tremendous national fortune. And in 1967, Norway officially became a welfare state when it introduced a national insurance fund. This was supposed to be self-sustaining via own contributions, but that precondition was unrealistic and it needed an outside boost. In long and in short, 1960s Norway was primed for its own version of a great leap forward.

Yet another factor was political, in the sense of policy and its making. Norway's uniquely conducive policy environment was spelled out in the 1960s by Stein Rokkan, a Norwegian sociologist whose work (his own and together with Seymour Martin Lipset) boosted Norway's visibility among social science comparativists. Best known for his work on Norway's center–periphery cleavages and European party systems, he also usefully distinguished between two types of democratic processes.

One was the familiar, competitive kind, pertaining to votes and elections, percentages and parliaments. The other was the cooperative kind, "corporate pluralism" being his term for the ingrained network of economic and corporate interests and the practice of behind-the-scenes discussion that influences policy outcomes—not just in Norway of course but notably there. "Votes count," he wrote in 1966, "but resources decide." It was an incisive comment three years before the big gusher. "The system" was already in place to handle the new bounty skillfully, to keep debate from getting too animated and, not least, to keep management in Norwegian hands. From fish and timber to hydropower, from the Middle Ages to the twentieth century, variants of this arrangement have a long Norwegian pedigree. It helps us understand the absolutely extraordinary, relatively nonpoliticized, discreetly overseen and oddly nonpublic role of oil in a Norwegian society underpinned by it.

Norway, say some, was additionally blessed with a generation of far-sighted politicians in the 1960s, who took shrewd long-range decisions in the misty dawn of the oil era. Just as important was the ingrained national feature of adaptability to circumstance. The wisdom of individual politicians can be debated, but an undoubted factor was the stability of Norwegian politics, in three senses. Postwar recovery encouraged centrist politics and banished most vestiges of the old extremism. The second factor was the dominance of the center-left Labor Party, which governed, mostly on its own, for two decades after 1945. (From the war up to the 1970s, the party never dropped as low as 40 percent of the vote.) The third, more complex element was the tempered ambitions of the political opposition. Winds of change in the 1960s opened the door to interparty cooperation aimed at creating political instruments that would simultaneously keep politicians' fingers mostly out of the pie. Wrong-footed for a whole generation, the nonsocialist parties had little scope for shaking the tree (or even uniting their forces to such an end) when they finally did come to power and when oil finally emerged, at just that time, as a national factor.

When it came to crucial economic decisions, Rokkan held, "the central area is the bargaining table." Annualized negotiations between government, management and labor were already such common practice that it meant more to "the lives of rank-and-file citizens than [did] formal elections." Behind-the-scenes collective bargaining—which can resemble corporate pluralism—may have operated in a "constitutional vacuum" but it also had staying power. It is not false government so much as layered governance. "It seems likely," he added presciently, "that the many years of uneventful bargaining will have set precedents that will be hard to break." The half-obscured, hazily political role of oil is the biggest and best manifestation of it.

The value of a solid, existing base of resource management expertise is another factor impossible to overstate. Engineering technology—via roads and tunnels in transportation and in communication radio, TV and later mobile telephony—has been a huge, multigenerational factor helping to unify a scattered and mountainous country. In turn, the physical challenges have required canny solutions to the problems of distance and mountains, forcing Norwegian industry to explore alternative ways of doing things and putting a premium on flexibility. This factor's origins can be traced all the way back to the *Hollandertid* and the beginnings of proto-industry built around worked timber.

Since the latter third of the nineteenth century, when industry made a late and disruptive entrance into Norwegian life, the first factories went up in sunless valleys, along rivers and in other challenging milieus, via hydroelectric and hydrochemical works especially. It was necessarily decentralized. (Even in Oslo we see the legacy in converted factories flanking the Akerselva, a smallish but scenic river.) At sea as well, Norway managed a rapid shift from sail to diesel, mostly skipping the transitional stage of steamships, which pushed its merchant marine from a lagging to a leading position in the world within a few decades. In both cases Norway's leaps ahead were primed as well as impressive. Norway's capacity for fast structural adjustment was emphasized by economists Jörberg and Krantz. An investment ratio traditionally highest in Scandinavia led to "a swifter structural change in production" than (for example) in Sweden.

Much modern Norwegian history is bound up in the arcana of applied science: the Soderberg electrode, the Pedersen process in aluminum oxide, the Birkeland–Eyde nitrogen-extraction process and others too. These didn't just prefigure the oil economy; they ensured a quick transition to it and enabled its mastery. Technical skill and management expertise abounded in postwar Norway, a country of inveterate tinkerers, and it proved transferable to an emergent new industry that heavily depended, at the outset, on foreign expertise and capital. This in turn promoted possibilities for Norway to secure itself, fairly early on, as an all-around producer and refiner, not just a commodity source.

As the oil age was dawning, Norway was boosted dramatically by developments in the wider world. The timeline tells it all. In 1971 the oil started flowing; in 1972 Statoil was created out of Norsk Hydro, on a mixed commercial–public basis. (Forty-six years later, in 2018, the company changed names to the less nationalist and less commodified Equinor.) Late that same year (1972) the Norwegian public rejected membership in the European

Economic Community, in a referendum that turned largely on questions of economy; and its unexpected result, against most establishment opinion, ensured resource independence and Norway's core economic autarky.

Within the year an Arab oil embargo led by OPEC, driven by resource nationalism and sparked by the 1973 Yom Kippur war, shifted the entire calculus of the global oil industry. Sharp increases in Norwegian outflows coincided with oil shortages and spiraling prices worldwide. A barrel of oil jumped from $3 (US) before the 1973 embargo to $36 by the end of the decade, after a second oil shock in 1979 that was sparked by the Iranian revolution. Oil price and production trends along with global political upheaval worked vastly, if sometimes uncomfortably, in Norway's favor. It created a temporary but strange Norwegian coincidence of acute short-term problems (for Norway too was hit by the market disruptions of the early 1970s) and immense long-term potential.

Much of this is well documented. Less known, but no less important, was the dramatic expansion of international seabed rights via the UN's conferences on the Law of the Sea, discussed in Part I. Progress by the 1970s (confirmed by a treaty in 1982) secured for the world's coastal states an Exclusive Economic Zone that gave them monopoly rights to exploit their continental seabeds, reaching out 200 nautical miles (ca. 320 km). With its sprawling sea exposure, Norway stood almost uniquely to gain.

The heady prospect of a Norway awash in oil had significant downsides. It hastened the ongoing decline of traditional industries like shipbuilding, manufacturing and especially agriculture. It shifted interest, attention and expertise to an oil sector that was still in its infancy. The transition was by no means smooth and the societal effects were deeply wrenching. It could be, and ultimately was, pulled off by a very Norwegian solution, a calculated risk decision (after the giddy first phase) to *rethink oil*: to use it not just as a source of immediate income but as a store of future value. It emerged as a form of collateral, something to borrow against, in anticipation of rising production and in hopes of higher world prices. Norway effectively became its own banker. The price bust of the 1980s was for many a rude awakening, but a useful one that forced the shift in thinking that in turn shifted the strategy.

By this point, Norway was a developed, export-heavy country with networks and institutional links both in Europe and transatlantically. On the powerful basis of the Marshall Plan from the late 1940s, Norway finally had dependable outside sources of capital, flowing from some powerful allies; its merchant marine boosted these too. Its membership in EFTA from the late 1950s plugged it into the European trading system. The oil bonanza arrived at a propitious moment for Norway internationally as well as domestically. It is remarkable, in this regard, how timing so often gets overlooked in explaining success. North Sea oil was also a huge, but almost entirely unrecognized, factor behind Margaret Thatcher's dominance of British political life throughout the 1980s.

The Iron Lady, a vocal champion of individual enterprise and rolling back the state, benefited hugely from the North Sea oil contributions to the British Treasury, which peaked during her 11 years in power. It brought a more animated British global presence, from the Falkland Islands to Brussels, while at home it emboldened her in confronting Arthur Scargill and his militant coal miners—presenting herself as a modernizer in opposition to Luddite defenders of a dirty and dying energy sector. Vaulting tax revenues produced years of budget surpluses that actually enabled the treasury to stop issuing government bonds (which, like an "iou," are promises to pay the lender back).

Norwegian politicians, unencumbered by British postcolonial remorse and retrenchment, mostly avoided any delusionary rhetoric that Norway's success was due to their foresight and resolution alone. It helped that Norway had a corporatist political culture as against Britain's "yah-boo" competitive system and that west coast Norway, while culturally distinct, was no separate national entity as Scotland is to England.

Yet another happy circumstance is the siting of Norway's finds. Oil rigs have been confined to offshore locations, mostly out of shoreline sight, leaving a picturesque landscape unmarred by belching smokestacks and gas flares. The absence of oil derricks in Norwegian fjords is another gift from the geological gods. You can tour Norway, or live there for years, while scarcely realizing that it is a multi-million-barrel-a-day oil producer, or the second-leading gas exporter to Europe. The defining reality of modern Norway, its oil-and-gas economy, is curiously and even astonishingly out of sight, removed from its other defining reality, its world-famous landscape.

All told, an almost uncanny coincidence of new treaty law, domestic politics, regional diplomacy, geology, market structures, organized trade connections, technology, domestic policy networks and a cultural propensity for taking things in stride launched Norway's life as an oil nation and kept it more or less on course. Add these intangibles—astuteness, vision, hard-earned skill, low-key management, flexibility, ingrained parsimony, a solid national brand name—and you have the makings of a serious winning streak, not just a lucky hand skillfully played.

A hugely important shift *within* the fuel economy, one from oil to natural gas production, is actively underway. Because of Norway's understated success in oil, and because oil is usually found with gas (long treated as expendable) it is widely assumed that the transition will be seamless. The reality is less easy. Transition to primarily gas production involves a change from an industry pattern marked by tankers, isolated platforms and spot markets priced in dollars to a very different one involving pipelines, liquefied gas (LNG) facilities and long-term contracts hammered out in advance. It also means a northward shift of the entire energy sector to areas mostly north of 62 degrees latitude, the traditional demarcation point for the North Sea. Prospecting in the Arctic is a major known-unknown, but huge new finds point that way as the Norwegian fossil fuel future.

Two other features are worth mentioning. One is the decentralized nature of the industry. It is easy to caricature a state-owned oil behemoth, but in fact Norway operates a widely dispersed industry with a huge array of small, private-sector suppliers, each with niche specializations in products I could not even begin to describe. The state orchestrates the whole arrangement—granting exploratory licenses, building infrastructure, regulating it all—but the supply chain is widely dispersed and impressively self-sustaining.

The other element, again drawing on the past, flows from the dramatic improvement in Norway's capital needs. From the earliest days of independence, governments were keen to restrict foreign ownership of natural resources, especially waterfalls and forests. The reason had less to do with xenophobia or even the overhang of poverty than with the requirements of long-term national investment: Norway chronically lacked the capital assets to make structural improvements. This left the country potentially beholden to foreign lenders and sources of funding that could disappear in a downturn. This was also one explanation for the slow advance of Norwegian shipping. Low-cost sailing predominated well into the steam era because capital needs could not be covered. Skippers and crews jointly owned the barques and clippers, not out of generous egalitarian spirits but out of the need to share costs in a flagship industry. After 1905, sovereignty notwithstanding, Norway's sense of vulnerability actually increased.

One analyst, Jack Hayward, distinguishes between small states with ready access to foreign capital and those having to cope mostly without—assigning Norway (of the twentieth century) to the latter category and Sweden mostly to the former. Even before 1905 this created linkages that helped ease the transition to independence; it was a dependency kind of relationship only in part. Swedish capital was an unseen factor behind Norsk Hydro, the country's first major conglomerate. Another rising star at the time, chocolate-maker Freia, became (under its unassuming but tenacious leader Johan Throne Holst) the first Norwegian company to turn the tables and take a leading position in the Swedish market, where it launched Marabou.

Still, Norway's inability to invest really began to bite in the 1950s, as expectations grew and the state took on new commitments under a dominant Labor Party. Norwegian efforts in many fields tended to flag, notably the country's scientific establishment and a faltering, long-distance presence in Antarctica. It's safe to say that a trillion-dollar oil fund has ameliorated that particular problem. Public parsimony is now a matter of free choice and an extension of historical lessons, as opposed to a crying and persistent national economic need.

While I've emphasized the national side of oil, the industry is thoroughly hooked into the world economy. Oil pumped in western Norway flows directly abroad. Norwegian expertise can be parlayed into other projects, whether in the Russian Arctic or in the Saharan sands. Such associations can get Norway into hot water; Statoil was harshly criticized for pumping money into dirty oil-sand and shale projects in the American upper Midwest and in Manitoba in south-central Canada. Yet its expertise is in demand whenever new deposits are being sought out, Cyprus being but one recent example.

Norway was able to ride sidesaddle on the Arab oil horse and use OPEC's sudden clout to accrue wealth while mostly skirting blame for a worldwide oil addiction and its political fallout. It was half-partner and half-outlier, as a European, non-OPEC oil producer, pumping the product like the other oil states yet keeping the whole operation seemingly and comparatively clean. All this allowed Norway to present itself as *the* responsible oil nation, the exception that proves the rule, the solitary defier of the oil curse. Even in the North Sea context, it played a quiet and contained second fiddle to Britain, escaping attention and skirting scrutiny, working its little-big role to great benefit.

Norway in the twenty-first century emerged as Europe's second-largest source of imported natural gas, after Russia, and much valued as a friendlier, closer and more reliable alternative. This gives it a strategic European role despite not being part of political Europe. Norway is also positioning itself for the day after tomorrow, beyond both gas and oil, by investing heavily in North Sea wind farms, often in tandem with Britain—something that King Harald pointedly mentioned in his toast to a visiting Prince and Princess of Wales in early 2018. "Hywind," a floating offshore wind project, is one example of Norwegian-inspired technology being shared out with neighboring lands (in this case Scotland). Norway seems to have turned a psychological corner in thinking ahead. One unlikely benefit is the seemingly perverse luxury of planning for a switch *away* from the product that transformed the country.

A mandated policy requirement, involving a ferry industry in a country reliant on water crossings, for low- or zero-emission vessels sped the appearance of Ampere, the world's first electric (battery-powered) car ferry, which debuted to wide acclaim—but still as a pilot project—in 2015, fittingly in the celebrated Sognefjord.

Oil wealth is not the sole reason for the country's expanding world role over the past half-century, any more than the *dansketida* was the sole determinant of the "little Norway" syndrome. But it was and is a major contributing factor. Given how money talks in a global economy driven by trade and capital, Norway's oil industry and oil fund provide a one–two punch that transcends the category of "soft power." It acts almost like a substantial moon, emitting a gravitational pull on the world whose economic axis tilts, ever so slightly, because of Norway.

Ample funds on tap also act as a reputational springboard for Norway. The seemingly casual decision in January 2017, by Prime Minister Solberg at the World Economic Forum meetings in Davos, to contribute to a $400 million rainforest fund set up by Bill Gates, handing over a fat check in front of the cameras, was a deft example of the sort of flexible contributor and effortless positive player that "official Norway" increasingly wants to be seen as.

Norway's unlimited spending power is countered by its limited willingness to spend. If anything, the popular Norwegian complaints that arise—and arise they do—revolve around the theme of miserliness, that Norway is thinking *too* far ahead while neglecting (for example) services even in downtown Oslo— like ice-clearing in winter, the annual budget for which tends, inconveniently, to run out in March. Norway's tram and train systems are distinctly poor cousins to the gleaming systems on display in the likes of Vienna and Munich. Pre-oil underinvestment, notably in rail, is part of the reason. But it may also be that an ingrained, old Lutheran fear of spoiling the citizenry is a factor behind this alleged stinginess.

Oil also enhances planning certainty in unrelated endeavors. Ambitious projects can be envisioned boldly, budgeted with confidence and funded from blueprint to completion. Modernization becomes a virtuous circle in such an environment. Big-ticket projects are immune to the sort of ruinous cutoff halfway to the finish line that project managers and creative artists everywhere dread with good reason. National budgeting itself benefits from continuity. Quality governance is easier to come by.

Programmatically, Norway has committed itself to the aim of a decarbonized future even as it works out the considerable details in practice. This is broadly in line with the EU's goal of reducing greenhouse gases by 40 percent in 2030 as measured from 1990 levels, including a 27 percent renewables share in the energy mix. Norway's aim is greater still—two-thirds of its energy mix by renewables—but its starting point is also much higher given its immense hydroelectric capacity.

Yet in the wake of the Paris 2015 climate change treaty, which pledged states to take concrete steps to limit a global temperature rise to "well below" 2 degrees Celsius in the industrial era, Norway's practices have been sharply scrutinized and even legally challenged. Norway is frequently called out for exporting its pollution while championing electric car use at home (where it's the highest in the world on a per-capita basis, thanks to generous tax advantages).

Inevitably, Norway gets fingered for running a greener-than-thou public policy, a smokescreen that shifts the blame from producer to consumer, bringing a reputational boost while enriching itself at the expense of a world addicted to oil. But measured against the country's long-term security, most in Norway seem to regard any reputational wobbles as a price worth paying. Wealth also compensates in another sense, since Norway's traditionally high foreign aid budget (and the work of committed globalists like Jan Egeland) partly shields it from criticism.

As of 2015, Norway was the second-highest per capita donor among OECD countries, at 1.16 percent, with Sweden highest at 1.36 percent. (World Economic Forum figures for 2015 put Norway at a more modest 1.05 percent and in third position after Sweden and the United Arab Emirates.) Along with this national visibility and clout comes the individual sort; the same WEF in 2017 chose Børge Brende, formerly Norway's foreign minister, as its chief. Perhaps, in the end, it really is a case of the end justifying the means. The world is better off with a rich and involved Norway, and that requires finessing the oil factor by planning earnestly and actively for its aftermath.

The fossil fuel economy has changed and transformed Norway, but it hasn't created a new one. Oil speeded an evolution rather than fanning a revolution. The stratospheric consumer prices broadly attributed to it are, in fact, a long-standing bane of Norwegian life. Even in 1799 a visiting Thomas Malthus noted import dependency as the reason "which makes living in Norway more expensive perhaps than any other part of the world."

A tidy Norwegian history could be written on an economic narrative alone. It would flow from a Viking history of raid and plunder, take in the Hansa lock on Norwegian fishing and include the timber bonanza of the *hollandertid*. It would cover the quixotic tax policies of Christian IV, the attitude-turning Napoleonic blockade and the post-Kiel debt poison. It would include the poverty-driven westward emigration and the early disruptions of industry. Not least, it could include two European debates (1972, 1994) which revolved around questions of financial autonomy as much as traditionally political ones concerning an overbearing Brussels.

Seemingly tight Norwegian attitudes to money have frequently animated the pens of travelers. Fredrika Bremer noticed sharp Norwegian commercial instincts. Mary Wollstonecraft, who went there partly to conduct business on behalf of her erstwhile partner, was categorical: everywhere "wealth demands too much respect; but here [in Norway], almost exclusively it is the only object pursued." Four years later, Thomas Malthus found that "those who could speak English were inclined to make us pay for the convenience." Half a century on, Bayard Taylor noted that Norwegians were "quick-witted whenever the spirit of gain is aroused," a tendency he deplored as "keen and grasping."

We should not read *too* much into such accounts; they were not only writer-travelers but also tourists on budgets, subject to the usual rude surprises when it came to settling the bill, and reliant on local goodwill while lurching across the countryside in their horse-drawn *carrioles*. And there are, as always, obviating opinions. W. E. Gladstone, British prime minister and admirer of Norway who spent a month there in 1885, hailed "its manners unspoilt, its self-respect uncorrupted by the insolence of wealth." Still, it illustrates varying mind-sets encountered at a time when rural poverty coexisted with pockets of coastal and urban wealth. And they confirm an understandable priority on money, or the lack of it, in the prototypical Norwegian mind, with reason and for a very long time.

A less charitable trait, tight-fistedness, has paralleled endemic poverty as another classic theme in Norwegian public life. This has been highlighted because the lack of organizations often meant individuals, notably artists, having to petition parliament directly in order to get grants to live or work on. In 1851, the great violinist Ole Bull despaired when his modest request for start-up money for a Norwegian theater in Bergen was voted down (unanimously) by the Storting. Henrik Ibsen's early poverty, and chagrin, was deepened by two failed requests for a state pension before he finally got one. Pioneering sociologist Eilert Sundt was more successful, but his short-term grants too eventually ran out. A generation later, a university request on behalf of Fridtjof Nansen for his Greenland expedition for 5,000 kronor (US$20,000 today) was in Huntford's words "summarily rebuffed" by the Storting in early 1888, causing the soon-to-be-world-famous explorer to find alternative funding in Denmark. Amundsen's *Gjøa* expedition was a debt-ridden operation that nearly didn't come off. And Norway's early Olympic teams were repeatedly stymied in their efforts to secure enough funding. The tightwad charges frequently leveled against the nineteenth-century Storting often centered on one Søren Pedersen Jaabæk, a figure "mostly remembered for his consistent policy of saving and making cut-backs," according to Schønsby, a medical researcher whose needy field sometimes bore the brunt.

Another huge background consideration is Norway's history of economic upheaval related to its reliance on primary resources. Cod and herring stocks came and went at mysterious intervals, causing entire shifts in fishing fleets; shoals that disappeared from the west coast in 1796 reappeared in 1808, while another disappearance around 1870 devastated many fishing communities. The timber trade cut itself down along with the forests. Whaling turned Svalbard into the world's unlikeliest boom town. Periodic crop failures during wet summers are the stuff of darkest Nordic history. Shipping is a famously up-and-down industry: resurgence in the 1860s and 1870s was followed, in the 1880s, by competition from abroad; boom in World War I led to postwar bust.

In 1899 the "Kristiania crash" ended Norway's century with a financial washout, prompted (it is said) by a talkative messenger boy who spread panic on the Oslo bourse along with a bankruptcy rumor. The resulting construction slump was still evident years later, making the great fire that destroyed Ålesund in 1904 an opportunity to reboot a depressed sector locally. The fallout from a mining catastrophe in the early 1960s shook up governments in Oslo. A quarter-century later Norway was knocked sideways by a global oil price collapse. Historically minded Norwegians are acutely aware of how fleeting primary economy wealth can be, and how violent the swings of fortune. And these were Norwegian-specific crises, aside from the better-known others that affected Norway along with the global economy, from the Great Depression to the 1987 market crash to the 2007–08 banking collapse (which originated partly in Norway's one-time colony of Iceland). It may have inculcated a deeper tolerance for risk, and greater expertise in addressing it. For example, Norwegians, unlike the other Scandinavians, typically buy real estate with adjustable-rate mortgages, not the more conservative, fixed-rate ones favored elsewhere.

The national oil "rainy day" fund is a powerful reflection of the need to minimize this historical vulnerability. It is also an outsized, globalized manifestation of an ingrained national parsimony. This proclivity has relaxed in private as well as public spheres, but there is equal evidence of an ingrained savings mentality (the *matpakke*, or lunchbox from home, being one indicator). A recycling (*pant*) tendency feeds a certain genius for improvisation and reflects economic and not just environmental considerations.

This has been a life-and-death matter at times that stirs the national blood. There is a vivid example in the Norwegian film *The Twelfth Man*, which follows a saboteur, Jan Baalsrud, fleeing for his life in wartime Norway. Some guardian angels who have risked their lives arrive at his isolated hut, rip apart a beached boat and pound together a sturdy sledge that eventually whisks him, with the help of reindeer, to safety in neutral Sweden. It is, and is intended to be, a classic Norwegian scene.

Yet it is impossible to avoid the impression that contemporary Norwegian life is thoroughly and often unsettlingly monetized. Life both public and private revolves very largely around cost, price and similar issues of economy. The flaunting of individual wealth is still frowned upon but no longer taboo, yuppification having made inroads already by the 1980s. Norway has become a scruffy-rich kind of place where money talks loudly and insistently. Wealth is Norway's new, or now not so new, unofficial aristocracy. It may even have slipped into that role more easily than it would have in Sweden, where old social divisions, faint but still alive, might have offset some of the effects.

Despite the expanding pie (or because of it), there's also a surprising amount of what appears to be economic envy, with samplings of excess wealth gleefully splashed across tabloid front pages. Celebrities take special care not to advertise their housing size; country houses are often more lavish than primary ones and are insistently called "cabins" even if they sport outdoor Jacuzzis. All this confirms an old truth, that what matters is not absolute but relative wealth: that no one else is getting too far ahead of you and that you, in turn, aren't seen to be gaining an undue advantage. It feeds the sense of a meritocracy without confirming the existence of one.

While wealth manifestations can be banal or downright obnoxious, the net effect is very far from negative. By all accounts and by most measures, Norway has become a much more pleasant place since the 1960s. But concentrated wealth does have a corrosive quality whose effects appear with a long lag time. The unveiling, in late 2017, of evidence that elements in the real estate industry had worked to manipulate an already frothy housing market was a disturbing example of a link between rising incomes, growing inequality and flagging ethical standards.

A few months later, unsettling revelations about rampant cost overruns in the Storting renovation project revealed unexpectedly lax standards in the field of public procurement and official contracts. The clash between the old and the new Norway is sometimes noisy. It is hard to avoid the sense of a latent sleaze factor. And those in the nonmonetary professions face different challenges in the form of forbidding tax levels and living costs. Life in contemporary Norway is a surprisingly tough and unedifying scramble to make ends meet for those without the benefit of a full-time salary—a growing portion of the workforce, beyond the comforting official statistics, with which I am wearily familiar. Yet another unseen element is the army of volunteers, most but not all retirees, who keep all manner of social services operating at minimal cost to the state.

Indeed one of oil's striking manifestations is that it has *not* eliminated anxiety and political bickering over money, while passing the production peak may well have increased a sense of foreboding. The policy of locking most of it away provokes endless second-guessing. Criticism of governmental policy is anyway hardwired into the Norwegian psyche, and both right and left (insofar as those old terms still apply) are happy to weigh in. From the left come demands to spend more on hospitals and trains, on welfare and infrastructure; free school meals became a hobbyhorse of Labor leader Jonas Gahr Støre. From the right come demands for income tax relief and a less onerous state. Tourists with wheels, for that matter, can only marvel over the sky-high price of fuel at the pump, which they think should by all accounts be cheap. It is—in Saudi Arabia.

Some Norwegian oil anxiety is safely future-oriented and some is overblown, but much is justified. There is fear over what will happen after the oil is gone. There is fear that the world will wean itself from fossil fuel *before* the oil is gone. There is fear of market disruption. There is fear of accident on offshore rigs ceaselessly bashed by stormy seas. There is fear that knock-on inflation is pricing the average family out of the housing market. There is fear that oil prospecting in vulnerable areas will bring environmental calamity and kill the golden goose, along with Norway's reputation for careful stewardship. There is fear that grasping immigrants are siphoning off Norwegians' hard-earned wealth and exploiting their well-funded welfare state.

There is also fear that wealth is making Norwegians privately intolerant even while they remain publicly tolerant. There is fear that wealth makes Norway a tempting target for cyber-terrorists and other malign forces. There is fear that a unique bounty is not being handled astutely enough—but also a parallel fear that future politicians will sense this, change the rules and make things worse through politicized bungling. There is (well-founded) fear that easy money is exacerbating drug and other social problems among young Norwegians spoiled by life in the bubble. There is fear that the saved wealth, along with their hopes, dreams and pensions, will shrivel in a global economic meltdown or be hit by scandal. There is fear that the old savings mentality that served Norway so well is fading.

There is also a relativist fear among many that, however well-off they might be, they are trailing their friends and neighbors in the good-life stakes. And there is fear of eroding values and trust in a country built on them: that the country is losing its ethical compass because of the very thing the nation depends on. These may be the fears of luxury, the frettings of princes over their realms not paupers over their next meal, but even crowns can weigh heavily. When you have risen high, there is more to lose.

An essential problem for Norway is the need to cultivate and balance two obvious needs that are also fundamentally at loggerheads: love of nature on the one hand and a need to exploit the resources under their feet on the other. It may seem as though Norway entered into a Faustian bargain when it leapt into the oil age, the devil's pact that Goethe made famous. But things are not so cut and dried as that. Norwegians are compelled, by the nature of things, to balance the two. Norway is both nature-blessed and oil-bound. It is a big and basic dilemma that has to be managed politically but which cannot be solved, almost like life itself.

The best that Norway can hope to do is to prevent its compromise from getting too messy by keeping industry as clean as it can, and by diverting the inevitable charges of double standards by actively planning for a nonfossil long-term future of wind farms and electric cars. Norwegians as a rule do genuinely revere nature; even in the eighteenth century, the wealthier set was relocating out of Oslo. But they are also a no-nonsense people in a capitalist society for whom *not* exploiting their fossil fuel for a world still eager to pay for it would seem like so much lunacy. It's a balance that comes with a reputational price, but for Norwegians that price so far has seemed eminently manageable. The sharpest moral dilemmas are certainly cushioned (and outside criticism blunted) by high disposable incomes.

The really ticklish time for Norway lies neither in the present nor in the distant future but in the medium term. The next 10–20 years, which will coincide with the long and bumpy transition away from fossil fuel, will also bring the last major phase of Norwegian fuel exploration and exploitation, in Arctic waters that are far more distant, stormier and less surveyed. Roughly a third of the world's undiscovered fossil fuel lies there, some inside Norway's exploitable economic zone. This carries inherent risk that can only be partly offset by tighter safeguards and better technology.

One major focal point is Lofoten, the scattered archipelago near Bodø, off Norway's northwest coast, and the even remoter Vesterålen, to its north. The question of whether to allow drilling there has animated political debate for a decade without real resolution—but also set against a bedrock expectation that it will happen eventually in some form or other, which gives a somewhat artificial flavor to the debate. New fields, like the Barents Sea's *Snøhvit* gas deposits, promise jobs and investment for distant outposts like Hammerfest. But the problems remain manifest. Not every ambitious oil engineer cares to relocate his family to the Arctic.

Lofoten is an especially delicate matter because its untapped oil is found in more accessible waters than those of the Arctic. The archipelago is doubly renowned for its fairytale landscape and its sliced cod (*klippfisk*) industry. An otherworldly setting for painters and poets does not easily mix with the wily world of the oil executive. The area's waters also spawned the legend of the *maelstrøm*, popularized by Jules Verne and Edgar Allen Poe. NRK, the Norwegian television system, once ran an all-day, real-time live streaming of the waters rushing in and out of the narrow tidal basin. There is an unmistakable mystique about the place.

Adjacent waters are vital spawning grounds and transit zones for fish, according to Norway's *Havforskning* (sea research) institute. Cold-water coral reefs symptomize this fragile bounty while helping to nurture it. Norway, of course, was a fishermen's country before it was the oilmen's or the timber cutters'. Lofoten, where you can view sea eagles and whales, represents an essential link in a timeless chain of life. Tampering with Lofoten is tantamount to fiddling with Norway's essence.

Marine science, when it overlaps with the tourist promise of a pristine paradise, puts an entirely different spin on an oil debate. Drills must pass through the sea before they reach the seabed, while the oil passes up the other way. This is not just a question of fishermen's livelihoods and the yearly catch; it concerns fragile maritime ecosystems that frame Norway itself like few other countries. The issue touches multiple raw nerves.

Drilling remains some way off. It was initially delayed by the need for a *Konsekvensutredning*, an impact study. Before it was voted out of office in September 2013, the Labor Party gave a surprising go-ahead for studying oil development off Nordland and Troms, including Lofoten and Vesterålen. But it also emptily pledged a revote in 2015 and has a vocally anti-drilling youth wing. The rural-based Center Party opposes more drilling. Awkwardly, Norway's oil minister in a previous center-left coalition, Center's own Ole Borten Moe, was bullish on Lofoten prospecting. The whole debate is conflicted because it raises serious value choices heading toward an uncertain future. Meanwhile a potentially bigger concern—loaded oil tankers (not all Norwegian) plying coastal waters, following an uncertain set of international shipping rules—easily gets overlooked. It's another layer in a multitiered ecology-versus-economy dilemma.

Typically Norway is a land of fruitful if painfully slow compromise. Oil prospecting is kept on a leash by strict safety standards. But the leash itself gets longer as you approach the Arctic and tends to loosen under an industry-friendly governing coalition. Meanwhile pressures are building to access distant fossil fuel, and quickly, as rigs further south are decommissioned.

The government announced in early 2017 that 97 new blocks of Barents seabed were being auctioned off to energy conglomerates for future exploitation. Norwegian environmental groups were up in arms. Its *Naturvernforbundet* (society for the conservation of nature) complained about the government's tin ear when it came to hearing out concerns about the Arctic environment. "It has never been so bad" was the dismal sum-up by one of its officials, Silje Ask Lundberg. The Norwegian Institute for Marine Research, a scientific body rather than an environmental pressure group, concurred over the potential dangers, saying more drilling meant unknown dangers for bird and fish life in some pristine northern waters.

As the oil age ages, life for many Norwegians gets better even as the future dilemmas they face get tougher.

11

The Meaning of Nobel

The whole of my remaining realizable estate shall be dealt with in the following way [...] one part to the person who shall have done the most or the best work for fraternity between nations, for the abolition or reduction of standing armies and for the holding and promotion of peace congresses [the prize] for champions of peace by a committee of five persons to be elected by the Norwegian Storting.
    Will of Alfred Bernhard Nobel, November 27, 1895

There is no simple formula for what makes a good choice.
                            Geir Lundestad, *Fredens Sekretær*

For more than a century, the Nobel Prize for Peace has piqued the world's interest and, for the most part, commanded its respect. Such is the impact of Nobel—a robust, granite-like name, Mt. Rushmore-worthy, impossible to forget—that the prize has become an institution in its own right. Norway fell into its role as chief public arbiter of this sensitive field. By exercising that role, Norway gets lifted up reputationally and subtly defined in the process. While the prize is a vital part of the national patrimony, it's also something less than permanent, and Norwegians are acutely aware of both facts.

The award has eclipsed the many others doled out each year for similar purposes but with far less élan. Like the Academy Awards, it is packaged in a televised ceremony; but unlike the Oscars there is less glitter and no Golden Globes to provide a warm-up act.

In its very considerable field, Nobel has effectively cornered the market. No other name seems to register or to matter.

While obviously impressive, this effective monopoly also traps the prize into something of a bubble. In spotlighting successes in this field it also subtly changes the way we understand and regard that field. The prize givers not only award peace efforts, they determine what types of peace efforts to award. Over time this can come to redefine what peace and peace-making are all about.

An award to honor those fighting against misuse of power has become, in a curious way, a power in its own right. It's an unaccustomed position for Norwegians to occupy, and it gives them a special kind of influence. The paradoxical side of the Nobel equation also fits in well with the national story. It came from a private bequest, from a Swede no less, built on a back story stranger than most fiction.

The downside of this success—or, perhaps, a second one—is that complicated considerations of war and peace get funneled into the patent artificiality of a single prize handed out every 12 months, one which carries the nicely rounded figure of a million dollars (depending on the going exchange rate).

Uniqueness is a quality that is often claimed but rarely earned. In this case it is. A certain magic attends the Nobel name, and within the elite circle of Nobel prizes, the one given for peace-making efforts seems to attract more media attention and public scrutiny than all the others combined—although Swedes, and chroniclers of the often contentious literature prize, would probably dispute this airy claim.

When something unique is also highly visible the result is fame, but fame of the easily tarnished sort. The singularity carries further still. The prize for peace was the only one that Nobel specifically entrusted to Norwegian care, and it's also the only one that he entrusted to an explicitly political body, Norway's Parliament. This makes it a focal point for Norway itself, given how central parliamentary democracy has been to the making of modern Norway. Its growth—measured in column inches, prestige, chat room chatter, institutional heft and a combustible mix of outside veneration and venom—closely tracks (and itself has fueled) the emergence of "big Norway" itself.

The prize ceremony, a fixture on the national calendar each December 10, is a distinctly Norwegian affair: solemn, low key, typically accompanied by mournful violin solos. Appalling numbers of learned people around the world still think that Sweden hands out the peace prize, and getting this point right has become the ultimate litmus test for an outsider's passing knowledge of Norway. The event, held inside the capacious and lavishly muraled city hall, marks the date of Alfred Nobel's death (as well as UN Human Rights Day, later so designated). It is a hot ticket in Oslo. The Nobel Peace Prize has been in growth mode since the outset, but the expansion hit a new gear in the twenty-first century.

Yet the process itself has not fundamentally changed. The committee meets in an elegant yet simply appointed room with paneled walls dotted with portraits of past laureates, on the second floor of the Nobel Institute's headquarters. In that hushed inner sanctum the five members plus the secretary whittle down the list of nominees, commission background reports, debate options and, sometime before the early October deadline, vote and decide. The noon announcement is brisk and sober.

The ceremony itself was once confined to the hushed and elegant, nineteenth-century villa on Drammensveien, just up the road from the royal palace, where the (Stockholm-based) Nobel Institute's Oslo headquarters have been situated since 1904. Few of the early award-winners showed up in person. Burgeoning interest in the prize, during a tumultuous twentieth century in which general peace proved elusive, forced a later move to the University Aula. In 1990, Western fascination with Mikael Gorbachev, the enigmatic and popular awardee that year, compelled another change of venue to its present location. That, at least, seems unlikely to change; there's no public space bigger in Oslo.

Among recent additions, but since abandoned, was an annual Nobel concert featuring invited artists and music ranging from classical to hip-hop, which turned it into a more popular, or at least populist, affair. Nobel has also been a Norwegian growth industry in a physical and financial sense. In 2007 the Nobel Peace Center was opened in the converted *vestbanestasjon* (the old western train station) across the harborside plaza from the City Hall, offering interactive displays of past winners for the visiting public, who come in droves. The bifurcated nature of Oslo, its *Vestkant* and *Østkant* split by a modest river, is nowadays reflected even in its Nobel infrastructure. Not a few visiting dignitaries, unaware of the split addresses, have been chauffeured to the wrong place.

The prize boosts Norway's visibility while strengthening its reputation for studious depth and considered reflection. This is not just a story about Alfred Nobel, or his prizes, or peace itself; it is also a story of Norway. In the (knowledgeable) world's eyes, it has become not just a prize given by Norwegians but *Norway's prize*—a very different sort of animal, and one that draws interpretive controversy.

One, admittedly counterfactual clue to this fusion of national and thematic focus is this: the option of *not* granting a prize in any particular year has seemingly vanished. The anticipation is too intense and the logistics of a big event too intricate to jeopardize the whole affair with the tantalizing possibility of a nondecision. This is a choice that was frequently exercised in the past, when the prize committee was deadlocked or circumstances militated against.

The awardee list reveals some striking nonaward years. Famously and sensibly, the committee refused to give out awards during either world war. Less known are the peacetime gaps. Some fell in consecutive years, most notably 1924 and 1925. In 1928, and again in 1932, nobody got the nod. As late as 1966–67 the prize was again retained for two years running. The most recent year of no decision was 1972. Nowadays it is practically inconceivable for this to happen. In Sweden too, home of *Nobelstiftelsen* (the Nobel Foundation), only exceptional circumstances will now stop the awarding. The 2018 literature prize was one, canceled because of a spiraling sex scandal at the Swedish Academy.

The Nobel awarding ceremony is the one annual event sure to draw foreign attention to Norway. Providing safe and functional arrangements for the whole event is a huge challenge for the city of Oslo that involves, apart from the panoply of sophisticated security detail, all manner of visitation and hospitality requirements that have to be planned far in advance while accounting for last-minute changes by visiting VIPs. There are now two full months for this, between October (when the winner is announced) and 10 December. The annual hubbub also contributes to the local economy, thanks to the influx of hundreds of high-fliers on generous expense accounts. There seems too much at stake now, too much latent pressure to deliver a decision, a winner and a successful event, for the committee to play spoiler and still keep their reputations and, perhaps, their jobs.

Prize recipients are guaranteed top billing for the day on CNN, BBC and other world news outlets. They are the subjects of gently probing and respectful one-on-one interviews, their speeches scoured for notes of controversy and nuggets of wisdom. Norway and its Nobel committee all reside in the middle-distance background, discreet players in the process, basking in the quiet glow of giving voice to those with universal aspirations finally getting their due, and all in the warmth of Christmas season. In a world of vanishing reverence for virtue, the peace prize retains something of the sacred cow. With due respect to skiing and oil, it is nowadays the biggest name, and possibly the most visible and revered, of all Norwegian exports.

For all its cachet, the prize is a source of interpretive frustration on multiple levels. A prize dictated by the calendar is also trapped in its own awkward timetable. It is supposed to go to the person who has done the most for peace *in the previous year*, but which year? Increasingly, this proviso is applied to the still-unfinished year drawing to a close, but that involves interpretive license since the deadline for nominations is 31 January. The obvious inconsistency in recognizing this cutoff doesn't much worry the committee, judging from Geir Lundestad's revealing memoir from his 25 years as Nobel secretary.

While some potential winners have been denied because of it (Jimmy Carter in 1978 is the most glaring example), others have received the nod in disregard of dates (the 1993 peacemakers in the Middle East). In the controversial case of Barack Obama in 2009, the cutoff date was rendered meaningless as he had taken office just 11 days before. One result is a split emphasis: winners tend to be either those with a hot-off-the-press breakthrough (as in a recent ceasefire deal) or else perennial peace advocates finally being recognized. In a 24/7 news environment, harking back 18 months is like reaching into the awkward middle past, so it easily falls through the cracks.

Interpretive issues run deeper. The prize's prestige hinges on its autonomy. Yet however strenuously the Nobel committee emphasizes its independence of action (both formal and factual) and its resistance to political interference whether foreign or domestic, such a claim is greeted in many places with arched eyebrows. It strikes many non-Westerners as a democratic pretense, one that exaggerates notions of (committee) autonomy and which is, in the end, hard to sustain on an absolute scale. To some this double trend of growth and creeping Norwegianization is a little ironic, since the whole thing fell into Norway's lap.

Alfred Nobel's intentions with regard to his peace prize even today remain hazy. The industrialist was a late-life convert to pacifism, a change of heart that is reflected in his correspondence with Bertha von Suttner, a prominent Austrian peace advocate (and future laureate). The significance of that relationship has been shown by Anne Synnøve Simonsen, who (alone among Nobel researchers) has scoured the extensive correspondence between the two in Nobel's last years.

The Nobel bequest has been the focus of endless speculation. As with the money, so with the man: Nobel was a global figure (who lived in Russia, Italy and France) and not-very-Swedish national who compiled a substantial fortune mass-manufacturing explosives and selling them to the armies of the world. It is almost too easy to think of the peace prize as blood money, a late act of atonement for a lifetime given over to the testing, patenting, packaging and selling of nitroglycerine and smokeless gunpowder to governments bent on arming themselves. Yet in his last decade he developed an interest in the international peace movements that were burgeoning in tandem with militarism before World War I. After seemingly wallowing, mostly alone and Scrooge-like, in the darkness he apparently saw the light, or was made to see it by others.

His final will, which nullified earlier ones, was dated November 27, 1895; he died at home in Italy a year and two weeks later. It caused a sensation when, in January 1897, it was opened. Its provisions specified that his various business interests were to be wound up, liquidated and put into a managed central trust.

A Nobel Foundation was to be built from scratch to manage the aggregated fortune.

In turn, four separate granting institutions were assigned the task of arranging decision-making bodies that would choose the winners, who were to be paid out of the interest earned on the capital. The chemistry and physics prizes were to be awarded by the Swedish Academy of Sciences; that for physiology or medicine by the Karolinska Institute; and that for literature by the Swedish Academy, all based in Stockholm.

The peace prize was different. It was to be handed out by a Norwegian committee, chosen by the Norwegian Parliament but supported by funds from Sweden. The potential for conflicts of interest was endless, and the tensions between Norwegian prize-givers and the Swedish paymasters are among the most revealing sections of Lundestad's work. Much later another, sixth prize was created, in the field of economics, given out (for the first time in 1969) by the Swedish *Riksbank*. The economics prize is sometimes dismissed as a quasi-Nobel, a gatecrashing addition meant for pioneering work in an unloved profession—the only social science so esteemed, as if to make up for the public drubbing economists regularly sustain.

As bequests go, this one was unprecedented. It immediately prompted fierce reaction, not least from an uncomprehending but influential and far-flung Nobel family. Some members tried, vainly, to overturn it. Those efforts reached up to the king of Sweden (and Norway), Oscar II, who intervened ineffectively. That failure at least marked a reassuring affirmation of law over politics.

Once settled, the will was quickly and rightly praised as visionary. Countless people have benefited and untold lives saved by the efforts honored by the prizes—works, perhaps, stimulated by the allure of the prizes themselves (the upside of fierce ambition and vanity, surely). Yet ever since, questions of fidelity have swirled around the peace prize in particular. What did Nobel mean and intend? How much interpretive leeway should the committee assume? What scope is there for the "peace" term to evolve? Are career politicians the right people to decide such things?

Much of the problem revolves around the question of original intent. Most bequests are fulfilled and then forgotten. Unusually,

Nobel's is deliberately open-ended, a sort of living will. It involves the continuation, now into the twenty-first century, of wishes inked before World War I. Clearly, thinking must be allowed to evolve; just as clearly, the spirit of Nobel must be respected. Many angry words have erupted over the extent to which interpretation has triumphed. And because that interpretation involves so much prestige, so much money and so much visibility at both ends of the prize-giving, the questions can get amplified, as happened in the early 2000s in the Norwegian debate.

The will specified three separate criteria for peace prize winners. Disarmament efforts and the holding of "peace congresses" are specifically noted. Encouraging "fraternity among nations," the first-mentioned criterion, is also the loosest. Awards have gone to people for works that are tangential to narrow war-and-peace issues—notably to environmentalists or people, like Al Gore, preaching it.

Such questions cropped up repeatedly during the very first decade. In the inaugural year of 1901, an award (already, and a little controversially, being shared between two people) went to the founder of the International Red Cross, Henri Dunant, who had fallen into obscurity but was being reputationally rehabilitated. The rap then was that Dunant was a humanitarian who tried to soften the blow of war, but never worked specifically to eliminate or hinder it; a healer not a crusader. Three years later, an organization (the Institute of International Law) was the unlikely recipient.

Two years beyond that, just after Norway's break with Sweden, the choice was Theodore Roosevelt who, as US president, had helped negotiate an end to the Russo-Japanese war in 1904–5 but who also, as a politician, bore a quasi-imperialist reputation. This raised a third locus of early controversy, whether to reward the act or the person. The person inevitably came to feature; that was the view of Halvdan Koht, an early committee member and distinguished historian who wrote a scathing dissent, arguing that Roosevelt was the antithesis of what Nobel intended. Thus from the start the committee was vaguely tainted with a notion of "original sin" that worked to its advantage; having strayed from the nest early on, so the logic went, they were free to keep doing so.

The singularity of Nobel's testament is underscored by its seeming strangeness, and controversy was preordained by its opaque origins. Nobel the man often felt and probably was misunderstood, despite being an indefatigable letter writer. The arms dealer by day was a scholar-poet by night. His status as a lifelong, childless bachelor hardly helped. Any misunderstanding is itself understandable given the nature of his profession and his apparent late-life change of heart (there are reasons to be skeptical of deathbed confessions and the like). The will itself took up just four pages, remarkably short for a man with his breadth of interests and full- or part-holdings ranging across Europe and Asia that added up to an immense but scattered fortune.

The passages pertaining to the prizes covered less than a page, yet the bulk of the estate was to pay for them. The mechanics were not planned out and never explained. He specified that outside institutions would bestow the prizes, yet he never inquired whether they wanted the responsibility, and he never floated the idea publicly before he died. If confusion about his intentions was natural, then irritation over executing them was inevitable. His stipulation for complete liquidation of his holdings created severe problems for others, including family members effectively forced into a fire sale of their own shares in part-owned businesses. The legal tentacles were not just intergenerational but multinational, and the losses substantial.

There is more. Nobel named as his chief executor his 25-year-old engineering assistant, Ragnar Sohlman, a man with no legal or financial experience or expertise. Sohlman was roped into this life-changing role without being told, asked or sounded out. (A second executor, Rudolf Lilljequist, older and more experienced but tangential to the proceedings, was also named.) Sohlman then waited half a century before telling his side of the story, and even that was published posthumously. Gaps and the unexplained permeated the whole process. Nobel wrote his will himself, in longhand, without accompanying indicative notes and without consulting a lawyer.

It took the scrupulous determination, resourcefulness and diplomatic skills of Sohlman himself—who along with Bertha von Suttner is the unsung hero of this story—to have the will respected and fulfilled. (His grandson, Michael Sohlman, later headed the Nobel Foundation for two decades.) That the willed fortune involved, at one stage, an escape from France at gunpoint, with millions stashed in suitcases, gives it a cheap-thriller aspect along with a tinge of Chaplinesque comedy.

In 1898, in the midst of the will controversy, Sohlman was drafted into the Swedish army. "Recruit 114 Sohlman" was forced to juggle the daily slog of an army grunt with the pressures of serving as legal executor for a deceased global industrialist. Unconscionably split between two worlds with little help, he had to improvise, furiously; sensitive phone calls were routed into the officers' mess, while he set up shop in a vacant room where he conducted his urgent business by night. Sleep was rare and fitful.

When Sohlman needed to take a three-day, will-related trip to Kristiania (Oslo), his commanding officer reputedly asked "What's that? What the hell has Recruit Sohlman got to do in Kristiania?" As real-life anomalies go, it is rivaled only by the case of T. E. Lawrence, who after he became world famous as Lawrence of Arabia enrolled (under the name of John Hume Ross) as an entry-level aircraftman in Britain's Royal Air Force, where he met illustrious friends like George Bernard Shaw on after-hour escapes from the base. But whereas Lawrence engineered his own anomaly, Sohlman was forced by circumstances into his. It was a classic case of an unprepared man rising brilliantly to the occasion.

Born in Stockholm, Alfred Nobel was Swedish in nationality but in little else. A lifelong expatriate, he left Sweden at 9, going first to Russia with his father. He returned to Sweden chiefly for visits, usually coinciding with the September birthday of a mother to whom Nobel was deeply devoted. His home there, at Bofors, was rarely used but proved critical in establishing Sweden, rather than France, as the jurisdiction of the will. Though Swedish was Nobel's native tongue, Sohlman intriguingly notes in his memoir that it was only the inventor's fourth best-written language after French, English and German. As the will was handwritten in Swedish, this might be thought a complicating factor given the sketchy outline of his intentions that suggested a late-hour brainstorm.

Coming off a sickly childhood, Nobel often suffered poor health, yet pursued a peripatetic and workaholic life that may have speeded his demise at 63. As an adult he lived chiefly in Paris, but had to leave for legal reasons, and lived out his last years in San Remo, Italy, where he died—alone except for servants with whom he couldn't even converse (his linguistic skills did not include Italian), adding a suitably tragic note to the story.

His patented inventions, factories, financial acumen and hands-on stewardship generated immense wealth, but it was a rocky ride with wild swings of fortune. In the popular telling Nobel, who suffered depression in his later years, was so afflicted because of a bad conscience, which led him to become beholden to activists, like von Suttner, pushing a peace agenda. Proponents of this view cite his earlier (1893) will that focused mainly on science prizes while treating the peace question via a separate and smaller bequest.

Worse, in the context of that male-centric world, some of those peace advocates, notably von Suttner, were women. In February 1898 King Oscar of Sweden-Norway summoned Emmanuel Nobel, the deceased industrialist's nephew, for a meeting, telling him that "Your uncle was talked into this by fanatics, womenfolk mostly," a revealing opinion in two senses. Yet after the will was settled, King Oscar became a strong advocate and even handed the (Swedish) awards out personally.

Why did Nobel involve Norway, and why did a nonpolitician rope the Norwegian Parliament into his designs? Evidence is anecdotal and suggestive at best; for example, he admired the writings of Ibsen and especially Bjørnson and was fond of Sohlman's Norwegian wife. A deeper explanation involves Norway's situation in 1895. Norway and Sweden were wrangling over their forced union, and Nobel may have wanted to share the wealth, and the responsibility, with the aggrieved junior partner.

Better still is the idea that he approved of the Storting's internationalist leanings, notably its championing of compulsory arbitration of disputes. Norway's was the world's first parliament to provide funding for its members to attend international conferences like the Inter-Parliamentary Bureau (later Union). He may have assumed a meeting of minds, but he was naïve with respect to the political stream into which he was plunging.

At the time the Storting was widely thought more "advanced" than Sweden's Riksdag, having made its crucial democratic breakthrough a decade before, in 1884. Suffrage was wider in Norway than in Sweden. Significantly, the Storting also had fewer responsibilities, especially in foreign policy, which was still Sweden's domain, and was pushing for a foreign voice. Majority political opinion in Norway was dominated by Venstre, the "left," which Nobel evidently felt more inclined to promote his cause and follow his wishes than was Sweden's politically more conservative (and German-leaning) establishment. In the context of the times his decision is not so surprising.

There seems little truth in speculation that he was trying to break up the union, not that one rich man's will, or a yearly prize, could manage that. But it added fuel to the fire, as shown by King Oscar's awkward efforts to prod Nobel's family to contest the will—not relishing the thought of large sums flowing out of the Swedish treasury to Norway.

And so it was that Norway—still short of independence, diplomats and democracy —found itself tasked, unbid, with deciding the peace award. The novelty (not to say timing) was remarkable, as were the multiple lacunae. Dissension over individual winners seems like small potatoes compared to the implications for a Norway that would pick them.

His chief influence, von Suttner, was an Austrian aristocrat who became an influential author, passionate advocate of disarmament and, in 1905, first female recipient of the prize. In an intriguing study of their relationship, Anne Synnøve Simonsen demonstrates her pivotal role as instigator of both the prize and its Norwegian home. It seems reasonable based not just on the evidence—Nobel seems to have found in his maturity a new cause beyond profits at Bofors, which he had bought some years before—but also on some very human circumstances that are not hard to fathom. Simonsen shows, for example, a deeply literary side to Nobel that few knew about and was drawing his attention in the 1890s, especially following his precipitate move to Italy, where he knew no one.

His circumstances reflected his loneliness, his peripatetic lifestyle and the obvious affection and respect he had for von Suttner (in sharp contrast to his recently soured relationship with Sofie Hess, a one-time flame and subsequent hanger-on who gave him no end of grief). Whether or how far he was "influenced" by a mature woman and peace activist is interesting but to some degree academic; the fact is that he legally mandated for the award to be set up, and the wider evidence indicates that he reached the decision over several years. This was no last-minute, scribbled-in alteration, and he was very much in charge of his faculties. Norway, too, was the considered choice, and his decision changed the way Norway would come to be viewed.

Fame and occasional fury have followed the award since its inception. Much of it relates to the decisions themselves. Awards to Yasser Arafat (1993) and Henry Kissinger (1973) sparked resignations and (mostly hidden) angry words because the awardees were thought, by dissenters inside as well as outside the committee, not to be peacemakers at all. Others, like that to Obama in 2009, were derided as unearned or emptily aspirational; earlier ones, like that to Carl von Ossietzky (an anti-Nazi dissident named in 1935), sparked committee resignations for foreign policy reasons. Still other choices, like that for John Mott (a founder of the YMCA) in 1946, raised objections that they weren't peace advocates as such. In Mott's case the committee's own longtime chairman, Gunnar Jahn, and another member were overruled.

Second-guessing of the annual prize, including from within, is a cottage industry in itself. At times it echoes the old Cold War game of Kremlinology, prompting avid speculation over decisions on the basis of informational scraps, hints of internecine fighting and unexplained resignations following eccentric choices. Discretion and candor are handmaidens in this annual decision.

The process has drawn detractors too and has sparked periodic changes in the rules. Some basics remain as they were laid down: a prize decided upon by a five-person committee elected by the Storting, its members sitting for six-year terms. Prestigious committee spots are ceaselessly angled for, while the body as a whole guards its independence zealously. Members vote their conscience and, once the argumental dust has settled, decisions are treated, at least publicly, as unanimous. Those involved quietly and firmly, if not always happily, close ranks. The most public of awards, given out by the most open and democratic of countries, has the most private of processes leading up to and following it.

The prize committee has been taken to task for shadowing the broad lines of Norwegian foreign policy or discreetly furthering its aims. Given its potentially incendiary subject matter, there are reasons why the whole effort is kept under wraps, yet this factor itself adds to the suspicions of overlapping objectives. The official ban on discussing decisions, debates, dissensions and even nominations is 50 years—longer than many countries' restrictions on publishing state secrets.

Yet over the decades there has been a clear trend *away* from overt political interference into the Nobel-picking process. In the early years the annual prize closely tracked Norwegian policy priorities; indeed in the years 1901–05 it effectively *was* Norwegian foreign policy, and continued in that vein for independent Norway up to World War I.

For some decades cabinet members, even prime ministers, often chaired the Nobel committee. In a bid to limit conflicts of interest, Parliament in 1936 disallowed committee membership for sitting members of the cabinet; since 1977, sitting members of Parliament have been barred too. Parliament as a whole now practices surprisingly little oversight. At the ceremony itself, careful distance is also maintained between the award and the Norwegian state; King Harald sits in attendance but does not hand the awards out (whereas the king of Sweden distributes the others in a separate Stockholm ceremony). The prize for peace being the only one entrusted to an overtly political body, extra cautions in protocol are deemed necessary.

A different sort of politics has, however, arisen over time. In 1948 an important rules change was made. In an effort to reduce wrangling over committee seats and credentials, Parliament decided to assign seats to the big political parties, on a proportional basis according to how they fared at the previous election (which is similar to how the seven-person Swiss executive, the Federal Council, is constituted). Since then the big parties have zealously guarded "their" seats, which has led to clashes over purpose.

One occurred in 2017, when the Progress Party—a notably nationalist group, resistant to immigration and not especially noted for advocating peace or disarmament—proposed a party grandee, Carl I. Hagen, for its seat. Hagen, a perennial lightning-rod for criticism, was howled down in public derision (and replaced by Asle Toje, a former research director at the institute). Nearly lost in the kerfuffle was the fact that Nobel committee seats, while appointed by Parliament, need not be professional politicians at all. The fact that they nearly always have been emphasizes how hard it is to separate the prize from the country that awards it—or from Norwegian politics as defined by Parliament or from political processes and pressures as such.

In his rather pointed memoir, historian Geir Lundestad highlighted still another and more insidious political question, the distinctly different styles, purposes and attitudes of the Norwegians and Swedes supposedly united in this common endeavor. All the prizes come out of the bequest administered by a common body, the *Nobelstiftelsen*. It doles out annual monies for the prize, administrative costs and building upkeep. Astonishingly, no Norwegian was represented on that body until 1985, when Odvar Nordli was finally picked; even then it helped that he was a former Norwegian prime minister, the Swedes being more preoccupied, in Lundestad's view, with "fine titles." Still, skepticism and different outlooks persisted. "We were preoccupied with our own thing," Lundestad avers, "and the less we had to do with the Swedes, the better." This he attributes to a Swedish *storebrormentalitet* (big-brother mentality) and a concomitant, equally obtuse Norwegian *lillebrormentalitet*.

Issues of war and peace, which are also matters of life and death, are contentious by definition. Committee seats are sought after, but the job cannot be easy. The committee is equally open to scrutiny for what it does and for what it fails to do. The apparent simplicity of its task—vetting possibilities and choosing an annual winner or (up to three) winners—is complicated by an imperfect world and an immovable deadline. Obvious winners are elusive; humans are human. Soldiers-turned-peacemakers who get the nod might have dubious credentials that include a killing past; those who are politically active might tarnish their own reputations and embarrass the committee, in the future (with Burma's Aung San Suu Kyi the standout twenty-first century example). Deserving candidates can go unrecognized, with Mahatma Gandhi permanently atop the list of grievous oversights. Others have died before they could be awarded. The problem of hewing to Nobel's guidelines is an equally dicey matter, as we'll see. An award, any award, is a subjective question over which well-meaning and thoughtful people can, do and often must vigorously differ.

Meanwhile the growth and the razzmatazz that increasingly surrounds the Nobel events each December draw its share of detractors who say that the whole affair has become too big, too commercial and too willing to play to the public gallery. Much of this criticism was directed at Thorbjorn Jagland, the director in Lundestad's last years. The committee has been accused of bending with the political wind, even with some choices that were tailor-made to Nobel's specifications; for example, the 1997 award to Jody Williams and the International Campaign to Ban Landmines was surely prompted by the shock death of Diana, the popular Princess of Wales, who had taken up the issue publicly. In that case the timing rather than the choice was eye-catching.

With dissent hardwired into the Nobel Peace Prize, any attention, good or ill, inevitably gravitates back to Norway and its custodianship. All this makes the whole subject a sensitive one, even after a century of remarkable growth. A latent fear lurks that too many controversies (like that over Hagen) or iffy choices will prompt new Swedish calls to pull the peace prize to Stockholm—the source of the prize money, the foundation's headquarters and the custodian of the other prizes. It is an annual tightrope walk. For that reason, institutional (including financial) autonomy is paramount to the Norwegians, and the lack of it clearly rankles. Here again we find a telling, leftover relic of a union with Sweden that, in this regard, never quite ended.

And then there is the ever-present prospect of choices that boomerang. Because the prize goes mostly to living, active people fiercely dedicated to their work (Dag Hammarskjöld's posthumous award in 1961 being a singular exception), changing circumstances and future embarrassment can only be feared, not anticipated. Awardees from the Middle East can fall into this category, as does Aung San Suu Kyi. An acclaimed choice in 1991, when she was under house arrest, she was a symbol of defiance, democracy and decency, with a helpfully gender-based angle to boot. She chose not to attend the ceremony, fearing forced exile. A handsome publication by the Nobel Institute in 2001, marking the centenary of the prize, was specifically dedicated to her. Yet raging controversy over ethnic cleansing of a Muslim minority in her native land, during which she was widely accused of passive complicity or submissive impotence, brought fierce second-guessing over a prize given, to near-universal acclaim, a quarter-century before.

Another matter specifically and awkwardly relates to this, alone of all the Nobel prizes. It touches on the ever-difficult nexus of politics and law, and is the focus of hard-hitting critique by a Norwegian peace advocate and lawyer, Fredrik Heffermehl. In a range of books and articles he has been a vociferous Nobel committee critic. He holds that Nobel's wishes have been disregarded by committees who assume the right to interpret "peace" in their own ways—in effect, creating new criteria by handing out prizes, for example, to environmentalists, political dissidents and human rights advocates who may be admirable people but were not "campaigners for peace" in the original meaning. "Respect for the testament [...] has dropped significantly," he argues, resulting in a "steep decline in loyalty to Nobel," while the appointment of what he considers retired party hacks to the committee on the basis of electoral strength is nothing short of "a betrayal of Nobel's trust."

Heffermehl regards this development as a legal breach of trust, not just a matter of free interpretation of "peace" or even playing loose with Nobel's stated intentions. As a lawyer he regards it as a violation of the nature of inheritance law given that the committee is charged, specifically and solely, with fulfilling the terms of Nobel's will—a narrow not a broad obligation, which rules out liberal interpretation just as surely as judges are barred from legislating from the bench. He even regards the committee's interpretive straying as tantamount to an act of theft—with an added touch of moral hazard, since it takes prize money away from chronically ill-funded groups that are specifically campaigning for peace or disarmament, while frequently honoring already well- (and publicly) supported groups or individuals who may be rich and/or famous already.

He also takes the Nobel Institute to task for monetizing the whole Nobel concept, going after sponsorships in ways that may boost Norway's Nobelist cache but subtly corrupts the spirit of Nobel and cheapens the proceedings. Lundestad was the evident target of much of his wrath, whom he more or less accused of pulling strings behind a weak throne, so that might be thought a time-sensitive (and rather weak) complaint. Yet the author is surely correct in holding that few of today's parliamentarians hew to Nobel's thinking as of 1895, for how could it be otherwise?

Yet another frequent criticism, one indirectly addressed by Heffermehl, is the alleged pro-American bias of the committee—which he takes as part-reflection of Norwegian foreign policy interests as a loyal NATO member since 1949. Joining the Western military alliance marked a basic departure from Norway's long-standing earlier interest—which was especially keen around 1890—in compulsory arbitration and international cooperation via groups (like the IPU) that promoted a peace agenda. More US nationals have been Nobel peace laureates than any other nationality, which, to some, detracts from the award given America's sometimes contentious military engagements from Korea and Vietnam to Iraq and Afghanistan. Certainly some of the more disputed awards have gone to American figures; long before Kissinger in 1973 there was George C. Marshall (1953), a retired general, later Secretary of State and founder of the Marshall Plan (from which Norway much benefited), whose choice literally drew catcalls at the announcement. Theodore Roosevelt in 1906 was the first American awarded and the first truly controversial choice.

It's a serious allegation for which the first decade of the twenty-first century seemed to provide traction, given that three Americans, all prominent national politicians (Jimmy Carter, Al Gore and Barack Obama) took home awards during a seven-year stretch. All were Democrats, so the committee, some suggested, was vaguely playing some American domestic card as well; in Obama's case, the committee's relief over the departure of George W. Bush was palpable. Yet few office-bound US heads of state have actually received Nobels; just two sitting presidents have been awarded, and they were separated by more than a century (Roosevelt in 1906, Obama in 1909). The Carter choice relieved the committee of a perennial headache. He was a walking model of public rectitude, but specific success in any one year was frustratingly elusive until 9/11 happened and Carter's interventions over a second Gulf War gained him new attention. These various choices illustrate the annual fuss, elevated reverence and lava-flow controversy that attend the whole prize affair, while the committee is only as competent as its latest decision.

It is not surprising that Norway so reveres the Nobel peace award and looks on it as a proprietary institution. That the Nobel Prize enhances Norway's international visibility is undeniable. That it also "enlarges" Norway, its status and reputation, may be more surprising. That it easily draws second-guessing is inevitable. Norway gets a backwash of blame when the award proves a clunker, as many thought in 2009, or hit with a severe foreign policy reaction, as happened in 2010 with the choice of Liu Xiaobo, a Chinese dissident.

Yet the prize also handicaps Norway. As the awarding nation, it is open to charges of favoritism whenever a Norwegian is in the running. Nobel specified that the prize should be non-national, but he did not reckon with unspoken prejudices built into a process that excludes far more than it includes. Sweden, of course, faces the same problem with its awards. Veiled criticism of the Swedish Academy when Tomas Tranströmer, a Swedish poet (and the *eighth* Swede honored overall), was given the literature award in 2011 showed how favoritism charges are almost inevitable. So Norway, despite its recent activism in peace-building, suffers restricted access to "its" own award. Any potential Norwegian candidate, for example, Jan Egeland, needs to be extra-qualified. In a way it involves a neat extension of *Janteloven* itself; a kind of forced self-abnegation is at work.

Sweden has produced five Nobelists for peace. Two were shared with another (those to Klas Pontus Arnoldson in 1908 and Hjalmar Branting in 1921), while the other three (Nathan Söderblom in 1930, Dag Hammarskjöld in 1961 and Alva Myrdal in 1982) were sole winners. Norway has had two winners, just one (Fridtjof Nansen) outright, and none since 1922. The two Norwegians were named in consecutive years; both were men. Otherwise they were diametric opposites. One, Nansen, was world famous, the other (Christian Lange in 1921) almost unknown even in his time; yet sticklers to Nobel's guidelines have argued that Lange, a lifelong peace advocate, was the more strictly deserving winner. Nansen was an indefatigable worker cited for his multipronged—but to some, prize-tangential—efforts to repatriate prisoners of war, provide papers for stateless persons, relieve famine in Ukraine and Russia, and arrange refugee exchanges across the Aegean.

Over time there has been an evolution away from what Nobel had in mind, which creates a constant need to imagine what Nobel *might* have wanted or approved of. As noted, assumed latitude is an inbuilt problem. So is the nature of politicians, who are habituated to be proactive, whereas deciding on prizes essentially is a passive role of reviewing activities and following instructions of a will. So effectively there are three built-in problems—the facts that mainly politicians do the deciding, that a national institution has to follow the wishes of a single man and that Norwegians were so instructed by a Swede—even beyond the expected complications relating to the winners. Is it any surprise that interpretation is so paramount, and so vexed?

It is an independent decision in theory, made with difficulty in practice. Lundestad, Heffermehl's one-time nemesis, himself alleged meddling by Norwegian officials. By far the most damaging controversy in recent times came via China's forceful reaction to the 2010 honoree, Liu Xiaobo. The Chinese state had no truck with notions that the Nobel is not an indirect organ of Norwegian officialdom and a subtle foreign policy tool. In Lundestad's view the Norwegian Foreign Ministry and its then-chief Jonas Gahr Støre (unsuccessfully) pressured the committee not to give the nod to Liu. China then retaliated against Norway, canceling meetings, hounding its diplomats, summoning ambassadors in protest and throwing up tailored tariff walls that lost Norway substantial trade income. The award to Liu touched an international chord and straddled a world fault line. Only at Christmas 2016, after six years of limbo, did Norway's then-foreign minister, Børge Brende, patch things up with Beijing. The following year Liu died, still unfree.

The peace prize makes Norway into a sort of universal symbol for humankind's higher aspirations. There is a "wisdom from the mountain" element in the whole process, of setting future standards in the abstract. This can land the process and the people involved in hot water precisely because the peace prize is even more emphatically a link to the past. It anchors this institution to a Norway that no longer exists: the preindependent country that lacked diplomats and sent its legislators to attend peace congresses and promote arbitration. This did not matter as long as Norway had no independent disputes to settle. If Nobel expected the Norwegian committee would be a selfless mediator of merit, an invisible conveyor-belt for his wishes, then he was underplaying the prestige and power that would accrue to any such decision-making body, and to the country then pushing to the brink with Sweden.

Norway draws prestige and luster from the prize-giving process. It reinforces the national role as the committed ethicist and bold internationalist. It even plays into a certain Norwegian penchant for benign mischief, often expressed in its ability to wrong-foot predictions with an unorthodox choice. The country enjoys a reflective glow and appears earnest and well meaning, making it an insistent presence in a global dialogue without being ostentatious or sanctimonious. But the sensitivity of it all never dies, and Norway itself is not a completely objective presence. The prize is used to push the world along, gently, and the world can occasionally push back, hard.

The China counterattack, which shook the Norwegian establishment deeply, was a vivid manifestation of "large Norway," of an engaged country with international visibility and heft. It reinforced a trend evident in recent years. Norway's impact has been demonstrated, rather awkwardly, in a growing tendency to attract criticism. Norwegians always seem taken aback when their country gets hit with one charge or the other. International opprobrium is still rare, given wide perceptions—both inside and outside the country—that the Norwegian approach is not just well-intentioned or right-minded but also *fundamentally right*. Feelings get a little bruised when that presumption is challenged.

Norway attracted severe criticism in the 1970s when the extent of sealing and whaling in the Arctic became publicized internationally in *Paris Match* and other picture-heavy publications. Outrage followed. Norwegians did not invent whaling, but their name became irrevocably associated with its modern age. Norwegians rationalize the continued culling of minke whales on environmental grounds (they are the "rats of the sea," getting too numerous) while sensitized Westerners take it, none too gently, to task.

The occasional, targeted criticism that Norway attracts, whether for these practices, for its oil or for clunky Nobel choices, goes hand in hand with visibility. Nations with a strong presence attract the most attention and the most criticism; it comes with the territory. Typically it is the "largest" countries—China, Russia, the United States, Germany, to some extent Brazil, Japan and India—that are most persistently in the news, dominate social science textbooks and attract the most searching scrutiny. Victorian Britain, successful, expansive and haughty, was in that position. Sweden under Olof Palme in the late 1960s and 1970s became a lightning-rod because of his vocal antiwar and anticolonial stances. Being a country professing ideals, as Norway is and does, makes this factor the more important. It automatically opens it up to insinuations of hypocrisy or woolly thinking.

If Norway only attracted the nodding, smiling approval of an indulgent world, it would signify marginality, not importance. That country would be a pleasant nonentity. And it is not necessarily the case that such criticism lowers Norway's standing in the world's eyes. Being criticized means being noticed, and as any advertiser will point out, attention itself, publicity, is the best advertisement. "Global resentment," the novelist Jonathan Franzen wrote in a 1996 essay about New York, "is the highest compliment a city can receive," but he could just as easily have been referring to his ancestral land of Norway. Being criticized is part of the drama of being a player; taking a stand is not for the faint-hearted. Critical attention is a sign of respect, in the sense of a world that is actually paying attention to what a country, in this case Norway (or a small part of it), does.

Attracting the ire of Russia (over fishing), of China (over Nobel) and of fellow Westerners (for Arctic whaling) certainly reinforced this element and even forced a cessation of Norwegian sealing. So has criticism of Statoil (now Equinor), Norway's state-run oil company, for its investment in shale-oil projects in the United States and Canada. Charges of double standards flew. In May 2016, alleged plans to dump waste in a Norwegian fjord attracted the critical attention of the *Financial Times*. The point is not the merits of the arguments but the tendency not to cave in so readily with the political correctness that also implies.

As with whaling and oil, Nobel is inextricably linked to Norway's world profile. But unlike those perennial industries, Nobel is both contrived and artificial; the prize is a slave to the calendar and provides but a minor service to the most perennial, and for many the most urgent, of activities. Perhaps this is why the late writer Christopher Hitchens called the prize a "bore" and lit into recipients for angling for it. His main target, perhaps predictably, was Mother Theresa, for harboring aspirations of sainthood—undoubtedly the ultimate ambition—coupled with a nun's unseemly lust for the limelight.

The Nobel itself, like its honorees, is far from perfect. It is a ballyhooed institution that lands Norway, annually and discreetly, in the news. Recent years have also shown that the Nobel establishment is alive to criticism and astute enough to adjust when it gets too shrill. Yet one constant remains: an ongoing (Norwegian) struggle to break the Swedish yoke.

12

Epilogue

Norwegians have come a very long way and are keenly and pridefully aware of the fact. The country that deigned to describe itself in 1950 (in the infamous *Oslo Book*) as "gray, colorless and dull, [which] has surely something to do with our national mentality" has been busily transforming itself. Norway has emerged, butterfly-like, as a land of entrepreneurial flair, quirky experimentation and prestige projects like a new national gallery so conspicuously immense (and costly, and squarish) that during construction it became, for many unimpressed locals and old-timers, a source of chagrin as much as pride.

In time they may warm to it, the way a past generation made its peace with its once-maligned neighbor, the city's Town Hall, when it was unveiled after World War II. Yet this is also a country and capital so headlong into expansion that a second major museum (to house the Munch collection) could be built at the same time yet hardly be noticed. Together the grudging acceptance and the double-time progress say a great deal about the Norwegian mental cosmos.

Evidently, Norwegians are reaping the fruits of a singular bonanza and displaying them with fetching enthusiasm. But it's not just that. They are also spinning an unusual patrimony into a strikingly different and open-ended national project. It can indeed seem as though Norway's traditional vexations of geography and history have been put to bed, or refashioned with wealth-fueled ingenuity into something like a new Norway able to wink at its old nemeses—the sort of place where celebrities can return to the land (as in the "reality" TV serial *Farmen*) and giggle their way through a cow-milking session on camera.

But it would be a mistake to see the twenty-first century Norwegian outcome, if an outcome it is, as some art-begets-life version of Askeladden, the idler of folk tales who wins the girl and the kingdom's keys. Luck is sweeter when it's earned, and Norwegians can make a fair case for achievement. The actual story is grittier but more appealing than that of Ash Lad's. It also features some connecting themes that lend perspective to today's Norwegian phoenix.

They include a knack for tackling structural obstacles with flexible mind-sets, an uncanny doggedness and, far from least, a flair for exploiting opportunities without seeming opportunistic. That Norway, a still major oil producer in a time of climate change frenzy, can be saluted for its ecological sensibilities is among its more unlikely achievements. The impetus for this going concern is found in the situational triad I've tried to dissect in these pages.

Geography traditionally dealt Norway a poor hand—locationally, latitudinally, topographically—that it finessed by adapting to the sea; using its fjords as mental and physical assets; developing savvy solutions for local application; and maximizing opportunities to engage with the world and satisfy that restless nomadism that forms such a distinctive national thread.

History delivered unpromising conditions that prioritized some similar adaptive tendencies. The fourteenth-century Black Death rearranged Norwegian reality without destroying older customs or incipient awareness of common cause. The controlling tendencies of foreigners (Hanseatics, Danes, Swedes) instilled the value of restrained and flexible response. Unusual opportunities, like those from the Dutch imperium and even the Danish *eneveld*, gave them openings to exploit and lessons to learn from. Being handcuffed to Sweden after 1814 politically helped them develop societally, and eventually turn the tables on their masters via relentless logic, dazzling art and people's democracy. And the fledgling world of sport gave it a chance to engage internationally on equal terms while keeping some essential integrity about a home-grown and cherished lifestyle like *ski-idræt*.

The three perennials of the final section underscore the value, for a smaller state, of excelling in a niche capacity. Norway's

Nordic nest, its oil economy and its peace prize are all accidents of location and the past. But they are also concentrated, limited-focus opportunities that could be managed adroitly because they draw on bedrock elements of Norwegianness, namely a propensity to act cautiously while thinking boldly. It helped that Norway was well attuned to exploiting energy resources in awkward locations, spreading its wings widely, planting the flag in some truly exotic places and bearing up to the long-domineering neighbors who now wait their tables at high-end restaurants.

Norwegians' ability to keep their heads down and zigzag their way out of trouble was patented during long postmedieval centuries. A Viking past, enthusiastically raked over, makes Norwegian history seem more exuberant than it often is, yet that history is the more impressive because of its paucity of fireworks. And it is the more unusual because it reflected a pattern of bold or charismatic individuals giving a spirited lead (often in finger-wagging form) to the nation. It was such tendencies that not only kept Norway from collapsing in crisis or exploding in revolution but rendered such extreme outcomes implausible.

When closing a complicated circle, it's tempting to pick an example that tells a bigger story. For me such a moment came the weekend before the 2018 Winter Olympics, as an expectant country relished the prospect of a national triumph that, in the end, outdid even the sky-high expectations.

But it was a preliminary that caught my attention. Starting on a Friday evening and running, without a single break, until early Monday, one of Norway's two national, noncommercial TV channels broadcast a telethon dedicated to a single man, Ole Einer Bjørndalen, newly retired from a career that mixed skiing and shooting a kind-of gun. (Admittedly he is a special talent: the most decorated male Winter Olympian of all time, he racked up 45 world championship medals, 20 of them gold, and 14 Olympic medals, the last one at 43.). The telecast ran *55 hours nonstop* including three consecutive all-nighters. It covered each of his 96 world cup wins from start to finish, interspersed with expert commentary in case some viewers missed the point.

Then again, what was the point? Norway's fixation on winter sport and its reverence for great home-grown athletes needed no reminder. It seemed that a mirror was being held up, part of a wider exercise that reflected Norway and not just an illustrious Norwegian. The quirkiness of the idea, the tendency toward obsessiveness, the against-all-odds celebration and the toss-off ability to produce and broadcast such reverential monotony without bothering too much about the costs all delivered a generously definitive statement about a country that is self-consciously and now self-confidently different. The national story, or a desired version of it, seemed encapsulated in the grit and triumph of a biathlete in the toughest of combined elite sports, multiplied by 96. Look how far we've come, the broadcast seemed to shout; behold the grand synthesis. Bjørndalen was the ultimate Norwegian metaphor.

This display of unabashed Norwegian pride also raises a flicker of concern. If triumphing (over others or their own limitations) has delivered the sweet spot of life—a debatable proposition for many, including in Norway—then what might come next? Norway is not necessarily primed for a fall, but assumptions that life will stop improving are being openly voiced. A "party's over" sentiment may prevail, but after-parties have a way of stretching out too, and Norwegians—inured to lifestyles beyond the wildest dreams of their parents, let alone grandparents—are not obviously inclined to relinquish the trimmings.

Norwegians tend to fret (inwardly), which is probably a good thing; so is a cultural predisposition that tempers grandstanding. Less edifying are other outward signs, like the vaguely blasé, self-absorbed atmosphere that continuous prosperity seems to bring, and which outsiders have reluctantly to accept. Another is a parallel and almost touching tendency among many to assume "the system" will address any deficiencies. Any tendency toward triumphalism is best tempered by awareness that Norway, which has friends and institutions lending a supporting hand, is not quite the heroic loner of the imagination (or the Bjørndalen telethon). Plenty of issues remain on the national plate, from the unevenness of the EU relationship to rising levels of private debt to rumblings of intolerance, without evident appetite to tackle them systematically.

Spring 2019 brought two unsettling reminders of how easily the societal balance can get out of whack in a place, like Norway, where nature still defends its corner. First, a fungal infestation led

EPILOGUE 331

to the massive culling of farmed salmon along the northern coast. The losses sent shock waves around a traditional fishing, exporting and fish-exporting country. Then a pristine mountain lake near Bergen was found to be polluted, prompting a nationwide alert over water purity in a country that takes pride in its water resources. The causes of both were complex, but they seemed to prompt a disquieting sense that basics had been neglected and standards allowed to slide.

In his book *Fishing in Utopia*, Andrew Brown looks back on a 1970s Sweden he once knew but which he found, on later return, to have vanished. It's a book written with sympathy but tinged with sadness. It offers a cautionary tale for a country at a genuine crossroads—an oil state facing a pivot away from oil—but an inexact parallel for Norwegians, who hold onto their customs more tenaciously and have a track record of adjusting, often abruptly, to circumstance.

The need to achieve a tougher modus vivendi than the one on skis is pressing on the twenty-first century. Norway sits at the crux of an energy economy and an ecological worldview, which makes it an emerging metric for a world debate over transitioning to a cleaner-energy future. Norway is increasingly a global touchstone for a hot-button issue, as its energy focus shifts toward the same Arctic that is animating urgent global warming concerns. *This* is the grand synthesis that Norway could help bring about, and the one that outsiders will be looking to for hints and guidance.

Norway is not used to the glare of publicity or the role of testing agent. Its successes have been those of small Norway, the niche player able to finesse its way to success. Now a bigger Norway is called for. Its shift from the slipstream to the front line—metaphorically in these twinned global issues, physically in the Arctic—will almost certainly bring wider attention while adding to expectation. Even that oldest of Norwegian staples, the fuel-reliant mobility that drove its development and still ties a distended country together, could attract unwelcome scrutiny.

Skiing excellence may be the amalgamated self-image Norwegians hanker for, but their ability to respond to the energy–ecology–Arctic challenge, with its global and local echoes, will ultimately determine the Norwegian image in the rest of the world. It is a huge and complicated question, but few countries can claim better preparation or the self-interested wherewithal to tackle it.

Still, this is undeniably a special time for Norwegians. Not many countries have the chance to contemplate a halcyon moment, much less parlay it into something substantial and lasting. That is Norway's privilege and challenge.

Bibliography

Preface

Davies, Norman. *Europe: A History*. Oxford and New York: Oxford University Press, 1996.
Galtung, Johan. "Norway in the World Community." In *Norwegian Society*, edited by Natalie Rogoff Ramsøy, 385–428. Oslo: Universitetsforlaget, 1974.
Goodhart, David. *The Road to Somewhere: The Populist Revolt and the Future of Politics*. London: Hurst, 2017.
Mikalsen, Knut-Erik. "Nordmenn er verdens-mestre i jobreiser." *Aftenposten*, September 24, 2016, 20–21.
Milne, Richard. "Environmental Hero?" *Financial Times*, May 6, 2016.
Tuchman, Barbara W. *Practicing History: Selected Essays*. New York: Ballantine Books, 1981.
World Happiness Report 2017, United Nations Sustainable Development Solutions Network, accessed June 19, 2017. http://worldhappiness.report/ed/2017/.

Chapter 1: Little Big Country

Aase, Andreas. "In Search of Norwegian Values." In *Norway: Society and Culture*, edited by Eva Maagerø and Birte Simonsen, 13–28. Kristiansand: Portal, 2008.
Area of Land and Fresh Water, Statistisk Sentrabyrå, accessed May 23, 2018. www.ssn.no/natur-og-miljo/statistikker/arealdekke.
Barr, Susan. *Norway: A Consistent Polar Nation?* Oslo: Fram, 2003.
Bore, Thor Bjarne. "Jonas Lied and Svalbard." *The Norseman* 45:5 (2005), 34–41.

Bromark, Stian, and Dag Herbjørnsrud. *Norge: et lite stykke Verdenshistorie.* Oslo: Cappelen, 2002.
Ellingsve, Eli Johanne. *Stedsnavn på Svalbard/Names on Svalbard.* Trondheim: Tapir Akademisk Forlag, 2005.
Enzensberger, Hans Magnus. *Norsk Utakt.* Oslo: Universitetsforlaget, 1984.
Ferguson, Robert. *Henrik Ibsen: A New Biography.* London: Richard Cohen Books, 1996.
Frydenlund, Knut. *Lille land, hva nå? Refleksjoner om Norges utenrikspolitiske situasjon.* Oslo: Universitetsforlaget, 1982.
Fulbright, J. William. *The Arrogance of Power.* New York: Random House, 1967.
Henningsen, Bernd. "The Swedish Construction of Nordic Identity." In *The Cultural Construction of Norden*, edited by Øystein Sørensen and Bo Stråth, 91–120. Oslo: Scandinavian University Press, 1997.
Hønneland, Geir. *Arctic Politics, the Law of the Sea, and Russian Identity.* Basingstoke: Palgrave Macmillan, 2014.
Ibsen, Henrik. *Ibsen: Letters and Speeches*, edited by Evert Spinchorn. New York: Hill & Wang, 1964.
Ingebritsen, Christine. *Scandinavia in World Politics.* Lanham, MD: Rowman and Littlefield, 2006.
Jespersen, Leon. "The Constitutional and Administrative Situation." In *A Revolution from above? The Power State of 16th and 17th century Scandinavia*, edited by Leon Jespersen, 31–181. Odense: Odense University Press, 2000.
Johnson, Paul. *The Birth of the Modern: World Society 1815–1830.* New York: HarperCollins, 1991.
Lie, Trygve. *Syv År for Freden.* Oslo: Tiden Norsk Forlag, 1954.
List of European Countries by Area, accessed February 17, 2017. https://en.wikipedia.org/wiki/List_of_European_countries_by_area.
List of European Countries by Population, accessed February 17, 2017. https://en.wikipedia.org/wiki/List_of_European_countries_by_population.
List of Urban Areas in Norway by Population, accessed February 17, 2017. https://en.wikipedia.org/wiki/List_of_urban_areas_in_Norway_by_population.
Lundén, Thomas. "Sweden's Territorial Organization: From Viking Frontier to Municipal Reforms." In *Placing Human Geography: Sweden through Time and Space.* Svenska Sällskapet för Antropologi och Geografi, 15–48. Stockholm: Motala Grafiska, 2010.
Millward, Roy. *Scandinavian Lands.* London: Macmillan, 1964.
Nansen, Fridtjof. *Nansens Røst: Artikler og Taler av Fridtjof Nansen II 1908–1930*, edited by A. H. Wisnes. Oslo: Jacob Dybwads Forlag, 1942.

Neumann, Iver B., and Sieglinde Gstöhl. "Lilliputians in Gulliver's World?" In *Small States in International Relations*, edited by Christine Ingebritsen, Iver B. Neumann, Sieglinde Gstöhl, and Jessica Beyer, 3–38. Seattle: University of Washington Press, 2006.
"En 'Norgesvenn' refser sitt land." *Aftenposten*, August 13, 2006.
Norges geografi, *Store norske leksikon*, accessed September 21, 2017. https://snl.no/Norges_geografi.
Norsk Idéhistorie: Et lite land i verden, Bind VI, edited by Trond Berg Eriksen, Andreas Hompland and Øystein Sørensen. Oslo: Aschehoug, 2003.
"Norway weighs giving Arctic peak to Finland." *The International New York Times*, July 30–31, 2016, 3.
Nye, Joseph. *Soft Power: The Means to Success in World Politics*. New York: Public Affairs, 2004.
Roberts, Peder, Klaus Dodds and Liza-Marie van der Watt. "But Why Do You Go There? Norway and South Africa in the Antarctic during the 1950s." In *Science, Geo-Politics and Culture in the Polar Regions: Norden beyond Borders*, edited by Sverker Sörlin, 79–110. London and New York: Routledge, 2013.
Russell, Bertrand. *Praise of Idleness*. London: Routledge, 2004.
Sangolt, Linda. "A Wealthy Outlier: Norway in an Age of Globalization and European Integration." In *Norway: Nature, Industry, Society*, edited by Grete Rusten, K. Polthoff and Linda Sangolt, 297–320. Bergen: Fagbokforlaget, 2013.
Singer, Marshall R. *Weak States in a World of Powers: The Dynamics of International Relationships*. New York: The Free Press, 1972.
Sogner, Sølvi. "Norwegian-Dutch Migrant Relations in the Seventeenth Century." In *Dutch Light in the "Norwegian Night,"* edited by Louis Sicking, Harry de Bles, and Erland des Bouvrie, 43–56. Hilversum: Uitgeverij Verloren, 2004.
Stolpe, Sten. *Dag Hammarsköld: A Spiritual Portrait*. New York: Charles Scribners, 1966.
Storeng, Ola. Hvorfor er Norge best? *Aftenposten*, Oktober 29, 2016, 2.
Taylor, Peter J. *Political Geography: World Economy, Nation-State and Locality*. New York: Longman/John Wiley, 1993.
Thomson, David. *Europe since Napoleon*. London: Pelican, 1966.
Torgersen, Ulf. "Political Institutions." In *Norwegian Society*, edited by Natalie Rogoff Ramsøy, 194–225. Oslo: Universitetsforlaget, 1974.
Urquhart, Brian. *Hammarskjöld*. New York: W.W. Norton, 1994.
Wollstonecraft, Mary. *Letters Written during a Short Residence in Sweden, Norway and Denmark*, edited by Carol H. Poston. Lincoln: University of Nebraska Press, 1976.
Wood, Denis. *The Power of Maps*. London: Routledge, 1993.

The World Bank in Small States, accessed April 18, 2018. http://www.worldbank.org/en/country/smallstates/overview/.

Chapter 2: A Directional Puzzle

Amundsen, Roald. *My Life as an Explorer*. Chalford: Amberley, 2008.
Botton, Alain de. *The Art of Travel*. London: Penguin, 2002.
Bown, Stephen. *The Last Viking: The Life of Roald Amundsen*. London: Aurum, 2012.
Bryer, Anthony. "The First Encounter with the West: A.D. 1050–1204." In *Byzantium: An Introduction*, edited by Philip Whitting, 83–110. New York: New York University Press, 1971.
Forte, Angelo, Richard Oram and Frederik Pederson. *Viking Empires*. Cambridge: Cambridge University Press, 2005.
Gibbon, Edward. *The Decline and Fall of the Roman Empire*, abridged by Dero Saunders. Middlesex: Penguin, 1981.
Hegge, Per Egil. *Den Norske Folkesjela: Ordene som Forteller hvem vi er*. Oslo: Kagge Forlag, 2016.
Herrin, Judith. *Byzantium: The Surprising Life of a Medieval Empire*. London: Penguin, 2008.
Heyerdahl, Thor. *The Kon-Tiki Expedition*. London: George Allen & Unwin, 1950.
Homer. *The Odyssey*, translated by T. E. Lawrence. Hertfordshire: Wordsworth Classics, 1992.
Huntford, Roland. *Nansen: The Explorer as Hero*. London: Duckworth, 1998.
Kipling, Rudyard. *The Works of Rudyard Kipling*. Hertfordshire: Wordsworth Editions, 1994.
Logan, F. Donald. *The Vikings in History*. London: Routledge, 1991.
Lovoll, Odd S. *The Promise of America: A History of the Norwegian-American People*. Minneapolis: University of Minnesota Press, 1985.
Madeley, John T. S. "Scandinavian Christian Democracy: Throwback or Portent?" *European Journal of Political Research* 5 (1977), 267–86.
Magnus, Bente. "Veien til og fra Miklagård: Kontakten mellom Norge og det østromerske riket før vikingtiden." In *Hellas og Norge: Kontakt, Kompasjon, Kontrast*, edited by Øivind Andersen and Tomas Hägg, 119–38. Bergen: det norske institutt i Athen, 1990.
Malthus, Thomas Robert. "From the Travel Diaries." In *Travellers Discovering Norway in the Last Century: an Anthology*, edited by B. A. Butenshon, 28–45. Oslo: Dreyers Forlag, 1968.
Mead, W. D. *A Celebration of Norway*. London: Hurst, 2002.
Nansen, Fridtjof. *The First Crossing of Greenland*. Edinburgh: Birlinn, 2002.
Norwich, John Julius. *A Short History of Byzantium*. London: Penguin, 1998.

Ostrogorsky, George. *History of the Byzantine State*, translated from the German by Joan Hussey. Brunswick, NJ: Rutgers University Press, 1992.
Parker, Philip. *The Northmen's Fury: A History of the Viking World*. London: Vintage, 2015.
Piovene, Guido. *In Search of Europe: Portraits of the Non-Communist West*, translated from the Italian by John Shepley. New York: St. Martin's Press, 1975.
Reynolds, E. E. *Nansen: The Life-Story of the Arctic Explorer and Humanitarian*. Middlesex: Penguin, 1949.
Runciman, Steven. *Byzantine Civilization*. Cleveland: Meridian, 1967.
———. *The First Crusade*. Cambridge: Canto, 1992.
Schultz, Kathryn. *Being Wrong: Adventures in the Margin of Error*. New York: Ecco, 2011.
Stang, Håkon. "Fra Novaja Zemlja og Varanger til Verdens Hjerte." In *Hellas og Norge: Kontakt, Kompasjon, Kontrast*, edited by Øivind Andersen and Tomas Hägg, 139–52. Bergen: det norske institutt i Athen, 1990.
Stenersen, Rolf E. *Edvard Munch: Close-Up of a Genius*, translated and edited by Reinar Dittmann. Oslo: Sem and Stenersen A/S, 2001.
Sturluson, Snorri. *Heimskringla: or the Lives of the Norse Kings*, edited by Erling Monsen. New York: Dover, 1990.
Theroux, Paul. *Fresh Air Fiend: Travel Writings 1985–2000*. New York: Mariner, 2001.
Trägårdh, Lars. "Statist Individualism: On the Culturality of the Nordic Welfare State." In *The Cultural Construction of Norden*, edited by Øystein Sørensen and Bo Stråth, 253–85. Oslo: Scandinavian University Press, 1997.
"The West Wind." *The Economist*, December 23, 2017, 107–9.
Wester, Thorbjörn. "Spårlöst försvunna i Arktis." *Populär Historia* 3 (2019), 48–55.
Wood, Michael. *The Story of England*. London: Penguin, 2011.
The Wordsmith Dictionary of Phrase and Fable. Hertfordshire: Wordsmith Editions, 1993.

Chapter 3: Meanings of North

Andersen, Hans Christian. *A Poet's Bazaar: A Journey to Greece, Turkey & Up the Danube*, translated and introduced by Grace Thornton. New York: Michael Kesend, 1989.
Aubert, Wilhelm. "Stratification." In *Norwegian Society*, edited by Natalie Rogoff Ramsøy, 108–57. Oslo: Universitetsforlaget, 1974.
Balchin, Jon. *To the Ends of the Earth: Journeys of the Great Explorers*. London: Arcturus, 2006.

Bjørnson, Bjørnstjerne. *Three Dramas*. London: J.M. Dent, 1911.
Black, Jeremy. *The British Abroad: The Grand Tour in the 19th Century*. Gloucestershire: Sutton, 2003.
Brox, Ottar. *Hva Skjer i Nord Norge? En Studie i norsk utkanntpolitikk*. Oslo: Pax Forlag, 1965.
Brun, Hans-Jakob. "Endless Night and Crystal Days." In *Vinterland: Norwegian Visions of Winter*, 11–18. Oslo: De Norske Bokklubbene, 1993.
The Complete Works of William Shakespeare, Vol. II, edited by W. G. Clark and W. Aldis Wright. New York: Nelson Doubleday (undated printing).
Conway, Roderick. *No-Man's Land: A History of Spitsbergen*. Oslo: Norbok, 1995.
Cunliffe, Barry. *The Extraordinary Voyages of Pytheas the Greek*. London: Penguin, 2002.
Desai, Anita. "Frozen in Frøya." In *Bad Trips*, edited by Keath Frazier, 92–100. New York: Vintage, 1992.
Douglas, John. *Norway's Arctic Highway: Mo i Rana to Kirkenes*. Surrey: Trailblazer Publications, 2003.
Ferguson, Robert. *Enigma: The Life of Knut Hamsun*. New York: Farrar, Straus and Giroux, 1987.
Finlay, Victoria. *Jewels: A Secret History*. London: Sceptre, 2005.
Herodotus. *The Histories*, translated by Aubrey de Sélincourt. Middlesex: Penguin, 1954.
Hibbert, Christopher. *The Grand Tour*. New York: G P Putnam's, 1969.
Holmes, Richard. *The Age of Wonder*. New York: Vintage, 2008.
Hooker, William Dawson. "Notes on Norway." In *The Lure of the North*, 5–33. London: Pushkin Press, 2016.
Houltz, Anders. "Displaying the Polar Nation: Nordic Museum Exhibits and Polar Ambitions." In *Science, Geopolitics and Culture in the Polar Region*, edited by Sverker Sörlin, 293–328. London: Ashgate, 2013.
Howard, Roger. *The Arctic Gold Rush: The New Race for Tomorrow's Natural Resources*. London: Continuum, 2009.
Huntington, Samuel. *The Clash of Civilizations and the Remaking of World Order*. New York: Simon & Schuster, 2011.
Ingstad, Helge. "Fridtjof Nansen and Vinland Research." Det Norske Videnskaps-Akademi, Nansen Memorial Lecture, October 10, 1977. Oslo: Universitetsforlaget, 1978.
Into the Ice: The History of Norway and the Polar Regions, edited by Einar-Arne Drivenes and Harald Dag Jolle. Oslo: Gyldendal, 2006.
Jenkins, Roy. *Churchill*. London: Pan, 2002.

Johansen, Øystein Kock. "Ottar the Viking—the Voyages to the White Sea and Wessex." In *Norwegian Maritime Explorers and Expeditions over the Past Thousand Years*, 18–31. Oslo: Index, 1999.
Kagge, Erling. *På Eventyr*. Oslo: N.W. Damm & Søn A/S, 1994.
———. *Silence in the Age of Noise*. London: Viking, 2018.
Kent, Neil. *The Sámi Peoples of the North: A Social and Cultural History*. London: Hurst, 2014.
Lagerkrantz, Olof. *August Strindberg*, translated from the Swedish by Ansell Hollo. New York: Farrar Straus and Giroux, 1984.
Linné, Carl von. "A Tour in Lapland." In *Classic Travel Stories*, edited by Fionna Pitt-Kethley, 566–77. London: Leopard/Random House, 1996.
Lowe, Emmeline. "Unprotected Females in Norway." In *The Lure of the North*, 35–71. London: Pushkin Press, 2016.
Lundholm, Kjell O., Østen S. Groth and Rolf Y. Petterson. *North Scandinavian History*. Luleå: Tryck/Grafisk Huset, 1996.
Montesquieu, Baron de. *The Spirit of Laws*. New York: Prometheus Books, 2002.
Nansen, Fridtjof. "The Norsemen in America." *The Geographical Journal* 38:6 (1911), 557–80.
———. *In Northern Mists: Arctic Explorations in Early Times*, translated by Sir Arthur G. Chater. London: William Heinemann, 1911.
———. *Farthest North: The Exploration of the Fram 1893–96*. Edinburgh: Birlinn, 2002.
Niemi, Einar. "North Norwegian Rising: Regionalism and Nation-Building in the North, 1900–1940." In *Internationalization in the History of Northern Europe*, edited by Richard Holt, Hilde Lange and Ulrika Spring, 37–53. Tromsø: Report of the Nordsaga 99 Conference, 2000.
Nietzsche, Friedrich. *On the Genealogy of Morals*, translated by Walter Kaufmann and R. J. Hollingdale. New York: Vintage, 1967.
Norge: Det Bestes Store Veiatlas. Oslo: Det Beste A/S, 1999.
The Norton Book of Travel, edited by Paul Fussell. New York: W.W. Norton, 1987.
Norwich, John Julius. *A Taste for Travel: An Anthology*. New York: Alfred A. Knopf, 1987.
Østergård, Uffe. "The Geopolitics of Nordic Identity—from Composite States to Nation States." In *The Cultural Construction of Norden*, edited by Øystein Sørensen and Bo Stråth, 25–71. Oslo: Scandinavian University Press, 1997.Otnes, Per. *Den samiske nasjon*. Oslo: Pax Forlag A/S, 1970.
Ousland, Børge. *Alone to the North Pole*. Oslo: J.W. Cappelen Forlag, 1994.
The Oxford Dictionary of the World, compiled by David Munro. London: Oxford University Press, 1995.

Pedersen, Torbjørn. "Nordområdene lever sitt eget liv." *Aftenposten*, September 3, 2018, 12–13.
Remarks by State Secretary Audun Halvorsen at High North Dialogue in Bodø, April 4, 2019, accessed May 18, 2019. www.regeringen.no/en/akktuelt/dialogue_north/id2640602.
Rokkan, Stein. *Citizens, Elections, Parties*. Oslo: Universitetsforlaget, 1970.
Skinner, Toby. "The Town that Sold Christmas." *Financial Times*, December 22, 2018, 7.
Smith, Laurence. *The New North: The World in 2050*. London: Profile Books, 2012.
Sobel, Dava. *Longitude: The True Story of a Lone Genius Who Solved the Greatest Scientific Problem of His Time*. London: Fourth Estate, 1998.
Taylor, Bayard. *Northern Travel: Summer and Winter Pictures in Sweden, Denmark and Lapland*. New York: G.P. Putnam, 1871.
Thrower, Norman. "A Primer on Projections." *Mercator's World* 5/6 (November 2000), 32–38.
Thubron, Colin. *In Siberia*. New York: Harper Perennial, 2000.
Ubåtjakten utenfor Norge er trappet kraftig opp." *Aftenposten*, January 30, 2019.
Urwin, Derek W. "The Norwegian Party System from the 1880s to the 1990s." In *Challenges to Political Parties: The Case of Norway*, edited by Kaare Strøm and Lars Svådand, 33–60. Ann Arbor: University of Michigan Press, 1997.
Wilford, John Noble. *The Mapmakers*. New York: Alfred Knopf, 1981.
Woodman, Richard. *The Arctic Convoys*. London: John Murray, 1994.
Wullschlager, Jackie. *Hans Christian Andersen: The Life of a Storyteller*. London: Penguin, 2000.

Chapter 4: A Fractured Timeline

Acemoglou, Daron, and James A. Robinson. *Why Nations Fail: The Origins of Power, Prosperity and Poverty*. New York: Random House, 2012.
Anderson, Benedict. *Imagined Communities: Reflections on the Origins and Spread of Nationalism*. London: Verso, 1983.
Barton, H. Arnold. *Sweden and Visions of Norway: Politics and Culture, 1814–1905*. Carbondale: Southern Illinois Press, 2003.
———. "The Discovery of Norway Abroad, 1760–1905." In *Essays on Scandinavian History*, edited by H. Arnold Barton, 227–41. Carbondale: University of Illinois Press, 2009.
Benedictow, Ole Jørgen. *Plague in the Late Medieval Nordic Countries: Epidemiological Studies*. Oslo: Middelalderforlaget, 1992.

Berger, Stefan. "Nordic National Histories in Comparative National Perspective." *Historisk Tidskrift* 95:1 (2016), 67–96.
Bishop, Morris. *The Middle Ages*. New York: Houghton Mifflin, 1968.
Bremer, Fredrika. *Strife and Peace: Or, Scenes in Norway*. London: Knight, 1843.
Cantor, Norman F. *In the Wake of the Plague: The Black Death and the World It Made*. New York: Harper Perennial, 2002.
Carr, Edward Hallett. *What Is History?* New York: Vintage, 1961.
Christian Frederiks Dagbok fra 1814. Oslo: Gyldendal, 1954.
Cohn, Samuel K., Jr. *The Black Death Transformed: Disease and Culture in Early Renaissance Europe*. Oxford: Holden/Oxford University Press, 2002.
Defoe, Daniel. *Journal of the Plague Year*. London: Penguin Classics, 1986.
Derry, T. K. *A History of Modern Norway*. London: Oxford University Press, 1973.
Elstob, Eric. *Sweden: A Traveller's History*. Suffolk: Boydell Press, 1979.
Ersland, Geir Atle, and Hilde Sandvik. *Norsk Historie 1300–1625*. Oslo: Det Norske Samlaget, 1999.
Ferguson, Robert. *The Sword and the Cross: A New History of the Vikings*. London: Penguin, 2010.
Forte, Angelo, Richard Oram and Frederik Pedersen. *Viking Empires*. Cambridge: Cambridge University Press, 2005.
Henrikson, Alf, Arne F. Andersson and Helge Seip. *Norge og Sverige Gjennom 1000 År: i feide og fellesskap*. Oslo: Gyldendal, 1985.
Holmsen, Andreas. *Norges Historie: Fra de eldste tider til eneveldets innførelse i 1660*. Oslo: Universitetsforlaget, 1971.
Jordan, William Chester. *Europe in the High Middle Ages*. London: Penguin, 2002.
Keay, John. *Eccentric Travellers*. London: BBC/Ariel Books, 1985.
Kent, Neil. *The Soul of the North: A Social, Architectural and Cultural History of the Nordic Countries, 1700–1940*. London: Reaktion Books, 2001.
Making a Historical Culture: Historiography in Norway, edited by William Hubbard, Ian Eivind Myhre, Trond Nordby and Sølvi Sogner. Oslo: Aschehoug, 1995.
Manchester, William. *A World Lit Only by Fire: The Medieval Mind and the Renaissance*. Boston: Little, Brown, 1992.
Munch, Peter Andreas. *Norges Historie i kort udtog for de første Begyndere*. Oslo: 1839.
Nansen, Fridtjof. *Norge og Foreningen med Sverige med Supplementary Chapter to Norway and the Union with Sweden*. Oslo: Åse Kleveland Forlag, 2005.
Njåstad, Magne. "Resistance in the Name of the Law." In *Northern Revolts: Medieval and Modern Peasant Unrest in the Nordic Countries*, edited by Kimmo Katajala, 90–117. Helsinki: Finnish Literary Society, 2004.

North, Michael. *The Expansion of Europe, 1250–1500*. Manchester: Manchester University Press, 2007.
Norwegian Folk Tales, Selected from the Collection of Peter Christen Asbjørnsen and Jørgen Moe. New York: Pantheon, 1982.
Osborne, Roger. *Civilization: A New History of the Western World*. London: Vintage, 2007.
The Oslo Book. Oslo: Aktieselskapet Realforlaget, 1950.
Printz-Påhlson, Göran. "The Scandinavian Ideology." In *Facets of European Modernism*, edited by Janet Garton, 219–42. Norwich: University of East Anglia, 1985.
Rousseau, Jean Jacques. *The Social Contract*, translated by Willmoore Kendall. Chicago: Gateway, 1954.
Sars, J. E. *Udsigt over den Norsk Historie*. Oslo: Universitetsforlaget, 1967.
Skomsvoll, Yngve. *Norges Historie*. Oslo: Kagge Forlag, 2004.
The Sound Toll at Elsinore: Politics, Shipping and the Collection of Duties, 1429–1857, edited by Ole Degn. Copenhagen: Museum Tusculanum Press, 2017.
Stenersen, Øyvind and Ivar Libæk. *The History of Norway from the Ice Age to Today*, translated from the Norwegian by James Anderson. Lysaker: Dinamo, 2003.
Toynbee, Arnold J. *A Study of History: Abridgement of Volumes I-IV*. Oxford: Oxford University Press, 1946.
Tuchman, Barbara W. *A Distant Mirror: The Calamitous 14th Century*. London: Macmillan, 1979.

Chapter 5: Long Night's Journey into Day

Amundsen, Bård. "Norway was controlled from the Pulpit." *ScienceNordic*, 27 November 2014.
Anderson, Perry. *Lineages of the Absolutist State*. London: NLB, 1974.
Christianson, John Robert. *On Tycho's Island: Tycho Brahe, Science and Culture in the 16th Century*. Cambridge: Cambridge University Press, 2003.
Derry, T. K. *A History of Scandinavia*. Minneapolis: University of Minnesota Press, 1979.
Diamond, Jared. *Collapse: How Societies Choose to Fail or Survive*. London: Penguin, 2011.
Gulick, Edward Vose. *Europe's Classical Balance of Power*. New York: Norton, 1955.
Gustafsson, Harald. "A Nordic Perspective: Why? Why Not?" In *Internationalization in the History of Northern Europe*, edited by Richard

Holt, Hilde Lange and Ulrika Spring, 7–21. Tromsø: Report of the Nordsaga 99 Conference, 2000.
Ibsen, Henrik. *Plays: Six—Peer Gynt and The Pretenders*, translated by Michael Meyer. London: Methuen, 1987.
Kent, Neil. *A Concise History of Sweden*. Cambridge: Cambridge University Press, 2008.
När Hände Vad i Nordens Historia, edited by Sven Rosborn och Folk Schimanski. Lund: Historiska Media, 1996.
Rian, Øystein. "Introduction." In *A Revolution from above? The Power State of 16th and 17th century Scandinavia*, edited by Leon Jespersen, 1–30. Odense: Odense University Press, 2000.
———. "State, Elite and Peasant Power in a Nordic Region." In *A Revolution from above? The Power State of 16th and 17th century Scandinavia*, edited by Leon Jespersen, 181–247. Odense: Odense University Press, 2000.
———. *Embetstenden i dansketida*. Oslo: Det Norske Samlaget, 2003.
———. *For Norge, Kjempers Fødeland: 12 Portrett frå Dansketida*. Oslo: Samlaget, 2007.
Riste, Olaf. *Norway's Foreign Relations: A History*. Oslo: Universitetsforlag et, 2001.
Ross, John F. L. "'Innumerable Others': Reassessing King James VI/I's Scandinavian Sojourn." *Temp: Tidskrift for Historie* 11 (December 2015), 5–25.
Vogt, Carl Emil. *Herman Wedel Jarlsberg: Den aristokratiske opprøreren*. Oslo: Cappelen Damm, 2014.

Chapter 6: Norway and the Dazzling Dutch

Badeloch, Noldus. *Trade in Good Taste: Relations in Architecture and Culture between the Dutch Republic and the Baltic in the Seventeenth Century*. Turnhout: Brepols, 2005.
Bernier, Olivier. *Louis XIV: A Royal Life*. New York: Doubleday, 1987.
Bochove, Christiaan van. *The Economic Consequences of the Dutch: Economic Integration around the North-Sea, 1500–1800*. Amsterdam: Aksent, 2008.
Bruijn, Jaap R. "The Maritime Industries of the Dutch Republic, in Particular the Timber Trade, in the 17th and 18th Centuries." In *Timber and Trade: Articles on the Timber Export from the Ryfylke-area to Scotland and Holland in the 16th and 17th century*. Aksdal: Lokalhistorisk Stiftelse, 1999.
Dico, Joy Lo. "Harmony after the Storm." *Financial Times*, December 15–16, 2018, 12.
Emmer, Dieter. *The Dutch in the Atlantic Economy, 1580–1880: Trade, Slavery and Emancipation*. Aldershot: Ashgate, 1998.

Galbraith, John Kenneth. *Economics in Perspective: A Critical History.* Boston: Houghton Mifflin, 1987.

Gascoigne, George. "The Sack of Antwerp by a Spanish Army, 4 November 1576." In *Eyewitness to History,* edited by John Carey, 116–21. New York: Avon Books, 1987.

Goodman, Jordan, and Katrina Honeyman. *Gainful Pursuits? The Making of Industrial Europe 1600–1914.* London: Edward Arnold, 1998.

Israel, Jonathan D. *Dutch Primacy in World Trade, 1585–1740.* Oxford: Clarendon Press, 1989.

———. *The Dutch Republic: Its Rise, Greatness and Fall 1477–1806.* Oxford: Clarendon Press, 1995.

———. "A Golden Age: Innovation in Dutch Cities, 1648–1720." *History Today* 45:3 (March 1995), 14–20.

Kirby, David and Merja-Liisa Hinkkanen. *The Baltic and the North Seas.* London: Routledge, 2000.

Kuijpers, Erika. "Poor, Illiterate and Superstitious? Social and Cultural Characteristics of the 'Noordsie Natie' in the Amsterdam Lutheran Church in the Seventeenth Century." In *Dutch Light in the "Norwegian Night,"* edited by Louis Sicking, Harry de Bles and Erland des Bouvrie, 57–68. Hilversum: Uitgeverij Verloren, 2004.

Lillehammer, Arnvid. "The Scottish-Norwegian Timber Trade in the Stavanger area in the Sixteenth and Seventeenth Centuries." In *Scotland and Europe,* edited by T. C. Smout, 97–111. Edinburgh: John Donald, 1986.

Lindemann, Mary. *The Merchant Republics: Amsterdam, Antwerp and Hamburg, 1648–1790.* New York: Cambridge University Press, 2015.

Lottum, Jelle van. *Across the North Sea: The Impact of the Dutch Republic in International Labor Migration c. 1550–1850.* Amsterdam: Aksant, 2007.

Løyland, Margit. *Hollendartida i Norge (1550–1750).* Oslo: Spartacus, 2012.

Milton, Giles. *Nathaniel's Nutmeg.* London: Penguin, 1999.

Moore, Jason W. "Amsterdam is Standing on Norway." Parts I and II. *Journal of Agrarian Change* 10:1, and 10:2 (2010), 33–68 and 188–227.

Norsk Økonomisk Historie 1500–1970, Band I: 1500–1850, edited by Ståle Dyrvik. Oslo: Universitetsforlaget, 1979.

"Norway Imports Christmas Trees." www.newsinenglish.no, December 24, 2016, accessed December 29, 2016.

Pye, Michael. *The Edge of the World: A Cultural History of the North Sea and the Transformation of Europe.* London: Pegasus, 2016.

Schama, Simon. *The Embarrassment of Riches: An Interpretation of Dutch Culture in the Golden Age.* London: William Collins, 1988.

———. *Scribble, Scribble, Scribble.* New York: Ecco/HarperCollins, 2010.

Sicking, Louis. "New Light on the Flight of Archbishop Olav Engelbrektsson: A Watershed in Norwegian History." In *Dutch Light in the "Norwegian Night,"* edited by Louis Sicking, Harry de Bles and Erland des Bouvrie, 13–41. Hilversum: Uitgeverij Verloren, 2004.

Sogner, Sølvi. *Ung i Europa: Norsk ungdom over Nordsjoen til Nederland i tidlig nytid.* Oslo: Universitetsforlaget, 1994.

———. "Norwegian-Dutch Migrant Relations in the Seventeenth Century." In *Dutch Light in the "Norwegian Night,"* edited by Louis Sicking, Harry de Bles and Erland des Bouvrie, 43–56. Hilversum: Uitgeverij Verloren, 2004.

Tjaden, Anja. "The Dutch in the Baltic, 1544–1721." In *The Baltic in Power Politics 1500–1990, Vol. I, 1500–1890,* edited by Göran Rystad, Klaus R. Böhme and Wilhelm M. Carlgren, 61–136. Lund: Lund University Press, 1994.

Toyne, S. M. *The Scandinavians in History.* Port Washington, NY: Kennikat Press, 1970.

Chapter 7: The Union of Weights and Wings

Andersson, Ingvar. *A History of Sweden,* translated by Caroline Hannay. London: Weidenfeld and Nicholson, 1956.

British Views on Norwegian-Swedish Problems 1880–1895: Selections from Diplomatic Correspondence, edited by Paul Knaplund. Oslo: Jacob Dybwad, 1952.

Bryne, Arvid. *They Painted Norway,* translated by Jean Aase. Oslo: Andresen og Butenschøn AS, 2004.

Daugstad, Karoline. "Agrarian Landscapes and Agrarian Heritage." In *Norway: Nature, Industry and Society,* edited by Greta Rusten, Kerstin Dotthoff and Linda Sangolt, 67–78. Bergen: Vignostad og Bjørke, Fagforlaget, 2013.

Drake, Michael. *Population and Society in Norway, 1735–1865.* Cambridge: Cambridge University Press, 1969.

Forsdahl, Anders. "The Remote Regions—Northern Norway." In *The Shaping of a Profession: Physicians in Norway, Past and Present,* edited by Øivind Larsen, 109–16. Canton, MA: Science History, 1996.

Glenthøj, Rasmus, and Morten Nordhagen Ottosen. *Experiences of War and Nationality in Denmark and Norway, 1807–1815.* Basingstoke: Palgrave Macmillan, 2014.

Gunther, John. *Inside Europe.* New York: Harper, 1938.

Ibsen, Henrik. "Three Poems by Henrik Ibsen," translated by Robert Bly. *Scandinavian Review* 4 (1978), 46–50.

Larsen, Øivind. "What is Norway Like?" In *The Shaping of a Profession: Physicians in Norway, Past and Present*, edited by Øivind Larsen, 17–26. Canton, MA: Science History, 1996.
Malmanger, Magne. *One Hundred Years of Norwegian Painting*. Oslo: Nasjonalgaleriet, 2000.
Meyer, Michael. *Ibsen*. Middlesex: Penguin, 1971.
Palmer, Alan. *Bernadotte: Napoleon's Marshal, Sweden's King*. London: John Murray, 1990.
Sandvik, Hogne. "Western Norway." *The Shaping of a Profession: Physicians in Norway, Past and Present*, edited by Øivind Larsen, 124–37. Canton, MA: Science History, 1996.
Schjønsby, Hans P. "The Establishment of a Public Health System." In *The Shaping of a Profession: Physicians in Norway, Past and Present*, edited by Øivind Larsen, 71–85. Canton, MA: Science History, 1996.
Scobbie, Irene. *Sweden*. London: Ernest Benn, 1972.
Sørensen, Øyvind. "What's in a Name? The Name of the Written Language of Norway." In *The Cultural Construction of Norden*, edited by Øyvind Sørensen and Bo Stråth, 121–37. Oslo: Scandinavian University Press, 1997.
Tissot, Louis. "The Events of 1848 in Scandinavia." In *The Opening of an Era: 1848*, edited by François Fejtö, 167–79. New York: Universal Library, 1973.
Weibull, Jørgen. "The Union with Norway." *Sweden's Development from Poverty to Affluence, 1750–1970*, edited by Steven Koblik and translated by Joanna Johnson, 68–88. Minneapolis: University of Minnesota Press, 1975.

Chapter 8: A Sporting Start

Allen, E. John B. "'We Showed the World the Nordic Way': Skiing, Norwegians, and the Winter Olympic Games in the 1920s." In *The Olympics at the Millennium: Power, Politics and the Games*, edited by Kay Schaffer and Sidonie Smith, 72–90. New Brunswick, NJ: Rutgers University Press, 2000.
Athenfærden 1906: Nordmændenes Deltagelse i de Olympiske lege. Kristiania: J.M. Stenersen, 1907.
Bliksrud, Liv. *Sigrid Undset*. Oslo: Gyldenhal, 1997.
Enoksen, Lars Magnar. "Glima and the Viking Martial Arts." In Torgrim Titlestad, *Viking Norway: Personalities, Power and Politics*, edited by Torgrim Titlestad, 365–70 (Appendix IV). Stavanger: Sagabok, 2008.
"From Day to Day, the Fever." *Embros*, April 13, 1906 (mimeograph).

Goksøyr, Matti. "Opplevde Felleskap og Folkelig Nasjonsbygging." *Historisk Tidskrift* 80:3 (2000), 307–29.
———. "Nationalism." In *Routledge Companion to Sport History*, edited by S. W. Pope and John Nauright, 268–94. London: Routledge, 2010.
Gottass, Thor. *Norway: the Cradle of Skiing*, translated from the Norwegian by J. Basil Cowlishaw. Oslo: Font Forlag, 2011.
Jørgensen, Per. "From Balck to Nurmi: The Olympic Movement and the Nordic Nations." In *The Nordic World*, edited by Henrik Meinander and J. A. Mangan, 69–99. London: Routledge, 2913.
Kardasis, Vassilis. *The Olympic Games in Athens 1896–1906*. Athens: Ephesos, 2004.
Kazantzakis, Nikos. *Report to Greco*, translated by P. A. Bien. New York: Simon & Schuster, 1965.
Lindroth, Jan. *När Idrotten blev folkrörelse*. Stockholm: Rabén and Sjögren, 1975.
Mallon, Bill. *The 1906 Olympic Games: Results from All Competitions, in all events, with commentary*. Jefferson, NC: McFarlane, 1999.
Miller, David. *Athens to Athens: The Official History of the Olympic Games and the IOC, 1894-2004*. London: Mainstream, 2003.
Miller, Stephen G. *Arete: Greek Sports from Ancient Sources*. Berkeley: University of California Press, 1991.
Nansen, Fridtjof. *Friluftsliv*. Oslo: Jakob Dybwads Forlag, 1940.
Nielsen, Niels Keyser. "Sport and Popular Mobilization in Nordic Societies, ca. 1850–1900." *Scandinavian Journal of History* 33:1 (2012), 69–86.
Olstad, Finn. *Norsk Idretts Historie: Forsvar, Sport, Klassekamp*. Oslo: Aschehoug, 1987.
Powell, E. Alexander. "The Olympian Games of 1906." *Badminton Magazine* 6 (1906), 667–83.
Ross, John F. L. *Olympic Homecoming: Greece's Legacy and the 2004 Athens Games*. Athens: Explorer Press, 2004.
———. "Parting Ways, Testing Waters: Norway's Early Olympic Ventures." *Journal of Sport History* 40:3 (2013), 413–34.
———. "Fridtjof Nansen and the Aegean Population Exchange." *Scandinavian Journal of History* 40:2 (2015), 133–58.
Sandblad, Henrik. *Olympia och Valhalla: Idéhistoriska aspekter av den moderna idrottsrörelsens framväxt*. Stockholm: Almqvist & Wiksell, 1985.
Schantz, Otto J. "Pierre de Coubertin's Conceptions of Race, Nation and Civilization." In *The 1904 Anthropology Days and the Olympic Games: Sport, Race and American Imperialism*, edited by Susan Brownell, 156–88. Topeka: University of Nebraska Press, 2008.

Shaw, David W. *Daring the Sea.* Secaucus, NJ: Birchlane Press, 1998.
Titlestad, Torgrim. *Viking Norway: Personalities, Power and Politics.* Stavanger: Sagabok, 2008.
Young, David C. *The Modern Olympics: A Struggle for Revival.* Baltimore and London: University of Johns Hopkins Press, 1996.

Chapter 9: The Reluctant Unionists

Arter, David. *Scandinavian Politics Today.* Manchester: Manchester University Press, 2008.
Booth, Michael. *The Almost Nearly Perfect People: Behind the Myth of the Scandinavian Utopia.* London: Vintage, 2015.
Churchill, Winston S. *The Second World War, Vol. I: The Gathering Storm.* London: Cassel, 1948.
Colville, John. *The Fringes of Power: 10 Downing Street Diaries 1939–1955.* New York and London: W.W. Norton, 1986.
Deutsch, Karl W. et al. *Political Community in the North Atlantic Area: International Organization in the Light of Historical Experience.* Princeton: Princeton University Press, 1957.
Hemstad, Ruth. "Fra 'Indian Summer' til 'nordisk vinter'—nordisk samarbeid og 1905." *Norsk-Svenske relasjoner i 200 år,* edited by Øystein Sørensen og Torbjörn Nilsson. Oslo: Aschehoug, 2005.
Huntford, Roland. *The New Totalitarians.* London: Allen Lane, 1971.
Ingebritsen, Christine. "Norm Entrepreneurs: Scandinavia's Role in World Politics." In *Small States in International Relations,* edited by Christine Ingebritsen, Iver B. Neumann, Sieglinde Gstöhl, and Jessica Beyer, 273–85. Seattle: University of Washington Press, 2006.
Kettunen, Pauli. "A Return to the Figure of the Free Nordic Peasant." *Acta Sociologica* 42:3 (1999), 259–69.
Kivimäki, Ville. "Between Defeat and Victory." *Scandinavian Journal of History* 37:4 (2012), 482–504.
Nissen, Henrik S. "The Nordic Societies." In *Scandinavia During the Second World War,* edited by Henrik S. Nissen, translated by T. M. Pettersen, 3–52. Oslo: Universitetsforlaget, 1983.
Nøkleby, Berit. "Adjusting to Allied Victory." In *Scandinavia During the Second World War,* edited by Henrik S. Nissen, 279–323. Oslo: Universitetsforlaget, 1983.
Ross, John F. L. *Neutrality and International Sanctions.* New York: Praeger, 1989.
Tingsten, Herbert. *The Debate on the Foreign Policy of Sweden 1918–1939.* London: Oxford University Press, 1949.

Turner, Barry, with Gunilla Nordquist. *The Other European Community: Integration and Cooperation in Northern Europe.* London: Weidenfeld and Nicholsen, 1982.
Vaughn, Richard. *Post-War Integration in Europe.* London: Edward Arnold, 1976.

Chapter 10: Well and Truly Oiled

Galbraith, J. K. *Annals of an Abiding Liberal.* New York: Meridian, 1980.
Hayward, Jack. 'Introduction." In *Industrial Enterprise and European Integration: From National to International Champions in Western Europe,* edited by Jack Hayward, 1–20. Oxford: Oxford University Press, 1995.
Hellevik, Ottar. *Nordmenn og det gode liv.* Oslo: Universitetsforlaget, 1996.
Hjalager, Anne-Mette, Grzegorz Kwiatkowski and Martin Østervig Larsen. "Innovation Gaps in Scandinavian Rural Tourism." *Scandinavian Journal of Hospitality and Tourism* 18:1 (2018), 1–17.
Jörberg, Lennart, and Olle Krantz. "Scandinavia 1914–1970." In *The Fontana Economic History of Europe: Contemporary Economics 2,* edited by Carlo M. Cipolla, 377–459. Glasgow: William Collins, 1976.
Katzenstein, Peter. *Small States in World Markets: Industrial Policy in Europe.* Ithaka: Cornell University Press, 1985.
Lipset, Seymour Martin, and Stein Rokkan, eds. *Party Systems and Voter Alignments.* New York: Free Press, 1967.
Rokkan, Stein. "Norway: Numerical Democracy and Corporate Pluralism." In *Political Opposition in Western Democracies,* edited by Robert A. Dahl, 70–115. New Haven, CT: Yale University Press, 1966.
Sarromaa, Sanna. *Norske Tabuer: Om likhetens tyranny, språk som religion og hellige mødre.* Oslo: Spartacus, 2016.
Sjøtun, Svein Gunnar. "A Ferry Making Waves: A Demonstration Project 'Doing' Institutional Work in a Greening Maritime Industry." *Norwegian Journal of Geography* 73:1 (2019), 16–28.
"Staten kan tape milliarder," *Dagbladet,* 23 mai 2018, 12.
Taylor, Stan. "The Politics of Unemployment." In *Politics in Western Europe Today,* edited by D. W. Urwin and W. E. Paterson, 33–58. New York: Longman, 1990.

Chapter 11: The Meaning of Nobel

Franzen, Jonathan. *How to Be Alone.* New York: Fourth Estate, 2002.
Furre, Berge. *Norsk Historie 1905–1990: Vårt hundreår.* Oslo: Det Norske Samlaget, 1992.

Heffermehl, Fredrik S. *The Nobel Peace Prize: What Nobel Really Wanted.* Santa Barbara: Praeger, 2010.
Lundestad, Geir. *Fredens sekretær: 25 år med Nobelprisen.* Oslo: Kagge, 2015.
Simonsen, Anne Synnøve. *Kvinnen bak Fredsprisen.* Oslo: Cappelen Damm, 2012.
Sohlman, Ragnar. *The Legacy of Alfred Nobel: The Story Behind the Nobel Prizes*, translated from the Swedish by Elspeth Harley Schubert. London: The Bodley Head, 1983.
Stenersen, Øivind, Ivar Libæk and Asle Sveen. *The Nobel Peace Prize: One Hundred Years for Peace.* Oslo: Cappelen, 2001.

Chapter 12: Epilogue

Brown, Andrew. *Fishing in Utopia: Sweden and the Future that Disappeared.* London: Granta, 2008.

Index

Note: The Norwegian letters æ, ø and å have been treated as a + e, o, and a respectively; the Swedish letters å, ä and ö are rendered as a, a, and o.

Aall, Jacob 105
Aamodt, Kjetil André 240
Aarhus 109
Aasen, Iver 208
ABBA 87
Act of Union (*Riksakt*) 193, 210
Adam of Bremen 73
Adler, Cort 183
Aegean Sea 54, 321; *see also* Mediterranean
Aftenposten 244
Ahlmann, Hans Wilhelmsson 27
Akerselva River 287
Åland islands 250
Alaska 39, 76, 77, 199
Ålesund 29, 109
Alexander I, Czar of Russia 87, 195, 196
Alexander II, Czar of Russia 210
Alexander III, King of Scotland 115
Alexandra, Queen of Great Britain and Northern Ireland 229
Alexandria 69
Alexios I Komnenos, Byzantine Emperor 57
Alfred, King of England 79
Algeria 71
Alps 5, 70
　Engadine 23
Alsace-Lorraine 19

Alta (town) 91
　(river) 82, 86
Älvsborg fortress 144, 173
Alvsson, Knut 137–38, 166
amber trade 69–70
Amboyna 170
Amstel River 162
Amsterdam 46, 162, 166, 167, 169, 178; *see also* the Netherlands
Amundsen, Leon 42
Amundsen, Roald
　as author 13, 233
　as explorer 82, 89
　Gjøa expedition 74, 76, 296
　Maud expedition 42, 179
　South Pole expedition 27–28, 39, 41–42, 237
Andersen, Carl 242
Andersen, Hans Christian 23, 67
Andersen, Hendrik Christian 192
Andrée, Salomon 81
Andrew, Prince of Greece 229
Anker
　Carsten 118, 192, 294
　family 160
　Peder 205
Anna, Byzantine Princess 56
Anna, Queen of England and Scotland 143

351

352 THE RISE OF LITTLE BIG NORWAY

Anne, Queen of Great Britain and
    Ireland 133
Anslo, Cornelis Claesz 185
Antarctica 25–27, 41–42, 291
    Treaty of 27
Arafat, Yasser 315
Archer, Colin 38
Arctic
    Norwegian interest in 28, 63–93
        passim
    oil and gas 108, 301–02, 331–32
    as region 5, 20, 35, 69, 72
Arctic Council 92, 262, 268
Arctic Highway 89
Arctic Ocean 87, 88, 90
Arcturus (Little Bear) 71
Arendal 11, 75
Argentina 28
Arkhangel 184
Armenia 16
Arnesen, Liv 27
Arnoldson, Klas Pontus 321
Asbjørnson, Peter 214
Åsgårdstrand 39
Askeladden 328
Astrid, Princess of Norway 27
Athens 43, 84
    as Olympic setting 226–33
Atlantic Ocean 35, 38, 49, 74, 89, 117
Aung San Suu Kyi 317–19
Australia 24, 187
Austria 291

Baalsrud, Jan 23, 297
Bærums Verk 145, 158
Baffin Island 33
Baffin, William 75
Baghdad 53
Bakunin, Mikhail 208
Balchen, Bernt 11
Balck, Viktor 229, 242
Balkans, the 53, 55, 71, 129
    wars in 231
Balke, Peder 82
Baltic countries 19, 266
Baltic Sea

    as amber source 69–70
    as cultural barrier 107, 139
    importance for Denmark 92, 136,
        143, 169
    importance for Finland 87, 92
    importance for Sweden 92, 217
    location 33, 38
    unimportance for Norway 33, 92
Barents Sea
    importance for Norway 29, 30, 92
    location 33
    as oil and gas source 77–78, 301–2
Basil I, Byzantine Emperor 53
Basil II, Byzantine Emperor 53,
        55, 56, 58
Barentsz, Willem 74, 143
Bartlett, Robert 33
Beerenburg, Mt. 26
Beethoven, Ludwig von 213
Belgica expedition 41
Belgium 165, 194, 252, 254, 271;
    see also Benelux
Benelux union 5, 252
Bergen
    location 21, 40, 46, 78, 137, 149
    as medieval center 36, 104, 116
Bergensbanen 35
Bergman, Ingmar 121
Bering Strait 75
Bernadotte; *see* Karl XIV Johan
Bernstorff, Count J. H. E. 154, 157
Birger Jarl, King of Sweden 118
Birger Magnusson, King of Sweden
    116, 118
Birka 109
Birkeland, Kristian 208, 287
Bjerke, Asbjørn 238
Bjørndalen, Ole Einar 239, 329–30
Bjørgen, Marit 239
Björling, Alfred 81
Bjørnson, Bjørnstierne
    as social analyst 7, 9, 67, 108, 208,
        211, 214
    as political figure 12, 220
Bjørset, Vilhelm 107
Bjurstedt, Molla 246

Black Death, the 119–28
  legacy in Norway 8, 108, 134, 145, 179, 328
Black Sea 57, 58
Blanche of Namur, Queen of Sweden and Norway 134
Blegen, Carl 232
Blekinge 134, 151
Blücher, Gebhard Leberecht von 198
Bodin, Jean 101
Bodø 78, 90–91, 300
Bohuslän 7, 19, 151
Bolt, Amund Sigurdsson 135
Bombelles, Count Louis Philippe de 198
Borg 109
Borgund 109
Borlaug, Norman 15
Bondevik, Kjell Magnus 98
Borre 113
Bosporus, 58, 61
Boström, Eric 221, 232
Bothnia, Gulf of 90
Bouvetøya 26, 28
Brahe, Tycho 145–46
Brandes, Georg 12, 204
Brandt, Enevold 153
Branting, Hjalmar 321
Brazil 24
Bredal, Peter 183
Breivik, Anders Behring 104, 240
Bremer, Fredrika 97, 295
Brende, Børge 294, 322
Brexit 266
Brömsebro, Treaty of 146, 148, 151
Brønnøysund 91
Brundtland, Gro Harlem 5, 281
Brunelleschi, Filippo 212
Bucharest 46
Buddenbrooks (Mann) 198
Bulgar Empire 53–55
Bull, Edvard 105
Bull, Ole 47, 192, 208, 211, 214, 295
Burke, Edmund 35
Bush, George Walker 320
Byron, George Gordon, Lord 227

Byron, Robert 232
Byzantine Empire 49, 50, 53–57 *passim*, 60, 231–32; *see also* Constantinople, Varangian Guard

Cabot, John 74, 167
Calvin, John 140
Canada
  comparison with N. 271
  location 34, 74, 83
  as oil state 292
  size 6, 24
Canary Islands 43
Cape of Good Hope 74
Cape Horn 42, 74
Caribbean Sea 19, 168, 169, 175
Carnegie, Andrew 244
Caroline Matilde, Queen of Denmark 153, 156
Carter, Jimmy (James Earl) 307, 320
Caspian Sea 51
Castlereagh, Robert Stewart 195, 197
Catherine the Great, Czarina of Russia 122, 154, 185
Celsius, Anders 80
Chamberlain, Neville 37
Charlemagne 70
Chaumont, Treaty of 195
Childs, Marquis 223
Chile 28
China 24, 73, 74, 77
  Nobel controversy 321–24
Christian I, King of Denmark, Norway and Sweden 136–37
Christian II, King of Denmark, Norway and Sweden 119, 137–38, 140–41, 166, 254
Christian III, King of Denmark and Norway 138, 140–42
Christian IV, King of Denmark and Norway
  interest in Arctic 75
  interest in Norway 8, 102–3, 142–48 *passim*
  and timber trade 172, 177, 179, 180, 187, 295

Christian VII, King of Denmark and Norway 153, 158
Christian VIII, King of Denmark 199; see also Christian Frederik
Christian August, Crown Prince of Sweden 196–97
Christian Frederik, King of Norway 105, 193–201
Christiania; see Oslo
Christiaens, Elsie 185
Christina, Queen of Sweden 122, 241
Christoffer II, King of Denmark 134
Chrysafis, Ioannis 231
Churchill, Winston 37–38, 70, 100, 260
Cicignon, Johan Caspar de 183
Clement VI, Pope 120
Clermont 56
Cold War 8, 16, 32, 85
Colombia 17
Columbus, Christopher 74, 167
Colville, John 260
Constantine, Crown Prince of Greece 226
Constantine the Great, Byzantine Emperor 50, 112
Constantine IX Monomachus, Byzantine Emperor 58
Constantinople 50, 52, 53, 56, 57, 59
Cook, Frederick 41
Cook, James 75
Copenhagen 24, 154, 172; see also Denmark
   Treaty of (1660) 148, 151
   Treaty of (1767) 153
Copernicus, Nicholas 145
Cork, County 33
Coubertin, Pierre de 229
Council of Baltic Sea States 266
Crete 53
Cromwell, Oliver 171, 186
Crusades 56–57, 111
Cruys, Cornelius 183–85
Custer, George Armstrong 4
Cyprus 46, 292

Cyril, St. 55
Dæhlie, Bjørn 239
Dahl, Johan Christian 22, 82, 208, 213
Dalarna 33, 151
Danzig 165
Davis, John 74
Davis Strait 33
Death in Venice (Mann) 23
Defoe, Daniel 124
Delos 68
Delphi 33
Denmark
   Arctic interest 77, 79, 84
   Baltic control 136, 169
   in Europe 263
   governance patterns in 100, 145–47, 204
   influence in Norway 8, 12, 127, 203–4
   landform 23, 39
   orientation 46
   rivalry with Sweden 7, 75, 169, 172–73
   Scandinavian ties 217, 249–68
   size 6, 9, 23
   sport 230–32
   tensions with Germany 12, 153, 203, 215, 257
   union with Norway 19, 84, 129–58, 163, 165, 168, 186
Désirée (Desideria), Queen of Sweden and Norway 210
Diana, Princess of Wales 318
Dias, Bartholomew 167
Didrickson, Mildred "Babe" 245–46
Diet of Worms 139
Dirksen, Everett 282
Dnieper River 57, 58
Dovrefjell 33, 97
Downing, George 171
Drake, Sir Francis 74
Dronning Maud Land 26–27
Dublin 23, 111
Dudley-Do-Right 66

INDEX 355

Dunant, Henri 310
Düsseldorf 44, 212
Dybeck, Richard 81

East India Company (VOC/Dutch) 170, 175, 182
 (English) 175
Easter Island 131
Edström, Sigfrid 227
Edward VII, King of Great Britain and Northern Ireland 229
Egede, Hans Poulsen 156
Egeland, Jan 294, 321
Eider River 70, 250
Eidsvoll (town) 160, 161, 190; *see also* Norway constitution
Einstein, Albert 244
"Eirik Rauds Land" 25
Elizabeth I, Queen of England 141, 143
Elizabeth II, Queen of Great Britain and Northern Ireland 229
Ellisiv 52, 58
Elsinore (Helsingør) 143, 169
Emperors' War 257; *see also* Thirty Years' War
Engadine; *see* Alps
Engels, Friedrich 101, 208
England 101, 155
 Dutch link 171–72, 175, 180–81
 search for northern passages 74–77
 importance for Vikings 49, 51, 109–15; *see also* United Kingdom, Scotland
Enlightenment, the 73, 98, 103
Erasmus, Desiderius 138
Erik Klipping, King of Denmark 116
Erik Magnusson, King of Sweden 116, 122, 134
Erik Menved, King of Denmark 118, 133
Erik of Pomerania, King of Denmark, Norway and Sweden 134–35
Erik the Red (Erik Thorvaldsson) 25, 45, 111

Erickson, Charles 246
Eriksen, Stein 239
Estonia 45, 100, 266
Euphemia, Queen of Norway 118
European Economic Area (EEA) 271
European Economic Community (EEC/EC) 18, 252, 255; *see also* EU
European Free Trade Association (EFTA) 18, 259, 289
European Union (EU) 18, 258–59, 293, 330
Eurozone 220, 263
Eyde, Samuel 287

Færoe Islands 19, 111, 194–95
Falkland Islands 289
Falköping, battle of 133
Fatima, shrine of 63–64
Fersen, Axel von 200
Finland
 Arctic role 66, 81, 87–88
 in Europe 263, 268
 forest industry 159
 history 8, 9, 19, 190
 migrations to Norway 4, 160, 187
 Norway, comparisons with 98, 129, 149, 194, 213, 269–70, 277
 physical orientation of 20, 30, 45–46, 48
 population 6, 23
 sport 32
 in World War II 48, 66, 196, 252
Finnmark 4, 20, 45, 77, 82
 role in N. development 84, 86, 144, 152
Finse 36
fjords 35, 37–40, 160, 165, 177–78, 289, 292; *see also* Oslofjord
Flåm 29
Folkunga dynasty (Sweden) 118
Forgotten Valley, the 29
Fram
 Amundsen voyage 39, 42
 Nansen voyage 34, 38, 65, 83
 Sverdrup voyage 83

France
  home of Gothic 72
  location 19
  opposition to Dutch 171–73
  relations with Sweden 79–80, 196–202
  Revolution 152, 154, 157, 190
  size 42
  Vikings in 111
Frankenstein (Shelley) 73
Franklin, John 76
Franks 111
Franz Josef Land 25
Frederick II, Emperor of Germany 110
Frederick William, Elector of Prussia 149
Frederik II, King of Denmark and Norway 142, 146, 177
Frederik III, King of Denmark and Norway 147–49
Frederik VI, King of Denmark and Norway 153, 158, 198–99
  as crown prince 154
Frederiksborg 143
Fredrik I, King of Sweden 80
Fredrikstad 143
Freia 12, 39, 291
Freud, Sigmund 191
"Fridtjof Nansens Land" 25
Frobisher, Sir Martin 74–75
Frydenlund, Knut 11, 89
Fulbright, James William 14
  Fulbright program 47

Galtung, Johan 19
Gandhi, Mohandas (Mahatma) 317
Garborg, Arne 208
Garborg, Hulde 208
Gates, Bill 293
Gävle 71
Geer, Louis de 173 (seventeenth century), 210 (nineteenth century)
Geneva 139
George, King of Greece 229

George III, King of Great Britain and Ireland 153
Gerhardsen, Einar 86
Germany
  Antarctic interest 26
  conflicts with Denmark 12, 19, 203
  as destination for Norwegians 82, 212–14
  impact of 15, 190, 215
  interest in Norway 116
  World War II occupation of Norway 15, 87–88
Gibbon, Edward 60, 116
Gibraltar 57
Gladstone, William Ewart 270, 295
global warming 7, 20, 29, 187, 261
Glomma River 143
Glorious Revolution 141
Goethe, Johan Wolfgang von 300
Gokstad 113
Gorbachev, Michael 305
Gore, Albert 310
Gorm, King of Denmark 12
Göta Canal 36, 154
Gothenburg 36, 144, 154
Gothic, image of 72
Goths 106
Gotland 134, 136, 151
Gran, Tryggve 26, 234
Grand Tour 56, 212
Gråtopp, Halvard 135
Great Depression 297
Great Northern War 48, 184, 257
Great Schism 54
Greece
  under Byzantium 54, 57
  as civilizational source 33, 68, 215, 236
  Bremer visit 97
  and Olympic Games 226–32
Green Revolution 15
Greenland
  as Arctic land 69, 81, 83, 156
  legacy of Vikings 15, 34, 45, 109, 115, 131
  as Danish possession 23

INDEX 357

map distortion effect 72
Nansen crossing of 40–41
Norwegian claims on 25–26
Norwegian loss of 136, 194–95
Grieg, Edvard 105, 208, 211–14
Grieg, Nordahl 18
Grimm, Jacob and Wilhelm 66
Gripenstedt, Johan August 209
Grotius, Hugo 172
Grundtvig, N. F. S. 104, 258
Gude, Hans Fredrik 39, 82, 208, 213
Gulf Stream 88–89
Gustav, Prince of Sweden 200
Gustav I Vasa, King of Sweden 138, 141, 144
Gustav II Adolf (Gustavus Adolphus), King of Sweden 141, 144–45
Gustav III, King of Sweden 80, 154, 155, 157, 231
Gustav IV Adolf, King of Sweden 156, 196
Gustav VI Adolf, King of Sweden 232, 241
Gutenberg, Johannes 103
Gyldenløve, Ulrik Frederik 150
Gyllenstierna, Christina 138

Haagensen, K. A. 229
Haakon VII, King of Norway 42, 91, 99, 225, 229
Haarlem 181
Hafgerdingar effect 33
Hafrsfjord, battle of 98, 113
Hafvilla effect 67
Hagen, Carl Ivar 316, 318
Håkon I (the Good), King of Norway 113
Håkon IV (Håkonsson), King of Norway 112, 115–16, 131
Håkon V (Magnusson), King of Norway 116–18, 133–35
Håkon VI (Magnusson), King of Norway and Sweden 99, 133–34, 136
Halden 20, 48, 113
Halland 134, 151

Hals, Frans 164, 183
Halti, Mt. 30
Hamar 127
Hamburg 67
Hamlet (Shakespeare) 101
Hammerfest 20, 92
Hammarskjöld, Dag 17–18, 318, 321
Hammarskjöld, Hjalmar 18
Hamsun, Knut 47, 85, 245, 275
Hans, King of Denmark, Norway and Sweden 137
Hanseatic League (Hansa) 77, 116–17, 132, 145, 151–52, 328
Hansen, Armaur 122, 208
Hansen, Bernhuff 246
Hansen brothers, Christian and Theophil 232
Harald Bluetooth, King of Denmark 12, 113–14
Harald I (Fairhair/Hårfagre), King of Norway 12, 79, 113
Harald III (Sigurdssson/Hard Ruler/Hardråde), King of Norway and Denmark 49, 51–61
Harald V, King of Norway 99, 292
Harbo, George 244–45
Hardangervidda 36
Härjedalen 19, 146, 151
Harold Godwineson 112
Harrison, John 71
Hastings, battle of 112
Haug, Thorleif 239
Hauge, Hans Nielsen 155
Hebrides, the 19, 111, 115
Hedeby 79
Hedin, Sven 210
Hedtoft, Hans 258
Hedvig Elisabet Charlotta, Queen of Sweden and Norway 211
Heffermehl, Fredrik 319–20
Hegel, Frederik 204
Hegel, Georg Wilhelm Friedrich 101
Heimskringla (Snorri) 103, 105
Hellqvist, Carl Gustaf 136
Helsingør; *see* Elsinore
Helsinki 45, 46, 71, 87, 254

Henie, Sonja 239
Henry VII, King of England 74
Henry VIII, King of England 141, 175
Herodes Atticus 228
Herodotus 68, 69
Herschel, Sir William 65
Hertervig, Lars 82
Hess, Sofie 314
Heyerdahl, Thor 38, 41, 49
Hillingar effect 33
Hitler, Adolf 15, 260
Hobbes, Thomas 183
Hoel, Adolf 26
Hofmo, Rolf 241
Holberg, Ludwig 188
Hollandertid 159–88, 287, 295; *see also* the Netherlands
Holmsen, Andreas 105, 123
Holst, Johan Throne 289
Holstein; *see* Schleswig-Holstein
Hønefoss 40
Hooker, William 82
Hudson Strait 73
 H. Valley 69
Hudson, Henry 75, 77, 143
Huizinga, Johan 170–71, 270
Hungary 56, 270
Hunger (Hamsun) 8, 275
Huns 55
Hurtigruten 21, 78, 91
Hven 146

Ibsen, Henrik
 attitudes to Norway 12–13, 296
 exile in Europe 215
 societal impact 108, 158, 188, 208, 211–15 *passim*, 222, 225, 313
Iceland 20, 24, 26, 67, 69, 78
 escapes plague 122
 in Europe 263
 as source of Norwegian history 103, 110, 194–95
 Vikings in 111
Ihlen, Nils Claus 25
IJsselmeer 177–78
Iliad, The (Homer) 54

Ilulissat Declaration 28
India 16–17, 51
Ingstad, Anne Stine 234
Ingstad, Helge 86, 233–34
Institute of International Law 310
International Campaign to Ban Landmines 318
International Committee of the Red Cross (ICRC) 310
International Maritime Organization (IMO) 33
International Olympic Committee (IOC) 227, 229, 230
Inter-Parliamentary Bureau (Union) 313
International Polar Year 83
Iranian revolution 288
Ireland 49, 79, 155, 270
Ismay, Gilbert 36
Istanbul 45, 53, 231; *see also* Constantinople
Italy 20, 21, 53, 84, 160, 196, 212
Ithaka 46
Ivan IV (the Terrible), Czar of Russia 49

Jaabæk, Søren Pedersen 296
Jagland, Thorbjørn 318
Jahn, Gunnar 315
James III, King of Scotland 137
James VI/I, King of Scotland and England 67, 133, 143, 186
James II, King of England 141
Jämtland 19, 146, 151
Jan Mayen 26, 28, 46, 78, 111
Jan Mayen 83
Janteloven 10, 13, 251, 264
Jarislav, Prince of Kiev 52
Jelling Stones 12
Jensen, Siv 281
Jerusalem 57
Johaug, Therese 240
Joseph II, Holy Roman Emperor 154
Jotunheimen 23
Joyce, James 23

INDEX 359

Julianne, Queen of Denmark and Norway 153
Julius Caesar 65

Kagge, Erling 65
Kallstenius, Evald 81
Kalmar Union 133–38 *passim*, 158, 256, 257
Karelia 19
Karl IX, King of Sweden 79, 144
Karl X, King of Sweden 147–48, 172, 257
Karl XI, King of Sweden 80, 150
Karl XII, King of Sweden 184, 210, 211
Karl XIII, King of Sweden and Norway 193, 196, 202
Karl XIV Johan, King of Sweden and Norway
  as French Marshal Bernadotte 196–98, 201
  and Kiel Treaty 196–99
  as Swedish Crown Prince 158, 257
  as Swedish King 202, 205, 208; *see also* Napoleon
Karl XV, King of Sweden and Norway 209
Karlstad, negotiations at 18, 48, 222
Karolinska Institute 309
Kaupang 109, 135
Kautokeino 90
Keel, the 20, 48, 151
Keilhau, Baltazar Mathias 83, 156
Key, Ellen 6–7
Keynes, John Maynard 107
Keyser, Jacob Rudolf 105
Kiel (town) 189, 190
  Treaty of 26, 80, 189–91
Kielland, Alexander 211
Kiev 49, 56
Kievan Rus 49, 111
King's Bay disaster 285
Kinnarodden 64
Kipling, Rudyard 51
Kirkenes 46, 78, 89, 92
Kiruna 84

Kirkwall 112
Kissinger, Henry 315
Kittelsen, Theodore 128, 213
Kjus, Lasse 240
Knåred, Treaty of 79, 144, 169
Knausgaard, Karl Ove 107
Knox, John 140
Knut, King of England and Denmark 112, 114
Koht, Halvdan 85, 105, 310
Kongsberg 145, 152
Konow, Magnus 242
Korean War 16
Korvald, Lars 5
Kragerø 43
Kristiania; *see* Oslo
Kristiania crash 296
Kristensen, Monika 27
Krohg, Christian 8, 208, 213
Krummedige, Henrik 137
Kyriolax 236

Lambros, Spyros 226
Lancaster Sound 75
Lapland 66, 80
Lapp Codicil 95
Lapua movement 84
Larsen, Carl Anton 38
Larvik 10, 38, 109, 135
Latin America 178
Latvia 266
Lawrence, Thomas Edward 312
League of Nations 15, 255
Lefort, Franz 184
Leghorn 168
Leif Eriksson 48, 111, 161
Leipzig 44, 197, 212
Lenglen, Suzanne 246
Leonardo da Vinci 212
Leonidas, King of Sparta 227
Lie, Trygve 16–17
Lie, Jonas 85, 214
Lied, Jonas 25
Lillehammer 5, 35, 71, 161
Lilljequist, Rudolf 311
Lillomarka 11

Lincoln, Abraham 215
Lindesnes 45
Lindisfarne 109
Linnæus, Carl (von Linné) 80
Lisbon 168
Lithuania 19, 266
Little Bighorn, the 4, 8
Little Ice Age, 79, 180
Livonia 169
Locke, John 165
Lofoten islands 91, 152, 300–301
London 47, 162, 167
Long Day's Journey into Night (O'Neill) 132
Longyearbyen 28, 83; *see also* Svalbard
Louis XIV, King of France 80, 148, 150, 171, 186
Louis XVI, King of France 154
Louis XVIII, King of France 200
Louis Philippe, King of France 64
Lovén, Sven 53
Løvenskiold, Severin 206
Lowe, Emily 217
Lübeck 116, 198
Lundberg, Silja Ask 22
Lundeberg, Christian 222
Lundestad, Geir 307, 322
Luther, Martin 139; *see also* Reformation
Luxembourg 185, 252
Lysaker Group 214

Macbeth, King of Scotland 67
Macbeth, Lady 66
Magellan, Ferdinand 40, 167
Magerøy 64
Magic Mountain, The (Mann) 23
Magnus I (Olavsson), King of Norway 59
Magnus VI (Lagebøte), King of Norway 115–16
Magnus Eriksson, King of Norway and Sweden 119, 123, 133–34
Magnus Ladulås, King of Sweden 116, 118
Malthus, Thomas Robert 38, 295

Man, Isle of 19, 110, 115
Maniaces, George 54
Manzikurt 54
Marco Polo 73
Margaret of Denmark, Queen of Scotland 137
Margrete I (Valdemarsdatter), Queen of Denmark, Norway and Sweden 133–35
Margrete II, Queen of Denmark 100, 253
Maria Theresa, Empress of Austria 154
Marie Antoinette, Queen of France 200
Marselis family 175
Marshall, George Catlett 320
Marshall Plan 47, 320
Märtha, Crown Princess of Norway 27, 47
Märtha Louise, Princess of Norway 68
Marx, Karl 101, 106, 208
Mary Rose 175
Massalias 69
Mathisen, Oscar 208
Maud, Queen of Norway 99, 225, 229
Maud 42, 179
Mauropus, John 55
Medieval Warm Period 79
Mediterranean Sea 33, 44, 55, 59, 69, 231, 262
Medvedev, Dimitri 30
Mercantilism 171–72, 177
Mercator, Gerardus 72
Mercouri, Melina 228
Mercouris, Spyros 228
Methodius, St. 55
Metternich, Klemens von 195, 201
Michael IV, Byzantine Emperor 52, 58, 59
Michael V (Kallifates), Byzantine Emperor 52, 58, 59
Michael VII, Byzantine Emperor 54
Michelangelo Buonarroti 212
Michelsen, Christian 208, 221
Minsk 46

INDEX 361

Mo i Rana 89, 91
Moe, Ole Borten 301
Monsen, Lars 32
Montesquieu, Charles de Secondat, Baron de 73, 101
Morgedal 239
Mother Theresa 325
Mott, John 315
Mozart, Wolfgang Amadeus 154
Munch, Edvard 39–40, 105, 208, 214, 222
Munch, Peter Andreas 103, 121
Munich 12, 44, 212
Munk, Jens 75
Muscovy Company 77
Mykonos 43
Myrdal, Alva 57, 89, 321
Myrdal, Gunnar 89

Nansen, Fridtjof
  as author 13, 29, 42, 65, 98, 233
  as diplomat 15–16, 194, 209, 231
  as explorer 82, 89, 223
  life 105, 234, 239
  Fram expedition 34, 38–39, 237
  Greenland crossing 38, 40–1, 237, 296
  Hardangervidda crossing 237
  as Nobel peace laureate 16, 321
  as *ski-idræt* advocate 237
Nansen, Hans 237
Nansen Office for Refugees 16
Naples 17
Napoleon Bonaparte 75, 114, 151
  importance for Denmark–Norway 130, 157–58, 193–201 *passim*, 203, 253, 257
  invasion of Russia 197
Narvik 37, 92
National Aeronautics and Space Administration (NASA) 70
National Romanticism; *see* Romantic Movement
Navigation Acts 172, 186, 216
Nazis 26, 87, 105
Nehru, Jawaharlal 16–17

Netherlands, the
  comparison with Norway 170–71, 270
  Golden Age 161, 164, 171, 179
  importance for Norway 40, 159–88
  role in Baltic 169, 174
  role in world trade 143, 167–68, 271
  size 4–5, 24; see also *Hollandertid*
neutrality, policies of 9, 17, 47, 100
  Leagues of Armed N. 154, 255
New York 169, 324
New Zealand 39, 187
Newfoundland 111
Nietzsche, Friedrich 101
Nigeria 284
Nobel, Alfred
  bequest controversy 308–11
  life 80, 311–15
Nobel, Emmanuel 313
Nobel Foundation 306, 317
Nobel Prize for Peace
  decision process 305
  importance for Norway 14–15, 219–20, 303–25
  no-decision option 306–7
  prizewinners 16, 17, 29, 307, 310, 315, 317–18, 320–25
  tensions built into 307–08, 315–23
Nobel Prizes (other) 305, 309
Nordek plan 259
Norden Society 260
Nordenskiöld, Adolf Erik 81, 83
Nordic cooperation 5, 7, 28, 203, 217, 235, 249–69; *see also* Denmark, Finland, Iceland, Norway, Sweden
Nordic Council 258, 260, 263
Nordic Inter-Parliamentary Union 260
Nordkalotten 87
Nordkapp 45, 63–4
  battle of 88
Nordland (Norway) 77, 78, 82, 86, 91
Norrland (Sweden) 68
Nordli, Odvar 317
Nordmarka 11

Norheim, Sondre 239
Normans 50, 54, 57
Norsemen; *see* Vikings
Norse mythology 23, 34–5, 68, 160–61, 238–39
Norsk Hydro 15, 217, 291
North Atlantic Treaty Organization (NATO) 9, 15, 47, 258, 260
North Berwick 67
"North Norway Rising" 83
North Pole 41, 65, 81
 Magnetic North Pole 67
North Sea 33, 38, 91, 143
North Star 64–65
North-East Passage (Northern Sea Route) 74, 77, 92
North-West Passage 41, 74–76
Northern League 84
Northern Lights (*Aurora Borealis*) 6, 65, 68
Norway
 Antarctic claims 26–28
 Arctic, importance for 4, 25–27, 29–30, 63–93, 300–302, 331–32
 Black Death in 119–28
 Christianization of 49, 113–18, 139
 Civil Wars 115, 117, 239
 1814 Constitution 9, 82, 190, 192–93, 199, 201
 Cultural flowering post-1814 14, 211–16
 Denmark, relations with 7, 129–58, 203, 256
 directional challenges 31–61
 Dutch period (*Hollandertid*) 159–88
 economic development of 149–52, 179–80, 216–20, 259–60, 286–87, 290–91, 296–97
 environmental sensibilities 6, 262, 292–94, 297, 300–2
 Europe, dilemmas over 44, 86, 108, 266, 287–88, 295
 expansionary impulses 14–15, 18–28, 115, 328
 films and TV 11, 22–23, 32, 68, 279, 328–30
 food 37, 231
 foreign aid 15, 294
 foreign representation 218–22, 226, 230–1, 316
 health issues 204–7
 historical fragmentation of 97–108
 independence (1905) 84, 87, 129, 221–22
 international non-Scandinavian comparisons with 269–71
 language issue 104, 108, 215, 269–70
 "little Norway" syndrome 7–14, 292, 331
 "long night" notion 129–32, 158
 monarchy as institution 99, 114–19, 133, 135, 145
 Nobel Prize, importance for 220–21, 303–25
 northern development 77–93
 oil fund 280–82, 297
 oil and gas industry 91–92, 271, 273–302, 331–32
 Parliament (Storting) role 201–2, 205, 313–16
 policymaking channels 285–86
 political parties 13, 16, 35, 85–86, 218, 286, 291, 301–2
 population trends 6, 8, 10, 121–24, 149, 203, 207
 reformation in 139–41, 145
 rural aesthetic 7–8, 171
 Russia, relations with 8, 29–30, 92
 size paradox 4–30, 292, 331
 skiing as national mirror 161, 238–41, 329–31
 sport, importance of 31–32, 225–46, 275
 Sweden, relations with 129, 188–223
 United Nations, policy in 17–18, 255, 262
 United States, relations with 9, 46–48, 215, 243–46, 260
 Viking age 49–61, 108–19
 welfare state 207, 285
 westward migration 44, 243–46; *see also* England, Finland, Oslo, Nordic cooperation, United Kingdom

INDEX 363

Norwegian Institute for Marine Research 302
Norwegian Polar Institute (NPI) 89, 92
Norwegian Sea 33, 89, 91
Novgorod 49, 58
Ny Ålesund 87
Nygaard, William Martin 204
Nygaardsvold, Johan 223

Obama, Barack 307, 315, 320
Odyssey, The (Homer) 46
Oedipus Rex (Sophocles) 228
Oehlenschlæger, Adam 258
Ofotbanen 84
Öland 173
Olaus Magnus 79
Olav I (Tryggvason), King of Norway 49, 57, 113
Olav II (Haraldsson), King of Norway (St. Olav) 49, 51, 52, 58, 79, 113
Olav III (Kyrre), King of Norway 114
Olav IV (Håkonsson), King of Norway and Denmark 133–34
Olav V, King of Norway 99
    as crown prince 27, 238
Olav Engelbrektsson, Archbishop of Norway 139, 166
Oldenburg dynasty 133, 136–37, 149; *see also* Denmark
Olga, Queen of Greece 229
Oliva, Treaty of 149
Olympia, Ancient 227–28
Olympic Games (modern) 5, 35, 225–33, 238–42; *see also* Lillehammer
O'Neill, Eugene Gladstone 132
Øresund 169
Organization of Petroleum Exporting Countries (OPEC) 288
Orkney Islands 19, 103, 111, 115–16, 137
Orienteering 31–32
Oscar I, King of Sweden and Norway 208–9, 216
Oscar II, King of Sweden and Norway 218, 221–22, 309, 313
Oseberg 113

Oslo [Christiania 1624–1876 Kristiania 1877–1924]
    character of 8, 24, 300
    development of 10, 106–07, 134–35, 137, 142
    location of 21, 32, 36, 38, 40, 45, 71
    as Nobel ceremony host 305–7
    as political center 83, 86, 92, 116, 118
    as Olympic host 239
Oslo Accords 18
Oslofjord
    character of 10, 38
    historical importance 113, 118, 119, 135, 142, 149, 161
    as Munch's base 39
    as conduit to world 38–9, 143, 165, 170; *see also* fjords, Oslo
Ossietzky, Carl von 315
Østfold 10, 20, 32, 38, 113, 135
Ostrogoths 55
Ottar (Othere) 45, 79
Ottoman Empire 43, 228
Ousland, Børge 65–66
Oxenstierna, Axel 144

Pacific Ocean 42, 44
Palme, Olof 324
Pan (Hamsun) 85
Pan-Scandinavianism; *see* Nordic cooperation
Paris 44, 85, 167, 200, 212, 230
    Treaties of (1815) 195
    Treaty of (2015) 294
Parry, William 76
Pasvik River 48
"People-Wandering Time" 50
Peary, Robert Edwin 41
Pechenegs 53
Peer Gynt (Ibsen) 105, 129, 214–15
Peerson, Cleng 46
Peter the Great, Czar of Russia 8, 28, 175, 184–85
Peter I Øy 26, 28
Petersen, Clemens 204
Philip, Duke of Edinburgh 229
Philip of Macedon 228

Phillips Petroleum (Conoco Phillips) 47, 284
Phoenicians 34, 70
Phokas, Nicephorus 53
Pietists 79
Pilgrim's Way 63, 79, 123, 139
Piraeus 59
Pleistocene epoch 40
Pliny 69
Poe, Edgar Allan 301
Poland 19, 101, 169, 196
Poltava, battle of 184
Polybius 69
Pomerania 194, 197
Portugal 33, 57, 63, 74, 269
Prose Edda (Snorri) 103
Protestantism; *see* Reformation
Prussia 149, 194, 197; *see also* Germany
Psellus, Michael 55
Ptolemy, Claudius 69, 71
Putin, Vladimir 30
Pyramiden 87; *see also* Svalbard
Pytheas 69

Quadruple Alliance 169
Quisling, Vidkun 104

Ragnhild, Princess of Norway 27
Ramstedt, Johan 222
Rasputin, Grigori 166
Realism, in art 213–14
Reagan, Ronald 244
Reformation 12, 52, 67, 79, 98, 137, 139–42
Rembrandt van Rijn 164, 183, 185
Renaissance 98, 232
Restauration 46
Rhine River 168, 173
Ribe 109
Rockne, Knute 243–44
Rokkan, Stein 36, 285–86
Rollo 112
Roman Catholic Church 49, 54–56
Romanos III Argyros, Byzantine Emperor 52, 58–59
Rome (city) 44, 215

Roosval, Baltasar 229
Roosevelt, Franklin 47
Roosevelt, Theodore 310, 320
Røros 48, 145, 175
Rosendal Barony 8
Roskilde, Treaty of 136, 148, 151
Ross, Sir James Clark 76
Ross, Sir John 76
Rostock 116
Rotterdam 177
Rovaniemi 66, 90
Rousseau, Jean-Jacques 14, 101
Rudbeck, Olof 5, 80
Runeberg, Johan 252
Ruskin, John 171
Russell, Bertrand 13
Russia (and as USSR)
  Arctic interest 25, 83–85, 87–88, 144
  budget 280
  delineation agreement with Norway 29–30, 92
  history 8–9, 48–49, 87, 100, 321
  orientation 8, 15, 19–20, 24, 68
  in winter sport 239
Ruud, Birger 239
Rye, Olaf 203

Saga era 49, 103, 112
Salem 67
Saltfjellet 78
Sami 68, 81, 82, 84–86
Samuelson, Frank 244–45
Samuil, Tsar of Bulgars 53
Santa Claus 10, 66
Santiago de Compostela 63
Sars, Johan Ernst Welhaven 105, 131, 157
Sars, Eva 105, 239
Saxo Grammaticus 103
Scandinavia; *see* Nordic cooperation, Denmark, Finland, Iceland, Norway, Sweden
Scandinavian Airlines System (SAS) 253
Scanian wars 186, 257
Scargill, Arthur 289

Scharnhorst 88
Schleswig-Holstein 19, 70, 79, 149, 153
Schubert, Franz 213
Schumann, Robert 213
Scotland location 45, 69, 84, 175
　trade with Norway 164, 176–78
　importance for Vikings 19, 109–11, 117
　parallel with Norway 292
Scott, Robert Falcon 42, 76, 234, 237
Sehested, Hannibal 146–49 *passim*
Seljuk Turks 54
Seventh Seal, The (Bergman) 121
Shakespeare, William 65, 67, 101
Shelley, Mary 73
Shetland Islands 19, 111, 137
Siberia 72, 77
Sicily 54, 71, 111, 231
Sigbritsdatter, Dyveke 137, 166; *see also* Willoms, Sigbrit
Sigurd the Crusader 57–59, 227
Sigurd Jorsalfar (Bjørnson) 214
Silk Road 73
Sinai 46
Skagerrak 33, 38, 47, 180
Skåne 134, 151
Skatteboe, Gulbrand 246
Skien 149
Skjalgsson, Erling 235
Skredsvig, Christian 214
"Sloopers" 46–47
Slyngstad, Yngve 280
small-state analysis 5
Smolensk 49
Snorri Sturluson 52, 69, 103, 214
Snøhetta, Mt. 69
Söderblom, Nathan 321
soft power 19, 240, 293
Sohlberg, Harald 48, 239
Sohlman, Michael 312
Sohlman, Ragnar 311–12
Solberg, Erna 36, 281, 293
Solheim, Erik 262
Soria Moria 214

Sound Tolls 136, 143, 146, 154, 169; *see also* Denmark
South Africa 27
South Pole 42, 65; *see also* Amundsen, Scott
Spain 44, 63, 74
　Armada 141, 143
　in Netherlands 148, 167, 172
Speyer, Treaty of 169
Spice Islands 169
Spinoza, Baruch 165, 174
Spitsbergen, Treaty of 87; *see also* Svalbard
St. Petersburg 45, 184
Staaff, Karl 222
Stamford Bridge, battle of 51, 109, 112
Statoil (Equinor) 287, 291–92
Stauning, Thorvald 223
Stavanger 21, 36, 98, 113, 127, 177
Steen, Johannes 220
Steenwinkel, Lorenz van and Hans van 179
Steinkjer 33, 78
Sten Sture
　the Elder 137
　the Younger 138, 257
Stettin, 70
　Treaty of 143
Stiftelsen for industriell og teknisk forskning (SINTEF) 282
Stiklestad 37, 52, 114
Stockholm
　development of 106, 203
　massacre of 138–39, 254
　Olympic Games host 241–42
　orientation 24, 36, 71, 109
　political situation 200; *see also* Sweden
Stoltenberg, Jens 28, 46, 88
Støre, Jonas Gahr 299, 322
Stradivari, Antonio 160
Strindberg, August 6, 68, 211, 217
Struensee, Johan Friedrich 151, 153–54
Sundt, Eilert 105, 296

Suttner, Bertha von 308, 311, 314
Svalbard
  history of 4, 46, 64, 77, 111
  importance for Norway 78, 82–83, 86–89, 156
  Svalbard Act 87; *see also* Spitsbergen Treaty
Sverdrup, Georg 105
Sverdrup, Johan 208
Sverdrup, Otto 82–83, 89
Sverre, Johan 229
Sverre Sigurdsson, King of Norway 115
Sweden
  Arctic connection 79–81, 84
  Baltic connection 169–76 *passim*
  Dutch links 172–73
  dynastic history 100, 133
  and Nobel home 305–6, 312, 325
  orientation 33, 45, 48, 71, 87
  as sporting power 241–42
  unions with Norway 18, 98, 129, 133–34, 189–223, 256
  wars with Denmark–Norway 48, 143–48, 150–51, 201, 257
Swedish Academy 306, 309
Swedish Academy of Sciences 309
Swedish *Riksbank* 309
Switzerland 99, 196, 229, 270–71

Tacitus 70
Talleyrand, Charles Maurice de 195
Tallinn 45, 100
Tampere 46, 277
Tasman, Abel van 187
Taylor, Bayard 82, 99, 187–88, 295
Tegnér, Esaias 104
Telemark 33, 278
Terboven, Josef 87
Terra Nova 42
Tessin, Nicodemus 80
Thams, Jacob Tullin 243
Thatcher, Margaret 289
Theodora, Byzantine Empress 58
Thessaloniki 55

Thirty Years' War 103, 140, 146, 149, 257
Thorpe, Jim 245
Thrane, Marcus 209
Thule 69
  Ultima *Thule* 69–70
Tidemand, Adolph 82, 208
Tierra del Fuego 40
Tigris River 50–51
Tilsit, Treaty of 196
Tingsten, Herbert 268
Toje, Asle 108, 317
Tolkien, J. R. R. 4
Tønsberg 10, 13, 40, 116, 119, 152
Tordesillas, Treaty of 74
Torell, Otto Martin 83
Torfæus, Tormud 103
Torstensson, Lennart 150, 257
Toynbee, Arnold 114, 164, 183
Tranströmer, Tomas 321
Trip, Elias 173
Troll (Lie) 68
Trollhättan 154
Trolle, Borge 144
Troms 77, 86
Tromsø 79, 81–82, 85, 91–92
Trondheim
  founding of 49, 57
  location 21, 33, 37, 78, 83, 90
  Nidaros as holy site 63, 79, 114, 134, 139, 225
Trondsen, Christoffer 166
Trøndelag 78, 113, 148, 151, 198
"Tulipmania" 182
Turku 71
Tysvær 165
Tzimisces, John 53

Ukraine 49, 321
Ulfeldt, Corfitz 146
Ullmann, Liv 132
Ulysses (Joyce) 23
Undset, Ingvald 232
Undset, Sigrid 49, 116, 232
United Kingdom (UK) 11, 21, 48, 91, 169, 289, 292

in Antarctica 27–28, 42
and Europe 259
monarchy 153, 229, 292
and Norwegian independence
 194, 220
in post-Napoleonic settlement
 194–97, 201, 203
reforms in 207, 216
tensions with the Netherlands
 171–73, 177, 186
war on Denmark-Norway 157–58
in World War II 11, 35–36, 47, 87–
 88, 90–91, 260; *see also* Scotland,
 England
United Nations (UN)
 Charter 15, 17
 Educational and Scientific
  Organization (UNESCO) 91, 136
 Human Rights Day 305
 Norway as member 16, 255, 262
 peacekeeping forces 17–18
 Sea-law treaty (UNCLOS) 28–30,
  78, 288
United States of America (US)
 geography 8, 14, 19, 22, 24, 35, 97
 impact on Norway 47–48, 215
 Norwegian immigration to 9,
  46–47, 243–46
 political history 78, 97, 99, 192, 210,
  216, 320
Untouchables, The 66
Utøya 11, 268
Utvær 45

Valdemar I (the Great) 115
Valdemar V (Atterdag) 134, 136
Valdemar, Prince of Sweden 116
Varangian Guard 52–53, 57–59, 231;
 see also Byzantine Empire, Harald
 Hardråde
Vardø 45, 82, 118
Värmland 7
Vasa dynasty 104; *see also* Sweden,
 Gustav Vasa
Vasa 175
Vega 91

Vega 81
Vejle 12
Venezuela 284
Venice 59, 174
Verdens Gang 36
Vermeer, Jan 164, 183
Verne, Jules 301
Verrazzano, Giovanni da 75
Versailles
 Palace 148
 Treaty of 87
Vespucci, Amerigo 167
Vesterålen 91
Vestfold 10, 38–39, 45, 119, 135
Victoria, Queen of Great Britain and
 Ireland 131
Vienna (city) 293
 1815 Treaty of 194–95
Vietnam War 14, 260, 320
Vikings
 athleticism of 227, 235–37
 exploratory reach of 26, 33–35, 45,
  49–61, 79, 108–18
 legacy 97–106, 158, 211, 227
 societal characteristics 73, 109–18
Vinje, Aasmund Olavsson 188,
 208, 214
Visby 136
Vladimir, Prince of Kiev 56
Volga River 51

Wagner, Richard 211
Wallenberg, Marcus 217
Waterloo, battle of 195
Waterton, Charles 121
Weber, Max 149
Wedel Jarlsberg, Fredrik 220
Wedel Jarlsberg, Herman 155, 194,
 205–6, 209
Welhaven, Johan 108, 208, 227
Werenskiold, Erik 208, 213–14
Wergeland, Henrik 108, 208
Wergeland, Oscar 190
Wessel, Henrik 185
Wessel, Peter (Tordenskiold) 151, 185
Wessex 79

Weston, Thomas 84
Westphalia, Treaty of 101, 186
Wetterstedt, Gustaf af 198
Wilder, Thornton 264
Wilderness, In the (Undset) 116
William the Conqueror 112
Williams, Jody 318
Willoch, Kåre 283
Willoms, Sigrit 137, 166; *see also* Sigbritsdatter, Dyveke
Wills Moody, Helen 246
Wilse, Anders Beer 22, 47
winds, meaning of 42–43, 46
Winckelmann, Johann Joachim 227
witchhunts 67
With, Witte de 172
Witsen, Nicolaas 184
Wizard of Oz, The (Baum) 66
Wollstonecraft, Mary
  compares Denmark with Norway 154–57
  criticizes Norwegian practices 36–37, 152, 187, 295
  observes Norway 7, 10, 73, 119
World Bank 24
World Economic Forum (WEF) 293–94

World War I 14, 18–19, 229, 259, 316
World War II 18, 47–48, 116
  as Nordic turning point 253–55, 258–60
  northern Norway affected by 23, 37–38, 85, 87–88, 91–92
  Norway strengthened by 11, 15, 223
World Wide Fund for Nature (WWF) 91

Xenophon 227
Xiliphinios, John 55
Xiaobo, Liu 321–22

Yenisei River 72
Yggdrasil 161, 188; *see also* Norse mythology
York 51, 109, 112
Young Men's Christian Association (YMCA) 315

Ziller, Ernst 228
Zoe, Byzantine Empress 52, 58, 60
Zuiderzee; *see* IJsselmeer
Zürich 140, 271
Zwingli, Ulrich 140

www.ingramcontent.com/pod-product-compliance
Lightning Source LLC
Chambersburg PA
CBHW032015230426
43671CB00005B/93